Cutting Jesus Down to Size

Books by G.A. Wells

Herder and After (1959)
The Plays of Grillparzer (1969)
The Jesus of the Early Christians (1971)
Did Jesus Exist? (1975; second edition, 1986)
Goethe and the Development of Science (1978)
The Historical Evidence for Jesus (1982)
The Origin of Language: Aspects of the Discussion from Condillac to Wundt (1987)
Religious Postures: Essays on Modern Christian Apologists and Religious Problems (1988)
Who Was Jesus? A Critique of the New Testament Record (1989)
Belief and Make-Believe: Critical Reflections on the Sources of Credulity (1991)
What's in a Name? Reflections on Language, Magic, and Religion (1993)
The Jesus Legend (1996)
The Jesus Myth (1999)
The Origin of Language (1999)
Can We Trust the New Testament? Thoughts on the Reliability of Early Christian Testimony (2004)
Cutting Jesus Down to Size: What Higher Criticism Has Achieved and Where It Leaves Christianity (2009)

Edited Works

Language: Its Origin and Relation to Thought (co-edited with D.R. Oppenheimer), by F.R.H. Englefield (1977)
The Mind at Work and Play (co-edited with D.R. Oppenheimer), by F.R.H. Englefield (1985)
J.M. Robertson: Liberal, Rationalist, and Scholar (1987)
Critique of Pure Verbiage: Essays on Abuses of Language in Literary, Religious, and Philosophical Writings (co-edited with D.R. Oppenheimer), by F.R.H. Englefield (1990)
The Old Faith and the New, by David Friedrich Strauss (1997)

Cutting Jesus Down to Size

What Higher Criticism Has Achieved and Where It Leaves Christianity

G.A. WELLS

OPEN COURT
Chicago and La Salle, Illinois

To order books from Open Court, call toll-free 1-800-815-2280, or visit our website at www.opencourtbooks.com.

Open Court Publishing Company is a division of Carus Publishing Company.

Copyright © 2009 by Carus Publishing Company

First printing 2009

All rights reserved. No part of this publication may be reproduced, stored in a retrieval system, or transmitted, in any form or by any means, electronic, mechanical, photocopying, recording, or otherwise, without the prior written permission of the publisher, Open Court Publishing Company, a division of Carus Publishing Company, 315 Fifth Street, P.O. Box 300, Peru, Illinois 61354-0300.

Printed and bound in the United States of America.

Library of Congress Cataloging-in-Publication Data

Wells, George Albert, 1926-
   Cutting Jesus down to size : what higher criticism has achieved and where it leaves Christianity / G.A. Wells.
      p. cm.
   Includes bibliographical references and index.
   ISBN 978-0-8126-9656-1 (trade paper : alk. paper)
 1. Bible. N.T. Gospels—Criticism, interpretation, etc. I. Title.
   BS2555.52.W45 2009
   226'.06—dc22

                                                2009012192

Contents

Preface	ix
Introduction	1
i. What This Book Is About	1
ii. The Jesus of the Early Epistles Is Not the Jesus of the Gospels	6

1 / BASIC FACTS ABOUT THE GOSPELS   23
  i. Mark   23
  ii. Matthew and Luke   33
  iii. John   41
  iv. More on 'the Jews' in the Gospels   51

2 / THE QUESTION OF MIRACLES AND THE WORK OF DAVID FRIEDRICH STRAUSS   57

3 / THE VIRGIN BIRTH   79
  i. Introduction   79
  ii. The Birth at Bethlehem   83
    a. Matthew's Account   83
    b. Luke's Account   86
  iii. Luke's Parallel between John the Baptist and Jesus   91

iv.	The Nativity as Fulfillment of Prophecy	94
v.	The Genealogies	99
vi.	The Origin and Purpose of the Christian Virgin Birth Traditions and Their Post-Scriptural Developments	105
vii.	Finale	108

4 / THE RESURRECTION — 113

i.	The Gospel Accounts	113
	a. The First Three Gospels	113
	b. The Fourth Gospel	126
ii.	Paul's Account	133
	a. Introduction	133
	b. To Whom the Risen Jesus Appeared	138
	1. Cephas	138
	2. James	142
	3. The Twelve	145
	4. The Five Hundred and More	149
iii.	The New Testament Evidence as a Whole and the Synoptic Burial Narratives	151
iv.	Recent Defenders of the Traditional Doctrine	156
v.	Recent Reinterpreters of the Traditional Doctrine	171

5 / THE GOSPEL OF MARK: HISTORY OR DOGMA? — 179

i.	William Wrede's Epoch-Making Book	179
	a. The Role of Disciples	179
	b. The Secret of Jesus's Status as Son of God	190
ii.	Mark and Community Tradition: K.L. Schmidt and Form-Criticism	195

6 / Q, THE SAYINGS GOSPEL — 207

7 / THE PRELUDE TO JESUS'S PUBLIC MINISTRY — 219

   i. Jesus and John the Baptist — 219
   ii. The Temptation — 234

8 / JESUS AS APOCALYPTIC PROPHET — 245

   i. The Transition from Prophecy to Apocalyptic Thinking — 245
   ii. From Reimarus to Schweitzer — 247
      a. Hermann Samuel Reimarus — 247
      b. Franz Overbeck, Johannes Weiss, and William Wrede — 256
      c. Albert Schweitzer — 264
   iii. The Fourth Gospel and Later — 274
   iv. An Appraisal of Relevant Passages — 278
   v. Recent Attempts to Cope with the Texts — 286
      a. Sundry Proposals — 286
      b. 'Meta-Narratives' — 291
      c. Coping with the Romans — 294
   vi. Finale — 297

Concluding Thoughts — 303
Epilogue: The Gospels and Eyewitnesses — 319
   i. Richard Bauckham — 319
   ii. P.R. Eddy and G.A. Boyd — 326
Notes — 333
Bibliography — 355
Index of New Testament References — 373
General Index — 385

Preface

Works mentioned or quoted (listed under their authors' names in the Bibliography) are referenced in my text and notes simply by the relevant page numbers, usually with also a date of publication.

Books of the Bible are quoted from the Revised Version (RV), published 1881–85 of the Authorized or King James Bible (AV) of 1611. On some few occasions I refer to more recent translations—the Revised Standard Version (RSV) or the New English Bible (NEB)—or have rendered the Greek text of the New Testament literally or adapted it to the syntax of my sentences.

The terms 'Mark', 'Matthew', 'Luke', and 'John' sometimes designate the author of the relevant gospel and sometimes that gospel itself. Which meaning is intended will be clear from the context. 'Luke' also designates the author of the Acts of the Apostles. Quotations from a number of New Testament books are referenced with abbreviations. These, in the order in which the relevant books are printed in modern Bibles, are:

Mt., Mk., Lk., Jn. (for the four gospels)
Acts (for the Acts of the Apostles)
Rom., 1 and 2 Cor., Gal., Ephes., Phil., Coloss., 1 and 2 Thess., and 1 and 2 Tim. (for epistles ascribed to Paul).
Rev. (for the New Testament apocalypse or book of Revelation).

I follow the usual terminology in calling the first three of the four canonical gospels 'the synoptics'. The term 'synoptic' means 'what can be seen at a glance' and owes its origin to the fact that, if the complete texts of all three are put side by side in parallel columns, one can see what material has been added, omitted, or adapted in one as compared with another.

I thank my wife Elisabeth for keeping things going at home while I worked on this book, and for helpful comments on my manuscript.

I thank Mr. D. Collins, Miss Edith Geissler, and Mrs. Elke Wagstaff for their careful typing of the original. I am particularly grateful to Elke, both because it is she who has done the bulk of this work and because latterly she has persevered with it under difficult conditions.

Introduction

i. What This Book Is About

What is called the 'higher criticism' attempts to determine the date, authorship, integrity, and character of the various books of the Bible. The term distinguishes it from 'lower' or textual criticism, which is concerned to recover the authentic text of these documents. The distinction should not be taken as a value judgement, for we do not have the originals of these texts, and trying to recover from later copies what their authors actually wrote is important and no mean task.

The detractors of the higher criticism—such as Gary North (1990) for whom it is no more than a 'hoax', and Hal Lindsey, who calls it wicked dogmatism inspired by Satan (1974, pp. 166–68)—suppose that it has been arbitrarily imposed from outside, from certain arbitrary assumptions, onto the scriptures. In fact, as we shall see, it is the careful study of the scriptures themselves which has prompted the questionings of the higher critics.

Although much of the higher criticism of the New Testament (particularly the gospels), continuous since the late eighteenth century, has been the work of Christian scholars, one result of it is that many doctrines, taught for centuries, are now abandoned by numerous spokesmen of the mainstream churches, who are reduced to justifying the old formulas by novel interpretations. But in spite of such critical work, there is today a resurgence of fundamentalist and ultra-conservative Christian belief, backed by scholarship of like kind. This book is essentially a response to such resurgence and to the defensive tactics of the more liberal commentators.

After my first chapter, outlining when the gospels were written and some of their tendencies, I turn in Chapter 2 to Strauss, one of the first of the major higher critics, and give particular attention to the question of miracles. Leslie Houlden notes, in the impressive 2005 handbook, *Jesus: The Complete Guide*, edited by himself, that Jesus is represented in the gospels as working miracles in the fashion of what was believed of others of his time. There is "nothing special", Houlden says, about him as a miracle worker: "The ancient world was accustomed to such men and wondered at them. Apollonius of Tyana is the best known, from his 'Life' by Philostratus (p. 423).

The discussion in Chapters 3 and 4 of the New Testament accounts of Jesus's birth and infancy, and of his resurrection, shows how subsequent scholars have built on, and continue to build on, some of Strauss's major insights. These chapters are updated and revised from my 1989 book—considerably so in the case of the resurrection; for while scholarly defence of the virginal conception is now relatively rare, the resurrection still excites endless discussion. These two chapters should suffice to show that even in New Testament times a welter of incompatible traditions were created and manipulated differently by different Christian groups. John Bowden, Anglican priest and former director of SCM Press, allows that the virgin birth and the resurrection are "two points where Christian tradition most wants to see miracles", but where there is in fact "a high proportion of pious legend" (1988, p. 160). If these two items are deleted as unhistorical, a very considerable gap is left in traditional Christian doctrine.

I turn next (Chapter 5) to Mark, the oldest of the four canonical gospels, and to the seminal work of 1901 on Mark by the German New Testament scholar William Wrede. N.T. Wright, now bishop of Durham, has summarized Wrede's view as: "Mark, used as a main source by the other gospels, is a theological fiction, which cannot be trusted to give us information about Jesus, but only about Mark's own theology." Wright contrasts this with Schweitzer's view that "the gospels gave us, more or less, information about Jesus, even if we had to do some sorting of wheat from chaff." (I discuss Schweitzer in my Chapter 8) Then—surprisingly for such a conservative Christian scholar—Wright allows that "the question at issue between Schweitzer and Wrede remains on the table to this day" (1992b, p. 8). In my Chapter 5, I also discuss the 1919 work of K.L. Schmidt, which gave Markan studies a new direction. Throughout this chapter I draw very substantially on the chapter on Mark in my 1996 book.

Chapter 6 discusses that considerable fraction of the material common to Matthew and Luke which they took neither from Mark nor from each other, and which represents their assimilation of a source document not now extant, known as Q (= *Quelle*, German for 'source'). It bears witness to Jesus as a Galilean preacher of the early first century who urged Jews to repent before an imminent and final judgment would overtake them. Q only implicitly takes some note of his death, as on a par with the hostility and violence suffered by prophets down the ages. It certainly does not regard his death as redemptive, and has no Passion narrative, nor mention of Pilate. It consists mainly of Jesus's sayings, and is in this respect similar to the Coptic Gospel of Thomas, discovered in 1945.

What is said about the Galilean activity of Jesus in Matthew and Luke is almost entirely taken either from Mark or from Q. Hence I am able to proceed in Chapter 7 to discussion of the Galilean prelude to Jesus's ministry in these gospels—a discussion which shows, among other things, how greatly the New Testament writers misuse and distort the Old Testament.

Chapter 8 is focussed on a very significant element in the ministry itself, namely that Jesus's preaching is flawed by the delusion that normal life on Earth was very shortly to come to a catastrophic end. In a typical passage, he declares:

> The sun shall be darkened, and the moon shall not give her light, and the stars shall fall from heaven, and the powers of the heavens shall be shaken. And then shall appear the sign of the Son of man in heaven: and then shall all the tribes of the earth mourn, and they shall see the Son of man coming on the clouds of heaven with power and great glory. . . . Verily I say unto you, This generation shall not pass away, till all these things be accomplished. (Mt. 24:29–34)

The recognition of the prominence of such views in the preaching ascribed to Jesus is traced, in this Chapter 8, through the work of Reimarus, Johannes Weiss, and Albert Schweitzer, to that of commentators of today. It is important to keep in mind that the synoptic gospels represent Jesus as foretelling catastrophes as imminent in his own time, not as shortly to occur in ours, as many of today's evangelicals suppose, and that this stamps him as a failed prophet. Although this is characteristic of the first three (the synoptic) gospels, very little material of this kind remains in the fourth, which presents a very different Jesus, albeit one that is open to criticism on other grounds.

Another flaw in the synoptic preaching is the inclusion of unethical or unrealistic maxims: for example, do not resist evil; be perfectly confident that God will always supply food, clothing, and whatever you ask in prayer; and hate your parents, wife, and children in order to be Jesus's disciple (Mt. 5:39; 6:25ff; 7:7–11; Lk. 14:26). At one point Jesus declares himself to be "gentle and humble-hearted" (Mt. 11:29—this from the speaker of so many harsh invectives!), yet he goes on to call himself "greater than Solomon" (12:42). There is nothing humble in "all that came before me were thieves and robbers" (Jn. 10:8). The two sayings I have just quoted from Matthew do not form a psychologically impossible combination; men who claim to be modest little fellows are quite capable of speaking and behaving as egoists. But the combination is hardly admirable. And much more disturbing is the way Jesus repeatedly stresses the terrible fate awaiting those who do not accept his claims. Leslie Houlden, in his 2005 handbook, observes that, although "we cannot be certain where the Master's voice exactly sounds", it would be foolish to doubt the "radical and startling character of Jesus's teaching", which has "continued to disturb all the attempts of later generations to tone it down or domesticate it to human convenience." He adds: "The End-time's nonappearance naturally caused the most drastic rethink" (p. 435).

Jesus, as thus portrayed is, in Schweitzer's phrase, "all too human". Theologians still strive to establish that he was (and is) nevertheless also one hundred percent divine. J.A.T. Robinson, in his immensely popular *Honest to God*, specified, as "the problem of Christology", "how Jesus can be fully God and fully man, and yet genuinely one person" (1963, pp. 64f). The simple answer is, of course, that the whole thing is an absurdity and that nobody in his senses should try to solve such a pseudo-problem. The real problem is, How did such a contradictory conception ever get into the minds of rational beings?, and this is a problem for the psychologist and the historian. It is the fourth gospel—discussed in my Chapters 1 and 8—which so heavily emphasizes Jesus's divinity, and which also almost eliminates his apocalyptic preaching.

I have not repeated the detailed account of the gospel Passion narratives which I gave in my 1989 book, but I wish to advert here to their links with the doctrine of the atonement—a doctrine less prominent in the gospels[1] than in the epistles, naturally enough, as the epistles are much concerned to interpret Jesus's death. What is so strange is that they represent it as deliberately willed by God. That the Son could suppose that, by voluntarily submitting to suffering, he could induce the Father to refrain from inflicting suffering, as punishment on others, would be psychologically intelligible, particularly if prompted by Isaiah 53:5: "He was wounded for our transgressions; he was bruised for our iniquities". But that God himself should victimize his Son, and then think that this enabled him, God, to redeem all who have faith in his Son, is very strange, even allowing for some musing on the next verse in Isaiah which tells that it is the Lord who "hath laid on him the iniquity of us all." Nevertheless, we read:

> It was the good pleasure of the Father . . . through him [the Son] to reconcile all things unto himself. . . . through the blood of his cross (Coloss. 1:19f). God designed him to be the means of expiating sin by his sacrificial death, effective through faith (Rom. 3:25, NEB). He spared not his Son, but delivered him up for us all (Rom. 8:32). Jesus gave himself for our sins . . . according to the will of our God and Father (Gal. 1:4).

The Acts of the Apostles is equally explicit: he was "delivered up by the determinate counsel and foreknowledge of God" (2:23; NEB "by the deliberate will and plan of God"). There is also the well-known passage in the fourth gospel: "God so loved the world that he gave his only begotten Son . . . that the world should be saved through him" (Jn. 3:16f). Even in the first three gospels, Jesus in Gethsemane asks God to "remove this cup" from him, that is, to spare his life, yet adds that God's will be done, not his own (Mk. 14:35f and parallels). As Adela Yarbro Collins observes, the implication of what follows (the arrest, trial, condemnation, and execution) is that "it is God's will that Jesus die" (1992, p. 65).

One can of course see how this strange idea arose. Jesus redeemed us, but our redemption could surely not have been in any sense fortuitous, and so must have been planned by God, who therefore sent him to Earth for the express purpose of getting him killed there. Apologists resign themselves to calling this, with F.R. Barry, who was bishop of Southwell, "a deep mystery" (1965, p. 134). And Stephen Sykes, bishop of Ely, called atonement theory an attempt to explain the fact that "what God did about human sin is both extremely surprising and gives rise to many questions and objections" (1997, p. 50). One such is surely: if Jesus's death was the working out of a divine plan for man's salvation, why blame the human agents who brought about this benefit? Even Judas is a mere implement in this divine schedule. Jesus is represented as acknowledging this, and as nevertheless condemning him: "The Son of man goeth, even as it is written of him; but woe unto that man through whom the Son of man is delivered up" (Mk. 14:21). Anthony Cane's recent exhaustive study of Judas's place in Christology admits that this "pairing of necessity and culpability" makes Mk. 14:21, and its parallels in Matthew and Luke, a "most difficult text" (2005, pp. 33, 57).

ii. The Jesus of the Early Epistles Is Not the Jesus of the Gospels

In the book my primary concern is with the four canonical gospels. In earlier books I discussed the wider problem of how Christianity originated, and for that purpose it was necessary to consider all early Christian documents in chronological order so as to ascertain how ideas about Jesus developed and changed quite drastically within a relatively brief period. I will not go over all the relevant details again here, but must briefly advert to the significance of the fact that the gospels are not the earliest of the Christian writings which have survived: the Paulines (letters written by Paul) are earlier, and numerous other epistles originated, if not earlier than the gospels, then at any rate before what they say had become widely known and accepted in Christian circles.

That the Paulines pre-date the gospels is well-known to New Testament scholars, but may surprise the average Christian, who finds them printed in the Bible *after* the gospels, and who is of course aware that they address *post*-resurrection situations in the early churches, while the gospels concentrate on Jesus's *pre*-resurrection life. Paul must have written these letters by A.D. 60, at any rate before the Jewish war with Rome, which began in A.D. 66 and culminated in Jerusalem's capture and destruction in A.D. 70; for he repeatedly mentions dealings he was still having (and planned further to have) with the Christian community there, which was obviously still untroubled by any such upheavals. And upheavals they were! Bart Ehrman writes: "The Romans sent in the legions from the north and within a year subjugated Galilee." A group of Galilean Jews fled to Jerusalem and "eventually provoked a bloody civil war against the priestly aristocracy" there.

> Once they acquired control, these 'Zealots' pressed the fight against the Romans to the end. The result was a horrifying three-year siege of Jerusalem, in which reports of starvation and cannibalism were rampant. The war ended in a bloodbath in which tens of thousands of Jews were slaughtered or enslaved, rebel leaders were crucified, much of the city was leveled, and the Temple was burned to the ground. (2000, pp. 224f)

As I show in Chapter 1 below, even Mark, the earliest of the gospels, is generally admitted to have been written only around A.D. 70, and certainly not in Palestine. This time gap between the Paulines and the gospels, although quite short, is very significant, since the Jewish War occasioned a decisive break in continuity. The Jewish Christianity known to Paul was dispersed and reduced to insignificance.

Altogether, what is said of Jesus in the gospels is very different from what is said of him in the Paulines and the other early epistles. In all these latter (Paulines and others) there are not only no references to his parables or miracles, but no Galilean ministry at all, nor Passion in Jerusalem, indeed no indication of time, place, or attendant circumstances. The words 'Calvary', 'Bethlehem', 'Nazareth', and 'Galilee' never appear, and the word 'Jerusalem' is never used in connection with Jesus, who figures as a basically supernatural personage who took human form, "emptied" then of his supernatural powers (Phil. 2:7)—certainly not the gospel figure who worked wonders which made him famous throughout "all Syria" (Mt. 4:24). He was indeed crucified for our redemption—indeed, Paul specifies this crucifixion as the very substance of his own preaching (1 Cor. 1:23 and 2:2)—yet the Passion is not as described in the gospels, for there is no cleansing of the temple (which, according to Mark and Luke was what triggered the resolve of the chief priests and scribes to kill Jesus), no conflict with the authorities, no Gethsemane scene, no thieves crucified with Jesus, no weeping women, no word about the place or time, and no mention of Judas or Pilate.[2]

The distinction between the two layers of tradition is constantly blurred by apologists. Typical is A.E. Harvey, who claims that the crucifixion "under Pontius Pilate" is "not only described in considerable detail in all four canonical gospels", but is also "referred to on countless occasions in other New Testament writings" (1982, p. 11), whereas in fact those "countless" other references are not to a crucifixion under Pilate, but to one in unspecified circumstances. Paul, for instance, says that it took place "in due season", "for our sins", thus saving us from "the wrath" (Rom. 5:6–9).

Paul is of course both the earliest and the most substantial single one of these early witnesses, as those of the letters ascribed to him which he really wrote (namely Romans, 1 and 2 Corinthians, Galatians, Philippians, 1 Thessalonians, and the brief Philemon) comprise a substantial body of literature. There are admittedly a few statements in them which, if read from prior knowledge of the gospels, can be taken to imply that he knew of Jesus's ministry as depicted there. I have discussed them in full in my books of 1999 and 2004. A favourite example adduced by apologists is the occasion when Paul uncharacteristically appeals to the authority of "the Lord" to support an ethical teaching (on divorce: 1 Cor. 7:10). It is, however, not necessary to suppose that he believed the doctrine to have been taught by the historical (as opposed to the risen) Lord; for, as M.E. Boring and others have shown, in Paul's day Christian prophets gave directives in the name of the risen one as the obvious way of supporting rulings they wished to inculcate. At a later stage it would naturally be supposed that Jesus must have said in his lifetime what the risen Lord had said through his prophets; and so the doctrine came to be put into the mouth of the earthly Jesus and recorded as such by the evangelists.

That Paul received communications from the risen Lord is beyond doubt. He expressly records (2 Cor. 12:9) what the Lord had said personally to him in answer to a prayer; and the speaker can only have been the risen Lord, for Paul did not know Jesus before his resurrection, and, as a Pharisaic persecutor of Christians, certainly did not then pray to him. The early documents reiterate the then importance of Christian prophets as spokesmen of the Spirit. In church, says Paul, "two or three prophets" may speak, while others "weigh what is said"; and "if a revelation is made to another sitting by", then the first should be silent, "for you can all prophesy, one by one" (1 Cor. 14:28–31). He repeatedly speaks of "revelations" which he himself felt impelled to pass on to the community (1 Cor. 2:13; 7:40; 14:37). Other early documents show how widespread the phenomenon was. Ephesians tells us what "has now been revealed to Christ's holy apostles and prophets by the Spirit" (3:5). The book of Revelation refers to prophets as integral to the church (22:9), and delivers logia of the risen Lord through his spokesman, the author (22:16 and 20). One can readily envisage how all manner of rulings and doctrines could have emerged on such a basis, and in time be ascribed not to the risen but to the earthly Jesus. Houlden puts this matter as follows:

> In the Spirit-laden atmosphere of many of the early congregations, it is no great distance from 'the Lord now says' to 'Jesus said'; from the present statement 'Lo, I come as a thief! Blessed is he who is awake' (Rev. 16:15), to the use of this figure and theme (in a different form) by the Jesus of the past (Mt. 24:43). (2004, p. 103)

The fact that these prophesyings were made in church, in an assembly of worshippers, enhanced their appeal; for when any situation arises which excites the emotions of a whole group, rather than of a few individuals, then the united expressions of emotion tend to increase the intensity of emotion in each individual. This is the psychological fact that underlies panic when fear is the emotion. It underlies the orgy where the sexual emotions are involved, and it underlies group situations where rejoicing or mourning is the occasion.

Paul's mystical experiences included a revelation to him by the risen Jesus of how the Christian cultic act of eating and drinking had come to be established. He reminds the Corinthians that he had learnt "from the Lord himself" (1 Cor. 11:23, NEB) that "on the night when he was delivered up" (not 'betrayed'! See note 2 to this Introduction) he had said: "this is my body, which is for you: this do in remembrance of me", followed by similar words about "the new covenant in my blood". Paul then adds his own assessment of the religious significance of the meal: "For as often as ye shall eat this bread and drink the cup, ye proclaim the Lord's death till he come." The meal was, then, both a memorial to Jesus's death, and a looking forward to his second coming. According, then, to Paul, the risen Jesus personally told him that he, Jesus, had, during his earthly life, instituted the eucharist in this way.

One would expect any knowledge of pre-crucifixion words of Jesus to have reached Paul by word of mouth from other Christians, after his conversion to Christianity. But he implicitly denies this, and says that this knowledge came to him "from the Lord". This can only mean a revelation from the risen Christ, just as he elsewhere insists that the substance of all his preaching derives not from any human source, but from "a revelation of Jesus Christ" (Gal. 1:11f). So even in this case, this was the origin of the message.

Once such a cultic act had been established, it would be natural to suppose, in time, that Jesus had ordained it. An act of this kind certainly already existed in both the pagan and the Jewish background. In the previous chapter of his letter to the Corinthians Paul had warned them not to join in pagan sacrificial meals: "Ye cannot drink the cup of the Lord and the cup of devils (*daimonión*). Ye cannot partake of the table of the Lord and of the table of devils" (10:21). It is clear from this passage, says Hurtado, that "the cult meal of the Christian congregation is emphatically one in which the Lord Jesus plays a role that is explicitly likened to that of the deities of the pagan cults" (1999, p. 85). As for the Jewish environment, VanderKam says, of the ritual meal described in the Dead Sea Scrolls, that however one interprets it, "its messianic character, the prominence of bread and wine, the fact that it was repeated regularly, and its explicit eschatological associations do recall elements found in the New Testament treatments of the Lord's Supper" (1994, p. 175).

What is taken as the strongest evidence for linking Paul's Jesus with the Jesus of the gospels is that his list of those who had seen the risen Jesus includes men known personally to Paul, and they—it is claimed—had known Jesus during his ministry. If so, it would be hard to believe that Paul had not learned from them much more about Jesus's earthly life than is apparent from his letters. As the claim rests on identifying as companions of Jesus persons named in Paul's list, it will occupy us in Chapter 4 below.

For the present we can note that the Paulines, substantial as they are, have very little to say about the earthly Jesus. And the early post-Pauline material, also substantial, is equally vague about him. It comprises:

i. 2 Thessalonians, Colossians, and Ephesians. These epistles are ascribed to Paul in the canon, but probably falsely. The New Testament scholar Christopher Tuckett endorses the "widely held view" that they are pseudonymous and that Paul's authoritative position "led to other people writing 'letters' in his name" (2001, pp. 70f, 88n3).

ii. The letter to the Hebrews, the epistle of James, the three epistles of John, and the first of the two epistles ascribed to Peter. (The second is of later date, as much as half a century later than the Paulines. I give the details in my 2004 book, where Hebrews and 1 Peter are also discussed.)

All the canonical post-Pauline yet early epistles are dated between A.D. 60 and 95 (that is, within the period when the gospels were being written). Nevertheless, although most of them stress one or more of Jesus's supernatural aspects (his existence before his life on Earth, his resurrection and second coming) they do not ascribe to him the teachings or miracles attributed to him in the gospels; and they give no historical setting to the crucifixion, which remains the one episode in his incarnate life which they mention at all. This suggests that there was an interval before the biographical material of the gospels became generally known and widely accepted by Christians. That older Christologies should have persisted in some quarters while new ones were emerging in others is hardly a matter for surprise. It would, however, be astounding if the authors of these early letters, portraying Jesus as they do, had in mind—as nearly all commentators suppose—a recently deceased human figure, namely Jesus as depicted in the gospels. For instance, Chapter 1 of Colossians stresses, even more than the Paulines had done, that "our Lord Jesus Christ" is fundamentally a supernatural personage, and designates him

> the image of the invisible God, the firstborn of all creation; for in him were all things created, in the heavens and upon earth; . . . all things have been

created through him and unto him; and he is before all things, and in him all things consist.

Tuckett allows that "quite how all this can be said of a human being living in the recent past is not quite easy to understand" (p. 79). Yet, in the manner of nearly all New Testament scholars, he does not query that this is in fact the case.

Significantly, later epistles, written after the gospels had established themselves, do show the kind of overlap with their substance that we might reasonably have expected from the Paulines and the other early documents if their Jesus were the Jesus of the gospels. These alter epistles include three falsely ascribed to Paul, namely the so-called Pastoral epistles 1 and 2 Timothy and Titus. Tuckett notes that "they are almost universally regarded as pseudonymous" and represent "an attempt to rewrite Paul's ideas so that they relate to the contemporary world" (pp. 84, 88). I discuss this in detail in my 1999 book. 1 Timothy records (6:13) that Christ Jesus "witnessed the good confession before Pontius Pilate." 2 Peter, a second-century work, likewise pseudonymous and probably the very latest of the New Testament books, alludes to the gospel episode of Jesus's transfiguration. And Ignatius of Antioch, writing around A.D. 110, mentions that Jesus was born of the virgin Mary, baptized by John, and crucified in the time of Pontius Pilate. He reiterates this dating in three of his epistles with an emphasis that suggests that not all Christians were then agreed on the matter—a disagreement one would expect, in view of the older Christologies.

Numerous scholars continue however to deny that there are any real differences in the Christologies, and find the silences of Paul (and others) insignificant because—so they claim—later writers are just as silent as earlier ones. "The fallacy of the argument from silence," says Wenham "is seen most clearly in the case of Luke. He knew all the Jesus-material of his gospel, yet when he came to write Acts he did not repeat it there" (1991, p. 219). Dale C. Allison Jr. quotes Leonhard Goppelt, approvingly, to the same effect: "Luke did not point back to the accounts of his Gospel in any of the missionary sermons in the book of Acts" (1997, p. 112). Did he not? The following details, on which the early documents are silent, and which give a quite specific geographical and historical setting to Jesus's life, are mentioned in Acts:

1. Jesus was "of Nazareth", performed many miracles and signs (2:22) and "went about doing good and healing all oppressed of the Devil" (10:38).

2. God anointed him "with the Holy Ghost and with Power" (10:38).

3. He prophesied the destruction of the temple (6:14), had twelve disciples, and one of them, Judas, acted as a guide to those who arrested him (1:16).

4. He was committed for trial by the Jews and repudiated by them in Pilate's court. Pilate wished to release him, but they insisted that he release a murderer instead (3:13–14). He was also tried by Herod and the trial took place in Jerusalem (4:27).

5. John the Baptist foretold that "there cometh one after me, the shoes of whose feet I am not worthy to unloose" (13:25). And "John baptized with the baptism of repentance, saying unto the people that they should believe on him which should come after him, that is, on Jesus" (19:4; Cf. Lk. 3:3, 16).

Concerning this point, it has been noted that John the Baptist "is identified by name eighty times in the canonical Gospels and nine times in Acts" (R.L. Webb 1994, p. 179n)—as against nil mention in the New Testament epistles.

There is, then, a disparity between all the early documents (Pauline and other) and the gospels which cannot be readily discounted. It is perverse when many scholars reduce the whole problem—if indeed they acknowledge it at all—to the silences of Paul, when so many others are equally silent about matters which, had they known of them, they could not but have regarded as important.

I have set out the relevant details concerning the whole problem elsewhere—most recently in my 2004 book *Can We Trust the New Testament?*, where I summarize:

> When we come to Christian documents, in and outside the canon, which are known to have been written late enough for the gospels (or at any rate some of their underlying traditions) to have been current, then we do find clear allusions to relevant biographical material about Jesus in a way that is earlier unknown. The later documents, from the first half of the second century, include, within the canon, 1 Timothy (one of the three Pastoral epistles ascribed to Paul, but . . . generally admitted to be later compositions) and 2 Peter (probably the very latest of the twenty-seven canonical books). Outside the canon there are . . . the epistles of Ignatius of Antioch, and also the short manual on morals and church practice known as the Didache, the epistles of Barnabas and Polycarp, the apocryphal Epistle of the Apostles, the Apology of Aristides, and the surviving fragment of Quadratus's

Apology . . ., the so-called second epistle of Clement, . . . and the two Apologies of Justin Martyr. . . . Significant biographical material is present in all these writings. . . . There is, then, no doubt that, in the first half of the second century, Christian writers refer to Jesus in a way quite unknown in the earlier documents. I have repeatedly insisted that, until this distinction is accepted as fundamental, there will be no adequate understanding of Christian origins. (p. 51)

It has often been claimed that one must allow the early Christian writers much more knowledge about Jesus's life than the sparse details they specify; for otherwise one would—absurdly—be imputing to them worship of some Mr-We-Don't-Quite-Know-Whom. The answer to this is that in fact they worshipped a personage whom they were convinced had appeared to them in resurrected form "in power" (Rom. 1:4), completely transformed from what he had been on Earth. That they gave him the name "Jesus" is no cause for surprise, as it means "Yahweh saves", an appropriate name for a supposed saviour. Even the relatively late gospel of Matthew betrays, at 1:21, that he shall be called Jesus "because he will save his people". The French biblical scholar Charles Guignebert, who died in 1939, suggested that the name 'Jesus' was a cultic title, meaning 'saviour'. The name of a god or supernatural personage, he said, was long supposed to express the essence of his being, and "the power of the name of the Lord Jesus is frequently borne witness to in the New Testament", notably in Phil. 2:9–10 where Paul, having reminded his readers that the Lord showed himself obedient to God even unto death, added: "Wherefore God also hath exalted him above all, and given him a name which is above every other name; that at the name of Jesus every knee should bow, of those that are in heaven, and on earth, and in hell". In other words, said Guignebert, "the name of Jesus has a peculiar power over the whole of creation, so that the spiritual beings of the world, who rule the elements and the stars, prostrate themselves at the sound of it" (1935, pp. 76f).

That a sacrosanct name 'Jesus' may have been current in Paul's time is further suggested by the fact that, in Greek, 'Joshua' is rendered as 'Jesus', and Joshua figures in Jewish religious thinking of the period between A.D. 40 and 60 as the model for some who claimed supernatural powers—the so-called 'sign prophets' who thought of themselves as able to replicate some of the miracles of Joshua and hence as something like *Joshua redivivus*. They believed that, if only a 'sign' of the Exodus-Conquest could be performed, it would force God speedily to bring salvation (cf. my 2004 book, pp. 10f).

Robert Van Voorst, in the 2005 handbook edited by Leslie Houlden (pp. 640f), follows Graham Stanton in saying that, to ascribe much significance to the silences of the early documents is quite ridiculously to suppose that, when an author does not mention something, he or she must have been ignorant of it. Of course silence does not always prove ignorance, and any writer knows a great many things of which he says nothing. Silence is significant only when it extends to matters obviously relevant to what an author has chosen to discuss. Writers who regarded Jesus's life and death as of supreme importance might be expected at least to indicate when and where he lived and in what circumstances he died, had they known of these things. I did not, as Stanton and Van Voorst allege, unrealistically expect precise and detailed historical and chronological references, but pointed to the almost total silence of the early epistles concerning what, according to the gospels, was the very substance of Jesus's teachings and behaviour when reference to these matters would have been of crucial help apropos of the matters under discussion.[3]

For instance, one of the issues confronting Paul was: should Christians be required to keep the Jewish law? One would never suppose, from what Paul says, that Jesus had views on this matter, as, according to the gospels, he had. Again, is Jesus's second coming, which will bring the world to an end, imminent? And will it be preceded by catastrophes or occur without warning? On these two points 2 Thessalonians (probably a little later than Paul, although it claims to have been written by him) contradicts the genuinely Pauline 1 Thessalonians. But neither appeals to any teachings, such as those detailed in the gospels. This is very hard to understand if Jesus had in fact spoken them, and supposedly only a decade or two earlier. As a further example, there is the failure of the early writers to claim that Jesus worked miracles, when they themselves regarded miracles as important testimony (cf. below, p. 61).

When I first addressed these problems, more than thirty years ago, it seemed to me that, because the earliest Christian references to Jesus are so vague, the gospel Jesus could be no more than a mythical expansion and elaboration of this obscure figure. But from the mid-1990s I became persuaded that many of the gospel traditions are too specific in their references to time, place, and circumstances to have developed in such a short time from no other basis, and are better understood as traceable to the activity of a Galilean preacher of the early first century, the personage represented in Q (the inferred non-Markan source, not extant, common to Matthew and Luke; cf. above, p. 2), which may be even earlier than the Paulines. This is the position I have argued in my books of 1996, 1999, and 2004, although the titles of the first two of these—*The Jesus Legend* and *The Jesus Myth*—may mislead potential readers into supposing that I still denied the historicity of the gospel Jesus.[4] These titles were chosen because I regarded (and still do regard) the virgin birth, much in the Galilean ministry, the crucifixion around A.D. 30 under Pilate, and the resurrection as legendary. What we have in the gospels is surely a fusion of two originally quite independent streams of tradition, namely, as Bultmann a good while ago intimated, "the union of the Hellenistic kerygma about Christ whose essential content consists of the Christ-myth as we learn it from Paul, . . . with the tradition of the story of Jesus" (1963, p. 347). The Galilean preacher of the early first century who had met with rejection, and the supernatural personage of the early epistles, who sojourned briefly on Earth and then, rejected, returned to heaven, have been condensed into one. The preacher has been given a salvific death and resurrection, and these have been set not in an unspecified past (as in the early epistles) but in a historical context consonant with the Galilean preaching. The fusion of the two figures will have been facilitated by the fact that both owe quite a lot of their substance in the documents to ideas very important in the Jewish Wisdom literature. I have dealt with this in the books of 1996, 1999, and 2004, and I revert to it in Chapter 6 below.

I regard it as of the utmost importance to keep in mind that, prior to their fusion in the gospels, the two streams of tradition were quite separate and independent of each other. Because so many endorse Leander Keck's judgment that "today only an eccentric would claim that Jesus never existed", it has become customary to assume that, not merely his historicity, but also the historical setting of his life, as given in the gospels, is to be accepted as integral to the early epistles, and that, in consequence, "the one indubitable fact of his life" is "that he was crucified on Pilate's orders" (Keck 2000, pp. 13, 17). The importance of keeping in mind, against this, that the early epistles and the gospels represent independent streams is highlighted when we find Stanton and Van Voorst making so much of the fact that, as far as we know, no one in antiquity actually denied that Jesus existed. But this—whether he existed or not—is surely one obvious result of the vagueness of the earliest Christian epistles about his life, and should not be allowed as a basis from which one can impute to the authors of these documents, and to some of their Jewish and pagan contemporaries, knowledge of and acceptance of the historical setting of that life given in the gospels. The figure of the early epistles, and the Christianity based on it, was too obscure to attract much attention. The major pagan critics of Christianity all wrote only after the gospels had become established, and gathered from them that Jesus was a teacher and wonder-worker of a perfectly familiar kind. Hence they had no reason to doubt the main outlines of the life there ascribed to him. It is clear from what Arnobius records of pagans' criticisms of the early fourth century that, like most people today, they assessed Jesus from the gospels, from which they gathered that Christians were foolish enough to worship a being who was born a man, behaved as an ordinary magician, and died a death which would have shamed the lowest of mankind. Here was substance enough for their rejection of him, and it is unrealistic to expect them to have pursued their investigation into what for them was obvious rubbish to the extent of discriminating the documents and recognizing the problems which thereby emerge—something which has been only slowly and painfully achieved in modern times. Indeed, it was not until the early twentieth century that some theologians both recognized the gulf between the Jesus of the gospels and the Pauline Christ and showed some awareness of its importance for theories of Christian origins. The Toronto theologian S.G Wilson admits, with characteristic frankness, that "it sometimes seems that the topic is instinctively avoided because to pursue it too far leads to profound and disturbing questions about the origin and nature of Christianity" (1984p. 3). More recently, the New Testament scholar Bart Ehrman, having noted that "Paul's epistles are in some ways more reflective of Christian beginnings than the Gospels" (p. 10), goes on to ask, in view of the discrepancies between the two: "Did the Gospel writers and Paul share the same religion?" He does not venture an answer, but, discreetly addressing his readers, says: "I must leave that for you to decide" (2000, pp. 332, 336). He certainly does not underestimate the problem. In his 1999 book he says, of the Paulines (p. 79):

> We hear nothing here of the details of Jesus's birth or parents or early life, nothing of his baptism or temptation in the wilderness, nothing of his teaching about the coming Kingdom of God. We have no indication that he ever told a parable, that he ever healed anyone, cast out a demon, or raised the dead. We learn nothing of his transfiguration or triumphal entry, nothing of his cleansing of the Temple, nothing of his interrogation by the Sanhedrin or trial before Pilate, nothing of his being rejected in favor of Barabbas, of his being mocked, of his being flogged, and so on.

Ehrman adds that the historian wanting to learn of the historical Jesus will also be not much helped by "the other authors of the New

Testament"—a rare acknowledgment that Paul's are not the only New Testament epistles that are so notably silent.

Ehrman is also aware that "there is not a solitary reference to Jesus or his followers in pagan literature of any kind during the first century of the Common Era" (p. 49). Appeal is still made—by Van Voorst and others—to Tacitus as having confirmed that Jesus suffered under Pilate. But even his testimony is too late to serve as such a confirmation. Since the eighteenth century it has repeatedly been pointed out that, when Tacitus wrote that "Christians derive their name and origin from Christ who was executed by sentence of the procurator Pontius Pilate in the reign of Tiberius" (*Annals*, 15:44), he was simply repeating uncritically what Christians of his day were saying.[5] The Catholic scholar J.P. Meier allows that Tacitus, and Pliny too, both writing around A.D. 112, "reflect what they heard Christians of their own day say" and are not "independent extracanonical sources." As for Jewish testimony, "no rabbinic early text . . . contains information about Jesus", and later ones "simply reflect knowledge of, and mocking Midrash on, Christian texts and preaching" (1999, p. 466). Meier does accept Josephus as an independent confirmatory source, and Alice Whealey, in her recently published account of the reception, from antiquity to the twentieth century, of the paragraph about Jesus in Josephus's *Antiquities of the Jews*, observes: "this text is often considered as the only extant extra-Biblical evidence to the historicity of Jesus" and has been called "the most discussed passage in all ancient literature" (2003, pp. xii–xiii). But Josephus too, like the pagan and Jewish authors already mentioned, was writing at a time (around A.D. 94) when at least some of the gospels were available, and at a place (Rome) where he could well have heard about Jesus from Christians. In any case, few allow that the obviously Christian words in the relevant paragraph are from the pen of this orthodox Jew. Had he believed what is here ascribed to him, he would not have confined his remarks on Jesus to a few lines. I have written at considerable length on Josephus in my books of 1996 and 1999, and will not go over this ground yet again here. The literature on this subject is truly illimitable, and so I cannot complain that Dr. Whealey makes no mention of this work of mine. She shows how, during the eighteenth century, the passage came to be regarded as a Christian forgery, and how the whole discussion was nevertheless re-opened by twentieth-century scholars, with the result, she claims, that "after four hundred years the question of [the] authenticity [of the passage] has still not been settled" (p. 195).

As I have said, my concern in this book is with the gospels rather than with the early epistles. But the significance of the enormous difference in what is said of Jesus in these two sets of documents should not pass unnoticed; and if in fact two different personages are being synthesized in the gospels, that in itself puts in question substantial features of what is recorded in them. Paul may well have thought of his "Christ crucified" as one of the victims of earlier rulers of the region. Josephus tells that Antiochus Epiphanes, king of Syria in the second century B.C., and the Hasmonean ruler Alexander Jannaeus, of the first century B.C., both caused living Jews to be crucified in Jerusalem (Antiquities of the Jews, 12:255–56; 13:380). He expressly notes that in these cases this punishment was not inflicted only after execution, as it often was. Both periods of persecution are alluded to in Jewish religious literature (for instance in the Dead Sea Scrolls), and Jannaeus's crucifixion of eight hundred Pharisees left a strong impression on the Jewish world. Paul's environment, then, would have known that pious Jews had earlier been crucified, although dates and circumstances would have been known by many only vaguely, if at all. Of course, Christianity could not have been based just on vague historical reminiscence. The earliest documents show that it was based on emotional needs, on mystical beliefs and contagious delusions, and was moulded in the meetings of the congregations under the influence of preachings, prophesyings, and speaking with tongues (cf. below, pp. 136f).[6] The craving for love and protection found satisfaction both in the community of like-minded persons and in the belief of a supernatural savior. Other religious brotherhoods of the time were equally anxious to believe that after death their members would be rewarded and compensated for all the unhappiness of this life. They were more concerned with salvation than with historical facts, and it was belief, not inquiry, that assured them of salvation. The creed of a given brotherhood served to identify it, and Paul's formula, "We preach Christ crucified" seems to have been just such a sectarian shibboleth. To understand his doctrine of union with Christ we need to be familiar with the psychology of mysticism rather than with the detailed history of Palestine.

Christian scholars understand clearly enough that to regard, as they do, the Jesus of the early epistles and the Jesus of the gospels as one and the same person entails accepting that a historical personage who was—in the formulation of Rowan Williams, Archbishop of Canterbury—something like an ancient equivalent of "a car mechanic from somewhere near Basra" came to be worshipped as God within a few decades of his death, "well within the lifetime and the neighbourhood of those who had known him intimately" (2007, pp. 58, 68). This Williams attributes to his having lived a life of "unconditional love". "What is seen in Jesus is what God is: what God is is the outpouring and returning of selfless love" (pp. 69f). Apart from the fact that this characterization is a very one-sided appraisal of the behaviour of the Jesus of the gospels, it leaves unexplained why the authors of the early epistles tell us next to nothing about this alleged life of unconditional love. It seems much more reasonable to suppose that the development really went in the reverse direction, that a supernatural personage, represented in the early epistles as briefly incarnated on Earth, was later given a detailed biography. This would have been by no means unusual. The old gods of Greece and Rome were all in due course furnished with biographies. It is surely harder to believe that a real human being, a Jewish preacher, could come so very rapidly, without such fusion with a supernatural personage originally quite independent of him, to be worshipped as God. I shall revert to this matter in section ii of the Epilogue below, in response to criticisms of me in the 2007 book by the theologians Eddy and Boyd.

More helpful than the Archbishop is the New Testament scholar Larry Hurtado. He of course retains the premiss that the authors of all the New Testament books write of one and the same Jesus, but sees that the—admittedly quite extraordinary—exalted evaluation of him in the earliest documents is due to the kind of visions and supernatural experiences detailed in them—rather than, we may add, to historical reminiscences. He writes:

> Within the Christian circles of the first few years . . . individuals had powerful revelatory experiences that they understood to be encounters with the glorified Jesus. Some also had experiences that they took to be visions of the exalted Jesus in heavenly glory, being reverenced in cultic actions by the transcendent beings traditionally identified as charged with fulfilling the heavenly liturgy (e.g. angels, the 'living creatures', and so on).

He adds here, in a note, that "key pre-Christian passages that reflected and stimulated traditions about such heavenly beings and their liturgical responsibilities include, of course, Ezekiel 1:4–28, Isaiah 6:1–5, and Daniel 7:9–10." He continues:

> Some received prophetic inspirations to announce the exaltation of Jesus to God's right hand and to summon the elect in God's name to register in cultic actions their acceptance of God's will that Jesus be reverenced. Through such revelatory experiences Christological convictions and corresponding cultic practices were born that amounted to a unique 'mutation' in what was acceptable Jewish monotheistic devotional practice of the Greco-Roman period. (2005, p. 203)

Hurtado realizes that, to grant all this was so "does not require that one accept the validity of either these convictions and this 'mutation' or the claims of those whose religious experiences were taken as divine revelations."[7] All that "sound historical method requires" is that "we understand the crucial role that has been played in notable religious innovations by powerful revelatory religious experiences." He adduces, as examples, "the Qumran 'Teacher of Righteousness', Muhammad, Baha Ullah, Guru Nanak and others" (p. 204). All this may well be found acceptable because it will still be assumed, with Hurtado, that those who experienced these 'encounters with the glorified Jesus' and who received corresponding 'prophetic inspirations' had prior knowledge of the kind of Jesus we meet in the gospels. They will indeed have believed, as Paul did, that Jesus had been incarnated as a man who was crucified. But I do not see that more than this was necessarily involved in their thinking.

To show the inadequacies of the gospels' witness is surely an important task in view of the considerable acclaim given to fundamentalist and evangelical insistence that behavior and policy must be founded on acceptance of biblical doctrine. It needs to be more generally known not only that, but also why, the gospel birth and infancy narratives are admitted (now even by some reputable Catholic scholars) to be legendary, and why numerous New Testament scholars have likewise come to set aside the resurrection accounts. If these openings and endings are deleted as untrustworthy, the gospels' substance (apart from their Passion narratives) is reduced to preaching and miracle working. The preaching of the fourth gospel is (as I show in Chapter 1) totally different from that of the synoptics, and this latter is flawed by expectation of a prompt and catastrophic end to the world, and by the inclusion of some unacceptable ethical precepts. The miracles are those of an ordinary magician. It all amounts to something very unimpressive. After twelve years at Christian schools, I myself remained unaware that very many reputable Christian scholars have agreed that the gospels cannot be regarded as simple narratives of events written from the testimony of eyewitnesses, but are compilations from various sources arranged and edited in accordance with the various purposes of four unknown narrators. I was equally unaware that there is near-universal agreement that the gospels were written later than the genuine Pauline epistles—a point that must bear significantly on our view of Jesus.

In pointing all this out, I shall no doubt be accused, as I have been in the past, of merely destroying without building up. Van Voorst tries to discredit me by supposing that I have written "not for objective scholarly reasons, but for highly tendentious antireligious purposes." It is of course much easier to impute motives than to give a full and fair account of somebody's arguments. Moreover, it is not even true that hostility to—or, for that matter, sympathy with—a given material, religious or other, necessarily warps the reasoning process. It may make the mind work all the harder to produce results which will stand up to searching scrutiny. The sociologist Stanislav Andreski, commenting on what had been written in his field, notes that "the most profound insights into the mechanics of social systems have come from people who either hated or admired them" (1972, p. 99). The very considerable industry required of a scholar cannot be long sustained without an underlying emotional drive of some kind: hence the *argumentum ad hominem* is seldom just.

If mankind is to grow mentally at all, some feelings must be hurt, and although in individual cases it may be expedient to conceal the truth, the systematic inculcation of questionable doctrines is another matter. It is often hard to know how best to be helpful to others, but one thing is surely indispensable, namely to find out the truth wherever possible. Strife in opinion there must always be, but the Basel theologian Franz Overbeck well expressed what is desirable when he wrote (to Treitschke, December 1st, 1869): "I favour sharp and uncompromisingly clear confrontation in matters of theory, while I want the peace kept in practice. And the more difficult it is to combine these requirements, the happier I am to make every attempt to do so."

1

Basic Facts about the Gospels

i. Mark

It was what the Toronto theologian F.W. Beare calls "second-century guesses" that gave the four canonical gospels the names by which we know them; for they were originally "anonymous documents" of whose authors "nothing is known" (1964, p. 13). Even as they now stand, there is nothing within them to indicate who their authors are, and to this the fourth gospel is, as we shall see (below, pp. 131ff), only apparently an exception. An eyewitness of the events narrated would surely, says Ehrman (2000, p. 53) have authenticated his account by appealing to personal knowledge—"for example by narrating the stories in the first person singular ('on the day that Jesus and I went up to Jerusalem . . .')." Ehrman also observes that "because our surviving Greek manuscripts provide such a wide variety of (different) titles for the gospels, textual scholars have long realized that their familiar names . . . do not go back to a single 'original' title, but were added later by scribes" (1999, pp. 248f).

Once Christian communities had come to acquire more than one gospel, it was natural that they should give them titles as a means of distinguishing them.[1] It was equally natural that these titles should not be colourless (such as 'document A' and 'document B') but ascriptions to persons believed to have been companions of Jesus, or at any rate of the earliest apostles. And so we find Irenaeus (bishop of Lyons about A.D. 180) naming all four as they are now named, and as the first to do so. R.T. France, who allows that "the headings 'According to Matthew', 'According to Mark', etc., are not part of the text of the gospels", adds that they "are generally believed to have been added early in the second century" (1986, p. 122). Late in that century would be nearer to the truth.

The earliest extant gospel is Mark's, used as a source by Matthew and Luke, each of whom was unacquainted with the other's work. Their two gospels are thus reworkings of a Greek gospel of a non-disciple. The fourth gospel, ascribed to John, is independent of the others, but clearly used sources which were in part identical with theirs. These statements oversimplify a complicated problem in that the exact relation of the gospels to each other defies final solution because of lack of evidence;[2] but what I have stated to be the case on the matter has justified itself by its utility as a hypothesis which has enabled commentators to make sense of the differences and similarities between the individual gospels.

That all four gospels were written between the commencement of the Jewish war with Rome in A.D. 66 and the end of the first century is what France allows to be "by far the majority view in twentieth-century scholarship" (p. 118). Mark wrote when gentiles could become Christians without having to obey the Jewish law. Hence what Paul had to battle hard for had, by that time, become accepted without question. Moreover, as we shall see in Chapter 5 below, "Mark's Gospel is now widely regarded as the product of a more or less creative editorial process among diverse and discrete oral (and possibly written) traditions which had circulated for a generation within the primitive Christian communities that transmitted them." It is thus "the product of 'community tradition' and not direct eye-witness testimony" (Telford 1995, pp. 2, 6).

Nevertheless some apologists still claim that eyewitnesses of Jesus's career, or at any rate persons who had heard their testimony, were still around when Mark was writing, and would have been able to veto any inaccuracy or invention in his narrative. This might be a plausible conjecture if it had been written in Palestine about the year 60. In fact, however, it is not addressed to Jews at all, but to an audience to whom the author found it necessary to explain Jewish customs, which he himself seems to have found finicky—traditions, he says, somewhat disdainfully, about "the washings of cups and pots and vessels of bronze" (7:4). His knowledge of Jewish practices is imperfect. An example commonly adduced is his statement at 7:3 that "the Pharisees and all the Jews do not eat unless they wash their hands, observing the tradition of the elders." Such handwashing was ritual, not hygienic, as hands raised in prayer must be clean. What Mark alleges may have been true of Diaspora Jews, exposed to the danger of ritual defilement from contact with pagans, but it was certainly not true of all Palestinian Jews, as practically any critical commentary will point out (for example Nineham 1963, p. 193; Anderson 1976, pp. 184f. Ehrman, 2000, p. 74, notes that, because of this misunderstanding, "many scholars have concluded that

Mark himself was not Jewish"). In the incident in which Mark's statement is embedded, Jesus is represented as trying to confute Pharisees, of all people, with a mistranslation of their own scriptures. He quotes the Greek (the Septuagint) of Isaiah 29:13 which makes his point just where it deviates from the Hebrew original, which reads: "The fear of me has become a mere precept of men, learned by rote." The Septuagint renders this as: "The doctrines they teach are but human precepts", quoted by Jesus at Mk. 7:7: "In vain do they worship me, teaching as doctrines the precepts of men." As Anderson notes (p. 182), this is "part of the polemic of Gentile Christians." They naturally read the Old Testament in the Greek version, and ascribed to Jesus the way it is understood there.

Mark's knowledge even of Palestine's geography is likewise defective. At 7:31 Jesus is said to go from the territory of Tyre by way of Sidon through the Decapolis to the Lake of Galilee. So he first went north (to Sidon), although his destination (the Lake) was to the east. Also, to go from either Sidon or Tyre via the Decapolis to the Lake would make sense only if the Decapolis lay between them and the Lake, whereas in fact it lies beyond it, further to the east. Anderson, endorsing Rawlinson, comments that this "is like travelling from Cornwall to London via Manchester" (p. 192)—or, as an American commentator has said, like stopping off in Boston on the way from New York to Philadelphia. Jesus's whole journey to "the borders of Tyre and Sidon", from which he is here returning to Galilee, is probably a construction of the evangelist, who thought it suitable to place the miracle story of his encounter with the Syro-Phoenician woman (7:24–30) in this Phoenician territory (cf. McCowan 1941, p. 66).

Kümmel (1975, p. 97) writes of Mark's "numerous geographical errors", and Nineham lists passages which have relevant "vagueness and inaccuracies" (1963, p. 40). Niederwimmer (1967, pp. 177–183) gives detailed criticism of Mark's "strange geography". I have dwelt on this matter as it is commonly brushed aside by the more conservative commentators. Mitton even assures us that "an indication of Mark's historical reliability is his accurate presentation of the social, historical, and geographical conditions in Palestine in the early part of the first century A.D." (1975, p. 74).

In sum, both Mark and his audience were too remote from Palestine to evaluate what they were being told about Jesus. "The original readers", says Räisänen (1990, p. 153), "knew even less about Palestinian geography than the evangelist did." Where Mark wrote is not known. Anderson (p. 29) finds that the best we can say is that his gospel "was composed for Gentile readers in some unspecified part of the Roman empire."

Precise dating is also not possible. At Mk. 12:1–12 Jesus is made to predict not only his own murder but also God's "destruction" of those responsible for it. This can perhaps be read as an allusion to the destruction of Jerusalem in A.D. 70, widely regarded in early Christianity as God's punishment of the Jews for killing him. At 13:2 Jesus predicts the destruction of the temple, which took place in that year. Telford, with many others, holds that the prophecy was put into his mouth after the event, that the fall of Jerusalem was so apocalyptic an event that it aroused expectations that Jesus's second coming or *parousia* was imminent. Mark, he says (1999, p. 13), wrote a little later, when these hopes had waned somewhat—a waning expressed in verse 10 ("the gospel must first be preached to all the nations"), also in the assurance that nevertheless "this generation shall not pass away, until all these things be accomplished" (verse 30), and in the insistence that constant watchfulness should on no account be relaxed (verses 33–37). Houlden's indeterminate "about A.D. 70" (2005, p. 574) is almost universally accepted as the gospel's date.

In Mark's Chapter 13 Jesus foretells the following sequence of events leading up to the end of the world:

1. false proclamations of the end (verse 6)
2. wars and rumors of wars (verse 7)
3. conflict of nations, earthquakes, and famines (verse 8)
4. persecution of Christians (verses 9–13)
5. "the abomination of desolation standing where he ought not" and flight of "those in Judea" to the mountains (verses 14ff)
6. tribulation, worse than ever before (verses 17ff)
7. signs of the end in the heavens (verses 24f)
8. arrival of the Son of man, who will come down from the clouds to effect a final judgment (verses 26f).

The phrase "abomination of desolation" (or 'desolating sacrilege', item 5 above) is taken from the book of Daniel, where it alludes to the heathen altar which the Syrian Seleucid ruler Antiochus Epiphanes erected in the temple at Jerusalem in 168 B.C. The author of Daniel was still alive when this happened, but pretends to have lived centuries earlier and to prophesy it. He refers to it in such a veiled way that Mark supposed that the "abomination" had not yet arrived, and that Daniel's 'prophecies' in fact referred to events which had still to occur—events presaging the end of the world; for, according to Daniel (and to Mark) the sacrilege is to inaugurate a final period of unprecedented distress (Daniel 11:31; 21:1).

Mark, then, is telling his readers that some event—connected surely with the persecution of Christians foretold in this same context (item 4)—will fulfil Daniel's 'prophecy', and that then "those in Judea" are to flee. As Mark was not writing for Judeans but for gentiles (and, as we saw, doing his best to explain Jewish customs to them), "those in Judea" may be a reference to Christians generally. Mark seems to warn against taking this verse 14 literally by intercalating into Jesus's speech the words "let him that readeth understand."

A well-argued explanation of verse 14 is Haenchen's (1968, pp. 444–48), namely that what Mark envisaged was an attempt by a Roman emperor to force pagan worship on Christians, as Antiochus Epiphanes had done on his subjects. Mark did not state this boldly, as open criticism of the imperial power might have been dangerous. Instead, he sounds a note of mystery with the intercalated words, clearly calling on readers to apply the 'prophecy' to their own situation.

Before studying Haenchen's argument further, let us scrutinize the references to persecutions in verses 9–13. They include the expectation that Christians will be brought into pagan courts on a capital charge because of their beliefs. "Before governors and kings shall ye stand for my sake, for a testimony unto them . . . And brother shall deliver up brother to death . . . and children shall rise against parents and cause them to be put to death." The earliest extant reference to Christian martyrdoms (as opposed to mere harassment) at pagan hands is to Nero's action against them in Rome in A.D. 64, when, however, they were indicted not for their beliefs, their Christianity, but because they had allegedly set fire to the city. This persecution was an isolated incident, confined to Rome and quickly terminated. The epistle known as 1 Clement alludes to it—unsurprisingly, as it was written from Rome in the 90s—but no other Christian writer does so before Melito, bishop of Sardis around 170. After Nero's suicide in 68, the Senate voided his legislative acts, and according to the Ecclesiastical History (iii, 17) of the fourth-century bishop Eusebius, Christianity then co-existed with the authorities until a deterioration set in under Domitian, around 90, although it may not have amounted to much (cf. Frend 1965, pp. 211–17). Pliny's letter to Trajan, and the emperor's reply, shows that, by 112, there was certainly some persecution of Christians just for being Christians, but we cannot tell how much earlier such sporadic incidents had begun. Christianity was indeed not an authorized religion (*religio licita*), and "if it drew attention to itself then its members were liable to punishment. Otherwise sleeping dogs would be allowed to lie" (Frend, p. 220).

Apologists who date Mark in the 60s argue that it was written in Rome shortly after the Neronian incident, to which, it is claimed, its references to persecution pertain. But Rome was first clearly stated to be this gospel's place of origin only by Clement of Alexandria in the late second century, and then by Origen in the third. Even after that, "Chrysostom, with equal assurance, says Egypt" (Nineham 1963, p. 42). 1 Clement, written in Rome in the 90s, shows no knowledge of Mark; and the gospel's "Latinisms" could be found anywhere in the Greek of the Roman empire. Rome was selected as the place of origin surely because of the tradition that Peter had been there, and that Mark drew his information from Peter. But, as I show in my 2004 book, the evidence that Peter was ever in Rome is very thin.[3] And Mark's faulty representation of Jewish customs, and his erroneous ideas of Palestinian geography, make it hard to believe he was briefed by the Palestinian Peter.

Persecution was a problem once it had become obligatory to take an oath by the emperor's genius, to offer libation and incense before his statue, and address him as *dominus* (Lord). There is some agreement that these practices—to which no convinced Christian could submit—could be demanded of Roman subjects from around 90; and refusal to comply meant death. Jews were exempt, and so Christians were safe until Christianity had become recognized as distinct from Judaism, and had come to regard itself not as just one more cult, but as the only true religion, divinely directed to oppose all others as diabolical.[4]

Returning now to Mark 13:14, we note that, as Judeans are there told to "flee unto the mountains" when they see the abomination, it is implied that, by fleeing, they will escape from it. Haenchen[5] interpreted this by pointing to 1 Maccabees, which gives an account of the reign of Antiochus Epiphanes. It tells (1:54) that "the abomination of desolation was set up on the altar" of the temple, that pagan altars were built throughout the towns of Judea, and that death was the penalty for refusal to comply with the king's decree to offer sacrifice at them. Evasion was possible only by "fleeing to the mountains" (2:28). Christians of the first century would not have suspected that the events reported here in this apocryphal work were the same as those prophesied in veiled manner in the book of Daniel. Nevertheless, the narrative of 1 Maccabees could have served to show Mark how state persecution—which he was expecting—might be implemented. And Mark's reference to the necessity of "fleeing to the mountains" (as, according to 1 Maccabees, the priest Mattathias and his sons had done after slaying the royal commissar), when the "abomination" appears, suggests that he had the incidents of 1 Maccabees in mind.

Haenchen decodes Mark's enigmatic message ("let him that readeth understand") to read: As soon as preparations (that is, the setting up of an image or altar) are seen being made for compulsory sacrifice to a pagan god or to the emperor himself—as soon, then, as the sacrilege is seen "standing where he ought not to be"—then those in Judea (that is, Christians) are to flee to the mountains. Judea is named because Mark regards the threatened Roman persecution as fulfilling the prophecy of Daniel, but his Christian readers will understand that Christians anywhere in the empire are meant. But it did not suit Mark's purpose to reproduce Daniel's statement that the desecration would take place in "the sanctuary" (the temple), and so he writes of the abomination (a noun of neuter gender) standing where he (masculine gender) ought not to be. This lack of grammatical concord seems deliberate, and due to Mark's envisaging the abomination as a picture or some representation of the god or of the emperor. According to Rev. 13:15 such a picture will even behave as a person by speaking. The writer had presumably come across the speaking images of pagan temples, constructed by the skill of the priests (see Sweet's comment on this verse, p. 216). Mark insists that flight is necessary when the abomination appears, for, if Christians wait until they are brought before this heathen image or altar, they will be left only with a choice between compliance or death.

Haenchen does not infer from all this that Mark was written as late as A.D. 90. He thinks that the evangelist looked back on the Neronian persecution of the 60s as a situation that could recur in the form of a more general persecution with which Christians would have to reckon. Of course, the passage beginning at 13:14 "presents the exegete with difficulties as great as any in the Gospel" (Nineham 1963, p. 351), and there is no agreed interpretation of its enigmatic words. But if Haenchen's suggestions are in any way correct, a date of composition some years later than 70 would be quite appropriate.

What is beyond doubt is that the historical situation in which Mark was writing was one in which "persecution is a very real possibility", and that "preparation of his readers for this possibility is a very real part of the Marcan purpose" (Perrin 1970, p. 52). The evangelist makes Jesus interpret his parable of the sower as meaning that what is sown is "the word", the Christian message, and that some accept it for a while, but stumble "when tribulation or persecution ariseth because of the word" (4:14, 17). This reference to persecution leading to apostasy of converts surely presupposes a situation well after the time of Jesus. Then, at 10:29f, Jesus says that those who have sacrificed everything ("house, or brethren, or sisters, or mother, or father, or children or lands") "for the gospel's sake" will receive ample compensation "now in this time" (presumably in the fellowship of the Christian community), albeit "with persecutions". In the New Testament, the word 'gospel' does not mean a written document, but 'good tidings' about the salvation of the world by the coming of Christ (as when Paul says that the Lord has ordained that "they which proclaim the gospel should live of the gospel": 1 Cor. 9:14). Here, in Mk. 10—as at 8:35: "whosoever shall lose his life for my sake and the gospel's shall save it"—the 'gospel' means the church's post-resurrection proclamation of Jesus who died for the sins of the world. Those who lose their lives in persecution because they affirm this 'gospel' will save their eternal lives. Since it would be an anachronism to make Jesus himself preach this 'gospel' before he suffered and died, Mark very often does not specify the precise content of his preaching. He is said to have "taught" (1:21) and "preached" (1:39) in such a way as to have "astonished" his audience (1:22) with an authoritative but unspecified "new teaching" (1:27). The significance of the silence about its content was noted already by Wrede (1971, p. 79).

Räisänen (1990, pp. 239f) finds that it is because Mark wants to portray Jesus as the model for later missionary preaching that he makes him say things which imply the kerygma of the later church. Mark cannot of course do this blatantly. Jesus as *proclaimer* of the message of salvation cannot plausibly be openly represented as *what it is that is proclaimed*. There must be a difference between *Jesus as preacher* and *the preached message*. So the message of the post-resurrection church cannot openly be put into his mouth. He can only refer to it allusively by speaking of "the gospel" that has to be preached, or by mentioning "the mystery of the kingdom of God" (4:11), which is surely the church's post-Easter doctrine that Christ has saved us if we believe in him. Matthew sensed how unsatisfactory it is to make Jesus's audience "astonished at his teaching, for he taught them as having authority and not as the scribes" (Mk. 1:22), when no indication is given of what was taught; so he turned this verse into a comment on the Sermon on the Mount (Mt. 7:28f), made when Jesus had concluded this discourse which is absent from Mark but spread over Chapters 5 to 7 of Matthew.

In a recent article, Houlden shows (2006, p. 280) that the way in which Mark and Matthew put doctrine of later Christian communities into the mouth of Jesus brings out how different was the attitude to the Christian life in the respective churches of these two evangelists. The question at issue was: are all comers to be accepted, or only those who satisfy stringent conditions? Mk. 9:38–41 makes Jesus the spokesman of the liberal alternative, summed up in his logion: "he that is not against us is for us". Matthew, who has hitherto been following Mark episode by episode, did not find this acceptable, and omits these verses in his Chapter 18. When he does address the same issue, he makes Jesus advocate a much more exclusive doctrine (in accordance with what we shall see to be the overall tenor of the teaching of this gospel), namely: "he that is not with me is against me" (12:30, of course not represented in Mark). Houlden wrote this article as a riposte to those who, even today, fail to appreciate that, in the New Testament period, Christians "differed radically from each other"—a failure typified by the man in the audience of one of his lectures, who told him that "God wrote the gospels with his finger."

A sustained attempt to establish a much earlier date for Mark than critical scholars are normally prepared to contemplate has recently been made by J.G. Crossley, a distinguished New Testament scholar of Sheffield University. He is not the kind of conservative Christian from whom such attempts commonly emanate. He justly finds that the early church traditions about Mark do not help to date it; and while he allows that its Chapter 13 gives the views of the early church rather than those of Jesus, he finds it equally unhelpful for dating this gospel. Its reference, for instance, to the threat of "the abomination of desolation standing where he ought not" could, he argues, as well refer to Caligula's threat around A.D. 40 to set up a statue of himself in the Jerusalem temple as to any later crisis.

Crossley believes that Mark was written between A.D. 35 and 45, that is, even earlier than the Pauline letters. He argues that all three synoptics portray Jesus as strictly observing the Jewish law, and that only from the mid-forties do we find indications of non-observance of some aspects of it among Christians (Gal. 2:11ff). To counter such developments, Matthew and Luke, he says, had to make it clear that Jesus was not challenging the law, but only the observance of expansions of it associated in particular with the scribes and Pharisees. Mark, however, had still been able to take it for granted that this was so, and did not have to be explicit about it. Hence he must have written before the controversies among Christians about observance of the law had arisen: "If Mark does not reflect the disputes of the mid-forties onwards, as Matthew and Luke so clearly do, and upholds the biblical laws, then it is possible that this is a gospel written earlier than the forties. In other words, Mark could assume what Matthew and Luke could not" (2004, p. 206).

Crossley's method is to take passages in Mark on an aspect of the Torah which make such assumptions, and to point to the significance of the changes made to them by Matthew and Luke. For instance, at Mk. 2:23–28 the Pharisees complain that Jesus's disciples are breaking the sabbath by plucking grains in a cornfield. Such behavior would break the sabbath law only if the disciples intended to gather the grains or carry them away, for that would constitute work, forbidden on the sabbath. Mere plucking and eating the grains at once in order to satisfy hunger was not against the law. Mark, says Crossley, was able to assume that readers would realize that this is what Jesus was allowing the disciples to do. Matthew and Luke, however, had to make changes in order to show unambiguously that this was so. Hence Mt. 12:1 states expressly (against Mk. 2:23) that the disciples were hungry and began to eat the corn.

As a second significant example, Crossley adduces Mk. 10:1–12, where—if we take the text at face value—Jesus prohibits divorce absolutely and without qualifications. Crossley, however, believes that allowance for divorce for sexual immorality was so obvious, and so completely in accordance with the law, that Mark did not need to mention it. Now we know from 1 Corinthians, written in the mid to late fifties, that there was controversy among Christians over marriage and sexual immorality. Hence, says Crossley, Matthew had to make it quite clear (at 5:32) that unchastity was a ground for divorce. This is Crossley's second major instance of the way in which Mark could make assumptions that could no longer be made from the fifties onwards.

Crossley is well aware that his arguments are very controversial. Since he holds that Mark must be dated before the mid-forties, and at a time when Christianity was largely law-observant, it follows that Mk. 7:1–23—where Jesus is said to "declare all foods clean"—must be read, against the scholarly consensus, as a passage that adheres to biblical law. He also has to show that "Mark's knowledge of Judaism is exceptionally well informed" (p. 209). And dating Mark earlier than the Paulines makes it very difficult indeed to understand how Paul, and the authors of other early epistles, could write of Jesus as they did if, as Crossley clearly supposes, they and Mark were all writing about the same Jesus figure, and do not embody two streams of tradition that had independent origins.

ii. Matthew and Luke

That Matthew and Luke, independently of each other, revised Mark's gospel in itself shows that they were not eyewitnesses of the relevant events; for eyewitnesses would not take so much of what they wrote—sometimes word for word—from someone else, let alone from the Greek gospel of a non-disciple. Matthew's Greek orientation is shown also when he uses the Greek translation of the Old Testament (the Septuagint) on occasions when the Hebrew original does not support his argument. Thus Psalm 8 has, in the Hebrew: "Out of the mouth of babes and sucklings thou has established strength." The context shows that the meaning is that the glory of God is reflected in that he has made such a puny and insignificant creature as man the master of all creatures. The Septuagint, however, has "perfected praise" instead of "established strength"; and this allows Matthew, at 21:16, to take it as referring to children praising Jesus in the temple.

That Matthew wrote later than A.D. 70 is clear not only from his use of Mark, but also from an allusion to events in that year in his version of the parable of the marriage feast (22:1–14). He surely drew the parable from tradition, for it is attested independently in two other gospels—in Luke (14:16–24) and in the Coptic Gospel of Thomas. In Matthew's version "the kingdom of heaven is likened unto a certain king who made a marriage feast for his son". The invited guests—the Jews, as the chosen people, are obviously meant—persistently refuse the invitation, and even kill the messengers sent with it (verse 6), whereupon the king sent armies to burn their city (verse 7). These two verses, which make the point that the city was destroyed, and as a punishment, are absent from the other extant versions of the parable; and Matthew's text runs on naturally if they are deleted, for after the military expedition, the preparations for the supper remain exactly as they had been. The two verses are, then, quite obviously an insertion, and have almost universally been taken as a retrospective reference to A.D. 70. Some have objected that a post-70 writer would have given more detail about the sack of Jerusalem. But an insertion into what was surely a pre-existing parable had necessarily to be brief. And brief though it is, it effectively brings up to date the history of God's dealings with the Jews. That the insertion was made by Matthew and not by a later hand into his gospel (thus leaving a pre-70 date possible for the gospel itself) is evidenced by the fact that it accords very well, as we shall see, with the fierce criticism of the Jews characteristic of his theology. Beare notes in his commentary (1981, p. 7) that it is "generally agreed" that Matthew wrote "after the fall of Jerusalem to the armies of Titus". Moreover, Matthew added a second part to the apocalyptic discourse of his Markan material. It is twice as long as the first part, and all the pronouncements and parables comprised in it reiterate the theme that readiness and watchfulness must be sustained, even though the "master is away for a long time" (24:48, NEB). Matthew, then, has not abandoned the hope of his second coming, but, obviously, there has been considerable unrest in the Christian community he is addressing at its failure to have occurred. He is concerned to allay such misgivings, and so must have been writing quite some time after the earlier, confident expectations were current. Houlden (2005, p. 592) follows many others in suggesting approximately A.D. 85 as the date and Syria as the place where this gospel was written.

At that time there were obviously already Christian scribes, as well as orthodox Jewish ones, as is clear from Jesus's mention of "scribes made disciples to the kingdom of heaven" (13:52). These are presumably 'our' scribes, in contrast to "their scribes", the non-Christian ones of 7:29, where we learn that Jesus taught the people with authority, and not as did "their scribes". Again, "your synagogues" are mentioned when he addresses Jews (for example 23:34), while in speaking to his own followers he calls the assembly places of the scribes and Pharisees "their synagogues". Matthew characteristically adds the word 'their' when the context itself fails to indicate that what is referred to belongs to those he calls "the hypocrites", meaning non-Christian Jews. Matthew's Christianity had, then, broken with the local synagogues. They are for him "the locations where the hypocritical scribes and Pharisees parade their piety in almsgiving (6:2) and prayer (6:5), and where they claim the best and most prominent seats (23:6)" (Sim 1998, p. 143. Beare, 1981, p. 165, notes that 'hypocrites' is a favourite word of Matthew, occurring fourteen times in his gospel, as against once in Mark, thrice in Luke, and not at all in the rest of the New Testament).

Correlatively, Matthew is the only evangelist who makes Jesus speak of an *ekklēsia*, translated as 'church'. "My church" of 16:18 is in obvious contrast with "their synagogues" of other passages. At 18:15–17 the *ekklēsia* is mentioned anachronistically as if it had already existed as a regulative body, with a discipline and an organization, at the time of Jesus's ministry; for he here tells his audience to report the misbehaviour of a persistently wayward brother to "the church", and adds: if the miscreant will not listen to the church, then treat him as you would an outcast, as a pagan ("a gentile") and "a tax-collector".

From all this it is clear that Matthew's church existed in an orthodox Jewish environment and was very much concerned to define itself in opposition to it. "The sheer intensity" of the polemic "can only be explained on the grounds that the evangelist is describing, whether accurately or not, contemporary opponents" (Sim 1998, p. 121). His hostility is "far too intense to be a matter of literary convention", and "some kind of unhappy contact with Pharisaism" is required to account for his vehemence (Hare 1967, pp. 98ff). That Judaism should have been hostile to people who worshipped a crucified Messiah and nevertheless regarded themselves as the true Israel need cause no surprise.

All this points to a date for Matthew some good time later than Jesus's lifetime; and a post-70 date is suggested by the escalation of Jewish hostility at Mt. 27:25. Here, it is not the crowd or mob (*ochlos*) of the immediately preceding verses, but—suddenly and implausibly—"the whole nation" (*pas ho laos*) who beg Pilate to kill Jesus, saying: "His blood be on us and on our children". This has notoriously been taken as proof that the Jews have voluntarily accepted eternal guilt for Jesus's death. But by these Jewish speakers of about A.D. 30 and their "children", Matthew surely had in mind not Jews of remote future times, but the generation which he knew had suffered appallingly in the devastation of the Jewish homeland from A.D. 66. He was certainly not looking ahead to future centuries, for he believed that "this generation shall not pass away till all these things be accomplished" (24:34), and follows this with exhortations to watch out for the catastrophic end of normal life, and the judgment (24:36–25:13; cf. 16:28). The evangelist was, then, thinking of "those descendants of the crowd who will exist in the brief span of time until the world ends" (Luz 1995, p. 135).

Matthew's Christian community will have been embattled and quite small—only few will be saved (7:13f)—and so could not tolerate even internal divisions: its members must, in consequence, not be judgmental towards each other (7:1–5), but humble (18:1–4) and forgiving (18:21f). Sim observes that all this shows the importance Matthew placed on social cohesion (1996, p. 237). The Sermon on the Mount, covering the whole of Chapters 5, 6, and 7, is relevant here. It begins by stressing the blessed nature of those within the community (5:1–16; verses 13f read "Ye are the salt of the earth, . . . the light of the world"). It then forbids anger towards any fellow member, ruling that even to call him a fool makes one "liable to the hell of fire" (verse 22). "Him that is evil" is not to be resisted so there must be no retaliation, but submission (verses 38–42). As for external enemies and persecutors, they should not be hated, but loved and prayed for (verses 43–47). This presumably reflects the fact that the community was too small and weak to confront aggressors; but other passages show that it could rest assured that God will condemn them to everlasting torment at the judgment (16:27, and 13:42, the interpretation of the parable of the good seed and the tares). Matthew takes grim satisfaction in anticipating their "weeping and gnashing of teeth"—a phrase for which he had a particular liking, for he introduces it on six occasions; and altogether he makes more of hell as a place of eternal torment than any other New Testament book, apart from the book of Revelation. There is irony in the fact that this grim and narrowly sectarian document, which taught the abiding validity of the Jewish law (5:18), came in time to be fully accepted by gentile Christianity, and even placed at the head of its canonical collection.

For all its hostility to non-Christian Judaism, Matthew is certainly the most Jewish of the four gospels. It opens with birth and infancy narratives which draw us into a world full of Jewish piety: Jesus is "the Messiah", the "son of David" with ancestry going back directly to Abraham; and he is the legitimate "king of the Jews" (2:2). Unlike its equivalent at the beginning of Luke, this Jewish tone continues throughout, with many quotations from the Jewish scriptures. Whereas in Mark Jesus's audience finds his teaching both authoritative and new (1:27), Matthew retains only the former of these two epithets (7:28f). For him, this teaching was not radically new, and he insists that not a letter or stroke of the Jewish law is to be abolished (5:17–19). But of course what is to be kept is the law as interpreted by Matthew, not what the Pharisees have made of it. He repeatedly quotes Hosea's dictum that God desires mercy, not sacrifice, and he seems to regard love of God and the Old Testament command to love one's neighbour (Leviticus 19:18) as the law's two most imperative stipulations (Mt. 5:43–48; 22:39f), in the light of which others must be reinterpreted. He studiously adds "thou shalt love thy neighbour as thyself" (19:19) to the verse in Mark (10:19) which he is there adapting. Such reassessment of an older body of tradition characteristically occurs as a religion develops, as we may see today in Christian reinterpretations of the resurrection and of other traditional doctrines.

Turning now to Luke, we find that the opening verses of his gospel have been frequently adduced in attempts to link it with eyewitness testimony. We read there that "the eyewitnesses and ministers of the word" (this latter phrase means 'preachers') reported "to us", in other words to Christians (verse 2), the events which "have been accomplished among us" (verse 1), whereupon "many" (not alleged to have been eyewitnesses) undertook to record them in writing.[6] The original followers of Jesus thus wrote nothing down but merely preached. The author owns that he himself is writing even later than the "many" who first made a written record, but he claims—I translate the Greek here literally—to have "followed all things accurately from the beginning". 'Followed' cannot be taken to mean 'participated in' (thus making the author a companion of Jesus), for one cannot participate in events 'accurately'. One can follow them accurately only in the sense of investigating them thoroughly, and the author is claiming no more than to have made a proper scrutiny of what his sources say about the relevant events from their inception onwards. Hence the RV renders the passage as: "Having traced the course of all things accurately from the first". As the Catholic scholar Joseph Fitzmyer concedes (1986, p. 289), "Luke writes as a third-generation Christian". Only one of his sources is now extant, namely the gospel ascribed to Mark; and if Luke had really regarded it as reliably based he would not have contradicted it as freely as he in fact does.

It is universally agreed that the gospel of Luke and the Acts of the Apostles were written by the same author. And evangelical writers still argue that—I quote Terry L. Miethe as typical of them—since Luke-Acts have been found to be "reliable historical accounts . . . about methods of travel, about the time it took to travel from place to place", it is quite unreasonable "immediately to rule them out when they talk about something 'spiritual'" (1987, p. 110). So if I write a story in which a man travels from one place to another in a plausible number of hours and by a feasible method of transport, I am to be believed if I say that persons who, on the way, touched his handkerchief were cured of disease (Acts 19:11–12). Miethe also claimed that, according to "the testimony of scholars throughout the . . . world", Luke-Acts offers reliable information about "what happened politically". In actual fact their author is in such complete confusion over the chronology of events that occurred in Palestine in the first half of the first century as to suggest that he was not close in time or place to them.

Let me give examples. In Acts 5, where the scene is Jerusalem about the mid-30s A.D., Gamaliel reviews bygone Messianic risings and mentions that of Theudas. But we know from the Jewish historian Flavius Josephus (who lived in this first century) that Theudas's Messianic promises were made when Fadus was procurator (A.D. 44–46) and so could not have been known to Gamaliel at the time when he is represented as speaking. So conservative a Christian as F.F. Bruce does not think that Josephus had got the date wrong, but supposes instead that there was another Theudas, who did much the same as the one in Josephus, but a few decades earlier (1952, p. 147). Gamaliel continues by saying that *after* Theudas there was a Messianic rising under Judas the Galilean at the time of the census. Luke knows of only one census, that under Quirinius (Lk. 2:1–2) of A.D. 6—forty years *before* Theudas. As we shall see, in his gospel Luke compounds the muddle by dating this census of A.D. 6 under Herod, who died in 4 B.C. Fitzmyer concedes that such errors in the dating of Palestinian events of the first half of the first century show that "on many of these matters Luke's information was not the best" (p. 15).

Acts details the missionary travels of Paul and was long supposed to have been written by a companion of him. From this premiss, Sir William Ramsay began his book *St. Paul the Traveller* (1895) by declaring Luke to be as reliable a historian as Thucydides. That he was a companion of Paul has been argued because of references in Acts to 'we' or 'us', meaning Paul and his companions (or sometimes just his companions). As I show in my 2004 book (pp. 103–114), there is widespread criticism of this interpretation of the 'we' passages. Each one of them begins with a sea voyage with Paul, and in part reads like a diary entry. Commentators have shown that, by the first century A.D., it was a convention of Greek literature to relate sea voyages in the first person, whether or not the author was an actual participant in the voyage, in order to make the description more vivid. Another possibility is that the relevant passages may have been present in some travel diary (not the author's own) from which he drew, and that he retained the 'we', and even inserted it into some passages where it is obviously inappropriate, in order to suggest that the narratives have an eyewitness basis. Talbert observes that the whole question is still "moot at the moment" (1997, p. 148). However, a linkage between Paul and Luke is surely out of the question, as what is said of Paul in Acts is quite incompatible with what he himself says in his epistles in circumstances where he has no motive for dissembling. Critical theologians have long been aware of this.

Luke obviously wrote some good time after A.D. 70, for he rewrote Mark's thirteenth chapter so as to give specific reference to Jerusalem's destruction and also so as to avoid any implication that it presaged the end of the world: Jerusalem is to remain in gentile hands "until the times of the gentiles be fulfilled" (21:24). Mark, we saw, had written:

> When ye see the abomination of desolation standing where he ought not (let him that readeth understand), then let them that are in Judea flee unto the mountains. (13:14)

Luke rewords this as:

> When ye see Jerusalem encompassed with armies, then know that her desolation is at hand. Then let them that are in Judea flee unto the mountains. (21:20f)

Luke again addresses Jerusalem at 19:41–44, again in a passage unique to his gospel:

> For the days shall come upon thee when thine enemies shall cast up a bank about thee and compass thee around, and keep thee in on every side, and shall dash thee to the ground, and thy children within thee; and they shall not leave in thee one stone upon another, because thou knewest not the time of thy visitation.

This mention of a 'bank' put round the city correlates well with Josephus's eyewitness account that the Romans erected siege works after failing initially to take the city by direct assault. And the final clause of the above quotation expresses the view that the city was destroyed as a punishment for its earlier failure to acknowledge Jesus. Again, in Luke, and only there, Jesus, on his way to execution, urges the "daughters of Jerusalem" to weep not for him, but for themselves and their children, because of the terrible fate coming to them (23:27–31). And only in Luke is it said that the Jerusalem crowd that witnessed the crucifixion went home "smiting their breasts" (23:48), obviously expecting divine retribution. In a later, Old Latin, version of Luke the implied reference to the fate of the city is made explicit when the crowd cries: "Woe to us for the things that have been done today on account of our sins, for the desolation of Jerusalem has drawn near" (Metzger 1971, p. 182; Lampe 1984, p. 164). That it could be ethically questionable to suppose that the 'God of love' had carefully arranged for the wholesale slaughter of the Jews of A.D. 70 as punishment for Jewish misbehaviour towards his son some forty years earlier does not seem to have troubled early Christians. All that was felt as a problem was that the punishment was not inflicted earlier. Origen accounted for the delay by regarding it as an opportunity given to the Jews to repent (see Chadwick's note, p. 199, to Origen iv, 22). The mentality underlying such interpretation of A.D. 70 persists even today to the extent that the long history of anti-Semitic persecution, including the Nazi Holocaust, has been explained by some Christian fundamentalists, "always with a flourish of biblical texts", as "part of God's 'chastisement' of his chosen people for their rejection of Jesus as the promised Messiah" (Boyer 2003, p. 539).

Among the tendencies of Luke is a marked sympathy with the poor and the deprived. Admittedly, the whole New Testament is "fairly thickly dotted with attacks on the rich" (Houlden 2004, p. 89), and already in Mark Jesus amazes his disciples by declaring (10:23f) how hard it will be for the wealthy to enter into the kingdom of God. But in Luke this attitude is more prominent. His Jesus blesses not "the poor in spirit" (Mt. 5:3), but "ye poor" (Lk. 6:20), and adds a curse on "you that are rich"—a clumsy addition in an address to disciples who have left everything in order to follow him. The parable of Lazarus and the rich man Dives is also unique to Luke, and is likewise prompted by the author's intense dislike of wealth. Dives goes to hell and is "in anguish in this flame". It is not said that he had been a man of bad character, but that in his lifetime he had "received good things" (16:24f). Luke thus threatens even those who had lived comfortably: "Woe unto you that are rich", unto you that are "full now", and who "laugh now", for you will hunger, mourn, and weep (6:24f). From these passages it might seem that heaven and hell have the function not of rewarding virtue and punishing vice, but that of redressing the misery or, as the case may be, the happiness of this life. But for Luke these will not have been two different functions; for in his view the world is ruled by evil forces, and those who prosper in it must necessarily be evil, empowered by such forces (Ehrman 1999, p. 148); and so there can be no such thing as honest wealth.

Luke is also distinctive both in his account of Jesus's death and in its significance. In Mark Jesus dies deserted by all—by his disciples from the time of his arrest—and mocked by all, even by his two fellow sufferers. Mark's purpose was surely to show how heavy was the burden he took upon himself for us, and that he bore it quite alone, with no help from any quarter, not even from God. Hence he dies with words of Psalm 22 on his lips: "My God, my God, why hast thou forsaken me?" (15:34). This gaunt account was obviously too much for Luke, so that what Jesus says on the cross depends on which gospel one is reading. Luke deletes his cry of dereliction and replaces it with three others: (1) "Father forgive them, for they know not what they do" (23:34). These words are, however, absent from some important manuscripts. They may have been added later, or they may be original and later deleted by scribes who found it outrageous to think that those who had crucified the Lord could be forgiven; (2) "Verily I say unto thee, Today shalt thou be with me in Paradise", spoken to the fellow sufferer who did not, as in Mark, mock him, and expressing Jesus's confidence that God would care for them both; (3) "Father, into thy hands I commend my spirit" (23:46)—a quotation from Psalm 31 (an evening prayer), introducing a note of tranquility and, again, confidence in God's care of him lacking in Mark. Evans comments, appropriately: "It is . . . presumably essential to what Mark thought he was presenting that Jesus should die in isolation with a cry of dereliction on his lips, and presumably it was also essential to what Luke thought he was presenting that he did not" (1977, p. 49).

As for the significance of Jesus's death, whether Luke regarded it as an atonement depends on which manuscripts of his account of the Last Supper are taken as giving the original meaning. Lk. 22:19b–20, which includes Jesus's statements that his body is "given for you" and his blood "shed for you", is absent from important ancient manuscripts, and is widely regarded as added by a later hand so as to bring Luke's version of the eucharistic words into line with that of Mark and Matthew. This view of the passage as an interpolation is supported by the fact that Luke eliminated Mark's statement (Mk. 10:45) that "the Son of man came . . . to give his life a ransom for many"—presumably because he found such atonement theory unacceptable, even though, for Luke-Acts, as we saw (p. 5), Jesus's death is important and was deliberately willed by God.

A further characteristic of Luke of note is the way it outdoes the other two synoptics in its coverage of the resurrection. Without Luke's final chapter, their testimony to this decisive article in the faith "would be jejune" (Evans 1990, p. 79).

iii. John

The fourth gospel is altogether very different from the other three. They have long passages in common, and hence are known as 'the synoptic gospels' (or simply 'the synoptics') because they can be 'seen together' (the meaning of 'synoptic' in Greek). They include very many of the same episodes, often in the same sequence, and often even in the same wording. But nothing in John's gospel is verbally identical with any whole passage in them. The historical setting of Jesus's life is of course the same in all four—he has contacts with John the Baptist and with Pontius Pilate, both attested as early first-century figures in non-Christian sources. But the fourth gospel has none of the parables of the other three, no exorcisms, no suggestion that Jesus associated with 'tax-collectors and sinners', no institution of the eucharist at the Last Supper, largely different miracles, very little eschatology—the doctrine of a future judgment is very much played down—and entirely different discourses comprising whole chapters in which Jesus expatiates on his own importance and closeness to "the Father". The Catholic scholar J.P. Meier justly concludes that this presentation of Jesus's ministry is too massively different from that of the other gospels to have been derived from them, and comes from an independent tradition with some similarities to theirs (1991, p. 44). This fourth gospel not only makes Jesus predict that his followers will be "put out of the synagogue" (16:2), but in two passages commits the anachronism of implying that at the time of his ministry the expulsion had already occurred (9:22; 12:42)—as it doubtless had by the time this gospel was written. John's characteristic designation of those who oppose Jesus is either "the Jews" or "the Pharisees", the only major Jewish party likely to have survived the war with Rome relatively intact, since Pharisaism, as primarily a lay rather than a priestly movement, was centred on the household and the study of the Torah, and so was not radically affected by the destruction of the temple. There is no mention of the Sadducees (the high priestly party) nor of 'Herodians', who in Mark and Matthew figure as opponents of Jesus. In John, the Pharisees are even represented as an authoritative body with powers of arrest: anyone who knows where Jesus is should inform them so that they can arrest him (11:57). In Jesus's lifetime, they had no such judicial powers, and it was only after A.D. 70 that they even became important (cf. Joan Taylor 1997, p. 189 and note).

Joseph Ratzinger, the present Pope (Benedict XVI) confidently declares that "papyri from Egypt dating back to the beginning of the second century" make it clear that the fourth gospel "must have been written in the first century, if only during the closing years" (2007, p. 219). He has in mind P^{52}, a papyrus fragment of a few verses from its Chapter 18, often put at between A.D. 125 and 150. However, paleography can never yield a precise date, as a scribe's handwriting may remain more or less constant throughout life, so that one must allow a fifty-year spread in dating any specimen of it. Moreover, Brent Nongbri of Yale University has recently shown that many of the characteristics of the writing of P^{52} "are present in papyri produced well into the third century". Hence this fragment "cannot be used to silence other debates about the existence (or non-existence) of the Gospel of John in the first half of the second century" (2005, pp. 32, 46). It remains true that there is no clear example of a literary relationship with it in any writing before A.D. 150. Earlier Christians of whom writings are extant (namely the author of 1 Clement, Ignatius of Antioch, Polycarp of Smyrna, and Justin Martyr) made no discernible use of it; and Papias knew, around A.D. 130, of the apostle John as a link in Christian tradition about Jesus, but not as the author of a gospel (see Haenchen 1980, pp. 5–15, for a review of the evidence; cf. also my 2004 book, pp. 63ff). Then, towards the end of the second century, the picture quite suddenly changes, and from the beginning of the third almost everyone agrees that the fourth gospel is acceptable and was written in old age by the apostle John, son of Zebedee, one of the twelve.

If this ascription is true, it is surprising, first that, while John is prominent in the synoptics, all the episodes in which he figures there are missing in the fourth gospel;[7] and second, that even the twelve play hardly any part in it. They appear only at 6:67–70, and are given but one further mention ("Thomas, one of the twelve", 20:24). Their names are not listed, nor are they sent out to missionize (as at Mk. 6:7 and parallels). They certainly have no authoritative function to be passed on to others: continuity with the later church is effected by those who are called 'disciples', and in this fourth gospel these include persons unknown to the other gospels—Nicodemus, Nathaniel, Lazarus, all of whom appear at decisive points, and also the "beloved disciple", who will occupy us below (pp. 130ff)—and Philip, who in the synoptics is indeed listed as one of the twelve, but no more is said of him. Haenchen noted (1968, p. 257) that such a discovery as the gnostic Gospel of Philip, found at Nag Hammadi in 1945, shows that Philip is important in relatively late tradition. Similarly, Thomas, who is of some importance in the fourth gospel (particularly in its resurrection narrative), is merely named in the synoptics, again in their lists of the twelve.

The reason why John was not named as the author of this gospel earlier than around A.D. 180 seems to have been that, in the second century, Valentinian gnostics used and valued it as support for their own aberrant views, with the result that some Christians even rejected it altogether as a heretical work (Details in Lindars 1972, pp. 28f). Moody Smith, summarizing, says that, if it "had been known or acknowledged in the second-century church as the work of John or of any apostle, its relative disuse among the orthodox in the second century and the outright opposition to it in some circles would be difficult to explain". He adds, discreetly: "Probably the almost simultaneous ascription of the Gospel to John and the wide acceptance and citation of it in the church were not unrelated" (1986, pp. 73f). Quite so. 'Apostles' were regarded as guarantors of the true and pure tradition, with the result that, from the early second century, there arose what has been called a vast array of literature ascribed to them, some of which survives, often only as fragments, in collections of New Testament apocrypha.

Obviously enough, the readers of the fourth gospel were not eyewitnesses of Jesus's ministry, for the author finds it necessary to explain Jewish items to them (1:41; 4:9, and many others). Hence the statement that "the Word became flesh and dwelt among us and we beheld his glory" (1:14) cannot mean that the writer himself was an eyewitness: the 'we' refers to all Christians who have rightly perceived the word of God in Jesus and have thereby beheld his glory. The 'we' at 21:24—the whole of this Chapter 21 is almost universally regarded as a later appendix to the gospel by another hand—states that "we know" that the witness of the disciple who wrote "these things" is true. This represents the endorsement of the community in which this gospel originated, and was added probably from fear that it would not easily win wide acceptance beyond this community, as indeed proved to be the case, for as we saw it was initially elsewhere appreciated primarily in heretical circles.

Jesus's miracles in the fourth gospel are enhanced as compared with those of the synoptics. None of the sick cured in them is said to have been ill for thirty-eight years (Jn. 5:5). The blind man who is healed had been blind from birth (9:1). Jesus walks across the whole lake (6:21), not just part of it. And whereas the daughter of Jairus and the son of the widow of Nain (neither of whom is mentioned in John) are raised on their day of death, Lazarus has been dead for four days, by which time "he stinketh" (11:39).

A much more significant difference between the synoptic miracles and John's is that the latter do not just give evidence of Jesus's magical powers. They are pointers to his true transcendent importance, namely his closeness to the Father. Thus he cures the man blind from birth in his capacity of "the light of the world" (9:5; cf. 8:12); and in Chapter 6, after he has fed the five thousand and walked across the lake, he complains that the crowds seek him merely because he had miraculously fed them (6:26), whereas they should realize that he is "the bread of life" (6:35), of eternal life, far superior to the wilderness manna. That did not prevent the Israelites from dying in due course (6:31f, 47–50), whereas "he that heareth my word and believeth him that sent me" has already "passed out of death into life" (5:24). To obtain this "bread of life", his audience should "believe on him" as the ambassador of God the Father (6:29). As such, he has no will of his own, but simply implements the Father's will (6:38), which is that "every one that . . . believeth on the Son should have eternal life" (6:40). Thus, when he says that "I and the Father are one", he means not that he is God, but that, as God's ambassador, he is a channel for God's will and has no independent initiatives of his own: "The word which you hear is not mine, but the Father's who sent me" (14:24), so that "he that honoureth not the Son honoureth not the Father which sent him" (5:23). God himself is not directly accessible, but those who discern Jesus as truly God's unique ambassador can in this way discern God. Hence he can say: "I am the way and the truth and the life: no one cometh unto the Father but by me" (14:6)—a dictum that has subsequently functioned often enough as justification for intolerance. His statement "the truth shall make you free" (8:32) is no advocacy of truth in general. The previous verse shows that here 'truth' means sectarian "abiding in" faith in him: and the following verses explain that this 'makes you free' in the sense of free from sin. His numerous "I am" sayings in this gospel—such as "I am the light of the world" (8:12)—are "an important ingredient of John's anti-gnostic Christology because they assert that it is only through belief in Jesus who is the life that salvation can be gained, not [as gnostic Christians supposed] through the discovery of light in oneself" (Koester 1990, p. 263). The Coptic Gospel of Thomas also has 'I am' sayings, and as Ismo Dunderberg shows in his 2006 book (on which see p. 331 below), this means no more than that both gospels were written about the same time against a common intellectual and theological background, not, as Elaine Pagels (2003, pp. 57ff) and others have argued, that the communities behind them were close to each other in some way.

There is also a predestinarian element in the salvific teaching of the fourth gospel. Jesus reiterates that the Father has ensured that not all are capable of accepting it:

No man can come to me except the Father which sent me draw him. (6:44)

No man can come unto me, except it be given unto him of the Father. (6:65)

I manifested thy name unto the men whom thou gavest me out of the world. (17:6)

I pray not for the world but for those whom thou hast given me. (17:9)

Such predestinarian stance may well have been prompted by the experience of preachers that many are indifferent to their message. Even the best sermons do not win over everybody and it is some comfort to suppose that God wills it to be so.

As the Father's ambassador, the Jesus of this gospel existed before being sent to Earth: "Before Abraham was, I am" (8:58). This pre-existence is what Paul had believed of Jesus in the 50s, but to have Jesus himself stating it in elaborate discourses in the 20s goes far beyond anything in the Pauline or other early epistles, or even in the synoptic gospels. Jesus, as Paul conceived him, "emptied himself" of all that was divine about him in order to come to Earth as a man (Phil. 2:6–11), and certainly did not go about proclaiming his supernatural status. For John, however, because Jesus was with God even before Earth was created, he can remind God of this fact (17:5) and can impart God's message to his audiences, which is simply that "ye believe on him whom he hath sent" (6:29). The message, then, is Jesus himself; and in Chapter 10 he speaks publicly to the Jews of his own importance in such a way that some of them, understandably, think him to be mad (10:20).

Chapters 13–16 consist of long farewell discourses to the disciples at a final supper—an informal meal "before the passover" (13:1), not a passover meal, as in the synoptics. The difference is theologically important, for it enables John to make Jesus die not after passover, but at its "preparation" (19:14, 31), when the lambs were being slaughtered in the temple. In this way he becomes the true paschal sacrifice, "the lamb of God which taketh away the sin of the world" (1:29). The supper discourses are unique to this gospel. They have no "take, eat" formula, nor mention of bread or wine. Instead, Jesus washes his disciples' feet, urges them to "believe in God, believe also in me" (14:1), and elaborates once again on his own importance ("I am the true vine", etc., 15:1), concluding with "I have overcome the world" (16:33), meaning that, by his immediately forthcoming death and resurrection, he has vanquished the demonic power hostile to God, "the prince of this world" (16:11). Then, throughout Chapter 17, he addresses God directly: "Father, the hour is come; glorify thy Son" (17:1).

I have quoted enough to show that the sayings material in John is very different, in substance as in manner, from that of the synoptics—from, for instance, the pithy sayings of Matthew's Sermon on the Mount. John has none of the synoptic sayings on marriage, divorce, property, and the state. In Mark, as we shall see in Chapter 5 below, a good deal of secrecy is characteristic of Jesus's teaching and behaviour. In John, however, the very reverse is the case. Early in his Johannine ministry, at the marriage feast in Cana, he miraculously turns a large amount of water into wine as the first of his "signs" which "manifested his glory" and led his disciples to "believe on him" (2:11. This is one of the many incidents in this gospel that are unknown to the others). His teachings are equally open. He tells the High Priest: "I have spoken openly to the world; I have always taught in synagogues and in the temple where all the Jews come together; and in secret spake I nothing" (18:20). And this teaching consists of long Christological disquisitions—very substantial compositions—quite different from what speeches there are in the synoptics. Hence, if both are authentic, Jesus spent his short ministry teaching in two different ways, and the synoptic tradition has transmitted the one style and substance of his utterances, and the Johannine tradition the other, with almost no overlap. It is more plausible to allow, as do most scholars, that the fourth gospel represents an advanced theological development in which meditations on the status and work of Christ are presented in the first person, as though he himself had said them. In Chapter 3, for instance, a speech by Jesus becomes, from verse 13, a speech about Jesus, and from a post-Easter perspective: "The Son of man must be lifted up, that whosoever believeth may in him have everlasting life. For God so loved the world that he gave his only begotten Son, that whosoever believeth on him should not perish, but have eternal life" (3:14–16). By "lifted up" his crucifixion is meant, as is made clear at 12:32f and 18:32. In his prayer in Chapter 17 he even speaks of himself in the third person as "Jesus Christ" (17:3). Lindars gives examples (1971, pp. 23f, 41, 61) of the way in which the evangelist uses no more than fragments of his source material—a phrase or even a mere word from the Old Testament or the Jesus tradition—and works them into narratives and discourses which are his own compositions. Starting with a small kernel from a source, he surrounds it with a whole chapter of his own theology.

To us it may seem dishonest that John composed speeches and put them into Jesus's mouth. But doubtless he felt that the spirit of Christ was upon him, and that he could therefore speak with the mind of Christ—as we know from 1 Cor. 2:16 that early Christian preachers did (cf. above, p. 8). If we accept Lindars's suggestion (1972, p. 51) that John's gospel is essentially an adaptation of homilies he delivered originally to a Christian assembly, possibly at the Eucharist—the discourse on the bread of life in Chapter 6 obviously suits this setting—then we can suppose that his function was to supply the assembly with revelation, knowledge, prophesying, or teaching, as in the early church alluded to in 1 Cor. 14:6.

There is a uniformity about the speeches in the fourth gospel extending even to others than those of Jesus. John the Baptist is made to speak exactly as Jesus does, propounding Johannine theology:

> He that cometh from above is above all: he that is of the earth is of the earth. . . . He whom God hath sent speaketh the words of God. . . . The Father loveth the Son and hath given all things into his hand. He that believeth on the Son hath eternal life; but he that obeyeth not the Son shall not see life, but the wrath of God abideth on him. (3:31–36)

In this gospel, the Baptist is no mere precursor, but a Christian preacher. At his very first meeting with Jesus, he identified him as "the lamb of God which taketh away the sin of the world" (1:29)—a conception of Jesus which surely can have arisen only after his death, not at the outset of his Galilean ministry. But the Baptist from the first knows not only of Jesus as atonement, but also of his pre-existence: "This is he of whom I said, After me cometh a man which is become before me: for he was before me" (1:30),

These discourses show that the writer's primary aim is to instruct, not to relate events. His gospel is primarily theological, not historical. The never-ending repetition of a few basic ideas, regardless of who is speaking or being addressed (even Pilate is regaled with Johannine theology; 18:36f), shows these speeches to be all alike free compositions of a single author, and also makes them almost unbearably monotonous. No one, said William Wrede, is more conscious of this than he who has the task of commenting on this gospel from its beginning to its end! (1903, p. 13).

The Jesus of the fourth gospel knows everything past and future. He is able to tell the Samaritan woman "all things" that ever she did (4:29). He knows from the first who it was who would "deliver him up" (6:64). His question to Philip, as to how they can feed the crowd, is not a real question, for he knows already what to do (6:6). Likewise, his thanking God for giving him miraculous powers is, he adds, mere pretence so as to impress his importance on the crowd (11:42). Without this added remark, his thanking might be understood as implying that he was uncertain as to whether God would support him.

Not only is Jesus's knowledge superhuman; the whole march of events in his life—what happens to him, as well as what he himself does—is directed supernaturally. His opponents repeatedly try to lay hands on him, but are unable to do so "because his hour had not yet come" (7:30, 44; 8:20). No one can harm him before the divinely preordained "hour" of his crucifixion. Such is his majesty that, when he admits, to the soldiers who have come with Judas to arrest him, that he is the man they seek ("I am he"), the whole cohort (*speira*) retreats and falls to the ground (18:6). It is clearly not easy for the evangelist to get him arrested at all! Even then, his death cannot be forced upon him against his will, and he dies only because he offers his life in accordance with the Father's command (10:18). Even Pilate has no power over him "except it were given . . . from above" (19:11). His death does not shame him, but is his glorification: "The hour is come that the Son of man be glorified" (12:23) and the Devil in this way defeated: "Now shall the prince of this world be cast out" (verse 31). "The prince of this world hath been judged" (16:11).

Small wonder that Schweitzer took the view that, in any reconstruction of the life of the real historical Jesus, the fourth gospel must be simply ruled out. More recent students of it who agree with this judgement express it less bluntly, as when Moody Smith says: "Although John doubtless contains chronological and topographical material worthy of historical scrutiny, it presents a picture of Jesus which, when placed alongside that of the synoptics, can be regarded as historical in only the most rarified sense of the word" (1984, p. 20). Nevertheless, the fourth gospel has not been ruled out: for many commentators perpetuate the traditional view of Jesus, dependent, as Martin Werner observed, on reading the synoptic gospels through Johannine spectacles (1957, pp. 62f).

As with Matthew and Luke, what is said of Jesus in the fourth gospel shows that it is not an early work. Indeed, the way it makes Jesus and his supporters confront those who are called "the Jews" is very strange. For instance, a man Jesus has healed on the sabbath is challenged by people described as Jews (5:10), which doubtless they were. But in this setting, everyone, including Jesus himself, is a Jew. Later, Jesus cures a man born blind, but the man's parents refuse to tell "the Jews" that it was Jesus who had cured him, "because they were afraid of the Jews" (9:22). But these parents were themselves Jews. In the other gospels the term is used, naturally enough, when non-Jews speak, as when the magi from the east inquire about one born "king of the Jews" (Mt. 2:2), or when Pilate designates Jesus as "the king of the Jews" (Mt. 27:37 and parallels). In John, however, the narrator somehow stands outside the orbit of Judaism, in that he seems no longer to consider himself, or even Jesus and his disciples, to be Jewish. This situation does not correspond to the time of Jesus, but more likely reflects a tension between the synagogue and the emerging Johannine Christian church in the latter part of the first century.

As John's church had been "put out" of the synagogue, it must earlier have been within it, and so surely included many Jews. Hostile feelings are apt to be strong between groups, or even individuals, who, although they have, or used to have, some doctrines in common, are now competing for support. People who had always been rank outsiders might be excused for not knowing 'the truth'; but those with whom one used to be in the same political or religious party, or even those who are still within it, but at the opposite end of it, can be charged with wilfully rejecting what is right. We see this from the fact that many books of the

New Testament include vilification not only of Jews, but of Christians who do not share the particular doctrinal niceties of the writer. Paul begins his letter to the Galatians, one of the very earliest Christian documents, by twice cursing Christians who do not agree with him (1:8f). The brief epistle of Jude consists almost entirely of vilification of rival Christians, who are said to follow their lusts, to commit shameful deeds, flout authority, pour abuse on things they do not understand, and to be grumblers and malcontents. To take this at face value would be like judging Catholics of the Reformation period from Protestant invectives. But in both cases the venom was strong and real.

Returning now to John, we find him very concerned that his church form a united front against the synagogue. He does not endorse the Old Testament injunction to love one's neighbour (Leviticus 19:18; Mk. 12:33 and parallels), let alone one's enemies (Mt. 5:44; Lk. 6:27), but makes his Jesus tell his addressees to love one another, that is, other Johannine Christians:

> Love one another. . . . By this shall all men know that ye are my disciples, if ye love one another. (13:34f)
>
> Neither for these only [my disciples] do I pray, but for them also that believe on me through their word, That they may all be one. (17:20f)

Houlden explains that, since John views 'the world' very negatively, for him the believer has duties "only toward those who like himself are saved from it." A man's moral duty "could only lie within the Christian circle, where alone 'meaning' was to be found" (2004, p. 36). The synagogue is outside this circle, and so "the Jews" are described in the harshest terms: their father is the Devil, a liar and a murderer, and their will is to do this murderer's desires (8:44). It is not surprising that the later church, understanding such passages as the voice of the Lord in his ministry of the 20s or 30s, and not as reflecting tension with synagogues of the 90s, should become violently anti-Jewish. John's gospel was particularly valued during the trinitarian controversies of later centuries, for it could be adduced as evidence for Jesus's divinity, and for the close relationship between the Father and the Son.[8] And so its harsh words about "the Jews" were not to be ignored.

It will not do to argue that the Johannine *Ioudaioi* are not really the generality of Jews, but only Judeans—at 6:41 and 51f "the Jews addressed" are Galileans—or alternatively merely the Jewish authorities; for Passover and Tabernacles are called "feasts of the Jews" (5:1; 7:2), and they are feasts of all Jews. The Torah is called "your law" in an address to Jews (8:17; 10:34), and it is not just the law of the rulers. For John, "God is spirit" (4:24), and must be worshipped "in spirit and truth", not with the paraphernalia of the Jewish law. This gospel is not a timeless meditation on eternal verities, but an indictment of Jews who do not accept Christological claims. Of course it allows that "salvation is from the Jews" (4:22), in that the incarnation takes place in a Jewish setting, and Christ is heir to promises made to Moses. "Moses wrote of me," says John's Jesus (5:46), but the benighted Jews fail to realize this. In this gospel, the opposite of 'the Jews' is not 'the gentiles', but true believers, Jesus's "own" (13:1), who accept his claims. While it would be a distortion to dub this anti-Semitic, it remains true, as Moody Smith concedes, that even now "no one who is Jewish is likely to find the Fourth Gospel congenial reading." He adds: "When read aright, it will scarcely comfort most nominal Christians." The evangelist's world-view is "evidently not our own" (1995, pp. 164, 169).

iv. More on "the Jews" in the Gospels

As hostility to Jews is still much in evidence today, it is appropriate to give a little further attention to attitudes to them in the early church, particularly in the gospels. Christianity certainly began within Judaism. Early Christian documents accept the God of Israel, the Old Testament, Jewish apocalyptic and angelology, and Jewish ideas about the Messiah. A non-Jewish origin for a religion which embraced all this is out of the question. It was perplexing that most Jews refused to accept the claims of Jesus, and Paul accounted for their intransigence by distinguishing the generality of Jews (the children of Abraham according to the flesh) from those who became Christians, for whom alone, he says, the Old Testament promises were meant (Rom. 9:6ff). Quite generally, the early Christians interpreted the Old Testament prophecies of doom as directed against the Jews, but its statements of hope and promise were seen as finding their fulfillment in the church (cf. Judith Lieu 1992, p. 85).

Commentators cannot agree whether Mark denigrates Jews as a whole or only their leaders. Telford concludes his discussion of this question by declaring it "hard to resolve" (1999, p. 240), from which we can reasonably infer that the evidence is inconclusive. Even Matthew, who attacks scribes and Pharisees quite ferociously in his Chapter 23 and elsewhere, begins that chapter with unreserved acceptance of their authority as teachers. They are said to "sit on Moses's seat", and so the Christian disciples should "do and observe all things whatsoever they bid you". Their fault is said to be failure to carry out their own teaching:

"They say and do not" (23:2f). This comes as a great surprise after the clear rejection of their teaching in earlier chapters. For instance:

1. At 12:1–8 Jesus rebuffs Pharisees who complain that his disciples "do what is not lawful on the Sabbath" and declares: "the Son of man is Lord of the Sabbath."

2. At 15:6–9 he complains that the Pharisees have "made void the word of God" by teaching "the precepts of men".

3. At 16:6 he warns the disciples against "the leaven of the Pharisees and Sadducees", and in verse 12, present only in this gospel, goes on to equate this leaven with their "teaching".

4. In Chapter 23 itself he calls scribes and Pharisees "blind guides" (verse 16)—hardly an endorsement of their teaching.

Here, as so often, uniform interpretation of all that an evangelist offers is impossible. Graham Stanton begins his 1992 detailed study of Matthew by admitting: "Individual verses still baffle me."

The denunciation of scribes and Pharisees as "full of hypocrisy and iniquity" (verse 28) which forms the main substance of Chapter 23 goes well beyond what the evangelist drew on this topic from Mark and even from Q (I discuss Q in Chapter 6 below) and constitutes a wholesale condemnation, without any hint of charity, of these two classes of men, many of whom may well have been as respectable and as well meaning as our bishops and clergy today. At any rate, when Paul said that, before his conversion, he had been "a Pharisee as to the law" (Phil. 3:5), he was certainly not confessing to former hypocrisy, but using the name as a title of honour, "claiming the highest degree of faithfulness and sincerity in the fulfilment of his duty to God as prescribed by the divinely-given Torah" (Beare 1973, pp. 107f). Matthew's attack on these his own neighbours is particularly incongruous, placed as it is immediately after endorsement of the Old Testament command "thou shalt love thy neighbour as thyself" (22:39)—placed too in a gospel where Jesus even enjoins love of enemies (5:44).

Modern Jewish scholars are appalled by Matthew 23. Samuel Sandmel, for instance, was "puzzled that Christians can read this chapter and still speak of Jesus as a kindly man" (1965, p. 125). But of course non-fundamentalist Christians have largely ceased trying to rescue even some of its polemic as authentic utterances of Jesus. Clearly, its hostility is best explained from the evangelist's end-of-century situation, when, as we saw, Pharisees were prominent in Judaism and conflict between them and Jewish Christians likely. Pharisees were hardly serious opponents much earlier. The Pauline corpus is indeed full of complaints about 'Judaizers' (Christians who wanted to retain Jewish practices), but includes no reference to Pharisees other than Paul's single honorable mention of his former Pharisaic way of life.

Luke's Jesus is, like Matthew's, not uniform in his attitude to Judaism. He does indeed denounce the Pharisees, yet on three such occasions he does so as the guest of a Pharisee who has invited him to a meal—a setting which does something to modify the anti-Pharisaic tradition which Luke inherited. Luke even records that "some Pharisees" gave Jesus friendly warning to leave town because Herod is out to have him killed (13:31). "There is nothing like this outside Luke, who certainly did not get it from Mark", where the Pharisees are aligned with "the Herodians" (Ziesler 1979, pp. 150–53). Even in Luke's Passion narrative there is no blanket condemnation of Jews. Weatherly has presented a detailed case for concluding that, "among Jews, Luke regards only the leaders of Jerusalem and the people of Jerusalem as responsible for the crucifixion of Jesus . . . Jewish leaders associated with Jerusalem instigated Jesus's death and . . . did so with popular assent" (1994, p. 271).

In Acts, also written by Luke, the Pharisees even appear as allies, especially of Paul, on the ground that they believed in resurrection. What they anticipated was of course a general resurrection of the dead at the end of the aeon; they did not look back to the death and resurrection of the Messiah in the recent past. Nevertheless, Acts represents them as speaking up for Christianity (5:34, 39) and as shielding Paul (23:6, 9). This is part of Acts' attempt to show that the overall Jewish opposition to Christianity is unwarranted and irrational, and that Christianity represents the true Judaism. It is as if the author were saying: the most pious of you Jews believe in resurrection; this is precisely what we Christians proclaim, and so your rupture with us is entirely your fault. This rupture is certainly a reality in Acts' account of the missionary work of Paul, where "the Jews" function as the natural enemies of the church. They "constantly oppose, harass and plot against the Christians, bend the ears of political authorities, and generally stir up trouble" (Wilson 1995, pp. 64f). The way in which Christian attitudes later further hardened is well illustrated by the fifth- or possibly sixth-century Codex Bezae, which imports numerous anti-Jewish and pro-gentile readings into the text of Acts (Metzger 1968, p. 50).

In sum it can be said that much in the synoptic gospels and Acts is harshly critical of Jewish religion and behaviour, but falls far short of expressing fundamental and systematic hostility towards all Jews of all time. As we saw, even Mt. 27:25, "his blood be on us and on our children", is not to be interpreted in this way. And the fourth gospel speaks for sectarians in conflict with the synagogues of the late first century, with Jews who rejected Jesus. The Johannine church will itself have included many Jews.

A significant factor leading to later hostility to Jews was the fact that Christianity rapidly became a gentile religion. In the first century it was a tiny, and originally Jewish minority within the Roman empire—what Bart Ehrman calls "a marginalized religious sect that had never been heard of by most people, and was scorned by most of those who had heard of it", whereas Judaism "not only had far greater numbers, but also visible public structures, wide public recognition, and prominent public representatives, some of whom had the ear of the highest officials in the empire" (2000, p. 358). But by the fourth century the roles had come to be reversed. Jews had become a relatively defenceless minority, hounded by the confident attack of a powerful Christian body, which read the gospels, particularly Matthew and John, not as reflecting disputes between different factions of Jews (those who accepted Jesus and those who did not), but as condemnation of all Jews as such.

As a result some of the greatest names in Christian history (Chrysostom, Augustine, Aquinas, and others) are found "advocating with frightening ferocity the right and even duty of Christians to dislike, hate, and punish the Jews" (Brown 1994, p. 385; cf. Casey 1996, p. 226 for some details). Protestants have been as guilty as Catholics here. In his tract of 1543, entitled *On the Jews and their Lies*, Luther encourages Christians to burn their synagogues and schools, raze their houses, confiscate their literature, abolish safe conduct for them on the highways, and put them to manual labour in communal, supervised establishments. In 1523, when he still hoped to convert them, he had protested (in a statement entitled 'That Jesus Christ was born a Jew') against the harshness of "imbecile papists and bishops" towards them. As so often, love became converted to hate when the message was not accepted. There was scriptural precedent for such a response to refusal to accept: "Whosoever shall deny me before men, him will I also deny before my Father which is in heaven" (Mt. 10:33; cf. Lk. 12:9).

On the Catholic side, vilification of the Jews was authoritatively and publicly repudiated only a generation ago, at the Second Vatican Council, in the declaration that what happened at Christ's Passion cannot be blamed upon all Jews then living, nor upon Jews of today. Haenchen notes (1968, p. 402) that the Coptic church even protested at this volte-face, and declared against it that holy scripture shows unambiguously that the Jews are murderers of God.

2

The Question of Miracles and the Work of David Friedrich Strauss

The history of belief in miracles seems to have taken the following course. There was originally no distinction between the normal and the miraculous, because the unsophisticated savage had no system of co-ordinated beliefs by which probability can be tested. The concept of 'abnormal', 'miraculous' arises as such generalized systems arise, and is a consequence of applying them. When the system is unclear, then the distinction normal/miraculous is correspondingly unclear. As experience and knowledge grow in certain fields, some general principles come to be recognized within these fields, and systems of belief begin to develop. The power of comparing propositions and determining their consistency is slowly developed in relation to the most frequently repeated daily operations. The everyday affairs of life, by their more continual operation, their constant opportunity for testing and experimentation, form the nucleus of what may be called the secular attitude, where humans foresee the consequences of their operations and feel surprise when their expectations are not fulfilled. It co-exists for a long time with the religious and magical attitude, but reigns over different spheres of life. As the secular sphere extends with the increase of knowledge, that other region of incalculable events becomes isolated and specialized. It becomes separated in thought as the realm of the miraculous. Gradually it comes to be associated with certain special occasions or aspects of life. More and more, miracles acquire a religious significance. And when religious philosophy begins to take shape, miracles are regarded as the special medium of divine revelation.

Now as long as divinities were merely tribal appurtenances, there was no tendency to claim any monopoly of marvels. But when rivalry between different religions begins, the miracles of the rival have somehow to be discredited. The first stage in this direction consisted in admitting the reality of rival miracles, but declaring them diabolical rather than divine. The next stage was denial of the authenticity of any miracles save one's own. The Protestants in Europe denied the reality of the Catholic miracles, and the Catholic enemies of the Jansenist Port-Royal refused to credit the miracle of the Holy Thorn.[1] Mutual criticism on the part of the champions of rival faiths tended to undermine and discredit the whole system of miracles. Attention was more and more directed to the possibility of error and fraud. Even those who could see no reason for rejecting miracles altogether could not help noticing their growing infrequency. This was sometimes explained by supposing that they ceased to be necessary once Christianity had gained definite ascendancy in the world.[2] From the eighteenth century, many apologists have gone even further. They reject ecclesiastical miracles from the second century onwards, and defend only the miracles ascribed to Jesus and the apostles. As J.M. Robertson noted, this thesis "is the childish one that in an age in which all cults claimed miracles, and none scrutinized them, we are first to accept Christian prodigies and reject all others, and then to reject all post-apostolic Christian ones but stand firm to the earlier" (1925, p. 66). That Jesus worked miracles was often represented as a justifiable inference from Christian doctrine as to his nature. In the early twentieth century, William Temple, who later became Archbishop of Canterbury, "swept aside . . . reasonable doubts about the New Testament miracle stories with the assertion that 'if a man is thus [like Christ] united to God, Nature is his servant, not his master, and he may (so the story tells us) walk upon the water'" (Kent 1992, p. 23). We shall see in Chapter 4 below that today Jesus's resurrection is sometimes defended in this way, as an allowable inference from Christology.

In 1971 C.H. Dodd, then doyen of New Testament scholars in Britain, showed himself well aware that the gospel miracle stories "are intended to affirm" that in Jesus God's presence and power made itself felt. As to their credibility, "with the flood of fresh discoveries about the behaviour of matter and mind, we hardly know what is, and what is not, possible" (p. 32). He discusses in detail not the walking on the water, but the immediately preceding feeding of the five thousand (Mk. 6:32–44 and parallels), "one of the most puzzling stories" of the gospels, which defies all attempts to make it "intelligible or credible by rationalizing it". Hence, he implies, we must accept that Jesus did in fact give "bread to the hungry crowd"—but "not so much as a miracle as a mystery", as a symbol of God's kingdom: "When the feast was spread, it was not difficult to read in it the proclamation 'the kingdom of God is upon you'." (The word 'symbol' occurs at every turn in Dodd's book, reflecting the tendency of literary critics—then as now—to interpret the texts on which they comment as replete with symbols.) Nevertheless, it was too difficult for the crowd to appreciate the symbolism. They failed to understand Jesus's message, for they were "patriots" who thought he would lead them in a rising against Rome. And so, in order to isolate his disciples from this dangerous gathering which was threatening to compromise his whole mission, he pressed them to go away across the lake by boat, while he persuaded the crowd to disperse (pp. 131–38. It was while the disciples were then rowing across the lake that he walked on the water towards them). On this exegesis, the historian Hugh Trevor-Roper commented (in *The Spectator*, 27th February, 1971): "If a secular historian told us . . . that an army of 5,000 men had gorged themselves on five loaves and two fishes, and that twelve hampers were needed to carry away the scraps, we should be very skeptical about anything else that he told us, even if he insisted that he had been there at the time."

Today it is fashionable for commentators to restrict themselves still further than Temple or Dodd did, in that they accept Jesus's miracles of healing, including the exorcisms, but not his 'nature' miracles (in Mark, the calming of the sea storm, the feeding of the five thousand and the four thousand, the walking on the sea, and the cursing of the fig tree). Weaver, concluding his survey of books on Jesus from the period 1900 to 1950, notes "near universal agreement that he was a healer", whereas "the other side of the miracle coin, the nature miracles, scared away most [almost] everybody" (1999, p. 361). The reason for this distinction is surely that the healings are regarded as believable incidents, morally motivated, which Jesus or his audiences could have taken for miracles whether they were truly supernatural or not, whereas the nature miracles seem simply bizarre, particularly when those of Mark are supplemented with the coin in the fish's mouth (Matthew) and the conversion of a vast amount of water into wine at a wedding feast (John).

A classic essay by T.H. Huxley of 1889 amply illustrates that there are plenty of miracles in which no one now believes which are much better attested than those of Jesus. Huxley discussed the writings of Einhard (a historian of intelligence and character at the court of Charlemagne) who about A.D. 830 reported numerous miracles from either first- or second-hand knowledge: for instance, a demon had taken possession of a girl and, speaking through her mouth in Latin to an exorcizing priest, named himself "Wiggo" and declared that he had long been a gatekeeper in hell before he set about ravaging the kingdom of the Franks. After the priest had cast him out, the girl could speak no more Latin, but only her own tongue. Huxley comments:

If you do not believe in these miracles, recounted by a witness whose character and competency are firmly established, whose sincerity cannot be doubted, and who appeals to his sovereign and other contemporary witnesses of the truth of what he says, ... why do you profess to believe in stories of a like character which are found in documents of the dates and authorship of which nothing is certainly determined ...? If it be true that the four Gospels and Acts were written by Matthew, Mark, Luke, and John, all that we know of these authors comes to nothing in comparison with our knowledge of Einhard ... If, therefore, you refuse to believe that 'Wiggo' was cast out of the possessed girl on Einhard's authority, with what justice can you profess to believe that the legion of devils were cast out of the man among the tombs of the Gadarenes? [Mk. 5:1–20 and parallel passages in Matthew and Luke].... It cannot be pretended ... that the Jews of the year 30 A.D., or thereabouts, were less imbued with the belief in the supernatural than were the Franks of the year 800 A.D. The same influences were at work in each case, and it is only reasonable to suppose that the results are the same.

And so, "where the miraculous is concerned, neither considerable intellectual ability, nor undoubted honesty, nor knowledge of the world, nor proved faithfulness as civil historians, nor profound piety, on the part of eyewitnesses and contemporaries, affords any guarantee of the objective truth of their statements when we know that a firm belief in the miraculous was ingrained in their minds and was the presupposition of their observation and reasoning."[3]

It is understandable that by the time the gospels were written, miracles had come to be attributed to Jesus. According to Jewish tradition, demonic power was to be crushed in the Messianic age, and Mark's miracle stories, where Jesus casts out demons from persons in whom they had lodged, were told—I quote the theologian Howard Kee—"in a community in which Jesus is regarded as an agent who has come in the end of time to defeat the powers of Satan" (1977, p. 36). Paul, however, the earliest Christian whose writings are extant, took a quite different view and held that Jesus had vanquished these powers not by standing up to them openly with miraculous displays of supernatural strength, but by submitting to a shameful death at their instigation, only to rise again in triumph over them (see my 2004 book, pp. 25f, 35–37).

As I have already intimated, if we wish to find out what the earliest Christians believed about Jesus, it is essential to study the extant documents in the order in which they were written, not in the order in which they are printed in the Bible. The earliest documents are those of the letters ascribed to Paul which were genuinely written by him, followed only a little later by several from other hands (listed above, p. 10). The epistle of James and the three letters of John may also be as early as these. In none of these documents is there any suggestion that Jesus worked miracles, even though in some of them miracles are regarded as of great importance for the spread of the Christian message. Blomberg says, justly, that "the nineteenth-century liberal quest for a miracle-free layer of Christian tradition has been all but abandoned." But when he adds that "the positive consequences for historicity should be acknowledged just as readily" (1986, p. 446), he blurs the question at issue, namely whether Jesus *himself* worked miracles; for the fact that, in the earliest documents, Christian missionaries are said to have done so is no corroboration of the gospel record concerning his own behaviour. Quite the contrary: it looks as though what was from the first attributed to missionary preachers was only later attributed to Jesus, as a result of a radical change in Christology, involving the abandonment of the Pauline view that Jesus had lived an obscure life of inconspicuous humiliation.

There is no mention of any miracle of Jesus even in the writings of the earliest Fathers (Clement of Rome, Ignatius of Antioch, and Polycarp of Smyrna—known as the 'Apostolic Fathers' because they were believed to be the immediate successors of the apostles). All this shows how wrong G.H. Twelftree is to claim that "both inside and outside the New Testament there is evidence that Jesus was remembered primarily as a very popular and powerful miracle worker" (2003, p. 123). Paul even comes close to actually denying that Jesus worked miracles when he insists that he can preach only "Christ crucified"—a Christ who submitted to a shameful death, not a Christ of signs and wonders (1 Cor. 1:22–23). One can of course respond by saying that if, as I have argued earlier in this book, the Jesus of the Pauline and other early epistles is so different from the Galilean preacher and magician of the gospels as to be a different personage, who lived at a more distant time, then one cannot expect much in the way of overlap between the activities of the two, and so the silence of these epistles does not tell against the authenticity of the material in the Galilean ministry, as portrayed in the gospels. However, apart from the fact that my premiss of two different personages is not conceded by defenders of Jesus's miracles, the silence of the Apostolic Fathers, who were certainly acquainted with life of Jesus material, as we know it from the gospels, remains significant. There is also the strange passage in Mark, where Jesus, in response to the Pharisees' request to show "a sign from heaven", replies: "There shall be no sign given unto this generation" (8:12). Haenchen thought (1968, p. 285) that Mark here himself betrays, without noticing it, that the miracle stories represent later tradition than this pericope.

N.T. Wright, bishop of Durham, deplores what he calls the post-Enlightenment "ruthless hermeneutic of suspicion" towards the gospels (2003, p. 19). But can we really be other than suspicious when we find that a miracle appears on practically every page? Jesus is born miraculously, as an adult he casts out demons, walks on the waves of an extensive sea, calms a storm, feeds multitudes, heals the sick, and raises the dead. All this should surely give us pause, quite apart from the failure of other relevant documents to confirm it. A very different view from that of Wright is expressed by his fellow Anglican priest Paul Avis, a member of the Church of England General Synod and Doctrine Commission, who declared (p. 8 of his opening article of the 1993 symposium he was editing): "In approaching the miracle stories of the New Testament we need to remind ourselves that there was nothing so fantastic that early Christian intellectuals could not believe it." With this in mind, we may plausibly remain skeptical of the recent (2005) attempt by Hugh Montefiore (who became bishop of Birmingham in 1978 after lecturing on the New Testament at Cambridge University) to show that many of the gospel miracles can be explained by crediting Jesus with para-psychological powers which enabled him to produce what are now regarded as paranormal phenomena. He suggests that Jesus fed five thousand "through the working of laws whose mechanism is completely unknown to us". The incident, he says, has "perhaps a faint analogy . . . to apports (objects which appear seemingly from nowhere)". Such "provision of material from nowhere is a well-attested paranormal phenomenon" (pp. 84, 86).

The question of miracles is of course only one aspect of the wider question of the authority of scripture and of the church. The Reformation famously discounted the church, as a merely human institution, and appealed instead to the authority of the Bible, the word of God. But this raised obvious problems. First, Protestant scholars themselves showed that biblical manuscripts can differ quite substantially, making it difficult to be sure what the original readings were. Much worse was that agreement on how to interpret what could be taken as the authentic text was quite impossible. Protestants found that their doctrine of *sola scriptura* ('scripture alone') was "proving itself to be the harbinger not of peace but of a sword; and a sword of such sharpness as to pierce to the dividing asunder of the joints and marrow of Protestantism" (Norman Sykes 1963, p. 178).

Small wonder that Catholics claimed that they could avoid these problems because their doctrines did not derive from an uncertain or ambiguous text, but were truly apostolic: Jesus taught the apostles, they taught their successors, who in turn taught theirs, and so on, so that the original faith, handed down undistorted, could finally be codified as Christian doctrine. Hence according to the fifth-century St. Vincent of Lérins, Catholics believe "what has been believed everywhere, always, and by all." Hence too Cardinal Newman could write in 1874 that "every Catholic holds that Christian dogmas were in the Church from the time of the apostles" (Quoted in Storr 1913, p. 308). 'Tradition' is the process by which the church hands on its faith to each new generation; and in a private letter of 1860, commenting on the devastating effects of Protestant reliance on the Bible, Newman rejoiced that Catholics were not tied in this way, but could appeal to tradition (Hanson 1975, p. 110). However, what actually happened in the course of church history was that any custom, rite, or belief not documented in the Bible, and thought to be older than living memory, was readily regarded as apostolic. Thus in the late second-century dispute about the appropriate day on which to celebrate Easter, both sides in this 'Quartodeciman' controversy claimed to be following the tradition handed down to them from the apostles; and by the fourth century the church regarded in this way practically everything of importance in its origin, worship, and teaching, so that there was an apostolic creed, an apostolic church hierarchy, and so on. Unfortunately, says Evans, this image of the apostle by which the church came to think of itself is "for us almost if not entirely fantasy, and the literature which promoted it is the literature of the imagination" (1971, p. 26).

Catholics and Protestants nevertheless agreed that the Bible is a divine revelation, even if, from the Catholic standpoint, it needed to be supplemented with the church's apostolic teaching and, of course, interpreted in the same light. But the status thus accorded to the Bible was bound in time to be questioned; and the most searching questioning of it to that date was published by David Friedrich Strauss in two volumes in 1835–36, which were particularly resented because of their treatment of the miraculous element in the New Testament.

Strauss's book is entitled, in the English translation of George Eliot, *The Life of Jesus Critically Examined* (1846. She translated the fourth German edition of 1840). The original was received, as Hans Frei notes, with "a virtually unanimous howl of condemnation by the theological profession"—not only because of its heavily critical substance, but also because it was virtually the first enquiry into the life of Jesus to be written with complete scientific detachment, "without the slightest stylistic echo of the topic's 'elevated' status or of emotional involvement with it" (Frei 1985, p. 223).

In 1864 Strauss followed this book with a 'Life of Jesus for the German People', addressed, then, to the laity, whereas the earlier book was intended for theologians. (The two-volume English translation of 1879 of this second *Life*, from which my references are taken, is called *A New Life of Jesus*.) Its final part is an effective abridgment of the earlier book, but is preceded by an attempt to reconstruct the character of the historical Jesus—unsatisfactory, since it is so difficult to be sure whether what an evangelist says represents the real Jesus or merely what a Christian community believed and ascribed to him. Strauss admitted this in his final work of 1872, translated into English under the title *The Old Faith and the New*. (My references are to the 1997 reissue of this translation—as two volumes in one—which includes an Introduction and brief explanatory notes by myself.) Strauss here says that the gospels are distorted at every turn by conflicting party ideals and interests, and we have no 'control' account from a neutral source. Furthermore, the supernatural powers they ascribe to Jesus make futile any attempt to describe his character in human terms (Volume 1, pp. 87ff). A man who can raise the dead, walk on water, and turn it into wine, and be resurrected after three days of death, is obviously no more describable in terms of human character than Samson, Hercules, or Venus.

The method of Strauss's major predecessor H.E.G. Paulus had been to set aside the gospel miracles as misunderstandings on the part of Jesus's entourage. The results were often grotesque. As a striking example Strauss notes (1840, section 28) the way Paulus explained Mary's pregnancy by supposing that someone visited her "in the evening or at night"; and that this was the angel Gabriel was merely "the subsequent suggestion of Mary's own mind". The healing miracles Paulus explains by positing special medicines known only to Jesus. The feeding of the five thousand occurred when he and his disciples shared their provisions with each other, thus setting the multitude an example which was promptly imitated, with the result that there was soon enough food for all. Again, according to Paulus, Jesus's resurrection was only apparent, for he did not die on the cross, but when laid in the cool tomb recovered consciousness. The earthquake rolled the stone away and enabled him to creep out unnoticed. From time to time he showed himself to his followers, until finally, on the Mount of Olives, a passing cloud came between him and them; they lost sight of him for ever and came to describe his departure as an ascension (after Horton Harris 1973, p. 44).

Strauss was convinced of the nullity of all this. He was particularly scornful about this explanation of the resurrection. Can we really believe, he asked, "that a being who had stolen half-dead out of the sepulcher, who crept about weak and ill, wanting medical treatment . . . could have given his disciples the impression that he was the Conqueror over death and the grave?" (1879, Volume 1, p. 412). The absurdity of Paulus's argument, he insists, follows naturally from his attempt to combine two incompatible premises: the modern scientific view that miracles do not occur, and the traditional view that the gospels were written by eyewitnesses of the events narrated in them. Combination of these premises means regarding the gospels as the work of men who had lived with Jesus and yet, with consummate stupidity, completely misunderstood all that he had actually said and done.

Strauss begins by challenging the assumption that the gospels are eyewitness reports. He notes that these works are in themselves anonymous, and that it is only their titles which ascribe them to named authors. But these titles, he adds, became established only in the latter part of the second century. And how little reliance can be placed on the ascription of any biblical book to a named author! Who now, he asks, believes that the book which records Moses's death and burial was written by him (with prophetic foresight), as its title ("the fifth book of Moses" in Luther's Bible) purports? How many Psalms bear the name of David even though they clearly presuppose the Babylonian captivity, which came only hundreds of years after his time? And Daniel, supposed to have been written at the time of this captivity, in fact shows a detailed acquaintance with the reign of Antiochus Epiphanes of nearly four hundred years later.[4]

Strauss realized that a very powerful argument against the ascription of the gospels to eyewitnesses is the presence in them of so-called literary doublets. Mark, for instance, includes accounts of two miraculous feedings, of the five thousand and of the four thousand. The sequence of events, and even the vocabulary, is in both cases remarkably similar (details in Nineham 1963, pp. 205f). That two separate incidents are involved is hard to believe, since in the second the disciples—who are reported as having recently witnessed the first—have so completely forgotten it that they think it impossible for food to be supplied to thousands in a desert place (Mk. 8:4). The doublet is best explained by assuming that a tradition of one such feeding existed, before Mark wrote, in two slightly different written forms, and that the evangelist, who drew on those written sources, incorporated both because he supposed them to refer to different incidents. If he supposed this, he obviously could not have been present as a witness of such a miracle. Different written and not merely different oral forms underlie such doublets, of which there are several in Mark. Two oral traditions that are slightly discrepant can be combined into one story. But as soon as a tradition is fixed in writing, discrepancies between it and kindred traditions can result in both these literary forms of the story being told.

Strauss discusses the doublets as they occur in Matthew rather than in Mark. In his book of 1835, he was not much concerned with the order in which the New Testament books were written, or whether the earlier ones were known to and used by the authors of the later. His purpose was to show that many narratives, no matter in which gospel they occur, cannot be accepted as historical. He has often been criticized for failing to discriminate the documents. But that was the work of his successors, to which his own was a natural preliminary.

Strauss, then, impugned one of the two premisses of Paulus, namely that the gospels are based on eyewitness reports. But he accepted the other premiss, namely that miracle stories cannot be literally true. He has often been criticized on the ground that his denial of the miraculous and the supernatural element in the world is never proved but merely presupposed, and that it was therefore arbitrary of him to treat the New Testament miracles as myths. But in fact his standpoint was one from which he could make sense of the evidence, and no more can be required of any hypothesis. It is, of course, true that he did not show by philosophical reasoning that belief in miracles is unjustified. But this is no defect, for the credibility or otherwise of a belief cannot be established by *a priori* rules. To say that all that happens must accord with the laws of nature does not settle everything, because these laws are, even today, very imperfectly known. An event may be improbable, but we should need extraordinary confidence in our own conception of the world to be able to determine, without regard to the evidence, that the report of an event, however marvellous, is false.

If all this is conceded, Strauss's argument remains unaffected. His point was that natural causation was accepted as applicable everywhere except in the case of the events portrayed in the Bible; and that it was therefore reasonable to see if these could also be explained on a natural basis. The same point was at issue in the protracted debate over Darwin's views later in the century. He and his supporters were accused of postulating, as an absolute and ultimate truth, that no causes have ever operated except natural ones. In fact, however, their assumptions did not pertain to absolute truth or ultimate reality. They argued only that, *if* inquiries were to be successfully carried on at all, it was necessary to exclude miracles from the argument. They were indeed told that, if science could not see the way to fitting miracles into the scheme of things, she should be content to 'bow her head and wait'. But that, as Ellegård notes, would have meant "giving up inquiry in those directions which theology wished to keep under its sway, thus preventing the confirmation of those scientific theories which were under debate" (1958, p. 146).

Strauss reached the conclusion that "in each instance of an ostensibly supernatural occurrence it was far more difficult to conceive the event so happening than certain causes which might have originated an unhistorical account of it" (1879, Volume 1, p. 34). Even if one allows the witnesses of an alleged miracle the best character, "it is absolutely impossible to conceive a case in which the investigator of history will not find it more probable, beyond all comparison, that he has to deal with an untrue account, rather than with a miraculous fact" (p. 200). He mentions the well-known story of Balaam's ass ("The Lord opened the mouth of the ass, and she said unto Balaam, What have I done to thee, that thou hast smitten me these three times?" Numbers 22:28) and says: even if Balaam himself had told us this, and we knew him as a man of good character, we would not accept his testimony that "an event should have happened contradicting all previous experience". And with the authors of the gospels, we are not dealing with eyewitnesses of miracles, but with persons who had received reports of them "from the tradition of others, and who show, by the whole tendency of their writings, that they were disposed to do anything rather than to try the traditions they received by a critical test" (pp. 199f). Quite so. The evangelists are advocates for their religious convictions, and advocates, then as now, state the case for their client. Furthermore—and this is a point of the greatest importance—if the New Testament miracle stories are to be accepted as genuine, they must be both well attested and internally coherent; and Strauss showed that this is quite emphatically not the case. External evidence of the gospels (that is, mention of them by other writers) is late; and their narratives include many contradictions, not just on minor matters, but on essentials. Strauss showed in great detail that this is true of such stories as the accounts of Jesus's birth, infancy, and childhood, the supernatural circumstances attending his baptism, the stories of his temptation, many of the stories embellishing the Passion, and above all the narratives of the resurrection and ascension. In my chapters on the virgin birth and the resurrection, many of the facts I adduce as relevant to their rejection as historical events were already noted by Strauss in his book of 1835–36.

Strauss, then, asked whether it was possible to explain gospel stories in a non-supernatural way without imputing gross stupidity or, in the case of H.S. Reimarus, his other major predecessor, even fraud to their authors. Like Paulus, Reimarus had held to the traditional view of eyewitness origin of the accounts, but had discounted their miracles, arguing, in the case of the resurrection narratives, that the disciples had stolen the body from the sepulcher and then fabricated, with slender agreement, stories of Jesus's return to life. In a lengthy assessment of Reimarus's work, Strauss pointed out that it is absurd to suppose in this way that they knew that there was no word of truth in their accounts, and yet proclaimed them with a conviction that sufficed to change the world (1861, p. 402). He found it all too characteristic of an eighteenth-century writer that Reimarus tended to explain religious phenomena in terms of deception or 'priestcraft', whereas in fact "all religions were founded by people who were themselves convinced." Strauss thought it much better to attribute the belief that Jesus was risen to the excited emotional state of the disciples, who "could not possibly think of him as dead" (p. 405).

One valuable part of Reimarus's account is, as Strauss recognized, his clear demonstration—unappreciated if not entirely novel at the time—that the resurrection narratives include real contradictions.[5] They do not agree "when, to how many, how often, where, and in what form" Jesus appeared, "nor as to what finally became of him" (Quoted in Strauss 1861, p. 368). Reimarus did not publish his findings, but, as we shall see in Chapter 8 below, part of his manuscript was issued posthumously by G.E. Lessing, between 1774 and 1778—anonymously as 'Fragments of an Unknown Writer'. If Houlden is right, Reimarus's failure to come forward publicly with his views "would still not be inadvisable in principle in some German universities, where the training of the clergy is the dominant purpose of undergraduate programs in theology" (art. 'Reimarus' in Houlden's 2005 *Guide*).

Strauss's argument was that many of the New Testament stories, and not only the ones involving miracles, are the outcome of Old Testament hopes. They "originated in a transference of the Jewish expectation of the Messiah into the history of Jesus" (1879, Volume 1, p. 205). If the evangelists believed, as they did, that Jesus was the Messiah, then they will also have believed that he must have been, done, and suffered all that they expected of the Messiah. He must, for instance, have been a descendant of David, born in David's city of Bethlehem.[6] Hence it was natural for stories to circulate in Christian communities giving him these qualifications. Since they were not based on fact they varied a good deal; and so we find that what one evangelist says on the subject is excluded by the narrative of another. Jesus's healing miracles are likewise constructions from the Old Testament. Isaiah 35:5 tells that "then the eyes of the blind shall be opened, and the ears of the deaf shall be unstopped; then shall the lame man leap as a hart and the tongue of the dumb shall sing." This passage, Strauss says (1879, Volume 2, p. 151), originated when the Babylonian captivity of the Jews was coming to an end, and describes how the exiles, overjoyed at the prospect of return, will forget all their sorrows. But when, after the return, the expected period of bliss did not occur, it was thought by later generations reading Isaiah that his reference was to miraculous healings which would occur in Messianic times. Hence the authors of the gospels, who believed Jesus was the Messiah, recorded incidents where he cures blindness, deafness, dumbness, and paralysis.

This way of accounting for the origin of numerous gospel stories (not only of those involving miracles) is today admitted to have been of decisive importance. Nineham calls it "indispensable to an understanding of the Gospels" (2000, p. xiii). Put in its most general terms, the principle is this: written descriptions (in the Old Testament or in any respected document) of some event (historical or imaginary) may be read by persons who know nothing of the real subject represented, and who may freshly interpret the document in accordance with their knowledge. In this way they may take the writing to refer to people and events entirely unknown to the actual writers. In the Psalms, for instance, the term 'the anointed' or 'the Messiah' is used to designate the reigning king. Later generations, reading the Psalms when the historical kingship had ceased to exist, nevertheless assumed that the meaning of the Psalmist had some relevance to present times; and that, since there were no more kings in the old sense, his reference must be to another king or Messiah, perhaps in heaven.

Since Strauss's time, the discovery of the Qumran Dead Sea Scrolls has provided evidence that non-Christian Jewish sectarians interpreted scripture in exactly this way. The Qumran Habakkuk commentary, for instance, interprets the first two chapters of the Old Testament text as applying to persons and events of significance in the life of the Qumran sect. Descriptions of the Chaldean invaders are reinterpreted so as to make them refer to new invaders, called "the Kittim", who can be identified as the Roman contemporaries of the sectarians.[7]

Strauss, then, holds that the writers of the gospels, and also the authors of the Christian traditions on which they drew, lived so entirely in the earlier history of the Jewish people, and in the sacred books in which it was laid down, that they found in them everything that subsequently took place, everywhere prophecies and symbols of what was to come. For the Jews of the first century A.D. all truth was contained in the scriptures; "and so science was entirely made to consist in a specially pitiful and arbitrary art of interpretation, of which we possess but too many examples in the New Testament" (1997, Volume 1, pp. 75f). As a minor example he instances (1840, section 135) Matthew's story that the rich Joseph of Arimathea buried Jesus in a tomb originally intended for himself. This, he says, was in part inspired by Isaiah 53:9: "they made his grave . . . with the rich in his death". And, of course, nothing but a tomb as yet unpolluted by any corpse would, for the early Christians, be good enough for their god-man, just as they considered it right that no one had ever sat on the ass which he used for his entry into the capital.

Strauss also holds that some New Testament stories resulted from a desire to represent Jesus as equalling or even outdoing the achievements of important Old Testament figures. Thus he had to supply food miraculously, and even to raise the dead, otherwise he would have been inferior to Elijah and Elisha. Strauss (1840, section 100) gives, as an example of the latter feat, Luke's story of how Jesus, happening to meet the funeral procession of the only son of a widow, took compassion on her and restored him to life. No other gospel gives the story, even though, according to Luke (7:17), the report of the incident "went forth . . . in the whole of Judea and all the region round about". Now Elijah had raised a widow's only son from the dead (1 Kings 17:17–24) and Elisha had performed a similar miracle (2 Kings 4:14–37). The evangelist is clearly anxious to show that the new prophet is in no way inferior to them; hence the bystanders are represented as saying: "A great prophet is risen among us" (7:16).

Some gospel incidents were, says Strauss (1840, section 107), invented in order to show that Jesus was a greater prophet than Moses. The forty days' temptation in the wilderness parallels Moses's time on Sinai; and since Moses had been transfigured upon the mountain top, Christ must also have a transfiguration to show that he was in no way inferior. All this, although it may still shock the laity, is barely disputed any more even by relatively conservative theologians. A.E. Harvey, in so *bien-pensant* a work as his 1970 *New English Bible Companion to the New Testament*, specifies a number of details peculiar to Matthew in the gospel transfiguration stories and says that "they perhaps show Matthew at work, deliberately presenting Jesus as the new Moses, the definitive lawgiver" (p. 70). That early Christians constructed their picture of Jesus from the Old Testament is obvious from the statement of Paul—the earliest extant Christian writer—that it consists of prophetic writings, written down for our instruction in order to elucidate facts about Jesus

(Rom. 15:3–4; 16:25–26). In other words, if study of scripture showed that the Messiah was to behave in a certain way, then, for early Christians, Jesus must have behaved in that way, whatever eyewitnesses or historical records said or failed to say. As Hoskyns and Davey put it, in their disarming way: "In the Church at the end of the first century the Life and Death of Jesus were recounted in the context of the Old Testament Scriptures" (1988, p. 60). F.C. Grant writes more bluntly of the evangelists' tendency to state the facts of Jesus's life "as they could be inferred from the Old Testament" (1959, p. 35). That ideas among Jews at the beginning of our era originated as a result of such musings on sacred texts is today obvious, as I have said, from the Qumran discoveries. Lindars has shown, in his 1961 book, that, like the Qumran scribes, the early Christians developed major aspects of their beliefs in this way, interpreting the texts in the light of their experience and their experience in the light of the texts.

It is, then, widely admitted that the historian must approach the gospels with what has been called 'a hermeneutic of suspicion'. Hence, says Robert Morgan in a Cambridge symposium on Jesus's trial, "the arguments from prophecy and miracle have lost all force" (1970, p. 136). This is due, in no small measure, to Strauss, who further, in 1872, insisted that a purely human Jesus on whom various elements from the Old Testament were subsequently foisted, is hardly compatible with any form of worship of him. Morgan also warns against uncritical acceptance of the non-supernatural elements in the gospels: "The sorts of motives which led to miracle stories being told about Jesus were also responsible for the preservation and transmission within the Christian communities of the passion narratives" (p. 139). This was also clear to Strauss, who warned in addition against uncritical acceptance of any non-supernatural elements included in the miracle stories. He wrote: "Every narrative, however miraculous, contains some details which might in themselves be historical, but which, in consequence of their connection with the other supernatural incidents, necessarily become equally doubtful" (1840, section 16). He reiterated this at the end of his essay on Reimarus, saying that the miraculous element is not a skin which can be stripped off, leaving a genuine piece of history (1861, p. 401). Even today, so many commentators assume that, even if a gospel story cannot be taken at face value, there is undoubtedly some kind of real event underlying it. In this spirit, historian Michael Grant declares that, although Jesus did not feed five thousand, he "must have done *something*" (1977, p. 42, Grant's italics). No historian treating a secular person or secular events would in this way rule out in advance the possibility that a given story in his sources is entirely legendary. Strauss gave great offence in setting much New Testament material aside as myth, pure and simple.

Jeffery John (now Dean of St. Albans Abbey) speaks for those who have altogether given up the quest for "what did or did not *happen*" (his italics) to prompt the gospel miracle stories. Although he is convinced that "there can be little doubt that Jesus himself did perform miracles", the question: what was the historical basis of these stories? is "unanswerable and therefore ultimately fruitless and boring" (2001, pp. 4, 17). The real question, he finds, is: what are the evangelists trying to say to their readers?; for each miracle story "in its present form is a literary creation with a theological purpose" (p. 5). Quite so, and to this extent Dr. John is in agreement with Strauss, like whom he finds that some of the stories figure Jesus as "a new Moses" while others make his actions recall those of Elijah and Elisha (pp. 5, 215f). But Dr. John differs from Strauss in finding "extraordinary complex . . . allusions" and "different levels of meaning" in them (p. 6). He is obviously among the many recent theologians who are beholden to the method of the 'New Critics' in literary criticism, who discern subtle hidden meanings everywhere in the texts on which they comment, and so represent them as 'polysemous', having multi-layered meanings capable of mediating many messages to their readers (cf. Wells 2004, pp. 161f). The result of such exegesis is a display of ingenuity, as when Dr. John declares that the turning of 120 gallons of water into wine at Cana and the feeding of the five thousand in a lonely place "point to a feast with Jesus that I can share in now, to a way in which I can be united with him now through receiving him sacramentally in bread and wine" (p. 24). In this type of writing one thing is frequently said to 'point to' another when the author wishes arbitrarily to posit some connection between them. Again, "whatever history may lie behind the stories of individual healings, their meaning and importance in the evangelist's mind is a universal, symbolical one: these miracles are about the potential of all of us to be healed of our age-old, inherited spiritual deafness and blindness" (p. 22). 'Inherited' in this context presumably shows proper deference to the doctrine of original sin. He adds:

> If Jesus once opened the eyes of a blind man, unstopped the ears of the deaf, loosened the tongue of a stammerer, so what? How can that help me? But if I find that his Spirit is still present and powerful to break down my own blinkered selfishness and make me see deep truths about God, myself, and the world; or if he can overcome my stupid prejudices and fears and chal-

lenge me to change my self-protecting hardened heart and open up in love to him and others; or if he can overcome my crippling self-enclosure and inability to relate to others, thus enabling me to speak out the truth he has shown me, then I too have been miraculously healed, and know what it means to be restored to the fullness of life. (p. 24)

Dr. John, respected and well liked though he is, judges himself so severely here surely because it has long been good Christian theology to regard mankind as depraved and so in need of the Christian specifics concerning redemption; and such thinking is perhaps not without influence on his New Testament exegesis, which nobody can say is unimaginative.

Strauss is aware that the argument that some New Testament stories are myths based on Old Testament expectations does not account for the crucifixion and resurrection. The former he does not need to explain away, for he includes the crucifixion under Pilate among the items of Jesus's biography he accepts as historical, and finds it sufficiently attested by Tacitus (1879, Volume 2, p. 356). The resurrection he of course does not accept, and he shows in detail that no stories could be more discrepant than the relevant New Testament narratives. But even the belief in the resurrection is, he held, to some extent traceable to musings on the Old Testament, for if our gospels are to be trusted in any way at all, we must allow that Jesus expected that he would soon return to Earth on the clouds (1997, Volume 1, pp. 91f). After his death, his followers would have reflected on this, and would have searched the scriptures for elucidation. There was, for instance, Psalm 16: "Thou wilt not leave my soul to sheol; neither wilt thou suffer thine holy one to see corruption." Whoever composed this Psalm certainly intended no statement about the Messiah, and expressed only his complete trust in God. But a Christian, who of course believed that David was the author, would argue that David could not be speaking of his own body, which did see corruption, and that the reference must be to Jesus. This is how Peter is represented as interpreting the Psalm in his Whitsuntide address to the Jews in Acts 2:27–28. And once the disciples were convinced that Jesus was still alive, it was but a short step to the conviction that he had appeared to them (1997, Volume 1, pp. 80–82).

We need to keep in mind that Peter's speeches in Acts—although they undoubtedly represent early Christian attempts to justify the resurrection—are not evidence of what was said or thought by a Peter who had been Jesus's companion. Ernst Haenchen, whose commentary on Acts is one of the outstanding achievements of post-World War II New

Testament scholarship, has shown that Peter and James repeatedly appeal in Acts to the Jews of Jerusalem with arguments which presuppose the Greek translation of the Jewish scriptures, and which are not available in the Hebrew original. From this alone it is clear that Peter's speeches in Acts cannot be taken as a true reflection of the ideas of the Jerusalem Christians he is supposed to have led, but could have been drawn up only in a Hellenistic community (cf. my 2004 book, pp. 89ff).

In spite of his destructive analysis, Strauss insists at the outset of his 1835 volume that the virgin birth, miracles, resurrection, and ascension "remain eternal truths, whatever doubts my be cast on their reality as historical facts." This kind of double-think is distressingly familiar from more recent apologists. Bultmann, for instance, held that, although the resurrection is "not an event of past history", it is nevertheless a "cosmic event", for it tells the truth that death has been deprived of its powers, so that we need not fear it, and can thus obtain "the possibility of authentic life", that is, life centred in God, not in the world, by, for instance, attachment to riches or honours (1972, pp. 19, 39–42). If today existentialism underlies such sleight of speech, Hegelianism performed the same function in Strauss's day, and it is in this aspect of his book that the Hegelian views he then held make themselves very apparent. He refers the reader to its concluding dissertation which, he says, demonstrates that "the dogmatic import of the life of Jesus remains uninjured". And so this elaborate treatise of 1,500 pages, written to disprove every supernatural occurrence connected with the life of Jesus, begins and ends with the assurance that it all makes no difference, and that those who think otherwise are "frivolous".

This looks like blatant insincerity, but in fact such philosophizing was as completely sincere with the young Strauss as it was the other day with Bultmann and with J.A.T Robinson's *Honest to God*. However, Strauss soon abandoned Hegel, and declared in a letter of 1839 that giving such philosophical support to Christian dogmas is vain affectation (quoted by Horton Harris 1973, p. 136). In his second *Life* and in his final work of 1872 there is no trace of double-think. Nothing that is set aside is brought back through another door. This is one reason why these later works have so frequently met with even more adverse comment than his first *Life*.

The publication of this first *Life* was promptly followed by Strauss's dismissal from his theological lectureship. In vain did he protest that his views were not unique, but represented, in the Protestant scholarship of the day, one trend, expression of which could appropriately be allowed to a member of a theological staff. Strauss not only lost his job, but was cut off from friends; for in those days "the Church was so bound up with society that . . . he could not openly visit them for fear of bringing them into disrepute" (Harris, p. 117). His isolation is well illustrated in the dedication to his merchant brother, years later, of his second *Life*, where he explains that he has hitherto avoided dedications so as not to compromise friends:

> But you, dear brother, are independent . . . by the happy privilege of commercial pursuits . . . [of] the favour or displeasure of spiritual or lay superiors. The appearance of your name on the foremost pages of a book of mine can do you no injury.

Although, then, his book of 1835 cost him so dear, he could never regret having thus made available its critical information. "Many a . . . man", he wrote in 1860, "who dates the liberation of his mind from the study of this book, has been grateful to me for this throughout his whole life" (quoted by Harris, p. 193). If this is less true today, it is only because, as a result of his work, so many more critical appraisals of the gospels are now available.

In his second *Life* Strauss does discuss the relative ages of the gospels, but simply accepts the view of F.C. Baur that, since Christianity arose from Judaism, and since Mattthew is the most Jewish of the gospels, it is therefore the earliest, and Mark wrote an abridgement of it (1879, Volume 1, pp. 152, 176). Mark's gospel is indeed much shorter than Matthew's, which includes a wealth of additional material. But this non-Markan matter is now regarded as added by Matthew to his edition of Mark; for whenever the two evangelists do overlap, when they tell the same story, it is nearly always Matthew who gives it in the shorter form. Matthew, then, abbreviated Mark, not vice versa, and supplemented his abbreviation with extraneous material. This view was argued as early as 1835 by Lachmann, and more decisively by Holzmann in 1863, but Strauss never accepted it.

In his final work of 1872, Strauss declares that he is no longer a Christian, and that Christianity survives among educated peoples only by dint of the corrections which secular reasoning has introduced into it. He goes on to say—what many theologians have since conceded—that the New Testament is, for modern man, an alien book. The Mainz theologian Herbert Braun, for instance, wrote in 1957: "Its statements are to a great extent legendary in character; it shares the ancient belief in demoniacal possession; it reckons on the world coming to a speedy end" (reprinted in Braun 1971, p. 288). Strauss declined to salvage it by symbolical interpretation: why these detours, he asks; why embroil ourselves at all with what we can no longer use, in order to finally reach what we need? (1997, Volume 1, p. 102). For the enemies of critical theology, this his last book is a classic illustration of the truth that all criticism leads inevitably to unbelief. Gladstone held it up to school children as an awful example of what they would come to if they once began exercising their own faculties.

The really weak points in this "confession"—as Strauss called his final book—are his naïve optimism and his exaggerated patriotism. He insists that anyone who thinks that the evil-doer is happy and the good man miserable in this life does not know how to distinguish appearance from reality (1997, Volume 1, p. 145). We might expect this sort of statement in theodicies of the eighteenth century, but in a writer of 1872 it may justly be called what Nietzsche called it—in a fiercely critical review of 1873, the first of his *Unzeitgemäße Betrachtungen* (Thoughts out of Season)—namely "philistine optimism", particularly when coupled with talk of "nature's great progress". For Nietzsche, these together with complacent patriotism, were deplorable aspects of the satisfaction engendered in German thinking by the victory over France in 1871. He did not see that Strauss's patriotism may fairly be regarded as an example of the natural willingness of innovators to be on a friendly footing with the majority at least on some questions, and hence unduly to stress what they do happen to have in common with that majority. During the war Strauss had found in the German cause a ground of union with his countrymen which for the first time put him into sympathetic relation with them after his long exposure to their Christian wrath. The open letter he wrote to Renan about the war aroused jubilation throughout Germany. And when the fighting was over, he said, in his final book, that it had been caused by "passion and unreason" on the part of the French—"a vain and restless people"—whereas the German decision to go to war had been purely rational.

Strauss seems to have expected that a book which included the patriotic views which had recently made him so popular would be acclaimed. But acclamation was not accorded to a theologian who had rejected Christianity and immortality and accepted Darwin's views (cf. below, p. 176). And so he found himself, in what were to be the final months of his life, relegated to his old status of ostracized apostate.

Strauss's view of the mythical nature of much in the New Testament was not completely new, but he was the first to work this view out in detail, as even Baur conceded (quoted by Horton Harris, p. 107)—Baur, who did so much to stress his own contribution to New Testament studies, and to minimize that of Strauss. Strauss, then, was original only as Colenso or Darwin were original. The Pentateuch had been criticized before Colenso, evolution advocated before Darwin. But it was they who argued their respective theses with such overwhelming evidence that the whole issue could no longer be brushed aside. That was what made all three of them so hated: they had let the cat out of the bag. Carlyle's attitude was typical. Although, so Allingham tells us, he was "contemptuous to those who held to Christian dogmas", he was nevertheless "angry with those who gave them up" and "furious with those who attacked them" (1907, p. 254). Hence, Allingham says (p. 211), he called Strauss's *Life of Jesus* "a revolutionary and ill-advised enterprise, setting forth in words what all wise men had had in their minds for fifty years past, and thought it fittest to hold their peace about".

Strauss was told—as Lessing was when he published fragments from Reimarus's criticisms of the scriptures—that none of this should have been set before the public, but issued, if at all, in Latin in decent obscurity. Writing as Strauss did, the impact of his first *Life* was enormous, and in later years he was able to note, with a touch of justifiable pride, that during a quarter of a century "not a significant line" had been written on the questions with which his book had dealt "in which its influence is not to be perceived" (quoted by Horton Harris, p. 193). A significant illustration of the truth of this remark is the way in which Renan came latterly to accept Strauss's position, declaring that "even as the life of Buddha is in some sort written in advance, so was the life of a Jewish Messiah traced *a priori*; one could tell what he ought to do, what he was bound to accomplish." He had to repeat and exemplify a hundred sayings of the prophets. He had to preach on mountains because "all the ancient theophanies had taken place on heights". "All the tissue of the life of Jesus was thus a special thing, a sort of superhuman arrangement disposed to realize a series of ancient texts held to relate to him" (quoted from the fifth volume of Renan's work on Christian origins by J.M. Robertson, 1924, p. 66, who wryly adds: "How, this being so, we can ever know that we are reading a real utterance of Jesus or an actual episode in his life, we are not told").

This influence of Strauss has been permanent. Hillerbrand, who in 1967 pointed to Strauss's career to illustrate the principle that radical criticism leads inevitably to agnosticism, nevertheless conceded that neither biblical scholarship nor theology have been the same since (pp. 129, 158). But Strauss's influence has been at best grudgingly acknowledged. The scientists of today speak of their predecessors with pride and appreciation. Thanks to the great and real progress that has been made, it is possible for them to look back on pioneers with sympathy for their difficulties and admiration for their achievements. But in theology there is no neutral vantage-point from which the student may survey dispassionately the successes and failures of the past. The hypotheses of his predecessors are still in competition with his own, and he must discredit them if he would establish his claim to have superseded them. Karl Barth, for instance, invokes derision for this purpose. "Proper theology", he says, "begins just at the point where the difficulties disclosed by Strauss and Feuerbach are seen and then laughed at" (1972, p. 568). Counter-arguments come less easily than laughter.[8]

Perhaps the most endearing feature of Strauss is his uncompromising honesty. He was clear that he could not have lived with himself had he suppressed or disguised his real views instead of publishing his famous book (quoted by Horton Harris, p. 193). Only once did he falter. The babble of voices opposing him led him to make concessions in the third edition of his first *Life*. They delighted the orthodox, not because they amounted to much, but as evidence that he had begun to contradict himself. And so, still *persona non grata*, Strauss realized that he had allowed criticism to lead him astray, and in the fourth edition of 1840 he reverted to the positions taken up in the first. George Eliot, whose fine English translation of this fourth edition appeared in 1846, met him in 1858, and found that he spoke as "a man strictly truthful in the use of language" (quoted by Horton Harris, p. 233). One may have a calling, he said in 1865, even if one has no professional position; and his calling, he added, is directed against make-believe ("Falschmünzerei") which he found rather prominent in the theology of the day. Have things changed much? Schweitzer wrote: "The apologists, as we learn from the history of the Lives of Jesus, can get the better of any historical result whatever" (1954, p. 233). And more recently Zahrnt has declared that, if historical study proved that Jesus had never lived, "even then we theologians would succeed in finding a way out—when have we not succeeded in the past?" (1963, pp. 102f). Strauss is today not gladly remembered because he finally declined all ways out.

3

The Virgin Birth

i. Introduction

We saw that the Pauline letters were written before the gospels; that the earliest extant gospel is Mark's, used as a source by Matthew and Luke, each of whom was unacquainted with the other's work; and that the fourth gospel, ascribed to John, is independent of the others, but clearly used sources which were in part identical with theirs.

The circumstances of the saviour's birth and infancy are narrated, within the New Testament, only in Matthew and Luke, and are not mentioned or alluded to in its other twenty-five books, where only wishful thinking has been able to discern anything of the sort.[1] None of the epistles nor the book of Revelation make any mention of it, and Mary and Joseph are never named anywhere in the New Testament except in the gospels. Paul believed that Jesus existed as a supernatural being before the world was created. He assisted God in the creation of all things (1 Cor. 8:6), but then humbled himself by being "born of a woman" as a Jew "under the law" (Gal. 4:4). Anything but a quite ordinary birth would go against this argument which is concerned to show his extreme self-abasement in adopting human existence. Pannenberg (1972, p. 72) notes that Paul was certainly familiar with the idea of a miraculous birth, for in this same chapter of Galatians he mentions it in connection with the birth of Isaac through Sarah (4:22–29); but he applies it not to Jesus but in an allegorical sense to Christians as heirs of the promise (verse 28). For Paul, Christ was "born of the seed of David according to the flesh, and designated Son of God in power according to the spirit of holiness by his resurrection from the dead" (Rom. 1:3f). Such a statement, says Parrinder, "can hardly be reconciled with the notion of a virginal conception by a holy spirit, for, on the contrary, it states that the spirit demonstrated that Christ was the Son of God by his resurrection" (1992, p. 70).

Of the four gospels, the earliest shows no knowledge of Jesus's origins and does not even mention Joseph's name. It introduces Jesus as an adult "from Nazareth of Galilee", coming to be baptized in the Jordan. The fourth gospel does not name his mother as Mary, and has nothing to say about his birth. It begins with a metaphysical prologue which states that, to those who believe in him, Jesus gave the power to become children of God, "which were born not of blood, nor of the will of the flesh, nor of the will of man, but of God" (Jn. 1:13). To see any allegation of virgin birth here would mean ascribing such a birth to all believers. Some early patristic writers tried to introduce a reference to Jesus by changing the Greek 'which' and the 'were born' into the corresponding singulars. Parrinder (p. 53) quotes Raymond Brown's observation that "this variant is not attested in even one Greek ms. of the Gospel, and is plausibly a change made in the patristic period in order to enhance the christological utility of the text." What the evangelist is really saying is that true Christians do not owe their becoming such to their natural origin, nor to any earthly conditions.

After this prologue, the fourth gospel introduces Jesus as an adult, called "the lamb of God" by John the Baptist; whereupon Philip describes him as "Jesus of Nazareth, the son of Joseph" (1:36, 45). In continuing his presentation the evangelist never disavows these statements that Jesus was naturally born and hails from Nazareth, not from Bethlehem. He even represents the Jews as rejecting his Messianic claims on the ground that he was not born in Bethlehem (7:42). In this gospel his brothers seem not to regard him as of supernatural origin, for "even they did not believe on him" (7:5).

The fourth gospel is not an early work, and its author may have known traditions that Jesus was virgin born and deliberately rejected them. However, that the doctrine is also absent from the epistles and from the earliest of the four gospels does suggest that it entered Christian tradition only at a relatively late stage. This is confirmed by non-canonical evidence, in that the earliest Christian writer outside the canon to mention the doctrine is Ignatius of Antioch, writing probably about A.D. 110. What he says on the subject shows that he was dependent on the same kind of traditions as Matthew had drawn on. He has, for instance, his own version of the story of the guiding star, saying that, "although the virginity of Mary and her giving birth were hidden from the Prince of this world", "our God Jesus the Christ . . . was manifested to the world" in that

> A star shone in heaven beyond all the stars, and its light was unspeakable, and its newness caused astonishment, and all the other stars, with the sun and moon, gathered in chorus around this star . . . (to the Ephesians, Chapters 18 and 19, as rendered in the translation of the Loeb Classical Library)

Even after Ignatius, Justin Martyr, writing about A.D. 150, still knows of Christians who regard Jesus as "made man of men" (*Dialogue with Trypho*, 48:2). It is thus obvious that there was "in the camp of the orthodox . . . still a good deal of latitude with regard to the doctrine of Christ's incarnation" (von Campenhausen 1964, p. 21).

The lateness of the virgin birth traditions is confirmed even more strikingly by the only two canonical gospels which do treat of the birth and infancy; for in both of them, the accounts of Jesus's ministry (his adult preaching and wonder-working) which follow the infancy narratives were clearly drawn from traditions which knew nothing of the infancy material. Let me illustrate.

According to Matthew's infancy narrative, Herod and all Jerusalem knew of the birth in Bethlehem of "him that is born King of the Jews" (2:2–3), and Herod proceeded to slaughter all the male children of Bethlehem who were less than two years old in order to eliminate him (2:16); yet when the adult Jesus comes to his "own country" and preaches there, he is regarded by the inhabitants as a familiar but totally undistinguished citizen, whose "wisdom" and "mighty works" take them completely by surprise. They say of him:

> Is not this the carpenter's son? Is not his mother called Mary? And his brethren, James, and Joseph, and Simon, and Judas? And his sisters, are they not all with us? Whence then hath this man all these things [i.e. this wisdom and these mighty works]? (13:54–56)

It is, then, precisely the "indisputable ordinariness" (von Campenhausen, pp. 12–13) of Jesus's home, occupation, and family relationships that is alleged to have stood in his way. Even Herod's son has no inkling of his origins (14:1–2). The foremost Catholic exegete of the nativity stories, Raymond E. Brown, has said that it is obvious from these and other discrepancies that "the stories of the ministry were shaped in Christian tradition without a knowledge of the infancy material", and Matthew "never really smoothed out all the narrative rough spots left by the joining of two bodies of once-independent material" (1979, p. 32). Brown adds that "if the first two chapters had been lost and the Matthaean Gospel came down to us beginning with 3:1, no one would have suspected the existence of the missing chapters" (p. 49). He shows that Luke's gospel displays the same discrepancy between infancy narrative and main body: "If John the Baptist was a relative of Jesus who recognized him even before his birth (Lk. 1:41, 44), why does John the Baptist give no indication during the ministry of a previous knowledge of Jesus and indeed seem to be puzzled by him (7:19)?" (p. 32).

Such residual discrepancies are the more striking because Matthew and Luke have obviously 'edited' the material about the ministry that reached them from Mark's gospel so as to eliminate any suggestion that Jesus was misunderstood by his own family who—if the birth narratives record historical fact—must have been well aware of his supernatural origin. Mk. 3:21 has it that "the ones from beside him" (or "those alongside him": NEB "his family"), went out to seize him, thinking he had lost his senses. Some older English versions translate the Greek here as though the reference were to 'his friends'. However, the meaning in this context is 'his family', for when they reach him in verse 31, they are identified as his mother and brothers. Matthew and Luke simply omit this story. Again, at Mk. 6:4 Jesus says: "A prophet is not without honour, save in his own country, and among his own kin, and in his own house." Matthew cuts out the words "and among his own kin", and Luke makes Jesus say merely that "no prophet is acceptable in his own country."

The New Testament epistles (and not only the Pauline ones) make it obvious that the earliest Christian preaching concentrated almost exclusively on the crucifixion and resurrection. As we saw, at this early stage, these events were simply alleged to have happened and not given any historical context. However one interprets this, it is clear that, by the time the earliest gospel was written, interest in the crucifixion had led in some Christian circles to the formation of a detailed Passion narrative. And it is understandable that, by then, interest had extended further to what Jesus had done and taught in his lifetime, so that this narrative is preceded by an account of his ministry. But only the yet later gospels of Matthew and Luke represent a stage where curiosity had reached out to his origins; and their accounts are so full of difficulties in themselves and so discrepant with each other as to suggest that there was no reliable information on the subject, that all that tradition provided was an allegation of a virgin birth at Bethlehem in the days of Herod the Great which speculation had free rein to develop—as free as we shall see to have been the case with the resurrection appearances.

ii. The Birth at Bethlehem
a. Matthew's Account

Unlike Luke, who introduces Joseph and Mary as residents of Nazareth from the first, Matthew implies that their home was in "Bethlehem of Judea"; for he begins his second chapter by recording Jesus's birth there, and he represents the holy couple as wishing to return there after their flight from Herod into Egypt. They failed to do so only because Joseph was warned in a dream that Herod's son Archelaus (who by this time had succeeded his father and reigned over the southern part of the kingdom) was an equal danger to them; and so they went instead to live in Nazareth in Galilee (2:21–23). Here, in the north, another of Herod's sons, Antipas, was ruler.[2]

Matthew represents the change of abode from Bethlehem to Nazareth not only as unexpected but also as fulfillment of prophecy; and he says the same of Herod's slaughter of the Innocents in Bethlehem. This massacre is not mentioned by Luke, nor by any ancient historian. It is in particular unmentioned by the Jewish historian Flavius Josephus, who in the first century A.D. recorded the history of Herod and his family, and even stressed its horrors. This particular horror would in any case have constituted a quite unnecessary action on Herod's part. Exotic magi from the east with royal gifts would have made a great impression in a small place like Bethlehem, and it would have been no great task for Herod's intelligence system to discover which child they had visited and then kill him. This would have been more to Herod's purpose than the hit-or-miss method of killing all the male children under two years in the place (cf. Brown 1979, pp. 188–89). Apologists have nevertheless argued that Herod was ferocious enough to have done something of this kind, particularly in the final years of his life, and that Matthew's account therefore rings true in respect of this detail. The answer must be that Matthew himself may well have had the same idea; that he knew enough about the reign of Herod to realize that ferocious acts could plausibly be attributed to him, and to anticipate that readers who also knew something (if not much) of him would find such a story believable.

Brown makes this point, and adds (pp. 227–28) that an Old Testament parallel to Matthew's story was ready at hand, namely the Pharaoh's massacre of Hebrew male children of Egypt (Exodus 1:22), from which the infant Moses nevertheless escaped. It has long been recognized that Matthew is much concerned to portray Jesus as a second—and greater—Moses. "The experiences of the leader of the Exodus are, as it were, recapitulated in the great Redeemer who will bring about the final deliverance of the people of God" (Beare 1981, p. 72).

Altogether there is much in Matthew's infancy narrative which, although "quite implausible" as history, is perfectly intelligible as "rewritings of Old Testament scenes or themes" (Brown, p. 36). For instance, the Joseph of the infancy narrative dreams (he is thrice advised in a dream, and on two of these occasions the advice is said to come from an angel). He also goes down into Egypt, the only man in the New Testament to do so. Precisely these two activities are associated with the patriarch Joseph, the hero of Genesis 37–50. Matthew's story of the magi, the "wise men from the east" (2:1) and their guiding star, seems to owe something to the story of Balaam in Numbers 22–24, where this soothsayer from the east is represented as foretelling the destruction of Moab and Edom at the hands of a future ruler of Israel, symbolized by a rising star.

> There shall come forth a star out of Jacob,
> And a scepter shall rise out of Israel,
> And shall smite through the corners of Moab,
> And break down all the sons of tumult.
> And Edom shall be a possession. (Numbers 24:17–18)

As noted in Metzger and Coogan's 1993 Oxford Companion to the Bible (art. Balaam), the oracle "may originally have applied to David", who first reduced Moab to subjection (2 Samuel 8:2), but later "was interpreted as the promise of a ruler who would come as a deliverer in the end time." Thus for Matthew it seemed appropriate that it should point to the Messianic child.

Matthew's magi are not said to be kings nor to be three in number—an idea that arose because they present three gifts (gold, frankincense, and myrrh) to the newborn child. They were not named "until Latin legends from the sixth century, when they were called Gaspar, Melchior, and Balthasar. . . . Later still they became saints, and their relics are said to be in Cologne cathedral" (Parrinder, p. 17). Their story is firmly set in a context of astrological belief. They observed the star "at its rising" (Mt. 2:2; cf. NEB: not "in the east", as older versions have it. When Matthew intends the relevant Greek noun to mean 'the east', he uses it in its plural form, as in the previous verse). "The moment of a star's appearance above the horizon was of prime importance in astrology. Probably it is assumed that the star appeared at the precise moment of the Saviour's birth or conception" (Beare 1981, p. 77).

On reaching Jerusalem the star turned south to Bethlehem—miraculously, as the apparent movement of all stars in the sky is from east to west. It seems an unnecessary miracle, as Herod has instructed the magi to seek the child at Bethlehem (2:8), and no star is needed to guide them across the five miles from Jerusalem to this known destination. The star is, however, made to perform a useful function by the further miracle of hovering "over where the young child was", or in other words, as the sequel makes clear, above the very house where he lay (2:9–11). A star which not merely turned south but also came to rest so as to point out a particular house would have "constituted a celestial phenomenon unparalleled in astronomical history: yet it received no notice in the records of the times" (Brown, p. 188). Noteworthy in this connection is that there is no suggestion in Matthew, as there is in Luke, that Jesus was laid in a manger because Joseph and Mary could not find accommodation in an inn. "When the astrologers find him, he and his mother are in a house, and the reader would naturally assume that it is their own house" (Beare, p. 76).

Apologists have tried hard to find some astronomical occurrence which might have been interpreted as the star of the magi. Halley's comet (visible every seventy-seven years) appeared in 12–11 B.C.; there was a rare conjunction of the planets Jupiter and Saturn in 7 B.C.; and Mars passed by in the following year. None of this makes Matthew's story into plausible history, for, as with his account of Herod's slaughter of the Innocents, he may have been drawing on some remembered phenomenon and linking it, with considerable distortion and embellishment, with Jesus's birth. Matthew wrote after A.D. 70, and what legends had then come to be told of astronomical occurrences of two or three generations earlier "in the days of Herod the King", might have prompted his story. Such a story was not unusual in the Mediterranean world, which had many a star, many a planet, to herald important births. Both Mithridates and Alexander Severus—to name but two examples—had their birthdays celebrated in this way.

If, as we have seen, the traditions of Jesus's ministry knew nothing of those embodied in the infancy narratives, the latter themselves, as they stand in the two relevant gospels, are composite and comprise elements of different provenance. For instance, at the beginning of Matthew's second chapter, the wise men are guided by the star to Herod at Jerusalem, and their question, "Where is he that is born king of the Jews?" leads, by means of an investigation of the scriptures, to the answer: in Bethlehem. But this place is in the sequel pointed out to them by the star, thus making the scriptural investigation unnecessary. On all this, Brown comments:

Why does the star, which eventually leads the magi to the house where Jesus is, not lead them directly to Bethlehem from the East, so that a stop at Jerusalem would not be necessary? We seem to have two different stories pointing to Bethlehem, one through investigation of the Scriptures, the other through the star. Herod's failure to find the child at Bethlehem would be perfectly intelligible in a story in which there were no magi who came from the East and where he had only general scriptural knowledge about Bethlehem to guide him. It becomes ludicrous when the way to the house has been pointed out by a star which came to rest over it, and when the path to the door of the house in a small village has been blazed by exotic foreigners. (p. 191)

b. Luke's Account

Although the infancy narratives of Matthew and Luke are quite independent, neither evangelist having read the account of the other, both were clearly acquainted with traditions which located Jesus's birth in Bethlehem during the reign of Herod the Great, and both knew from Mark's gospel that he spent his adult life in and around Nazareth and in Galilee generally. But on these bases they build very differently. Matthew, we saw, makes Bethlehem the home of his parents, and solves the problem of the family's later departure from that place with his stories of persecutions and angelic warnings, which are unknown to Luke. Luke however makes the parents resident in Nazareth, so his problem is to get them to Bethlehem for the birth. His solution is to make Joseph and Mary go there because Augustus had ordered a census of the whole Roman empire: "Now it came to pass in those days there went out a decree from Caesar Augustus, that all the world should be enrolled" (2:1). By enrollment is meant the registration of names and property as a basis for taxation.

There is in fact no evidence for a census of the whole empire under Augustus. Obvious authorities, such as the *Monumentum Ancyranum*, Dio Cassius, and Suetonius are silent on the matter, and the only witnesses who speak of such things are Christians, from the sixth century onwards, which creates "a very strong suspicion that they simply drew their information from Luke" (Schürer 1973, p. 409). How hard put apologists are for evidence to the contrary is shown when some of them appeal to a register of the resources of the whole empire which Augustus, as a careful financier, compiled. Tacitus tells that it recorded "the strength of the citizens and allies under arms, the number of the fleets, protectorates and provinces; the taxes, direct and indirect [tributa aut vectigalia]; the needful disbursements and customary bounties"

(*Annals*, Volume 1, 11, Loeb Library translation). This is no more than a summary of the military and financial resources and expenditure of the empire, and has nothing to do with censuses (Schürer, pp. 407f and note 36 on p. 408). The imperial census thus seems to be "a purely literary device used by Luke to associate Mary and Joseph, residents of Nazareth, with Bethlehem" (Fitzmyer, p. 393).

By the phrase "in those days" (2:1) Luke means "in the days of Herod, king of Judea" (1:5). This verse in Chapter 1 introduces the story of Mary's kinswoman, the aged Elisabeth, telling how the angel "Gabriel who stands in the presence of God" announced to her husband, a temple priest, that John the Baptist would be born to them. (That Gabriel is one of the 'angels of the presence' reflects "the speculative theology of angels that had developed in Judaism": Evans 1990, p. 151.) After the angel's announcement—the precise interval is not indicated, but there is no suggestion that it is long enough for Herod to have died in the meantime—Elisabeth duly conceived and "hid herself five months", surprisingly (but, as we shall see, for the needs of Luke's story), for she believed that her pregnancy had removed her "reproach" of barrenness "among men" (1:24f). A month later, Gabriel visits Mary, informs her of her kinswoman's condition, and tells her that she herself will conceive Jesus miraculously; whereupon Mary "arose in those days", went to Elisabeth, and stayed three months with her (1:39f, 56). Such a journey of some eighty miles would probably have taken four days, and that a lone woman would undertake it is surely motivated only by the evangelist's literary need to "bring the two women together, as both being involved in a single plan of God, which would later take effect in the relationship between John and Jesus" (Evans 1990, pp. 168f). On Mary's arrival Elisabeth addresses her as "the mother of my Lord" and says, "Blessed is the fruit of thy womb" (1:42–43), clearly indicating that Mary herself is also pregnant. Chapter 2 takes up Mary's story when she is about to give birth to her child. This will be six months later, and it was "in those days" that Augustus decreed the census (2:1). Thus Luke's initial "in the days of Herod" (1:5) is followed by the phrase "in these days" (1:39) and "in those days" (2:1), with no clear indication of a significant gap in time in the intervening events. Hence "for all its vagueness", this phrase "dates the birth of Jesus in 'the days of Herod'" (Fitzmyer, p. 399).

Now a Roman census in Palestine in Herod's time was out of the question. Although then under Roman influence, it was not made part of the empire until A.D. 6, ten years after Herod's death, when Augustus deposed Herod's son Archelaus and incorporated his territory into the province of Syria. Herod was a client king, holding his title and authority from Caesar and the Senate; he had to defend the imperial frontier and was not allowed to make treaties or wage war at pleasure, but was permitted freedom in his management of Palestine's internal affairs. A client ruler such as he may have paid a lump sum as tribute to Rome, although it is "improbable" that he did so: such exactions were more likely in the later period of the empire, when the political power of the *reges socii* was more restricted; and in any case payment of a tribute has no bearing on the possibility of a Roman census on his territory (Schürer, pp. 317, 416n, 417n). Moreover, if the Romans had—contrary to their known policy—carried out a valuation census on his territory, this would have been extremely unpopular, would have "offended the people to the quick", as Schürer says; in which case we should expect it to be recorded by Josephus, for "on no other period is Josephus so well informed, on none is he so thorough, as on that of Herod's last years" (p. 418). But he makes no mention of it.

Luke not only alleges a Roman census on Herod's territory in his lifetime, but also says: "this was the first registration, Quirinius being governor of Syria" (2:2). Herod died in 4 B.C., but Quirinius became governor of Syria only in A.D. 6 (Schürer, p. 420).[3] His career "is fairly well known and defies all attempts either to attribute to him two censuses in Judea or to date the start of his leadership of Syria to any other period than A.D. 6–7" (Fitzmyer, p. 402).[4]

Josephus mentions a census under Quirinius in the year A.D. 6. This was quite in order, for Judea had just been converted into a Roman province, and the imperial legate needed to make a list of the inhabitants and a reckoning of their landed property for the purpose of apportioning the taxation. Josephus says that this census was the first and that it was altogether novel for the Romans to raise a tax in Judea. (The passages are quoted by Schürer, p. 419.) He also says that it caused the Jews to revolt, under the leadership of Judas the Gaulonite of Gamala. The Acts of the Apostles, written by the author of the third gospel, refers (5:37) to "Judas of Galilee in the days of the enrolment" (*apographē*, as at Lk. 2:2). He would not have referred to this census of A.D. 6 as *the* enrolment if he had known of an earlier one. Hence we must infer that in his gospel he had in mind the census of A.D. 6, but antedated it and supposed it to have occurred in Herod's lifetime. Attempts to escape this conclusion are totally unconvincing.[5]

It is not hard to see how this error could have happened. The death of Herod in 4 B.C. and the Roman annexation of Judea in A.D. 6 were both "striking events in Palestinian history which would leave their mark in the minds of men" and "serve for approximate dating in a society not given to exact documentation".[6] It would be all the easier to confuse the two, as each was followed by an uprising. According to Josephus, Varus, then legate of Syria, had to intervene in 4 B.C. with the whole of his army. But the uprising of A.D. 6 was the more sharply remembered because it was then that Roman rule and taxation were imposed.

A further objection to Luke's account is that even the census of A.D. 6 would not have affected Galilee, where Mary and Joseph were living. When Herod died, the southern part of his kingdom (Idumea, Judea, and Samaria) was given to Archelaus, but Galilee in the north was put under another of his sons, Antipas. Archelaus was deposed in A.D. 6 and his territory annexed to the empire, but Antipas remained in office and ruled Galilee until A.D. 39. Luke implies that the inhabitants of Galilee were affected by a Roman census that in fact applied only to the more southerly provinces. Again we see that he is not concerned with accuracy of historical detail. His purpose is to get Mary from Nazareth to Bethlehem in time for the birth of her child. In obedience to the imperial decree:

> All went to enrol themselves, every one to his own city. And Joseph also went up from Galilee, out of the city of Nazareth, into Judea, to the city of David, which is called Bethlehem, because he was of the house and family of David: to enrol himself with Mary, who was betrothed to him, being great with child. (2:3–5)

We are thus required to believe that the 'own city' to which everyone was required to go was the place where his family originated; and that Joseph therefore went to Bethlehem, eighty-five miles away, because a thousand years earlier his ancestor David had been born there. But the practical Romans had no such cumbersome custom. "In a Roman census, landed property had to be registered for taxation in the locality within which it was situated", and "the person to be taxed had to register in the place where he lived or in the chief town of his taxation district" (Schürer, p. 411). It would have been ridiculous to make a man give his returns miles away from his home, where the authorities would be unable to check the entries he made. In any case, Schürer adds, "it is very doubtful whether a registration according to tribes and genealogies was possible; many were no longer able to establish that they belonged to this or that family."[7] Nor would Mary have needed to accompany Joseph, for the particulars needed for a Roman census "could be supplied by the father of the family." In any case, Joseph went to Bethlehem only because he was descended from David. Mary, however, was not: she was kindred to Elisabeth (mother of John the Baptist) who "was of the daughters of Aaron" (1:5), and so a Levite of the priestly tribe.

From all these considerations we can hardly avoid the inference that Luke has invented the journey of Mary and Joseph across some eighty miles of difficult country in order to have Jesus born in the place which, he stresses, is "David's city" (2:11), as he thought was expected of the Messiah.

We can see already by now that the infancy narratives of the two evangelists cannot be harmonized. In Matthew an angel announces the virgin birth to Joseph in Bethlehem in a dream. In Luke the angel, named as Gabriel, comes to Mary in Nazareth, and not in a dream but in person. The exalted status of the child is attested in Luke by an angel's words to shepherds and the song of the heavenly host (neither of which is mentioned in Matthew), but in Matthew by the appearance of the star (not mentioned in Luke). The child receives his first adoration in Luke from the shepherds who go unmentioned in Matthew, and in Matthew from the magi (unmentioned in Luke). In Matthew the holy family lived originally in Bethlehem, but in Luke they go there only because of a census of the people (not mentioned by Matthew). After the birth they went, according to Luke, to Jerusalem, when the time came for "*their* purification" according to "the law of the Lord" (2:22f, italics added). Luke here betrays "ignorance of Jewish custom", where only the mother, and "neither the father nor child were involved in purification: *their* . . . is . . . likely a clumsy device of Luke to bring the child into the proceedings" which "are said to be about him and not the mother's purification, which plays no further part in the story" (Evans 1990, p. 212). This story tells that in the temple, the pious and aged Simeon hails the child as "a light to lighten the gentiles", and the prophetess Anna thanks God for his birth. Then the holy family went straight back to Nazareth (2:39), where by the grace of God the child's early years were passed in uninterrupted growth (2:40). None of this is known to Matthew, who represents these early years as disturbed by perils and changes of abode. Matthew implies (2:16) that the child was a little under two years old when the family fled from Bethlehem to Egypt, and obviously older, perhaps years older, when they left Egypt to settle in Nazareth. As Brown notes, their flight into Egypt "is quite irreconcilable with Luke's account of an orderly and uneventful return from Bethlehem to Nazareth shortly after the birth of the child" (p. 225). "In Egypt today there are six sites where the Holy Family is said to have rested" (Parrinder, p. 18).

iii. Luke's Parallel between John the Baptist and Jesus

Luke's narrative begins with the story of the priest Zechariah, visited in the temple by the angel Gabriel who tells him that his aged wife Elisabeth "shall bear thee a son, and thou shalt call his name John" (1:13). Old Testament material has obviously been remodelled here. Luke is "reviving the pattern of the birth of Old Testament promise-bearers and saviours—Isaac, Samson, and Samuel—who are likewise miraculously born to old and barren women through the unexpected intervention of God" (von Campenhausen, p. 27). And Luke's description of Zechariah and Elisabeth "is taken, at times almost verbatim, from the Old Testament description of Abraham and Sarah" (Brown, p. 36).

Zechariah is struck temporarily dumb as a punishment for questioning Gabriel's announcement; and Elisabeth, on becoming pregnant, hides herself for five months (1:20 and 24). Both these events are dictated by what Creed calls "the necessities of the narrative" (1930, p. 12); for when Gabriel subsequently visits Mary and promises her a child he needs a sign with which to dispel her incredulity, and this sign consists in his assurance to her: "Behold, Elisabeth thy kinswoman, she also hath conceived a son in her old age; and this is the sixth month of her that was called barren. For no word from God shall be void of power" (1:36–37). Obviously, but for Zechariah's dumbness and Elisabeth's seclusion, Mary would have come to know of her kinswoman's pregnancy, which thus would not have been available as a trump card to Gabriel.

If the conception of John the Baptist required a miracle, that of Jesus requires an even greater one, a virginal conception. The parallelism between John and Jesus in this chapter is what Fitzmyer calls a "step-parallelism", that is, "a parallelism with one-upmanship. The Jesus side always comes off better" (p. 315).

Gabriel comes to Mary in Nazareth and tells her: "thou shalt conceive in thy womb" (1:31). She takes this as implying a natural conception, for she replies: "How shall this be, seeing I know not a man?"—a question which can only mean: 'I have no acquaintance with any man as might lead to the fulfillment of this prophecy'. But the exact opposite of this is involved in the actual situation. She is betrothed to Joseph (1:27) and must necessarily have looked to the fulfillment of the prophecy through her marriage with him. Mary's question is thus not how a woman in her situation would have reacted to the angel's announcement, but is perfectly intelligible from the needs of Luke's narrative. The real purpose of her question is to "advance the dialogue" (Fitzmyer, p. 350), "to give the writer an opening for the angel's prophecy as to how the conception is to come to pass" (Creed, p. 19). And so the angel is able to answer by telling her that "holy spirit will come upon you", and the child to be born "shall be called holy, son of God" (1:35). The Greek does not have '*the* holy spirit' or '*the* son of God' here, in the manner of most translations, as if Luke had been beholden to later trinitarian theology! (Likewise there is no 'the' at Mt. 1:20: Joseph is told: "that which is conceived in her is of holy spirit.")

Luke's second chapter may well have been drawn from a different tradition—one which knew nothing of a virgin birth. The chapter combines three incidents which may have been originally independent stories: the homage of the shepherds, Simeon's recognition of Jesus as the saviour, and the temple-teaching of the twelve-year-old. Each of these stories—they are all found only in Luke—shows when Jesus's true significance was recognized, and Luke has simply combined them into a sequence.

The story that the twelve-year-old amazed the learned doctors in the temple records also Mary's lack of comprehension at the behaviour of her child (2:48–50). This blank failure to understand that the child was abnormal is not what one would expect from a mother who had been visited by an angel and told that he would be born of "holy spirit", be "great", and be given the throne of David to "reign over the house of Jacob for ever; and of his kingdom there shall be no end" (1:32–35). Mary's entire oblivion in the temple of all these stupendous circumstances does seem to imply that the temple story comes from some pre-Lucan source which knew nothing of the traditions represented in the annunciation. Fitzmyer observes that it may belong to "a tradition which grew up about the childhood of Jesus and that continued to manifest itself in the apocryphal gospels, such as the *Infancy Story of Thomas*, which tells what Jesus did or said at the ages of five, six, eight, and twelve" (pp. 435–36).

Returning to Chapter 1 we note that it contains the Benedictus or joyful song of Zechariah at the birth of his son (1:67–79) and the Magnificat which Mary is represented as speaking in exultation at her own pregnancy when she visits the pregnant Elisabeth (1:46–55). Since these two songs are only loosely connected with their context and are full of Jewish ideas (they mention Israel, David, "our Fathers", and God's covenant with Abraham), there is some agreement that they are Jewish or Jewish-Christian hymns which Luke has incorporated into his narrative (with perhaps a few verses of his own composition to adapt them to the context). If the Magnificat were omitted, the account of Mary's visit to Elisabeth (1:39–45) would terminate naturally with 1:56 ("and Mary abode with her about three months and returned unto her house"). Likewise, if the Benedictus were omitted, 1:57–66 (the birth of John and his naming as John, with the final statement that "the hand of the Lord was with him") would terminate naturally at 1:80 ("And the child grew and waxed strong in spirit and was in the deserts till the day of his showing unto Israel"). Much of the substance of both hymns has little relevance to the situation of the persons Luke represents as speaking them. That Mary has conceived a child gives her no ground for the martial tone of the Magnificat (the proud have been scattered and the mighty put down). Brown thinks that we have here "a hymn that describes Israel, specifically the poor and oppressed remnant" (p. 340). Similarly, most of the Benedictus has little relevance to John the Baptist. It is a Messianic hymn, rejoicing in the horn of salvation that has been raised up in the house of David, to the discomfort of the Jews' enemies; whereas John is not of Davidic descent at all, but of the priestly line.

It is doubtful whether the evangelist even meant the Magnificat to be spoken by Mary; for although all Greek manuscripts introduce it with "and Mary said", some old Latin manuscripts have here, instead, "and Elisabeth said", and this may well have been the original reading (unless, as the NEB suggests, "the original may have had no name" and have simply been "and she said"). For, first, it is hard to see why a copyist should change 'Mary' to 'Elisabeth', while the opposite change is quite intelligible as prompted by increasing Mariolatry. Second, Elisabeth's position as an aged and barren woman resembles that of the long-childless Hannah (mother of Samuel), whose song of 1 Samuel 2 the Magnificat to some extent follows. Elisabeth, not Mary, is the one who, like Hannah, has been raised from the humiliation of childlessness. Third, the words immediately following the Magnificat at Lk. 1:56 are "more natural and grammatically better if Elisabeth is the author of the hymn" (Elliott 1982, p. 12). The verse reads: "And Mary abode with her about three months." If Elisabeth had hitherto been the speaker, it makes good sense that Mary is actually named here, as the subject of the verb, and that Elisabeth is referred to with the pronoun 'her'. But if Mary had been the speaker up to verse 55, it is most unnatural that Elisabeth should then be called 'her' (cf. Creed, p. 22). If, then, the Magnificat is Elisabeth's song of thanksgiving, the evangelist meant it to apply to John the Baptist, not to Jesus, and it then becomes a true parallel to the Benedictus, which in Luke's understanding is the thanksgiving song of Elisabeth's husband for the birth of John.[8]

In the present chapter I am concerned only with the relation between Jesus and John as it appears in Luke's infancy narrative. What dealings the two men are supposed to have had as adults will occupy us in a later chapter, and we shall see that this is a matter that is handled very differently in the different gospels.

iv. The Nativity as Fulfillment of Prophecy

Matthew represents five details in his infancy narrative as fulfillment of 'prophecies', but in fact the relevant Old Testament passages bear no relation to the events which he describes as fulfilling them. Let us study the details.

(a) When the angel has told Joseph that Mary will bring forth Jesus "of holy spirit", the evangelist adds:

> All this came to pass, that it might be fulfilled which was spoken by the Lord through the prophet, saying, Behold the virgin shall be with child, and shall bring forth a son. And they shall call his name Immanuel; which is, being interpreted, God with us. (1:22–23)

The reference is to Isaiah 7:14, where the prophet is addressing Ahaz (King of Judah about 735–715 B.C.) in Jerusalem. At this time, the united kingdom of David and Solomon had been divided into Israel in the north, ruled over by Pekah, and Judah in the south. Pekah had allied himself with Rezin, king of Damascus (Syria), intending a revolt against Assyria, the super-power of the day, and wanted Ahaz to join them. When he refused, they attacked him in Jerusalem, "but could not prevail against it" (Isaiah 7:1). Isaiah assured him that he really had nothing to fear from these two adversaries, and that, before a child shortly to be born to a "young woman" will be old enough to tell good from evil, "the land whose two kings thou abhorrest shall be forsaken" (7:16). As early as the child's birth, the political and military situation will be so much improved that his mother will give him a name of good omen, Immanuel (verse 14).

The AV and the RV render Isaiah 7:14 as "a virgin shall conceive and bear a son". But the Hebrew text makes no reference to a virgin and uses the word 'almah', meaning 'young woman', which is the rendering given in recent scholarly English versions such as the RSV and the NEB. (American fundamentalists burned copies of the RSV because of this change.) It is the Septuagint (an influential Greek version of the Old Testament) that uses the word meaning virgin, and renders the passage: "the virgin shall be with child and thou [the husband] shall call his name Immanuel." Brown notes that both the standard Hebrew (Masoretic) text and the Septuagint, and of course Matthew, use the definite article (*the* young woman or *the* virgin, not *a* young woman), so that it is "likely that Isaiah was referring to someone definite whose identity was known to him and to King Ahaz, perhaps someone whom the king had recently married and brought into the harem" (pp. 147–48). Even in the Septuagint version, nothing supernatural is asserted. Isaiah is simply saying to Ahaz that a woman who is now a virgin will (by natural means, once she is united with her husband) conceive the child.

Isaiah, then, did not suppose that this child would be the Messiah, to be born about seven hundred years later. In any case, Messianism as we know it from later Jewish history did not exist in his day. Messiah simply meant 'anointed' and was used to designate kings and high priests who were always anointed with oil. Saul, the first Israelite king, is called "the Lord's anointed" (1 Samuel 24:6). The term at this stage did not indicate a future redeemer. But when the Babylonian exile of 587–539 B.C. brought the monarchy to an end, expectations that the anointed kings of the house of David would deliver the Jews from their enemies or from catastrophe were transferred to an anointed king of the indefinite future; "and thus hope was born in the Messiah, the supreme anointed one who would deliver Israel" (Brown, p. 67n). When such expectations developed, many Old Testament passages were reinterpreted as references to this coming Messiah. But even then, Isaiah 7:14 was not understood in this way in Jewish usage.

In sum, Isaiah's oracle "does not predict a miraculous birth from a virgin, nor does it bear upon the birth of a Messiah still more than seven centuries in the future. It is an assurance to King Ahaz, terrified as he is by the threat of an invasion from the north, that the danger is negligible." And the name Immanuel "is to be given by way of a thankful acknowledgement that God has made his presence known among his people by removing the danger that has threatened" (Beare 1981, pp. 71–72).

(b) Herod is troubled to learn from the wise men that a "King of the Jews" has been born. He "gathers together all the chief priests and scribes of the people" to inquire from them the relevant locality. (The author obviously knew nothing of "the bitter opposition that existed between Herod and the priests, nor of the fact that the Sanhedrin was not at his beck and call": Brown, p. 188.) They tell him:

> In Bethlehem of Judea: for thus it is written by the prophet,
> And thou, Bethlehem, land of Judah,
> Art in no wise least among the princes of Judah:
> For out of thee shall come forth a governor,
> Which shall be shepherd of my people Israel. (2:5–6)

The first three lines of the citation are drawn from a textual tradition of Micah 5:2 that is identical neither with the Masoretic text nor the Septuagint. This indicates the multiplicity of texts available in Matthew's day—"variant Hebrew wordings, Aramaic targums, and a number of Greek translations" (Brown, p. 103. The Targums were Aramaic versions read in the synagogue as an interpretive translation of the original Hebrew). The final line has been added from 2 Samuel 5:2, where David is reminded that "the Lord said to thee, Thou shalt feed my people Israel". This, of course, *pace* Matthew, cannot belong to what was said by "the prophet" Micah, but it does serve to associate Jesus with David, which was doubtless the evangelist's intention. He was clearly also very much concerned to insist that the credentials of the Messiah include birth in Bethlehem rather than in some other city such as Jerusalem; but the passage in Micah says only that from the insignificant clan of Ephrathah, which included Bethlehem—the text reads "Bethlehem Ephrathah", little "among the thousands (clans) of Judah"—a ruler of Israel shall come forth. A few verses later there is mention of deliverance from an impending Assyrian invasion, and the writer seems to have had in mind not a Messiah of the remote future, but a leader who would deliver Judah from the Assyrian. Also, he does not say that Bethlehem will be his birthplace, only that he will come forth as a leader from it. The Old Testament makes David a native of Bethlehem, but does not suggest that he was there as king; in Jewish tradition up to Matthew's time, Jerusalem, not Bethlehem, was the city of David. Micah's prophecy of a ruler emerging from Bethlehem does not seem to have been understood by pre-Christian Jews as referring to the Messiah, for it is interpreted messianically only in the Targum of Micah (about A.D. 300) and not, for instance, at Qumran, even though Micah was used there. Hence, as Burger notes (1970, p. 24), the location of the Messiah's birth at Bethlehem was not common Jewish tradition ready and waiting for Christians to assimilate. However, both Matthew and Luke, in their wholly independent infancy narratives, make Jesus born there, and so this must have been a widespread tradition among the early Christians, perhaps inspired by "the tendency to imagine that the Messiah Son of David must recapitulate the experience of his famous ancestor" (Beare, p. 79).

(c) Joseph, warned in a dream by an angel to flee from Herod into Egypt, remained there with Mary and the child until Herod's death, "that it might be fulfilled which was spoken by the Lord through the prophet, saying, Out of Egypt did I call my son" (2:13–15). This is cited from Hosea 11:1, where the prophet is reminding the people of Yahweh's loyalty to them in the past when he delivered them from Egyptian captivity: "when Israel was a child, then I loved him, and called my son out of Egypt." Here, 'my son' means the nation, not the Messiah, and the reference is to a past deliverance (the Exodus), not a future one. Matthew's use of the passage well illustrates his complete lack of concern with historical interpretation of the scriptures. It sufficed for him that, since Jesus was the Son and had been in Egypt, what Hosea said fitted the facts.

(d) When Herod saw himself foiled, he had all the male children of Bethlehem and its environs killed. "Then was fulfilled that which was spoken by Jeremiah the prophet, saying,

A voice was heard in Ramah,
Weeping and great mourning,
Rachel weeping for her children;
And she would not be comforted,
because they are not. (2:17–18)

Rachel was Jacob's second wife, mother of Joseph and Benjamin, and according to one tradition she was buried at Ramah (near Jerusalem). Commentators explain that Jeremiah envisages her weeping in her tomb (31:15) "as she watches the columns of captives ('her children') marching along the road into exile, under the guard of the victorious Assyrians after the fall of the (northern)Kingdom of Israel (2 Kings 17:6)" (Beare, pp. 82–83; cf. Brown, pp. 205–06). For Matthew she has come to represent the mothers of Bethlehem weeping for their murdered children, and the historical context of the passage in Jeremiah has been wholly lost.

(e) Joseph is warned in a dream to avoid Herod's son Archelaus, ruler of Judea, and so "withdrew into the parts of Galilee, and came and dwelt in a city called Nazareth: that it might be fulfilled which was spoken by the prophets, that he should be called a Nazarene" (2:22–23). No such passage exists in the Old Testament, and Matthew's ascription of it to "the prophets", rather than to a particular prophet, may indicate that he did not have in mind any passage that would exactly bear him out.

There are, however, a number which, with some manipulation, can be made to yield the meaning desired. One suggestion, favoured by Howard C. Kee, is that Matthew, who will have known from Mark of Jesus's connection with Nazareth, produced a prophecy about Jesus's coming from that obscure hamlet by taking the consonants of the Hebrew text of Isaiah 11:1, which promises a 'shoot' (n-tz-r in Hebrew), later interpreted as the Messiah, and providing it with different vowels, which can be done readily in Semitic languages (1983, p. 186n).

In sum, Matthew is clearly much concerned to prove from the Jewish scriptures that Jesus really is, according to his origin and home, the expected Messiah. That the passages he adduces for this purpose are not to the point typifies the use of the Old Testament made by the authors of the New Testament. The latter "tear passages out of context, use allegory or typology to give old stories new meanings, contradict the plain meaning of the text, find references to Christ in passages where the original authors never intended any, and adapt or even alter the wording in order to make it yield the meaning they require" (Morna Hooker 1981, p. 295). This is the verdict not of some rationalist 'scoffer', but of the Lady Margaret Professor of Divinity in the University of Cambridge. The argument that the Old Testament can be read as prophecy of Jesus has lost all force, and, as Brown says, "has disappeared from most serious scholarship today", which recognizes that "the OT prophets were primarily concerned with addressing God's challenge to their own times" (1979, p. 146).

Richard Holloway, the former bishop of Edinburgh, has spelled out—as a *reductio ad absurdum*—exactly what the traditional 'argument from prophecy' really implies, namely that, for instance, Isaiah 7:14 LXX, "a virgin shall conceive", etc. was not just spoken by the prophet so as to stiffen the backbone of a frightened king of Judah, who was being invaded by his northern neighbours; but that these words were placed there by God, as a secret message for future readers who had the insight to see that they evidenced his careful long-term plan to bring salvation to mankind. They "pointed ahead to the day when God would embed himself in humanity by being born of a virgin in order to save us from our sins" (2004, p. 76). In sum, we are to believe that "God planted clues to his intentions in books written hundreds of years before the birth of Jesus Christ" (p. 77). Holloway understandably finds "the imaginative stretch required by this theory" all too great. Nevertheless, the gospels' view of prophecy is still enshrined in much of Christian liturgy, and this worries John Bowden, because of Christianity's anti-Semitic record:

At a time when we are being urged in some quarters to recover the 'traditional' faith in all its richness, it is worth remembering some of the 'richness' which that faith contains. Along with the virgin birth comes the argument from the 'prophecies' to Christ in the Old Testament, repeated each year at Christmas in countless carol services, an argument which infers that the Jews were blind and deaf because they could not see the Messiah who was prophesied so clearly in their own scriptures. It does not take much historical research to see where that leads. (1988, p. 13)

v. The Genealogies

Both Matthew and Luke give genealogies which purport to show that Jesus is descended from David. Old Testament passages which had come to be regarded as prophecies concerning the distant future were interpreted to mean that the Messiah will come from the line of David, and so anyone who had come to be regarded as the Messiah might well be held to belong to it. Jesus can be descended from David only through Joseph, for while Matthew is silent about Mary's ancestry, Luke states that she is kindred to Elisabeth, who is "of the daughters of Aaron" (1:5), that is, of the tribe of Levi, not of Judah, as was David. It is in fact Joseph's ancestry that is traced in both genealogies, not Mary's. Luke's table (3:23ff) does not even mention her, and Matthew names her only as the partner of Joseph, the descendant of David. But according to these evangelists, Jesus is not born of Joseph at all, but of holy spirit, and so the whole genealogical apparatus which aims at showing his descent from David fails to do this because the virgin birth story has been grafted onto it. Von Campenhausen says:

> Both the Lucan and the Matthean genealogical trees show that they originated in communities that as yet knew nothing of the virgin birth and regarded Jesus as Joseph's child. . . . Only in the last link of the chain have the evangelists attempted an artificial twist by way of correction, so as to accommodate it to the virgin birth. (p. 11)

Thus Matthew, having said that "Abraham begat Isaac", and so on down to the father of Joseph, finishes by saying, not 'Joseph begat Jesus', but that Joseph was "the husband of Mary, of whom was born Jesus, who is called Christ" (1:6). And Luke, who begins his table with Jesus and works back to Abraham and beyond, says Jesus was "the son (as was supposed) of Joseph, the son of Heli, the son of Matthat", and so on (3:23–24). Von Campenhausen adds that the manuscript variations of these passages show how little the text satisfied its readers, even in very early times.

The reply has often been made that, to the Jewish way of thinking, legal paternity completely took the place of natural paternity, so that Jesus can be regarded as son of David even though Joseph was only his legal father. Beare takes this position (pp. 61, 67), but von Campenhausen dismisses it as "a makeshift for which there is no adequate basis" (p. 11). It certainly fails to account for the insistence of Paul—the earliest extant Christian writer, who of course knows nothing of the virgin birth—that Jesus was "born of the seed of David according to the flesh" (Rom. 1:3). And the fourth gospel represents some Jews as saying that "the scripture said that the Christ cometh of the seed of David" (Jn. 7:42). This seems to have been the Jewish expectation, and mere legal paternity could hardly have fulfilled it.

Be that as it may, the genealogical trees given by Matthew and Luke are irreconcilable with each other. They agree quite well from Abraham to David, as one would expect, for the ancestry of David was available from the Old Testament (1 Chronicles 1 and 2, and Ruth 4:18–22).[9] However, from David to Joseph each table has its own names, the only ones common to both being Shealtiel and Zerubbabel his son, both well known from traditions concerning the Babylonian captivity. This section of Luke's table, apart from containing different names from those given in Matthew, also has about twice as many as are recorded there. As early as 1835 Strauss inferred from this that the genealogies are unhistorical, that Jesus's lineage was in fact utterly unknown, and that tradition, under these conflicting forms, attempted to prove his Davidic descent because it had come to be supposed that he was the Messiah, who was expected to be so descended. Leander Keck is being less than frank in saying that the two genealogies "do not agree completely" (2000, p. 6).

That Matthew's list begins with Abraham betrays its artificiality, for, as Beare has noted, "no ancient society kept records which extended unbroken over so long a period as extends from Abraham to Christ" (p. 62). Further artificiality is apparent when the evangelist divides the list into three series, each of fourteen names, pointing out that the end of each series coincides with an important historical event—the reign of David, the Babylonian captivity, and the birth of Jesus. His series, together with other information they contain, are shown on the facing page.

The second series consists of fourteen names only because four kings have been omitted from the list given in the Old Testament. This could well have been an error made in good faith: for although I have spelled the names in all three series as they are given in the RV, manuscripts make it clear that Matthew took them from the Septuagint. (Even in the RV, the third name in the first series is given as 'Jacob', as in the

Abraham	Solomon (whose mother was "her that had been the wife of Uriah", that is, Bathsheba)	Jechoniah
Isaac	Rehoboam	Shealtiel
Jacob	Abijah	Zerubbabel
Judah	Asa	Abiud
Perez (whose mother was Tamar)	Jehoshaphat	Eliakim
Hezron	Joram	Azor
Ram	Uzziah	Sadoc
Amminadab	Jotham	Achim
Nahshon	Ahaz	Eliud
Salmon	Hezekiah	Eleazar
Boaz (whose mother was Rahab)	Manasseh	Matthan
Obed (whose mother was Ruth	Amon	Jacob
Jesse	Josiah	Joseph, "the husband of Mary, of whom was born Jesus, who is called Christ"
David the King	Jechoniah "at the time of the carrying away to Babylon"	

Septuagint of 1 Chronicles 1:34, whereas the standard Hebrew (Masoretic) text gives it as 'Israel'.) The Greek forms of some of the royal names are similar and are also followed by names which have identical initial letters, so that the evangelist's eye could easily have glided from one name to another further on in the list, just as modern typists or compositors sometimes omit material occurring between two identical words in a passage.[10]

Matthew then begins his third series by repeating the name Jechoniah. This too—although it spoils his neat scheme of 3 × 14—could have been prompted by his reading of the Old Testament; for the

Septuagint of 1 Chronicles 3:16–17 states that Jechoniah had a son, Zedekiah, but, then, instead of naming his descendants, reverts to Jechoniah, naming his son as Shealtiel. As Burger says (p. 97), Matthew thus accurately reproduces the intention of the Chronicler in making the post-exilic line issue from Jechoniah.

With Zerubbabel, the son of Shealtiel and the last descendant of David of historical importance, Matthew leaves the guidance of the Old Testament, even though 1 Chronicles could have supplied him with eleven more generations. The next nine names in this final series of fourteen (up to but not including Joseph) are otherwise unknown and are far too few for the long period thus covered. Zerubbabel was born about 570 B.C., so that there are only twelve names (including his) from this time to that of Jesus, which makes each generation as long as fifty years, instead of the normal 25–30 years. (There were, for instance, eighteen generations of kings of Judah in the four hundred years between David and the Babylonian exile.) It seems clear that Matthew is here forcing his list into agreement with the overall scheme of 3 × 14 for which he has settled (1:17). As Brown observes, "even God did not arrange things so nicely that exactly fourteen biological generations separated such crucial moments in salvation history as the call of Abraham, the accession of David, the Babylonian Exile, and the coming of the Messiah" (p. 74)—apart from the fact that there were not, in history, fourteen generations in the second series and that the third achieves fourteen only by repeating the final name of the second. Beare notes that Matthew probably saw a mystical meaning in the number fourteen, which is "the sum of the numerical values of the three letters that make up the name of David in Hebrew.... In his mind, this number reflects the thought that in Jesus the promises of God to Israel are brought to fulfillment, and that the appointed channel of fulfillment is the Davidic monarchy in the person of the 'son of David' who will be acknowledged also to be the Son of God." Beare adds that this kind of number symbolism was "not unusual in the world in which Matthew lived" (p. 63).

My table above (p. 101) shows that Matthew includes four Old Testament women (Tamar, Rahab, Ruth, and Bathsheba) in the genealogy—quite unnecessarily, as Jesus's descent is traced through the male line. All four were aliens and three of them guilty of some kind of unchastity. Tamar was a Canaanite widow who disguised herself as a prostitute and offered herself to her widower father-in-law Judah, as a result of which she gave birth to Perez (Genesis 38). Rahab was a harlot of Jericho who sheltered Israelite spies (Joshua 2).

There is no support in the Old Testament for Matthew's statement that she was partnered by Salmon or in any way connected with the Davidic line, but in two Talmudic passages a section of the genealogy of Judah (as given in 1 Chronicles 4:21–23) is applied to her by a play of words (Johnson 1969, p. 164). Ruth was a Moabitess who, as the wife of Boaz, became the grandmother of Jesse. Bathsheba was the wife of Uriah the Hittite and David's mistress. She became his wife and bore him Solomon after he callously contrived her husband's death. All four women, then, contributed to the advancement of Israelite interests, and so bear comparison with Mary, who brought the Messianic hope to fulfillment. Whether this was Matthew's motive for including them can only be guessed. In spite of the irregularity in the lives of three of them, all four, according to Brown, "came off quite well in the Jewish piety of Jesus's time", so that there is "little likelihood that Matthew's readers would have understood them as sinners" (p. 72). Johnson has given evidence that, in pre-Christian Judaism, the four women "had come to occupy a traditional place in the ancestry of the Davidic Messiah", and that Matthew, who believed firmly in a Davidic Messiah, included them in his genealogy for this reason (Johnson 1969, pp. 178, 209).

Luke traces Jesus's ancestry not merely to Abraham, but right back to Adam, "the son of God". His tree does not emphasize numerical features as Matthew's does, and the sum total of ancestors may not even be a multiple of seven (eleven times seven), as there is considerable manuscript variation. The many unknown persons listed will have invited scribal tampering, so that the total varies from 72 to 78. My diagram on the following page shows that, while Matthew makes his table run from David to Solomon and then through the line of kings, Luke selects Nathan from among the sons of David, and so traces Jesus's descent through a line not royal. He nevertheless rejoins the royal line after the fall of the monarchy by listing Shealtiel and Zerubbabel; and against 1 Chronicles 3:17, he makes Shealtiel the son of an otherwise unknown Neri, instead of the son of the last king, Jechoniah. His motive in avoding the royal line until the Exile was probably theological: it would have led him to Jechoniah (given, as we saw, a prominent place in Matthew's table). Jeremiah had passed judgment on this wretched king, saying "no man of his seed shall prosper, sitting upon the throne of David" (22:30; cf. 36:30–31). As Luke expressly says that God will give Jesus "the throne of his father David" (1:32), he thus had reason to avoid making Jesus a descendant of this king.

THE TWO GENEALOGIES, FROM DAVID TO JOSEPH

Matthew 1	Names common to Matthew and Luke	Luke 3
	David	
Solomon		Nathan
Eleven others		Seventeen others (none identical with Matthew's line, and all otherwise unknown. Some anachronistically with patriarchal names).*
Josiah		Melchi (otherwise unknown)
Jechoniah		Neri (otherwise unknown)
	Shealtiel	
	Zerubbabel	
Eight others (otherwise unknown)		Seventeen others (none identical with Matthew's line, and all otherwise unknown
Jacob		Heli
	Joseph	

My diagram shows that the two evangelists diverge already in their naming of Jesus's grandfather. Even a Catholic scholar can now admit that all attempts to explain the discrepancies away "solve nothing", that the two genealogies "resist all harmonization", and that "most commentators realize today that we have in them neither official public records nor treasured family lists" (Fitzmyer, pp. 496f).

---

* "The custom of naming children after the patriarchs did not develop until after the Exile" (Brown, p. 92).

vi. The Origin and Purpose of the Christian Virgin Birth Traditions and Their Post-Scriptural Developments

Nothing in the Jewish scriptures suggests that anyone was or was to be born of a virgin, but in the Graeco-Roman world in which Christianity originated such an idea was not uncommon and was derived from much older cults. Some of the goddesses who gave birth without carnal intercourse were not virgins, but were called so by way of adoring flattery, just as nearly all male gods were at times deemed beneficent, whatever the cruelty of their supposed deeds. There is surely little difference between Matthew's story that Mary was found pregnant of holy spirit (1:18) and an Egyptian belief reported by Plutarch (*Life of Numa*, 4), that "it may be possible for a divine spirit so to apply itself to the nature of a woman as to inbreed in her the first beginnings of generation."

By the beginning of our era, the idea of divine impregnation, continually obtruded on the Jews by their pagan neighbours, had begun to affect their own outlook, with the result that some Old Testament worthies came to be regarded as born in this manner. Thus Philo, the Alexandrian Jew born about 20 B.C., tells that "the Lord begat Isaac", who is "to be thought not the result of generation, but the shaping of the unbegotten". He records similar views about Leah, whose husband is "the unnoticed", Zipporah, found "pregnant but by no mortal", and Samuel, whose mother "received divine seed" (Enslin 1940, p. 325). Christian apologists claim that such stories of birth without male concourse do not imply birth from a *virgin* mother. If in fact this was a detail added in the Christian legend, the reason for such an addition is not hard to discern: for the idea that birth from a virgin enabled Jesus to be born without any suggestion of "the lust of the flesh" is expressly stated in an apocryphal Christian work known as the *Epistula Apostolorum*, which purports to be a letter from the eleven disciples after the resurrection to Christians of the four regions of the Earth, and may date from the mid-second century (Hennecke 1973, pp. 190–93). Boslooper typifies the apologists who insist that only the Christian legend tells of "divine conception and human birth without anthropomorphism, sensuality, or suggestions of moral irregularity". For Boslooper, the story inculcates the sanctity of sex, premarital chastity, heterosexuality, and the necessity of monogamy and fidelity in marriage; and it had to consist of a mythical narrative "since it was only in this form that primitive peoples could grasp these truths" (1962, pp. 185, 234–36). He here relies on the familiar principle that revelation had to be 'accommodated' to the mentality of its recipients, and that this is why it often appears very strange to us of a later age.

The purpose of the infancy narratives is to show that exalted status pertained to Jesus not merely in virtue of his resurrection, but from his very conception. As Rowan Williams, the present Archbishop of Canterbury, allows, "we can see too clearly for comfort what *job* the story is meant to do."[11] The earliest gospel suggests that Jesus was chosen to be the receptacle of "the spirit" already at his baptism (Mk 1:10). But even this was, for later tradition, not enough, and Matthew and Luke felt it necessary to have him literally begotten of spirit. The fourth gospel outdoes this in a prologue which asserts that he was with God as "the word" even before the creation of "all things". This evangelist thus has no need of a miraculous birth on Earth, and is able simply to say that he "became flesh", and then to introduce him as a grown man.

The traditional date of Jesus's birth is entirely without scriptural warrant. The primitive church was far more interested in his death and resurrection than in his incarnation, and felt no need to celebrate his coming down to Earth at all. But by the middle of the fourth century, 25th December had emerged as a Christian festival at Rome and in North Africa, while elsewhere a similar festival existed instead on 6th January. "Through a process of interchange," says Paul Bradshaw, "the two eventually spread to become virtually universal observances throughout the Church." He adds that there have been two main theories to explain these dates. It was felt that Jesus must have lived on Earth for an exact number of years; and so those who regarded 25th March as the date of the crucifixion argued that he must have been conceived on that same day of the year, and hence born nine months later, on 25th December. Those who placed the crucifixion on 6th April, by the same reasoning had him born on that day of the year. An alternative to this 'computation hypothesis' explains the Roman choice of 25th December as due to the fact that, in the pagan world, this was the day of the winter solstice in the Julian calendar, and was regarded as the sun's birthday, since the days begin to lengthen and the power of the sun increases from this turning point in the year. The emperor Aurelian had in A.D. 274 made this day the birthday of the Unconquered Sun; and after the Peace of Constantine, the victory of Christ, the true sun, over this heathen cult was to be made manifest in this way. Bradshaw finds the computation hypothesis the more likely of the two, but allows that neither is without difficulties (2002, pp. 187–89).

The infancy stories, prefaced as they are in the two relevant gospels to accounts of Jesus's adult ministry, left the faithful wondering how he spent the intervening years; and "when people are curious, they usually take steps to satisfy their curiosity; so we should not be surprised that members of the early Church drew up accounts of what they supposed must have taken place" (Metzger 1987, pp. 166f). Hence a number of apocryphal gospels refer to the early years of Jesus's life. If the canonical ones do at least include one incident within this period (Lk. 2:41–51), they are totally silent as to what he accomplished between death and resurrection; and so other apocryphal gospels tell of his descent into the underworld. Metzger adds that "popular yearning" for such additional information has not subsided, "as is witnessed by the continuing production of still other 'new' gospels" (169n; cf. Goodspeed 1931 for details). Today, in *The Da Vinci Code*, Dan Brown tells that Jesus married Mary Magdalene, that she was pregnant with their child at his crucifixion, that she subsequently bore him a daughter and fled to France, where Christ's ancestral line was continued through the ages. Although all this is stated in a novel, it purports to be historically accurate. As a result, many of its millions of readers will suppose that they are not just amusing themselves but imbibing the truth.

The doctrine of the virgin birth initiated the devotion to Mary that has subsequently grown to such great proportions—not because evidence supports it, but as a result of believers' emotional needs. Wiles is able to quote both a Protestant and a Catholic authority who admit as much. The Protestant tells that, although "the weighty theologians" tried to contain the growth, "the pious monks and the simple devotion of the people kept pushing along the glorification uncontrollably until today we have, even officially, the doctrine of the Bodily Assumption" (Pius XII's 1950 edict that, having completed her earthly life, the virgin was, in body and soul, assumed into heavenly glory). The Catholic says, in effect the same, but without any implied negative judgement on the whole development, which he calls "one of the most touching cases of piety being in advance of science, stimulating science to ratify the intuitions of love" (Quoted by Wiles, 1967, pp. 89f). It is a most instructive example of the forces from which creeds are made and sustained.

Devotion to Mary was also responsible for the Catholic doctrine of the immaculate conception, with which the doctrine of the virgin birth is often confused. The former was prompted by awareness that, even if a human father had no part in generating Jesus, original sin could have been transmitted to him through his mother. Hence the church supplemented the doctrine of the virgin birth from Mary with that of the 'immaculate conception' of Mary herself from her mother—not in the sense that she had no human father, but that, as soon as she was conceived in her mother's womb, the Holy Ghost cleansed her from the original sin inherited from her parents. Pius IX's Bull of 1854 maintains that this doctrine is "revealed by God and therefore to be firmly and steadfastly believed by all the faithful." It had been flatly denied by Thomas Aquinas, who found that it was to the greater glory of the Virgin that she should not have been exempt from original sin (*Summa Theologiae*, tertia parts, quaestio 27—de Sanctificatione Beatae Virginis). A little earlier, St. Bernard had condemned the doctrine as a presumptuous novelty. But in time, the pious could not bear to think that Mary was under the influence of the Devil, even for a single moment.

vii. Finale

Protestant scholars have long admitted that the two gospel birth and infancy accounts are irreconcilable and that each one is replete with historical problems. Many of these, as I have set them out above, with the endorsement of recent Christian scholars, were already specified by Strauss in his epoch-making book of 1835. The second volume of the 1879 English version of his second *Life* of 1864 begins with a summary, extending over some hundred pages, of the objections to be made against the two genealogies, the birth in the city of David, the role of holy ghost, the annunciation and birth of the forerunner John the Baptist, and so on. Strauss was able to say there (p. 113) that, by that time, many theologians had come to "give up as untenable . . . the historical character" of all this, and to regard it as a tissue of "Christian legends and fiction". He added that this surrender was often made from belief that the material comprises mere "outworks", which can be burnt down without damage to the remaining gospel contents; whereas in fact much—but, he insisted, by no means all—of the remainder is equally vulnerable (p. 115).

How pervasive criticism of the birth and infancy narratives had become is evidenced in the sharply critical article 'Nativity' in Cheyne and Black's four-volumed *Encyclopaedia Biblica*, a clerical work first issued at the end of the nineteenth century, which the editors introduced as comprising "criticism which identifies the cause of religion with that of historical truth".

Catholic scholars have now reluctantly begun to follow their Protestant colleagues. Hans Küng acknowledges that the birth and infancy stories "are historically largely uncertain, mutually contradictory, strongly legendary and, in the last analysis, theologically motivated" (1976, p. 441). But Catholics have to be very careful. The updated 1993 edition of Brown's 1979 book includes a lengthy 'Supplement' where he tells how an article by a Spanish Jesuit, published in the 1970s and suggesting that the virginal coneption should be treated as a legend, "brought indignant petitions by over 10,000 Spaniards, a restatement of belief by the Spanish bishops' commission on faith, . . . and a warning from the Jesuit General" (p. 701).

Among Anglican scholars J.A.T. Robinson obviously found both the doctrine of Jesus's pre-existence "before all worlds" and that of his virgin birth somewhat embarrassing, for he exerted much ingenuity in trying to prove that both were introduced into Christian thinking only by the Fathers (1973, pp. 50ff, 151).[12] And the latter doctrine he salvaged, as many still do, by means of symbolical interpretation: "This symbol can only legitimately mean that Jesus's whole life was 'born not of the will of the flesh, nor of the will of man, but of God'" (1963, pp. 77). He concedes that this quotation from Jn. 1:13 refers to "Christians", and that it is they, not Jesus, who are there said to be born in this way (cf. above, p. 80).

Belief in Jesus's virgin birth has often been regarded as a necessary inference from Christian doctrine. Vincent Taylor found "the ultimate considerations which determine a true estimate of the Virgin Birth traditions" to be "doctrinal". He quoted Charles Gore's 1896 statement that "being what He was", viz. God, "His human birth could hardly have been otherwise than is implied in the virginity of his mother" (Taylor 1920, pp. 127f). But is parthenogenesis necessarily implied in the incarnation? Could not God assume the form of man without this? If gestation and embryonic development are submitted to, why not also fertilization, which is surely not more objectionable than all the subsequent processes? Surely it is clear that parthenogenesis is insisted on only because it belongs to the Christian record, which, Taylor admits, yields only "the verdict 'Not proven'."

Eric Franklin, admitting the fragility of the Christian record—the gospel accounts "cannot really be harmonized" and "cannot of themselves bear the weight of vigorous historical enquiry"—appeals instead to "the tradition to which they bear witness and from which they spring"—this tradition being in turn validated by "its own strength, its conformity to the whole life of Jesus, its continuing ability to inform, its appropriateness to Christian truth and the inner assent both of the community and its individual members" (1994, p. 73). Many a myth could be validated in the same way. That Wilhelm Tell founded the Swiss Confederation in the face of foreign oppression is a strong tradition, conformable to the (supposed) whole life of the sturdy, independent Tell, and appropriate both to national truth and to the assent of the Swiss people.

I shall later again allude to the Tell story as it is a good example of the myth-making process, and so may appropriately be kept in mind apropos of some features in the gospels—even though W.P. Weaver has recently dubbed it "bad taste to compare the Jesus story to the William Tell legend" (1999, p. 300). Tell's historicity is denied on the grounds that (1) his alleged deeds, such as the apple shot, had been told of previous heroes; (2) there are discernable motives for the circulation of the stories; (3) the silence of contemporary documents is remedied by interpolations and forgeries; (4) although the contemporary testimony is nil, references which assume the existence of the hero become legion within two hundred years of his supposed existence; (5) the later documents give more precise details (such as exact dates and names) than the earlier. Some of these considerations are certainly relevant to the doctrine of Jesus's virgin birth, and to the way in which it is sometimes defended today.

Theologians are still apt to claim, as they did in Strauss's day, that the narratives of Jesus's ministry and Passion are much more reliable than the birth and infancy ones, which therefore can, at a pinch, be surrendered. In fact, however, they illustrate very well the type of difficulty and problem presented elsewhere in the gospels: namely that earlier silences are superseded by narratives which contradict each other, are sometimes self-stultifying, are uncorroborated by external testimony, and also display willingness to invent incidents as fulfillment of prophecy.

Outright defence of the birth and infancy narratives is still mounted by evangelicals. Not that Jesus's virgin birth is particularly important in their overall theology; but to affirm belief in it signals religious correctness, freedom from a critical attitude to the sacred texts, and "willingness to believe in a quite extraordinary event on the basis of scripture alone" (Barr 1981, p. 176). W.A. Elwell, editor of the 1996 *Evangelical Dictionary of Biblical Theology*, introduces this work by saying that its contributors "honor the Scriptures as the Written Word of God", as "God's very words to us." Unsurprisingly, then, the entry 'Virgin Birth' expresses confidence that "the alleged historical discrepancies involving the census of Quirinius, Herod's massacre of the infants, the star and visit of the magi, the appearance of angels, the location of Jesus's parental home, the genealogies, the independent traditions of the two infancy narratives"—that all these "have reasonable explanations defending their historicity". Such explanations are not specified, but the entry concludes with a brief bibliography which includes the books on the subject by Thomas Boslooper and Raymond Brown. It is clear from my quotation from Boslooper above, that he is of little help to evangelicals,[13] and from my many references to Brown, the foremost Catholic exegete of the texts, that he helps them even less. He finds it "quite impossible" to harmonize the two stories and declares that we have "no reliable information" about the source of either (1979, p. 7). He is unimpressed by the standard defence that they are sober in tone (in spite of their many miraculous elements) compared with what we find on the subject in apocryphal gospels; and he asks, appositely: "Is this a difference of kind (history vs. fiction) or a difference of degree?" One might, he adds, "argue that both canonical and non-canonical narratives result from the attempt of Christian imagination to fill in the Messiah's origins, and that in the case of the apocryphal narratives the imagination had a freer and further exercise" (p. 33n).

Yet Brown's position remains ambiguous, for he declares that Jesus may nevertheless have been conceived without a human father, and that it is "easier to explain the NT evidence by positing a historical basis than by positing pure theological creation" (pp. 527f). Another New Testament scholar, James P. Mackey, who teaches at a Catholic university, regards this as too conservative a position, since "Brown is as adamant as anyone that the principal point of the nativity stories is to establish the presence of the divine spirit at the very conception of Jesus and the corresponding confession that he was the Son of God." For Mackey, there is nothing about his arrival on the human scene that would enable us to use that title of him, for his origins "were obscure in the extreme. . . . He was a most ordinary man" (1987, pp. 98f).

Critical questionings have not militated against the popularity of these charming stories, which continue to be recited and re-enacted every year. Church attendance at Christmas is far greater than at other times, and few celebrants will think to question whether their god-man was actually born in this way, and whether the accompanying miracles ever took place—any more than most Greeks, hundreds of years earlier, will have questioned whether their hero Hercules, still in his cradle, actually strangled the serpents sent by the goddess Hera to destroy him. To ask: 'Are these stories true?' would be a tactless intrusion on joyful occasions. Hence Franklin can say that our carol services and midnight eucharists "can help to bring out the best in men and to be an expression of the greatness of human love, of the worth of the family, of the hope for better things, even of a momentary glimpse of wonder and awe which can contribute so much to the quality of man's god-given life" (p. 127). No amount of criticism impairs the powerful effect which the Bible has on such formal liturgical occasions.

4

The Resurrection

i. The Gospel Accounts

a. The First Three Gospels

According to Karl Barth, we "rightly turn up our nose" at the many inconsistencies "in the attempts of liberal theologians to explain belief in the resurrection naturalistically" (1956, p. 340). If inconsistencies are a ground for scornful rejection, then it will fare ill with the New Testament accounts of the resurrection. A.E. Harvey notes in his 1970 *The New English Bible Companion to the New Testament* (p. 297)— hardly a sceptical work—that "all the gospels, after having run closely together in their accounts of the trial and execution, diverge markedly when they come to the circumstances of the resurrection, and it is impossible to fit their accounts together into a single coherent scheme." Fuller gives a brief summary of what he calls the "palpable inconsistencies" (1972, pp. 2–5), and a full hundred years ago they were set out in detail by the Zürich theologian P.W. Schmiedel, who gives ample evidence that on this matter "the canonical gospels are at irreconcilable variance with each other" and that the non-canonical notices "serve to show how busily and in how reckless a manner the accounts of the resurrection of Jesus continued to be handed on."[1] Karl Barth's way out of all this is that we ought not to ask for evidence for the resurrection, but should believe on faith alone; to which another theologian, Paul Badham, has appositely replied: "A faith which claims that something which happened in the past is important cannot evade historical scrutiny of that claim" (1978, p. 19).

Strauss emphasized how glaring the contradictions are when he declared, of the resurrection: "Rarely has an incredible fact been worse attested, or one so ill-attested been more incredible in itself" (1997, pp. 82f). Matthew records one appearance of the risen Jesus to his disciples and locates it in Galilee, while Luke records several but sites them all eighty miles away, in Jerusalem and its environs. (The final redactor of the fourth gospel tries to harmonize such discrepant traditions by appending a chapter with a Galilean appearance, John 21, to a chapter of Jerusalem appearances.) I know that witnesses of an event can give discrepant accounts of it, but one would not expect the discrepancies to extend to essentials. If one witness of a street accident affirmed that it took place in London, we should not expect another to site it in Birmingham. If we were faced with such discrepant reports, and also had no other evidence that there had been an accident, we should dismiss the whole thing. But this is our position in regard to the resurrection. As Elliott has said: "There is no independent witness to the Easter events outside the New Testament" (1982, p. 84).

The documents make it clear that the Christophanies were not vouchsafed to enemies, only to those who either already believed or subsequently became believers. As Elliott puts it: "Jesus in his resurrected state is visible only to those who have faith" (p. 86); or, in the wording of the New Testament itself, only to "witnesses who were chosen before of God" (Acts 10:40–41). According to Acts, the appearances of the risen Jesus went on for forty days. This feature contradicts even Luke (by the same author), which implies that Jesus's ascension occurred on Easter day. There, a number of appearances to his disciples on that day culminate in his declaration "Behold I send forth the promise of my Father upon you" (Lk. 24:49), followed by his instruction (in the same verse) that they are to remain in Jerusalem until they receive this promise, until, that is, they are "clothed with power from on high". All this sounds very solemn and final; and then, in the very next verses, with no suggestion of an interval of time, he "led them out" to somewhere near the neighbouring locality of Bethany and, while blessing them with uplifted hands, "parted from them and was carried up to heaven." Some manuscripts have only "he parted from them", hence the following words are relegated to the margin in the NEB. If they are nevertheless original—Fuller finds them "textually Lucan and integral to the narrative" (p. 122)—they will have been deleted by some copyists in order to suggest that the parting was only temporary, and thus to avoid obviously contradicting Acts, where the author seems to be drawing on a tradition not available when he wrote his gospel, and one on which he gladly seized because, while occasional appearances of the risen one might be dismissed by sceptics as hallucinations, a sojourn of forty days, during which he presented "many proofs" (Acts 1:3), was more substantial. However, even without the words at Lk. 24:51 which make the ascension explicit, the solemnity of the parting remains—the procession to Bethany and the blessing with uplifted hands—and surely indicates that it was final. Nor is there any suggestion in Luke's gospel that Jesus returned to the eleven, for its following final words, after the parting at Bethany, record their joyous return to Jerusalem and their continual presence in the temple, praising God. Even Acts—although it goes on to speak of the forty days, and of the ascension as following them—begins by allowing (1:2) that Luke's gospel records all that Jesus did and taught "until the day in which he was received up." Naturally, there were scribes who did their best to get rid of this 'received up' (See the discussion of the manuscript evidence for this verse in Metzger 1971 and Haenchen 1971).

Conservative apologists admit what they call "apparent discrepancies" in the evidence for the resurrection, but point out that certain cardinal facts are independent of them: all the accounts agree, for instance, that Jesus was crucified and subsequently raised. But this amount of agreement is frequently found in stories admittedly mythical. Historians agree that Wilhelm Tell is a legendary figure, but there are chronicles enough telling discrepant stories of how he founded the Swiss Confederation. Reverting to my example of a street accident, I would note that the conservative position implies that, although those who claim to be witnesses disagree even as to where it happened, and although there are no injured people, damaged vehicles or indeed any evidence apart from their discordant testimony, we are nevertheless to believe that an accident did occur.

The discrepancies in the gospel accounts of the resurrection events are not mere muddle but arise because one evangelist pursues theological purposes alien to another. For Luke, Jerusalem is of great theological importance, and in order to place the appearances there he amends the Markan narrative at two points. First he omits the record at Mk. 14:28 of Jesus's prediction (during the walk to Gethsemane after the Last Supper) that after his resurrection he would go before his disciples into Galilee. Then he rewords what Mark had recorded as the instruction to the women at the empty tomb. Mark has:

> Go, tell his disciples and Peter, He goeth before you into Galilee; there shall ye see him, as he said unto you. (16:7)

Luke adapts this so as to make it into merely something Jesus had said, while he was still ministering in Galilee, to the effect that he would, after his death, be resurrected:

> Remember how he spake unto you, *when he was yet in Galilee,* saying that the Son of man must be . . . crucified, and the third day rise again. (24:6–7)

Luke has thus made a prophecy about a future event in Galilee into a statement about Jesus's past teachings there. Having thus eliminated the suggestion that the disciples should go to Galilee, Luke goes on to make the risen Jesus appear to them and tell them to remain in Jerusalem "until ye be clothed with power from on high" (24:49), which he represents (at Acts 2:1–4) as happening at Pentecost, that is, some fifty days later.

Luke, then, repudiates Mark's statement that the disciples would see Jesus in Galilee. Mark's idea was surely that they should establish themselves as a Christian community there. Luke replaces this with a Jerusalem-oriented mission partly because, for him, Jerusalem represents continuity between Israel and the church. The initiation of the church there shows that Christianity had not broken readily or lightly from its Jewish roots. Indeed, for Acts the eventual rupture was entirely the fault of the Jews. Thus the disciples initially frequent the temple and even convert the Jews of the city by their thousands (Acts 2:41; 4:4). In the first fifteen chapters of Acts, every area missionized is subordinated to Jerusalem in one way or another.

Theologians speak, apropos of the changes Luke made in revising Mark, of his 'editing'. But we can hardly feel confidence in a writer whose theological purpose leads him to adapt a source so as to obliterate its plain meaning. As Evans has said, "it is not natural confusion but rather the lack of it, and the influence of rational reflection and apologetic" which have given rise to such contradictions (1970, p. 129).

The best manuscripts of Mark end at 16:8. The remainder of Chapter 16 is an appendix (distinguished as such in the RSV and the NEB) which makes the risen Jesus promise (among other things) that believers will be able to handle snakes and drink deadly poison without coming to harm. Up to 16:8 there have been no appearances of the risen one. The women visitors to the tomb have discovered it to be empty, and have been instructed there by "a young man arrayed in a white robe" to tell the disciples that they will see Jesus in Galilee. In Luke, the "young man" becomes "two men in dazzling apparel", and in Matthew he is called an "angel". Commentators point out that this is the meaning in all three gospels, as 'young man' sometimes designates an angel in ancient Jewish literature, and in the New Testament men in white or radiant clothes are always heavenly beings. In John (20:12) there are two angels. The women visitors also differ in the gospel accounts, only Mary Magdalene being common to all four. Perhaps it is this her prominence in the gospel resurrection stories that has prompted the endless speculation as to what role she might have played in Jesus's pre-crucifixion life. On that, however, the canonical gospels tell us as good as nothing. There is only the one single notice (Lk. 8:2–3) that she was among the women who accompanied him as he journeyed in Galilee, and who provided for him and for the twelve out of their own resources.

The initial verses of Mark's Chapter 16 include a statement that the women were too afraid to deliver the young man's message to the disciples, so that "they said nothing to anyone". Many think that the empty tomb story is no part of the early tradition, but a later legend, first introduced by Mark into the narrative; and it has often been suggested that his motive for making the women keep silent was to account for the fact that, as he well knew, there was no already existing tradition about an empty tomb when he wrote. As Lampe says: "The fact that the women do not pass the message on may suggest that the evangelist, or his source, knew that the story of the tomb and the angel was not part of the original Easter proclamation and had only developed at a relatively late stage in the tradition" (1966, p. 48). The New Testament scholar Paul Badham has pressed this argument, saying that Mark's comment that the women said nothing to anyone

> cannot make any kind of sense unless the story of the women finding the tomb empty was no part of the original Easter kerygma. If everyone knew that the women had reported finding an empty tomb, Mark's comment would have been an absurdity. It makes sense only on the supposition that Mark was consciously adding something to the original kerygma, and hence had to give some explanation as to why no one had previously heard of the empty tomb story before. (1993, p. 32)

Fuller rejected such reasoning as altogether a "too rationalistic" account of the way Mark had written and hence alien to the mind set of the early church, which was not worried about "conflicting historical evidence" (p. 53). But I have already given a striking example of Luke adapting his Markan material to the requirements of his own theology in a very 'rationalistic', meaning deliberate, way; and we shall be seeing that the careful arguing of apologetic concerns is prominent in the resurrection stories of both Luke and Matthew. There is no reason to believe that Mark was less rationalistic.

Whatever Mark's motive may have been, Luke reworded what his gospel says at this point so as to lead in to the appearances in and around Jerusalem that he has added to it:

Mark 16:8	*Luke 24:9*
And they went out and fled from the tomb; for trembling and astonishment had come upon them: and they said nothing to anyone; for they were afraid.	And they returned from the tomb and told all these things to the eleven, and to all the rest.

I do not mean to suggest that Luke is here concocting a narrative he knew to be false. As he was convinced that it was "beginning from Jerusalem" that the Christian mission went forward to "all the nations" (Lk. 24:47), he will naturally have supposed that his predecessor had got his facts a bit wrong, and so will have amended the Markan narrative in perfectly good faith. One thing that this kind of 'editing' clearly indicates is that Mark's gospel was not regarded as authoritatively based on reliable eyewitness information.

When in Luke's narrative the disciples are told by the women that the tomb is empty, they dismiss this as "idle talk" (verse 11). Then, in many manuscripts, there follows:

> But Peter arose, and ran unto the tomb: and stooping and looking in, he seeth the linen clothes by themselves; and he departed to his home, wondering at that which was come to pass. (verse 12)

This verse is relegated to the margin in the RSV and NEB. It is obviously related in some way to the account in the fourth gospel where Peter (and the 'beloved disciple', known only to the fourth gospel) run to the tomb and find it empty. The two accounts may derive from a common source. The effect of this verse is that, instead of being left with what has been dismissed as the "idle talk" of untrustworthy women, we have an authentication of their story from the stolid male prince of the apostles.

There follows the first of the Jerusalem appearances in Luke. It occurs in the story, unique to his gospel (24:13–32), of a walk by two disciples (Cleopas and an unnamed one) to Emmaus, said in the text to be a village near the city. Jesus joins them on their journey and, as there seems to be nothing out of the ordinary in his appearance, they take him for some traveller unknown to them. They proceed to tell him that Jesus of Nazareth, "a prophet mighty in deed and word", has just been condemned and crucified, to the disappointment of all their hopes, although his tomb has been reported to be empty and he has been said to be alive. The stranger responds by explaining that all these events happened in accordance with prophecy; and "beginning from Moses and from all the prophets, he interpreted to them in all the scriptures the things concerning himself"—without disclosing his identity. The whole point of this story is clearly to establish in this way that the Passion and resurrection, central to the faith of the church, are firmly grounded in God's overall plan. Jesus does not here actually specify any Old Testament passages, and certainly none that foretold his resurrection, for only with very considerable strain can anything in the Old Testament be made to yield something pertaining to that event. As Richard Harries, former bishop of Oxford, concedes: "The story reflects the experience not just of two disciples, but of the church as a whole, in knowing Christ through the [Old Testament] scriptures" (1987, p. 56). The church will have accumulated supposedly relevant passages only over a period of time; but here Jesus is represented as already being able to recite them all.

The failure of the two disciples to recognize Jesus straightaway is problematic in this story of a quite concrete encounter with a corporeal Jesus, but it is an essential element in its effectiveness. It alone makes possible the irony of the situation where the 'stranger' is told in detail of events of which he himself has been the victim. Yet although Luke needs this element, he did not find it easy to introduce it into the tale; for how can the two disciples be plausibly represented as failing to recognize a man they have known so recently and so well (particularly if we recall that, in all three synoptics, Peter had no difficulty in recognizing Elijah and Moses as present at the transfiguration (Mk. 9:5 and parallels) even though he can never have seen them before)? To motivate their failure, Luke has to attribute it to some unspecified (but presumably supernatural) power: "Their eyes were holden that they should not know him" (24:16. The verb rendered as 'holden' is *kratein,* 'to secure forcibly'). Not until the very end of the story is this impediment removed: "And their eyes were opened and they knew him" (verse 31), whereupon he vanished.

Luke is certainly very concerned to convince us that the resurrection appearances were not hallucinations, and to this end he stresses the physical reality of the risen one. Although the Emmaus story ends with Jesus "vanishing" into thin air and then reappearing equally independently of physical means to the eleven in a room in Jerusalem (cf. Jn. 20:19 and 26 where he is expressly said to enter through closed doors), he then convinces them that he is nevertheless no insubstantial ghost by inviting them to "handle" his "flesh and bones" and by eating "a piece of broiled fish" in their presence (Lk. 24:31–32, 36–43). Both the Emmaus story of his walking in earthly form, and his subsequent eating fish and inviting physical touch, are unknown to the earlier accounts and are evidently meant to answer the objection that what the disciples had seen was merely a ghost. These corporeal and tangible features are introduced even though they are quite inconsistent not only with the Pauline tradition, but also, as Lampe points out (1966, pp. 50–51), with other elements incorporated into Luke's own narrative, such as the sudden appearance within a room. Wiles has the same inconsistency in mind when he notes, discreetly, that "the differing degrees of physicality" implied in the records of Jesus's resurrection are "puzzling features" (1974, p. 138).

As Ernst Haenchen pointed out (1968, p. 554), we shall not understand Luke's Chapter 24 unless we realize that the Christian preaching of Jesus's resurrection had met with some opposition, which is there countered with evidence that the resurrection experiences were not insubstantial hallucinations, and that the very scriptures show that the resurrection was willed by God.

If we turn from Luke to Matthew, we find similarly a narrative shaped by conscious purpose. He has it that, on the Saturday morning, after the Friday crucifixion, the chief priests and the Pharisees—the latter appear here for the very first time in the entire synoptic Passion story—come to Pilate and ask, successfully, for a guard to secure Jesus's grave, so that his disciples will be unable to steal his body and then pretend that he had risen from the dead (27:62–66). If it had been felt necessary to secure the tomb in this way, a guard would have been needed for the first night, as well as for the second and subsequent ones. Moreover, the Saturday would have been a Sabbath. "Matthew avoids pointing this out by saying that it was the day 'after the Preparation' . . . The Pharisees would surely be violating their strong sabbatarian principles if they chose that day to send a deputation to Pilate, in company with the chief priests, for any purpose" (Beare 1981, p. 539). If there had in fact been a guard, this would have made the story, as given by the other three evangelists, quite impossible. But because he has supplied a guard, Matthew cannot accept Mark's statement that the women expect to enter the tomb (to anoint the body). He has to represent them as intending merely to visit it (28:1). Before they can look inside it, the guard has to be put out of action; hence the need for the "great earthquake" of the next verse—caused not by any natural seismic conditions, but by the descent from heaven of "an angel of the Lord" who rolls away the stone sealing the tomb, then sits on it and petrifies the guards with fear, so that they "become as dead men". Strange that only Matthew knows of these stunning events. But earthquakes are a familiar feature in Jewish apocalyptic literature, as a sign that the end of the world is near. And this is why, in Matthew's gospel and only there, "the earth did quake" also at the moment of Jesus's death (27:51), showing that that too presages the end. But why did not the guard of soldiers at the tomb, once they had recovered, tell of what they had seen and thus make it difficult for the Jews to deny the fact of the resurrection? To provide an answer to this question, Matthew has it that the chief priests persuaded the guards with bribes to pretend that they had slept and thus had given Jesus's disciples a chance to steal the body. The guards "took the money, and did as they were taught". Sleeping on duty would make Roman soldiers liable to severe punishment; and that they agreed to pretend that they had done so in order to please the Jews—who are also implausibly represented as being able to "put things right" with Pilate, so that the soldiers will not suffer punishment (28:14)—is not credible. In any case, "whoever has seen an angel descending from heaven, with an appearance like lightning (28:3), is not going to say—even for a considerable sum of money—that he was asleep and saw nothing" (Haenchen, pp. 549–550). Nevertheless, the saying that this is what happened was "spread abroad among the Jews and continueth *until this day*" (28:15)— a phrase which betrays the whole narrative as late apologetic—recall that Matthew wrote only after the destruction of Jerusalem in A.D. 70, by which time the supposed tomb was not open to inspection. His Christian community had serious disagreements with orthodox Jews, who may well have accused Christians of stealing the body and making up the story of the resurrection. His account of guards who did not sleep, but kept watch until an angel knocked them out, is the Christian response. Lampe has noted that what he calls Matthew's "legend" of the guard has "no historical value", is "very much in the manner of the later apocryphal gospels", and reflects controversy with the Jews (p. 51).

We may note that all the incidents which Matthew has added to Mark's Passion narrative are quite fanciful. They include not only the request for a guard (with its repercussion on this evangelist's resurrection narrative), but also a story that Judas hanged himself, thus fulfilling a prophecy of Jeremiah. Beare calls this "surely the most extravagant example of Matthew's handling of scriptures as proof texts" (1981, p. 526); and the story is incompatible with the account of Judas's death in Acts 1:18–20, which in its turn is said to fulfil a prophecy in the Psalms. Matthew's additions here to Mark further specify a dream by Pilate's wife, which led her to warn him not to proceed against Jesus, "that righteous man", and Pilate himself "washing his hands" to distance himself from Jewish malice and declare himself innocent of Jesus's blood. There are more additions besides, and Raymond Brown finds that they are all the stuff of nativity and Passion plays, "popular dramatization through storytelling, much like expanded infancy and passion narratives ever since" (1994, p. 60).

Returning now to Matthew's resurrection narrative, we find that at 28:7 the women at the tomb are told, as in Mark, that the risen one will appear in Galilee. But, diverging from Mark's account, Matthew makes them "run to bring his disciples word" of this. Also, on the way, they are intercepted by Jesus. Matthew may have added this detail because he feared that the testimony of the angel at the tomb, which is all that Mark offered, could be dismissed as hallucination. It is hard to see any other reason for this added episode, for in it Jesus effects no more than to repeat the angel's message that he will appear in Galilee. The women, however, introduce something novel in that at this point "they took hold of his feet and worshipped him." This kind of physical contact with the risen one is characteristic of the stage of tradition represented by the gospels, but excluded, as we shall see, by Paul, who also knows nothing of appearances to women. These, by the way, are also unknown to Luke. He records the women's visit to the tomb and their encounter there with "two men in dazzling apparel" (24:1–10), but says nothing of any appearance to the women, and goes on to imply at 24:22–24 that, up to that point, no one had seen Jesus.

At Mt. 28:16–20, the eleven disciples—Judas has defected—repair to Galilee and Jesus instructs them, on a mountain there, "to make disciples of all the nations". This is the only resurrection appearance to the disciples that Matthew records. Such words could have been put into Jesus's mouth only when the fierce controversy about the gentile mission that dominates the earliest Christian literature was not only over and done with, but even barely remembered. The eleven are here further instructed to baptize all the nations "into the name of the Father and of the Son and of the Holy Ghost". This again can only be late, for—as already Reimarus noted—there is no suggestion in the early literature (not even in Acts' account of the church's early history) that this formula was used. At Acts 2:38 Peter urges potential converts simply to "be baptized in the name of Jesus Christ" (cf. Acts 8:16; 19:5 and 1 Cor. 6:11). Fr. O'Collins concedes that Matthew makes Jesus "cite the trinitarian formula used by Christians in his [Matthew's] own day" (2003, p. 87). And when Jesus goes on to asssure the eleven: "Lo, I am with you, even unto the end of the world", this, says O'Collins, echoes the faith of the

Matthaean Christians "in the exalted Christ's presence which they experience vividly at their liturgical assemblies."

Matthew's risen Lord also instructs the eleven to teach converts "to observe all things whatsoever I commanded you". This represents a special theological interest of Matthew, who presents his gospel, with its five carefully constructed Jesuine discourses, as the new Torah; and 'all that I commanded you' is meant to refer back to these (cf. Fuller, pp. 88–89). It is with such facts in mind that Evans has said (1970, p. 67) that, not only does the risen Lord not say the same things in any two gospels, but also it is hardly the same Lord speaking: "In Matthew it is evidently a Matthaean Lord who speaks, in Luke a Lukan Lord and in John a Johannine Lord". Each gospel was written for a different Christian community, and—as Fuller puts it (p. 172)—"the words spoken by the Risen One are not to be taken as recordings of what was actually spoken by him, but as verbalizations of the community's understanding of the import of the resurrection". For this reason one should not—as so many apologists do—select bits and pieces from the different narratives and try to make them add up to a plausible story; for each of these narratives is a whole, independent of the others, so that one would be combining "not a number of scattered pieces from an originally single matrix, but separate expressions of the Easter faith" (Evans, 1970, p. 128).

In the Matthaean passage the risen Jesus speaks, we saw, on a "mountain". This is not meant as a geographical datum, but as the typical site for a revelation—as was the location of the Sermon on the Mount (5:1) and the transfiguration (17:1). The precedent for such mountain sitings was, of course, God's revelation to Moses on Sinai. This final revelation in Matthew includes Jesus's declaration "all authority hath been given unto me in heaven and on earth." C.H. Dodd allows that the intention here is "clearly to introduce the risen Christ as King of the World". He suggests that the passage nevertheless has a ring of authenticity because it is "notably sober and almost matter-of-fact in tone", entirely lacking "the conventional symbolism of apocalypse" (1968, pp. 116f). He also hints that the gospel resurrection accounts altogether lack the mythical tendencies of much ancient literature—this when, as we saw, Matthew tells that an angel descended from heaven, rolled away the stone sealing the tomb, and sat on it. Although Dodd was certainly concerned to represent these narratives in the best possible light, in his 1971 book—widely hailed on its appearance as the distillation of a lifetime of study—he concedes that whether "Jesus had in some way left his tomb" is a question on which "the historian may properly suspend judgment" (p. 167). If we are to accept the miracle of the resurrection, we need grounds more positive than this.

Defenders of the synoptic resurrection narratives take comfort, with Pannenberg, in the thought that "the legends created by excessive criticism have been less credible than the biblical reports themselves" (1987, p. 134). He is here alluding to the theory that Jesus did not die but merely "swooned" on the cross, recovered consciousness in the cool tomb, crept out unnoticed when the earthquake rolled the stone away, and showed himself from time to time to his followers. Such nonsense is, as we saw (above, p. 65), not the result of 'excessive criticism', but of yielding up only some of the traditional assumptions while clinging obstinately to others. In this example, belief in miracles has been surrendered, but the view that the gospels are based on eyewitness reports is retained, so that the miracle of resurrection is construed as a misunderstanding on the part of Jesus's entourage.

It is equally unsatisfactory to trace the gospel resurrection narratives to deliberate lies by eyewitnesses of the crucifixion who concocted resurrection stories they knew to be false—the position to which Reimarus felt himself driven (cf. above, p. 68). Schmiedel shows how such stories as the sepulchre guard (unique to Matthew) and the empty tomb could have arisen in stages in perfectly good faith.[2] He imagines a Christian confronted with the charge that the disciples had stolen the body. The obvious retort would be: "The Jews, we may be quite certain, saw to the watching of the sepulchre; they could very well have known that Jesus had predicted his rising again on the third day". Another Christian, hearing this, might take it not for conjecture, but for a statement of fact, and pass it on as such. But if soldiers guarded the tomb they must have witnessed the resurrection. What, then, did they see of it? The attempt to answer this would give rise to the story of the angel coming down from heaven and rolling away the stone. This again might well have originated as conjecture, but have been passed on as fact. And in order to explain why the soldiers did not tell of their experiences, it would be said that the Jewish authorities bribed them to suppress the truth and circulate instead the rumour that the disciples had stolen the body. A similar series of processes could have led to the story of the empty tomb. If Jesus was risen, his grave must have been empty. "Therefore no hesitation was felt in declaring that, according to all reasonable conjecture, the women who had witnessed Jesus's death had wished to anoint his body and thus had come to know of the emptiness of the grave". But why should not the disciples have gone to the sepulchre? Schmiedel answers: "The earlier narratives represent them as fleeing and deserting Jesus at Gethsemane (Mark 14:50, Matthew 26:56), and remaining in concealment while they were in Jerusalem." Luke's narrative changes this by very significantly omitting Mark's statement that they dispersed at Jesus's arrest, and by saying that "certain disciples" (24:24) did in fact go to the sepulchre. John expands this, naming the visitors as Peter and the beloved disciple, and reporting on their rivalry. It is clear that if, for some reason, the belief that Jesus was risen was once established, all these other traditions could have arisen in the way indicated.

In sum, that the divergent gospel accounts could have been written by persons who had already come to believe that Jesus rose from the dead is perfectly plausible; that their narratives provide any basis for such belief is not. The events alleged in the narratives did not form the basis of the faith, but the stories resulted from the faith and bear witness to a veritable flood of local traditions. These, as I have here and elsewhere stressed, were not deliberate lies. Years ago, the justly respected Catholic commentator Clifford Longley ascribed to me the view that the New Testament accounts of the resurrection are "dishonest fabrications"—as if I were something of a latter-day Reimarus. And recently Dr. J.M. Gilchrist has published a partially erroneous and completely misleading summary of my views under the overall heading "Tricks and Skulduggery" (2007, p. 106). I have never been among those who so totally lack understanding of the processes by which myths are formed as to argue that, either a tradition is true, or else it must have been maliciously invented by cynics who knew the facts to be otherwise. I referred Longley to Schmiedel's article, from which I have just been quoting, for a juster view.

If Jesus's tomb was empty, he did not leave his flesh and bones in his grave; and so either they had been transformed into something else, or else he rose in physical body. Paul, as we shall see, takes the former view, and the gospels (other than Mark's, which gives no evidence either way) the latter. They refer to the "flesh and bones" of the risen Jesus (Lk. 24:39), who "eats and drinks" with his disciples (Acts 10:41) and invites Thomas to touch him (cf. Lk. 24:39 where he invites the eleven to "handle" him). It is on the basis of such evidence that the fourth of the Church of England's Thirty-Nine Articles affirms that he ascended into heaven (where he now "sitteth") with "flesh and bones". His risen body has to be solid enough to support clothes, as no one supposes that the gospels would have us believe that he manifested himself (to ladies among others!) naked. Yet, as the bishops of the General Synod of the same Church of England have recently noted, this risen body must have been "of a very unusual kind", for it enabled him to arrive within closed doors (in spite of the solid fish he had eaten) and to vanish at will.[3] Badham has stressed what he calls the "internal incoherence" of the narratives here (1978, p. 37). The body is represented as solid for some purposes but not for others.

b. The Fourth Gospel

In the fourth gospel two chapters are devoted to the resurrection, although the second of these, the final Chapter 21, is obviously an appendix, presumably from a later hand. The women visitors to the tomb are reduced to the sole figure of Mary Magdalene, who on Easter morning finds the stone there already rolled away. There was no mention of any stone in the burial narrative of this gospel, and so here, in 20:1, John seems to be following a tradition independent of the one on which he had drawn there. Furthermore, a natural continuation of this verse comes only with verse 11, where Mary, still standing outside the tomb, looks into it and sees two angels inside. The intervening verses (2–10), however, tell how she ran from the tomb—she is not said to have looked into it before doing so—and told Peter and the "disciple whom Jesus loved" that the body had been removed and that "we know not where they have laid him". She obviously thinks that the body had been stolen. That she knows it to be missing suggests that this unit of tradition (verses 2–10) assumes that she has already inspected the tomb; but the unit has here been inserted into a story (verses 1 and 11ff) which makes her only subsequently inspect it.

It is also strange that she reports (verse 2) that we (plural) do not know what has become of the body. This suggests that the evangelist is here adapting (so as to make it refer to her only) a tradition similar to Luke's story that a number of women found the stone rolled away on Easter morning. John continues: "Peter therefore went forth". The verb here is singular in the Greek, but the evangelist nevertheless adds: "and the other disciple, and they went toward the tomb."

Clearly, a story concerning Peter has been clumsily expanded so as to include the beloved disciple. On arrival they both entered the tomb, and the beloved disciple "saw and believed". It is not said that Peter believed. On the other hand, it is implied that belief was no obvious matter, for they did not then realize that the Old Testament had predicted Christ's resurrection (verse 9). The two men are then said to return home (verse 10), after which the narrative returns to Mary Magdalene at the mouth of the tomb, as in verse 1, as if the intervening incidents had not happened. As Haenchen has noted (1968, p. 556) the whole intervening story can serve only the purpose of increasing our respect for the beloved disciple. He "believed" in spite of his ignorance of the supposed Old Testament prediction.

Peter was the first of the two disciples to enter the tomb, and he saw there the "napkin" which had covered the body's head "not lying with the linen cloths" which had been wrapped round the rest of the body, but "rolled up in a place by itself" (20:7). This seems to be a clumsy attempt to intimate that thieves had not removed the body—they would not have troubled neatly to have folded the napkin. One is of course not supposed to ask who it was that did this! Haenchen notes wryly that the evangelist's guiding spirit did at least prevent him from alleging that the remaining "linen cloths" were also folded (p. 556).

In the sequel, Mary is, as we saw, outside the tomb, and is weeping. When she looks into it, its occupants (here two angels) do not (as in the synoptics) give her the message that "he is risen", but merely ask her why she weeps. She says it is because the body has been "taken away", that is, stolen. But Jesus himself then appears to her, and, in the narrative of this gospel, she is the first to see him in his risen state, although she does not at first recognize him and takes him for the gardener (20:15). Here we have once again, as in Luke's Emmaus story, the motif of non-recognition. Once she realizes that it is her "master", he tells her not to touch him, for he is "not yet ascended unto the Father"—a strange saying: how can she touch him after he has ascended, unless he then returns to allow his followers physical contact? If so, why must he first ascend? At Mt.28:9 he did not object when the women "took hold of his feet and worshipped him". Here in John he tells Mary that, instead of touching him, she is to "go unto my brethren" and tell them that he is ascending. This is surely drawn from an old ascension tradition. His prohibition "touch me not" (20:17) clashes with his invitation to Thomas in a later episode in this chapter (verse 27). Ashton observes that each of the four episodes, combined as a sequence in this chapter, "taken on its own constitutes an effective ending to the gospel" (1991, p. 504). The four may, then, have been put together from originally disparate traditions. The episode we are at present considering terminates with Mary obeying Jesus's instruction: she goes to the disciples, tells them "I have seen the Lord", and reports what he had said to her (verse 18)—including, presumably, his statement that he is ascending. Ashton comments: "Here we have the quintessence of the early Christian mission: a proclamation, by a witness, that Jesus is risen. Nothing further is required: John could have ended his gospel here" (p. 509).

The narrative nevertheless continues with Jesus appearing, through closed doors, that same evening to the disciples gathered together. He instructs them to missionize: "As the Father hath sent me, even so send I you", and he then breathes upon them, thus imparting "holy spirit" to them (20:21f). In Acts, Chapter 2, 'holy spirit' comes upon them in quite different circumstances—at Pentecost, fifty days after Easter. All that the two accounts have in common is an underlying conviction that there was a clear divide between the time of Jesus's earthly existence and the time when holy spirit was available—as compensation for his absence from Earth—to the Christian community. That the divide is portrayed in two such different ways does not suggest that there was an underlying historical occurrence.

Thomas was not present at the appearance to the disciples recorded at Jn. 20:19–23, and did not believe their report that Jesus was risen until, eight days later, he again entered through closed doors and, in the presence of the other disciples, bade Thomas touch his wounded side. (Only the fourth gospel records that he was speared in the side while on the cross.) Convinced by this visible evidence, Thomas addresses him as "my Lord and my God". Although the word 'God' is rarely applied to Jesus in the New Testament—Titus 2:13 and Hebrews 1:8f are the only sure cases outside the fourth gospel—and although Thomas addresses him in this way only after the resurrection, a similar confession "could really have been made at any moment in the Johannine ministry by one who had eyes to see" (Brown 1970, p. 220), for throughout this gospel God is represented as visible in Jesus (cf. above, p. 45). "The restraining influence of rigid Jewish monotheism is beginning to weaken" (Lindars 1972, p. 615); and the doctrine of the trinity to restore it is not yet in sight. There are indeed New Testament references enough to Father, Son, and Spirit, but they are not said to be one. (The Comma Joanneum, 1 Jn. 5:7f, "these three agree in one", is admitted, even by Catholic authorities, to be an interpolation—"an expository expansion of the text" or, in Gibbon's plainer language, "a pious fraud".)

Thomas's confession does not please Jesus, for it was made "only because thou hast seen me: blessed are they that have not seen and yet have believed" (20:29)—a clear pointer to the early churches that what matters is not tangible evidence but faith. Modern believers follow suit. A recent book on the fourth gospel, having "doubted the wisdom" of trying to reconcile the relevant gospel accounts, rules that the resurrection "is to be apprehended by living faith (or not at all)" (Ruth Edwards 2003, p. 83).

Doubt is also expressed elsewhere in the gospel appearance stories, and one can see why. Critics will have said: Your risen Jesus was mere hallucination. Christians will have retorted: That suspicion arose among the very first disciples, and was refuted by the risen Jesus himself, who at Lk. 24:36ff dispels their doubts by eating fish, and at Mt. 28:17ff by his magisterial words.

An obstacle to the faith recommended in Chapter 20 of John is what Ashton calls the "fairy-tale" atmosphere of the stories there. Each one of them presents "some very odd images: a corpse that, apparently unaided, slips out of its burial-wrappings, angels who ask a single question and disappear, a man whom Mary now knows to be Jesus rejecting physical contact because he is about to ascend to heaven, and so on". Ashton's conclusion is that "neither the resurrection itself nor the stories told to illustrate its significance are historical in any meaningful sense of the word" (pp. 511f).

There follows, as a solemn conclusion to this gospel:

> Many other signs therefore did Jesus in the presence of the disciples, which are not written in this book: But these are written that ye may believe that Jesus is the Christ, the Son of God; and that believing ye may have life in his name. (20:30f.)

The next and final chapter is a strange appendix. It is the only chapter in which there is mention of the two sons of Zebedee, James and John—a fact which does not suggest the authorship of the whole gospel by one of them, particularly when, as we saw, all the incidents in which John figures in the other three gospels are absent from the fourth. Moreover, Nathanael, who has not been heard of since his call to discipleship in Chapter 1, and who is not mentioned at all in the other three gospels, suddenly reappears here in Chapter 21. Even more striking is that the disciples are here represented as having returned to Galilee to "go fishing"—as if, following Jesus's death, they had given up all the hopes they had placed in him; whereas in fact, in Chapter 20, he, already risen, had obviously dispelled their despair by coming through closed doors into their midst in Jerusalem, instructing them to go out as missionaries, and giving them holy spirit so that, in their work, they can forgive sins or withhold such forgiveness. Their behaviour in Chapter 21 gives no indication that they were aware that anything of the kind had happened, although the author of this chapter tries to bring it into line with the previous one by saying that it records "the third time that Jesus was manifested to his disciples" (21:14). The Archbishop of Canterbury,

Rowan Williams, has called this appendix a "Galilean fantasia",[4] fragmentary and isolated as it is from the rest of the fourth gospel, where the disciples have not even been represented as fishermen who had been called from their nets.

The first incident in this chapter is a miraculous catch of fish after a night of fruitless toil at sea. The story is so similar to the one at Lk. 5:1–11 (itself without parallel in Mark and Matthew) that the two must be related. In Luke the incident gives three fishermen, Peter and the two sons of Zebedee James and John, their motive for abandoning their trade and following Jesus, while here, at the end of the fourth gospel, it is a resurrection appearance to seven disciples, including these three. The other four are Thomas, who is named in the lists of the twelve in the other gospels, Nathanael, who is mentioned only in John's, and two who are unnamed. One of these seven is "the disciple whom Jesus loved" (21:7), but we cannot tell which one.

Only the fourth gospel mentions such a "beloved disciple". In its previous chapters he figures as a kind of superior counterpart to Peter. Although Peter was present at the Last Supper, it was the beloved disciple who was "at the table reclining in Jesus's bosom" (13:23). At the crucifixion, where Peter is not so much as mentioned, it is to the care of the beloved disciple that Jesus entrusts his mother (19:26f); and when both men go to the tomb, it is he who, as we saw, is first said to believe in the reality of the resurrection (20:8). As all three of these incidents have parallels in other gospels where he plays no part, the fourth gospel has here presumably drawn on source material similar to theirs, but reworked it so as to introduce him. This is particularly clear, as we saw, in the case of the visit to the empty tomb.

The second-century church naturally assumed that this beloved disciple must be one of the inner group of three who, according to the first three gospels, were Jesus's most privileged companions, namely Peter and James and John, the sons of Zebedee. These three alone were present at the raising of Jairus's daughter (as related by Mark), at the transfiguration (as related by all three synoptics) and at Gethsemane (as related by Mark and Matthew). Furthermore, it was obvious that, of these three intimates, Peter cannot be the beloved disciple as the two are mentioned as different persons in the fourth gospel; and since James was, according to Acts, martyred early (and so would not have survived long enough to have authored the whole gospel, as is claimed of the beloved disciple at 21:20, 24), it seemed clear to the church Fathers that the beloved one could only be John, who, they believed, had written the fourth gospel in his extreme old age at Ephesus.

Unfortunately for this theory, the incidents which represent Peter, James, and John as particularly close to Jesus occur only in the first three gospels. In the fourth, (where alone the beloved disciple figures) there is no raising of Jairus's daughter, no transfiguration, no Gethsemane agony—in fact no mention of the sons of Zebedee until the appendix (Chapter 21). Indeed, Peter, James, and John, although prominent in the other gospels, play but a minor role (or none at all) in John where, as we saw, prominence is assigned to disciples unknown to the other three.

The next incident in Chapter 21 of John is a dialogue between the risen Jesus and Peter which serves to rehabilitate this disciple; his earlier threefold denial is counterbalanced by threefold affirmation of his love for Jesus, who thereupon gives him leadership status with the injunction "feed my sheep." There follows a veiled forecast of his martyrdom—the writer may have known a tradition that he had been martyred—and a dialogue about the future of the beloved disciple where Jesus alludes to the belief, quite uncharacteristic of the fourth gospel, that some of the disciples might remain alive until his second coming (verses 22f). Jesus, says Dodd (1970, p. 431) is here made to subscribe to a "naive conception of his second Advent. . . . unlike anything else in the Fourth Gospel".

Up to this point, the fourth gospel, like the other three, has been anonymous. But at 21:24 we are told that it was the beloved disciple "who beareth witness of these things and wrote these things, and we know that his witness is true." The author thus refers here to the beloved disciple as an eyewitness, but speaks of him as someone other than the 'we', the Johannine community (cf. above, p. 44). The intention is clearly to represent the whole gospel as authenticated by an eyewitness. But this suggestion carries no weight, not only because it occurs only in an appended chapter, but also because, as we saw, the author of the first twenty chapters had to rework older material in order to introduce the beloved disciple at all.

The whole appendix is brought to an end with a verse which tries to achieve an even more grandiose allusion to unrecorded further deeds of Jesus than that which concluded Chapter 20:

> And there are also many other things which Jesus did, the which if they should be written every one, I suppose that even the world itself would not contain the books that should be written. (21:25)

There is no manuscript evidence whatsoever for the omission of Chapter 21 of this gospel; yet the view that it was written by the author of the other twenty is—in Haenchen's words—"as good as abandoned in today's critical scholarship" (1980, p. 594). Its presence in all the manuscripts (dating from the late second century) merely indicates that it cannot be a late addition.

Before passing on to Paul's account, it is of interest to note that even the prominent Catholic exegete Hans Küng admits to a good deal of legend in what the gospels say of the resurrection. He finds that, in those later than Mark, some practices and beliefs that were current in the early church are given a supposed grounding in the behaviour and instructions of the risen Jesus. In Luke the walk to Emmaus culminates in a meal where he "took bread and blessed and broke it, and gave it" to the two disciples (24:30). Every reader, says Küng, must be put in mind of the eucharist. (Fr. O'Collins also allows that Luke is here telling us that Christians "will grasp the risen Christ's presence when they gather for the eucharist". 2003, p. 88.) Similarly, baptism and the gentile mission are enjoined by Matthew's risen Jesus, and the importance of Peter and the power to forgive sins by John's (Küng 1976, p. 351). He finds that altogether the sepulchre narratives are no more than "legendary documentations" of the one item that is really significant, namely the message that God has awakened Jesus from the dead. Nor would the Christians' proclamation of this in Jerusalem have evoked any challenge from the authorities there as to whether there really was a tomb that was empty; for even the idealized portrait in Acts limits the Christian community of Jerusalem to some 120 persons (1:15) when the resurrection was first preached there, and this, in a city of some 25,000 or 30,000, was too insignificant a body to prompt any checking of its claims (p. 354). Likewise the New Testament scholar Martin Dibelius called the Jerusalem Christians a small and unobtrusive group, "a band . . . gathered together in a common belief in Jesus Christ and in the expectation of his coming again, . . . leading a quiet and, in the Jewish sense, 'pious' existence", sustained only by the "victorious conviction of the believers" (1956, p. 124).

Küng's suggestion, that a religious community may well ground beliefs and practices important to it by writing legendary stories which are meant to authenticate them, is widely recognized as significant. "Surely", says Crossley, "some degree of suspicion should be aimed at the historical accuracy of grounding the Gentile mission, something of great importance for the early Church, in the words of the bodily raised Jesus on a mountain (Mt. 28:16–20). . . . If we are going to take Christianity seriously in its Jewish and pagan contexts, then we must expect the Gospel writers to make up stories just as Jews and pagans did" (2005, pp. 181f). Those who doubt the fiction-creating capacities of early Christians can be referred to the tale that, at Jesus's death, tombs were opened and ancient worthies exited from them and promenaded in Jerusalem (Mt. 27:51–53). The gospels give examples enough of "creative storytelling, including the grounding of present beliefs in the life, death and resurrection of Jesus" (p. 186).

ii. Paul's Account

a. Introduction

When Paul wrote, Christian leaders established their authority by claiming to have seen the risen Lord. For Paul, an 'apostle' was precisely a person who had had such a vision and had been called to the Lord's service in consequence of it; for it is on this basis that he declares himself to be as much an apostle as were rival Christian teachers: "Am I not an apostle? Have I not seen Jesus our Lord?" (1 Cor. 9:1). The psychological predisposition to such visions can hardly have been absent if there was such a strong motive for claiming them.

One reason why this is not known to the general reader is that the word 'apostle' puts him or her in mind of the 'twelve apostles' and so suggests that only someone who had been a close disciple of Jesus during his lifetime could be an apostle. In fact the first author who uses the term fairly consistently in this sense is Luke (both in his gospel and in Acts). For earlier Christian writers, and for those of about the same date as Luke but ignorant of the gospel traditions, the term had no such implications and meant no more than 'Christian missionary'. For instance, at Rev. 2:2, the church of Ephesus is congratulated for having tested "them which call themselves apostles and . . . are not". If 'apostles' here meant (twelve) companions of Jesus, they could have been identified without being put to the test and "found false".

Paul ascribed the utmost importance to Jesus's resurrection and held that, without it, Christian faith is pointless, for death would not then have been defeated, nor man redeemed: "If Christ hath not been raised, your faith is vain; ye are yet in your sins" (1 Cor. 15:17). Earlier in this same chapter he gives a detailed statement of the basis of this faith (verses 3–8):

> (3) For I delivered unto you first of all that which also I received, how that Christ died for our sins according to the scriptures;

(4) and that he was buried; and that he hath been raised on the third day according to the scriptures;

(5) and that he appeared to Cephas; then to the twelve;

(6) then he appeared to above five hundred brethren at once, of whom the greater part remain until now, but some are fallen asleep;

(7) then he appeared to James; then to all the apostles;

(8) and last of all, as to one born out of due time, he appeared to me also.

This simple series of statements is the earliest extant evidence concerning the resurrection. Paul introduces them by saying that they comprise the substance of what he had preached to the Corinthians, the fundamental tenets, belief in which ensures their salvation (verses 1–2).

The first part of what Paul here says he "received" and is now handing on is widely agreed to be an early credal summary. Each of the statements in verses 3, 4, and 5 is introduced with the word *hoti* (stating 'that' something is the case), as would be appropriate in stating the propositions of a creed. These verses also include a notable number of words which Paul does not use elsewhere (specified by Dale C. Allison, 2005, p. 234), and this too suggests that these verses are not his own composition, but a formula he is quoting.

The passage does not locate the crucifixion in time. It places the resurrection three days after the death, but does not say when the death occurred. It is the appearances which Paul says are recent, made as they were to himself and to his contemporaries, and people who claim to see a ghost do not necessarily take it for the wraith of someone recently deceased.[5] Of the death and prompt resurrection he merely says that they were "in accordance with the scriptures." This of course does not mean the gospels, which did not, when Paul. wrote, exist, but the sacred books of the Jews. He is not able to quote them to support his claim. We saw in the previous chapter how New Testament authors twist and torture the most unpromising Old Testament passages into meaning something about Jesus; but "the resurrection seems to have baffled them, and no adequate Old Testament passage is ever produced" (Elliott 1982, p. 82).

The mention of the burial (verse 4) need not be taken to imply knowledge of a tomb, empty or otherwise. Paul may simply be emphasizing the reality of Jesus's death, as when we say someone is 'dead and buried' (cf. Evans 1970, p. 75 and note). The words 'he was buried' are "attached to the death of Jesus, not his resurrection, and confirm that the former occurred, just as the appearances then provide support for the assertion of Jesus's resurrection" (Wedderburn 1999, p. 87). That he was actually buried is important theologically for Paul, who regarded the death, burial, and resurrection as reflected symbolically in Christian baptism of total immersion: into the water constitutes death, under the water, burial; and out of the water resurrection (cf. Rom. 6:3f and Coloss. 2:12, where references to Jesus's burial are explicit). In 1 Corinthians Paul was writing to Christians who were denying that there was a resurrection of the dead, and had he known of an empty tomb, he would surely have been glad to adduce it as evidence of resurrection, instead of merely saying, as he does, that Christ was buried and then raised.

As we have seen, in the gospels Jesus's tomb is empty because he rose in physical body. Paul, however, has a quite different view of rising from the dead and roundly declares—in this same chapter where he writes of Jesus's resurrection and subsequent appearances—that "flesh and blood cannot inherit the kingdom of God" (1 Cor. 15:50). It is "clear enough", says Archbishop Carnley, that in verses 3–8 Paul understands Jesus's resurrection as "a truly representative sample of the resurrection of all believers", to which he makes reference in this later verse. In the same context (verse 43) he writes of the dead being raised "in glory"; and at Phil. 3:21 he argues directly from the resurrection body of Christ to the future resurrection body of believers: Christ "will change our lowly body to be like his glorious body". It is unclear from some passages (such as 2 Cor. 5:1–10) whether Paul believed that Jesus's body was *changed* into a glorious one, or *exchanged* for an entirely new glorious one. Richard Carrier has argued in a lengthy article (2005, pp. 105–231) that Paul took the latter view. If so, then Jesus's earthly body will have remained buried, and the question as to the emptiness of any tomb would not even arise. Be that as it may, since Paul certainly believed that Christ's resurrected body was not of flesh and blood, he could not have accepted any tradition that Jesus rose in physical body and ate and drank. Any claim to have eaten and drunk with the exalted one (Acts 10:41) would surely have seemed blasphemous to him.

Paul seems to suppose that Jesus ascended at once on being resurrected, and with a body of heavenly radiance, so that his subsequent appearances were made from heaven or by the glorified Jesus descending from heaven. So much is implied in Acts' version of Jesus's appearance to Paul who sees "a light out of heaven" (Acts 9:3ff) and hears a voice. And Paul's own account in no way suggests that the appearance to himself was in any way different from those made to the other persons in his list. In a recent study, A.W. Zwiep has spelled this out very clearly, saying that in earliest Christianity—in the epistle to the Hebrews as well as in the Pauline letters—Jesus's resurrection means "resurrection to heaven", "from grave to glory"; and his journey from the grave to the right hand of God was "not interrupted by interim appearances" (1997, pp. 129f, 143). Hence, the "appearances were *ipso facto* manifestations of the already exalted Lord, appearances from heaven". For Paul, says Guignebert, "*resurrection* means *exaltation* to *the presence of God, glorification*. It is curious that in the only passage in which the Apostle explains in detail his ideas on the being and nature of Christ from his pre-existence to his exaltation (Phil. 2: 5ff), no positive mention is made of the resurrection but only of the *exaltation*." Guignebert added that, had such a belief continued to prevail generally, there would have been no need for the gospel stories of bodily appearances, which their contradictions betray as secondary apologetic (1935, pp. 525, 528f). In the gospels there is even a trace of the belief that Jesus ascended to heaven directly from the cross; for at Lk.23:43 he says to the penitent criminal being crucified with him: "Today shalt thou be with me in Paradise." This is the only passage in the gospels which gives voice to such a tradition. It was not sustained, so obviously is it in conflict with the idea of a resurrection on the third day. That the appearances involved a descent from heaven is nevertheless implied in two other gospels. In Matthew several days must elapse between the appearance to the women in Jerusalem (28:9) and that to the disciples in Galilee, for they have to travel there (28:16) and could not have completed the journey more quickly. Even more strikingly, in the fourth gospel a whole week is said to pass between an earlier appearance and one which includes Thomas (20:26). It was presumably not supposed that Jesus had sojourned somewhere on Earth during these intervals—any more than that this had been the case with the intervals between the appearances to different persons recorded by Paul.

The appearances convinced Paul that the general resurrection of the dead, and the final judgment of both living and dead, already heralded by Christ's (not so recent) resurrection, were now very near indeed. Christ, raised from the dead was, then, the first indication that this general resurrection was forthcoming; it was "the first fruits of those who have fallen asleep" (1 Cor. 15:20). But now that he was not only risen, but had also begun to manifest himself from heaven, the final events which would bring the world to an end could not be long delayed. Early Christianity was certainly a charismatic movement where ecstatic experiences were, as the Finnish New Testament scholar Heikki Räisänen has said, "daily bread" (1987, p. 233). Paul and his fellow Christians were convinced that they were receiving messages from Jesus (cf. above, p. 7). They possessed "the Spirit of Christ" (Rom. 8:9), and at their gatherings this Spirit prompted them to speak words of "wisdom" or "knowledge", or to utter "prophecy" (1 Cor. 12:7–10). They could in this way speak "either by way of revelation, or of knowledge, or of prophesying, or of teaching". A 'prophet' is not necessarily a foreteller, but one who brings the message of a divinity, whatever it might be. In this same context, and in a later chapter (14:6, 24ff), Paul says that they could also "speak in tongues", that is, say things which they themselves cannot understand, but which others, present at the gathering, can interpret. The Spirit which prompted all this speech is not an abstraction, but, as Shaw says, "a sign both of Jesus's continuing life and of their inclusion in that life" (1983, p. 166). It was, then, in such a milieu that they had their visions of the risen Jesus. Like Shaw, John Macquarrie allows "a continuing sense of the presence of Christ" to be a factor which prompted belief that Jesus had been raised from the dead (1998, p. 113). Shaw, himself an Anglican priest, thinks it "unlikely that Christ was raised to life anywhere other than in Paul's imagination" (p. 96). Macquarrie does not dispute that the evidence for the resurrection is inconclusive (p. 112), but insists that, if it were necessary to accept that there was no sequel to the crucifixion—and he leaves his readers with the choice of believing that the cross was in fact the end—nevertheless, "the two great distinctive Christian affirmations would remain untouched—God is love, and God is revealed in Jesus Christ" (1990, pp. 406, 412, 414).

Any discussion as to what prompted Paul's views concerning Jesus's resurrection must take cognizance of the fact that the idea that a martyr's death could function as an atoning sacrifice, to be followed by his immortality, was not unfamiliar in the Hellenistic environment. The Jewish literature included what has been called 'the wisdom tale of the innocent righteous one'—no particular person is meant—who will be persecuted but vindicated *post mortem*. In the Wisdom of Solomon his enemies have condemned him to "a shameful death" (2:20), but he confronts them as their judge in heaven, where he is "counted among the sons of God". Cognate is the martyrological book 2 Maccabees, with its belief in the resurrection of the faithful; and 4 Maccabees adds to this the idea that someone steadfast in the faith unto martyrdom can benefit others because God will regard his death as "a ransom" for their lives, as an expiation for their sins (6:28–29; 17:21–22).

What is striking about the whole passage I have quoted about the appearances from 1 Corinthians 15 is, as Elliott says (p. 83), that "Paul does no more than provide a list. There are no details of how, where or when the Easter encounters took place or what happened." Also, he makes no mention at all of women witnesses. Apologists have often said that this is because in those days women's testimony carried no weight. To this, Schmiedel retorted (as cited, col. 4059) that, if Paul had believed that women had been substantially involved, he would have regarded this not as a matter of chance, but as willed by God, and would not have been ashamed of it, any more than he was ashamed to proclaim what he called the—by worldly standards—sheer foolishness of the doctrine of the cross (1 Cor. 1:20–25; Rom. 1:16). Moreover, the items he does list correlate very poorly with the record of appearances in the gospels. To show that this is so, I will first discuss Paul's naming of Cephas, James, and the twelve (verses 5 and 7) as recipients of appearances, as these persons are normally taken to have been close companions of Jesus during his lifetime, as that is depicted in the gospels. In fact, however, there is reason to think that they had no more been personally acquainted with him than Paul himself had been. Let us study the details.

b. To Whom the Risen Jesus Appeared

CEPHAS

Paul uses the name 'Cephas' in four chapters of 1 Corinthians and in the first two chapters of Galatians. He mentions 'Peter' as what is normally taken for an alternative name for this same person only at Gal. 2:7–8 (although some manuscripts have replaced 'Cephas' with 'Peter' in some of the other passages). It would certainly be strange that two different names are used within this single sentence for one person, and in my 1999 book I noted (p. 53) John O'Neill's 1972 suggestion that 'Peter' is here a post-Pauline gloss; introduced so as to substantiate the view (based on interpretation of Mt. 16:18) that Peter, not James, was the leader of the Jerusalem church. The German New Testament scholar Ernst Barnikol pruned the text even further. As they stand, verses 6–9 read, in literal translation:

> (6) Those who were of repute added nothing to me,
>
> (7) but on the contrary, seeing that I have been entrusted with the gospel *of the uncircumcision, just as Peter with that of the circumcision,*
>
> (8) *for the [one] operating in Peter to an apostleship* of *the circumcision* operated also in me to the gentiles,
>
> (9) and knowing the grace given to me, James, Cephas, and John who were reputed to be pillars, extended to me and Barnabas the right hand of fellowship, so that we [go] to the gentiles, they to the circumcision.

The words I have italicized are present in all the extant manuscripts, but these are considerably later than the original, and if the italicized passage is excised, Paul never mentions Peter anywhere.

Barnikol gives three principal reasons for regarding the italicized words as later additions to Paul's text. First, 'operating in Peter' and 'operating in me' is expressed in the Greek here by the relevant verb followed by the noun or pronoun in the dative case, without intervening preposition, and this usage with this verb is non-Pauline. Second, the references to two contrasting gospels, with two contrasting but equally valid apostleships, cannot be original, since in the previous chapter Paul has insisted, in the strongest possible terms, that there is only one gospel (1:6–9). If these references are removed, there remains an acceptable text in which the three "pillars" of the Jerusalem church recognize that Paul has been "entrusted with the gospel", and where they have "added" no conditions or restrictions to his preaching it to gentiles.

Barnikol's third reason for amending the text in this way is his weightiest. In Europe, he says, the text had been expanded to its present form by the time of Irenaeus, who appeals to it (*Adv. Haer. iii,* 13) as refuting the views of the heretic Marcion. But in the Bible of the North African church, the original text survived at least until the time of Tertullian; for he wrote five books to refute Marcion's claim that only Paul was a genuine apostle, yet he never once appeals to Gal. 2:7–8 which, as it stands in our manuscripts (and as cited by Irenaeus), completely undermines Marcion's position, in that here Paul is represented as granting to Peter a status equal to that which he claimed for himself. Tertullian's failure to adduce verses 7–8 is very striking, as he does refer to verses 1–5, and more than once to the second half of verse 9 (where Paul's mission to gentiles is welcomed), and then to what follows in verse 10, and so on. The necessary inference, says Barnikol, is that in his Bible verses 7–8 must have lacked their present references to Peter, which were interpolated some time in the late second century for the very purpose of discrediting Marcion's one-sided championship of Paul. They express the "classic anti-Marcionite church dogma of the harmonious parallel work of both apostles" (1998, pp. 296, 298).

In the gospels it is the name Cephas that is rare, while 'Peter' and 'Simon Peter' occur repeatedly. Cephas is mentioned only at Jn. 1:42, where Jesus tells Simon "You shall be called Cephas", and the evangelist adds "which means Peter". (The Greek *petros* is equivalent to the Aramaic *kepha*.) In the other three gospels, where there is no mention of Cephas, Jesus names Simon as Peter.

Today any interpolation hypothesis tends to be regarded with suspicion, as in the past it has been all too common to set aside in this way any passage which seemed inconvenient. But, as W.O. Walker observes, the widespread presence of interpolations in ancient literature—classical, hellenistic, Jewish and Christian—is "virtually certain"; and, in the case of the Paulines, the surviving manuscripts themselves, though late, "bear witness to numerous alterations, including short additions to the text." Moreover, the period between the actual composition of these letters (mid-first century) and the date of the earliest extant manuscript of them (P^{46}, from the late-second century) was "precisely the time during which the letters would have been most susceptible to alteration" (2001, pp. 43, 49). Standardization came only considerably later. (On this whole issue, Ehrman's 2006a book is very informative.) It must not be forgotten that, whereas today printed copies of a book are all identical, in the ancient world, where books were copied by hand, every individual copy was a newly created scribal artifact, which could be as faithful or as deviant as the scribe or his patron chose.

Even if we take the whole of Gal. 2:6-9 as genuinely Pauline, as Bart Ehrman does, it still does not, in his view, indicate that Cephas and Peter are one and the same; for it is difficult, he says, to see why the Peter of verses 7b and 8 should suddenly be called by a different name in the list of verse 9 ("James, Cephas, and John"). Ehrman observes that early Christian scribes "recognized this problem and rectified it by changing the text of verse 9", while modern commentators account for Paul's interchange of names in ways that are "as numerous as they are ingenious" (1990, p. 467). He also observes that many Christian writers from the second century and later, did in fact take the two names as designating different persons.

Dale Allison finds that this latter fact is of little significance, since—as Ehrman was himself well aware—Christian writers will have had an apologetic motive for such exegesis, namely to establish that the colleague whom Paul condemned for unreasonably opposing him at Antioch (Gal. 2:11ff) was not Peter, the prince of the apostles, but a less significant person named Cephas. In this way the embarrassment of having to admit that the two most prominent leaders of the early church had been at loggerheads could be avoided, and thereby "a great stumbling block removed" (Allison 1992, p. 490). Allison also suggests that Paul may have used two names for the one person, Peter, because repetition of the single name could be felt as stylistically inelegant. But his most forceful point is that, according to verse 9, Cephas, like James and John, is to go "to the circumcised", and this completely accords with what is said of Peter in verse 8.

Here we see the importance of allowing, as neither Ehrman nor Allison do, that verses 7b and 8, where alone Peter is mentioned, are to be set aside as interpolated. Moreover, verse 9, which Allison adduces as substantiating verse 8, surely gives a misleading summary of what had actually been agreed at the discussion Paul and Barnabas had with the three leaders of the Jerusalem church, James, Cephas, and John. Haenchen's assessment (1977, pp. 450f) of the agreement which had concluded this discussion is probably correct, namely: the Jerusalem three had, as a quite remarkable concession, given Paul the freedom to missionize gentiles without insisting on their circumcision, while making it clear that they themselves would continue to insist on the whole Jewish law being kept. Haenchen observes that, if Paul were to say clearly that this was the agreement, he would place himself as having been the subordinate party in the discussion, whereas in Galatians he is most anxious to represent his status as equal to that of the three. Hence he words the agreement as: they go to the Jews, we to the gentiles— really a division quite impossible to fulfil in practice, as all Christian communities in the diaspora will have been recruited from both sources. It can, then, come as no surprise that, when Paul goes on to mention his later quarrel with Cephas at Antioch (Gal. 2:11—14), we find that Cephas is there associated with Christians some of whom had been converted from paganism. He incurred Paul's fury because, under pressure from "certain persons from James", he refused to continue taking his meals with gentile Christians. It is easy to see that, once such converts had been allowed to step outside the Jewish law, it might plausibly be argued that keeping the law was unnecessary for any type of Christians; and James, and those who could be made beholden to him, were having none of that.

In sum, Paul refers to Cephas not as to a disciple of the historical Jesus, as was the Peter of the gospels, but as a resident of Jerusalem and one of the three leaders of the church there, who had had some visionary experience of the risen Jesus and, presumably on that basis, had been converted to Christism. The quarrel at Antioch was not between 'Peter' and Paul, but a confrontation between the Jerusalem Christianity, insisting on maximum conformity to the Jewish law, and Pauline Christianity not beholden to this law (Ehrman, p. 474). When, three years after his own conversion (and not until then), Paul paid his first visit as a Christian to Jerusalem, and was in touch with Cephas there for a fortnight (Gal. 1:18), his purpose was perhaps to discuss missionary strategy, but surely not to brief himself about the historical Jesus. If Cephas had been in a position to supply Paul with such knowledge, Paul's almost complete silence about it throughout all his epistles would be even more puzzling than it already is.

To judge from Paul's references, Cephas must have been a significant figure in the Jerusalem church. He is named as the first in Paul's list: the risen Jesus "appeared to Cephas, then to the twelve"; and I shall argue (below, p. 146) that it was Cephas's experience which prompted this subsequent experience of the group which Paul designates as 'the twelve'.

Gal. 2:11ff shows, as I have intimated, that the accord between Cephas and Paul did not last, that Cephas was threatening what mattered most to Paul, who here condemns his behaviour in the strongest terms. Anxious as he was to resist Cephas's pretensions, he would surely have alluded to one or other of the discreditable incidents in the career of the Simon Peter of the gospels, if he had had in mind this person, who was rebuked by Jesus as "Satan", fell asleep in Gethsemane, and went on to deny his master in cowardly fashion. It is also of interest that, while Paul places an appearance to Cephas as the first of all those which he records, in the gospels Peter plays only a very minor role in the appearances. They contain no *account* of an appearance to him. At Mk. 16:7 an appearance to "the disciples and Peter" is promised by the "young man" in the white robe at the empty tomb; and Luke 24:34 mentions, in a surprisingly casual manner, that an appearance to Peter had occurred without making it clear whether this was the first the risen Jesus had made. The eleven disciples and others with them are there reported as saying: "The Lord is risen indeed and hath appeared to Simon". This, says Eduard Schweizer, "sounds like a set formula and shows by its brevity that this is all Luke knew about an appearance to Peter" (1971, p. 364). The other two gospels are completely silent on the subject of an appearance specifically to him.

Finally, I note that the Jewish scholar Samuel Sandmel says: "I do not think that Peter-Cephas-Simon are historically one person; they are at least two" (1970, p. 52). Arguments to this effect have of course found little favour. Even Ehrman, in an end-note to a chapter on Peter in one of his later books (2006c, p. 262), queries whether he had been right to argue that Peter and Cephas were different persons. He does not actually repudiate this view, although his account in that book does not so distinguish them.

JAMES

Paul names the only other apostle he met during his fortnight with Cephas as " James the brother of the Lord" (Gal. 1:19); and at 1 Cor. 9:5

he mentions a group called "the brethren of the Lord". As the gospels supply Jesus with brothers, Paul is taken to be referring to members of Jesus's family. But it is quite possible that he meant members of a 'brotherhood', a group of Messianists which included James (and was perhaps led by him) and whose members were not related to Jesus but zealous in the service of the risen Lord (brethren "of the Lord", not of Jesus. Rom. 10:9 shows that 'the Lord' is a title associated with the resurrection).

2 Cor. 8:18 mentions a "brother", meaning a fellow Christian, who is "famous among all the churches for his preaching of the gospel" (RSV). The "brethren of the Lord" might well denote a group equally zealous in the risen Lord's service. In Acts, the Jerusalem Christians are called "the brethren", and the James who led them is not called Jesus's brother, nor even 'the brother of the Lord', although he is clearly the person whom Paul designated in this way. Neither in his gospel nor in Acts does Luke suggest that Jesus had a brother of this name, although he must have known that this was so if Mk. 6:3 was already present in his copy of Mark. In this verse the people of Jesus's "own country" call him "the carpenter, the son of Mary and brother of James and Joses and Judas and Simon". This is the only verse in this gospel which actually names Jesus's brothers and James as one of them. It is also remarkable for being the only verse in Mark where his mother is named as Mary—although quite well attested is a reading which eliminates her altogether, and has him called "the son of the carpenter".

On some half dozen occasions Paul appeals to 'words of the Lord'. Although he uses the name 'Jesus' 142 times, he never presents a saying as a saying of Jesus (Boring, 1991, p. 114); and above (p. 8) we saw reason to believe that his 'words of the Lord' can be understood as communicated to him by the risen one, as what Furnish calls "words of the risen reigning *Christ,* the church's *Lord*" (1968, p. 56). Likewise, 'Lord' in Paul's phrase 'brother/brethren of the Lord' may well designate the risen Lord rather than the historical Jesus.

In this connection it is of interest that Paul mentions a faction at Corinth whose members called themselves "of Christ" and who were not in full agreement with other Christian groups there, differently named (1 Cor. 1:11–13). If, then, there was a Corinthian group called 'those of the Christ', there may well have been a Jerusalem one called 'the brethren of the Lord' whose members were as little related to or personally acquainted with the pre-crucifixion Jesus as were the Corinthians.

It is also of relevance that in two gospels that are independent of each other (Matthew and John), the risen Jesus is made to call followers who are not his blood relatives "my brethren". Since elsewhere Matthew seldom and John never make Jesus call his disciples this, the two evangelists may well here be drawing on a common source, a story in which the risen Jesus made some statement about 'my brethren' in the sense of a group of followers. In his commentary on John's gospel, Lindars says that the words "go to my brethren and say to them" at this point in the resurrection narrative (20:17–18), considered together with Matthew's "go tell my brethren", "require the supposition that John was using a source which also lies behind Mt. 28:10" (1972, pp. 596, 607). This would be evidence for an early (pre-gospel) use of the words 'my brethren' as a way in which the risen Lord was believed to have designated a group of followers unrelated to him.

Readers of the New Testament naturally assume that, for Paul, Jesus was the Galilean preacher crucified under Pilate, and hence someone quite recently deceased. But if we pay due regard to the vague way in which Paul refers to the earthly life of Jesus (cf. above, pp.7ff), it is quite possible that he regarded him as a more distant figure. In the Pauline and deutero-Pauline letters the crucifixion is an event, at an unspecified time and place, carried out by unnamed personages, which ensures the salvation of believers because, in the upshot, it thwarted the evil cosmic forces which stood between them and God (cf. Coloss. 2:14–15, 20). This gives no basis of plausibility to the idea that the event had occurred in Jerusalem, involving well-known Jewish and Roman officials, as recently as a few decades before these early documents were written. If, then, Paul did regard Jesus as a more distant figure, this would make good sense of his references to James. Whoever he was, what Paul says of him shows that he preached the same Jesus as Paul (the two exchanged "the right hand of fellowship", Ga1. 2:9) and was able, at least until around A.D. 60, to preach unmolested in Jerusalem that this Jesus was the Messiah. This would be very surprising if he had been the blood brother of a Jesus recently executed as a Messianic pretender (as king of the Jews according to some gospel passages) by the authorities there. If they had recently found Jesus objectionable and dangerous, it is not plausible that they would have left unmolested, for a generation or more, his brother in that same city, who was implicating himself in all that he had stood for by proclaiming that his resurrection had vindicated him as God's Messiah, and that he would shortly return to inaugurate his kingdom. If, on the other hand, we regard Paul and the Jerusalem Christians James and Cephas as worshipping the risen form of an obscure and historically somewhat distant figure who was probably quite unknown to the authorities of the time, this will at any rate make it understandable that James was long allowed to survive untroubled.

Acts' attempt (8:1) to show that "a great persecution arose against the church in Jerusalem" and scattered it all to regions in Judea and Samaria is muddled and unconvincing. For it admits that the apostles were left unmolested (8:1), and at 9:26 the disciples are back in the city, and the church there is "built up" (9:31)—even though, according to 11:19, "those who were scattered because of the persecution" (the whole Christian community apart from the apostles) are still abroad, missionizing in Phoenicia, Cyprus and Antioch. Paul's epistles show that there was no significant persecution of Christians in Jerusalem before the Jewish War with Rome, which culminated in the destruction of the city, and hence the elimination of its Christian community, in A.D. 70. For he was able to visit the Jerusalem church several times over a long period and find there a stable and continuing organization.

In sum, Paul writes of "James the brother of the Lord", who was one of the Christian leaders at Jerusalem; and Luke (in Acts) writes of a James who is not specifically defined, but who led the church at Jerusalem and had (Chapter 15) negotiations with Paul, which obviously represent Luke's version of the negotiations between James and Paul mentioned in Galatians. In none of these texts is it necessary to regard James as Jesus's brother. But this would be an easy and natural inference for anyone who tried to harmonize them with Mark or Matthew.

Unlike Paul, the canonical gospels do not record any post-resurrection appearance of Jesus to James. Such an event is however included in the apocryphal Gospel of the Hebrews (Hennecke 1963, p. 159), where James vowed at the Last Supper (where, according to our four evangelists, he cannot even have been present) to eat nothing until he should have beheld Jesus after his resurrection. Jesus accordingly appeared to him first, brought bread and gave it to him.

THE TWELVE

Paul's mention of an appearance of the risen one to "the twelve" has often been taken as an undeniable reference to the twelve companions of Jesus's ministry who are specified in the gospels. However, in them, Jesus does not appear to twelve, but to eleven (Mt. 28:16), since Judas had defected and was replaced by Matthias only after the appearances had ceased with the ascension (Acts 1:9, 26). A post-Easter appearance of the Lord to the pre-Easter twelve of the gospels would make Judas part of the post-Easter group. As this is out of the question, the post-Easter twelve in the credal formula which Paul is quoting is surely not the pre-Easter twelve of the gospels: We need to keep in mind that Paul is not making some casual statement of his own, saying twelve and perhaps overlooking the fact that it was eleven, but quoting a Christian creed, where the wording was not casual, and where twelve really meant twelve. Who, then, were this twelve in Paul's credal formula? If they had been an important group, he would surely have mentioned them elsewhere, and would not, as he does, have named the leaders of the Jerusalem church as Cephas, James, and John. This "almost complete absence" of any kind of twelve from Paul's letters has been called "one of the most disconcerting elements in these letters when they are compared to the Acts of the Apostles" (Bernheim 1997, p. 195), which tries to represent twelve who had been companions of Jesus's ministry as a body of great importance in the early Jerusalem church—an account which cannot be said to be successful, since Acts gives no more than the names of nine of them. Of the other three, only Peter has any significance, and, at the midpoint of the narrative, all twelve are dropped (they are not again mentioned after 16:4) and replaced, without explanation, by the elders and by James—not James the son of Zebedee who, according to Acts 12:2, has already been executed, but by a James of Jerusalem whose identity is not, in Acts, further defined.

Schmithals finds that "there is no passage in the New Testament which makes it plain that the twelve played any special role either in Jerusalem or later on. They have their significance as witnesses of the resurrection. With this, our knowledge about them as a closed circle is exhausted" (1971, p. 70). He argues that the creed from which Paul was quoting in 1 Cor. 15:3–5 knew the twelve not as companions of an earthly Jesus, but as a group of enthusiasts who, having heard of the appearance to Cephas, interpreted it as Paul did (1 Cor. 15:20), as presaging. a general resurrection of the dead. In this exalted state of mind, the group will have become convinced that Jesus had appeared also to them; but as the hope of a general resurrection was not fulfilled, it will have disbanded, and so is not again mentioned in any New Testament epistle, Pauline or other.

A substantial number of New Testament scholars have likewise stamped the twelve as a short-lived phenomenon of the post-Easter community. Beare adduces Wellhausen, Bultmann, and Klein in this connection (1981, p. 240), and Schneemelcher points in addition to Vielhauer (1965, p. 28). Since then, their arguments have been pressed by Guenther (1985). Even in the gospels, the twelve are marginal. We are told nothing of most of them except their names, on which the documents do not even agree completely. As Beare observes "the list of names shows some variation in all four times that it is given in the New Testament" (1981, p. 239), namely in Mark (3:16–19), Matthew (10:2–4), Luke (6:14–16) and Acts (1:13). The names are not even listed in the fourth gospel, where, as we saw in Chapter 1, the twelve make only one appearance.

A notable number of eminent New Testament scholars have pointed out that Mark seems to have had some difficulty in imposing references to the twelve onto his material. Christopher Evans says that, in Mark, "any distinction between an inner group, a larger entourage, and the multitude has become blurred"; and that Mark's picture of Jesus permanently accompanied by a vast train of personal adherents is not historically plausible. He has clearly been made into "a paradigm of the Lord and his Church in Mark's own day" (1968, p. 57). Vielhauer agrees, saying that one minute Mark will speak of "the twelve" who in the next minute become simply "the, disciples" (1965, p. 69. He compares 11:11 with 11:14, and 14:17 with 14:12, 14). Nearly all Mark's references to the twelve occur in passages which Bultmann (1963), followed by Vincent Taylor (1966, p. 620), describe as "Markan constructions". For instance, 11:11 ("as it was already late, he went out to Bethany with the twelve") was written by Mark himself to serve as a link between two independent episodes which he took from his sources, namely the triumphal entry into Jerusalem (verses 1–10) and the cursing of the fig tree (verses 12–14). Neither episode mentions the twelve, but only 'the disciples'. The absence of any reference to the twelve in the second episode (after the linking verse which does mention them) struck Vielhauer, as we have just seen, as very instructive. 'They' are said (verse 12) to return from Bethany the following morning and to hear Jesus cursing the tree; but in verse 14 'they' are identified not as 'the twelve' but as 'his disciples'. Vielhauer adds that sometimes references to the twelve are obviously secondary insertions, as at 4:10: "When he was alone they that were about him, with the twelve, asked of him the parables". It seems odd that the evangelist finds it necessary to add that, when few were with him, they included his twelve close companions; and this clumsiness is explained if the original was simply 'those who were about him', and the reference to the twelve added later, in accordance with the idea that they always accompanied him. Again, at 9:31–35 he is in the presence of disciples who had been disputing who among them was greatest; yet he has to "call the twelve" as audience for his reproof of this.

Such evidence has suggested to many commentators that Mark's material resisted such references, and that he was importing a post-

Easter group into Jesus's lifetime. It must have been a very short-lived group, for, as I have noted, Paul does not mention it outside the credal formula he quotes, and it is never mentioned in any other New Testament epistle, nor in the letters of the Apostolic Fathers, who refer often enough in an imprecise way to "apostles". Not until the epistle of Barnabas do we find a clear statement that "those whom Jesus empowered to preach the gospel were twelve in number, to represent the tribes of Israel, which were twelve" (Chapter 8). This idea appears also in the one solitary reference to twelve in Q, namely that "you who have followed me will sit . . . on thrones judging the twelve tribes of Israel" (text reconstructed in J.M. Robinson et al. 2001, p. 151, from Lk. 22:28, 30 and Mt. 19:28). The number 'twelve' was obviously so significant for Jews that an early Christian group of twelve is an intelligible formation. The hesitation of Christian commentators in dating it earlier than Easter is illustrated by the way R.H. Fuller pushes this historical question into the background, saying, in his discussion of the Pauline mention of an appearance to the twelve: "Whether or not the twelve already existed as a body prior to the crucifixion need not . . . concern us" (1972, p. 35). Guignebert had been quite sceptical on the matter. He did not believe in the mission of the twelve (Mk.. 6:7–13 and parallels) and said he had "little more faith in the choice of Twelve by Jesus". When the Catholic scholar Lagrange called these doubts "an audacious denial, opposed by the evidence of the whole tradition", he replied: "Since in this case the whole tradition amounts to very little, the charge is hardly a grave one" (1935, p. 221). How fluid the tradition was he found illustrated by, for instance, the call of the first disciples, told differently in different gospels, and also quite artificially: "It is hard to believe", with Mk. 1:16–20, "that people who are supposed never to have seen or heard Jesus would have obeyed him at the first sign, to the point of leaving everything to follow him, without knowing why or whither" (pp. 217f).

This completes my discussion of Paul's claim that the risen Christ appeared to Cephas, to James, and to the twelve; and we have seen how poorly it correlates with the resurrection narratives of the gospels. This is not surprising if I am right in arguing, as I have done briefly in the Introduction to this book, and in more detail in other books, that Paul's Jesus is a figure much more distant from him than the Jesus of the gospels, who lived and died only a few decades before Paul wrote. When the real Paul mentioned those in Jerusalem "who were apostles before me" (Gal. 1: 17), he did not say that they had known Jesus personally. But this is of course what subsequently came to be generally presupposed; and so he is corrected by the pseudo-Paul of the apocryphal third letter to the Corinthians, which makes him speak of "the apostles before me who at all times were with the Lord Jesus Christ" (Hennecke 1965, p. 375). The real Paul's personal acquaintance with 'James the brother of the Lord' is unjustly taken to settle the matter in this sense, notwithstanding how very little there is in the early epistles, Pauline and other, to support such a view. But where nine tenths of the evidence points in one direction, and the remainder can be taken to establish an entrenched position contrary to it, one must acknowledge—in the manner of Samuel Butler's Professor Hanky—that people "would not be flesh and blood" if they "did not ignore the nine points and insist only on the tenth".

THE FIVE HUNDRED AND MORE

In verse 6 of his account of the appearances, Paul states that Christ was additionally seen by "above five hundred brethren at once", most of whom were still alive. This seems out of place in a list which otherwise names only notable personages of Christian communities. As we saw, in the earliest Christianity an apostle's authority depended on his having seen the risen Lord; and so the list, without the five hundred, may have been originally compiled as evidence of the credentials of the persons named in it, and the reference to the five hundred added later when the list came to be understood not as stating who had apostolic credentials, but as evidence for the resurrection. (This view is argued in Price 1995, pp. 82–83.) This addition could even be post-Pauline, for an appearance to five hundred was surely too good a piece of evidence to be ignored, and had it been early tradition it would presumably have surfaced in some form in the gospels, even though they, as later documents embodying later traditions, present a quite different account of the appearances from Paul's.[6] The appearance to James is admittedly also not in them, but it did not disappear from the tradition completely, for, as we saw, it is represented in the apocryphal Gospel of the Hebrews.

As, according to Paul, Christ appeared on several occasions to numerous persons at once, some apologists hold that there really must have been some external reality to be perceived. It would still not follow that what was there was interpreted correctly. Tyrell shows in his book on apparitions that there are examples enough of collective perception of what were taken for ghosts (1953, pp. 8, 109, 114). The evidence offered by sworn eyewitnesses at witchcraft trials likewise suggests that what people observe depends at least as much on their habits of thought as on what is actually there. A firm belief in the miraculous and in the ceaseless efforts of the Devil was presupposed in the observations and reasonings of witnesses and judges alike at these trials, and, as Huxley noted (cf. above p. 60), the number of witnesses counts for very little when all are affected by the same underlying beliefs.[7]

More recently, at the battle of Mons (1914), angels "varying in number from two to a platoon" were widely believed to have fought on the British side (A.J.P. Taylor 1970, p. 34). The virgin Mary is alleged to have been seen by two children at La Salette (France) in 1846 and by three children at Fatima (Portugal) in 1917, complaining in both cases of neglect of sacred rites. These are widely regarded as instances of the type of popular piety that in Romance-speaking areas was linked with nineteenth-century revivalist movements. At Fatima the initial appearances were followed by "an awed crowd of 30,000" seeing "first Our Lady of Sorrows, followed by Our Lady of Carmel, then Saint Joseph holding the Holy Child in his arms, and lastly the Lord Jesus". A "solar prodigy"on the same occasion (13th October, 1917) was "witnessed by thousands of people within a twenty-five-mile radius": the sun spun three times, then "moved away from its natural axis, and falling from side to side plunged down towards the earth at tremendous speed, zigzagging wildly as it came", but then finally resumed its normal place in the sky and shone forth peacefully (Jeffery and Dunn, pp. 39f). One wonders why the millions outside the twenty-five-mile radius did not report seeing anything abnormal.

It is of course true that hallucinations, even when induced by some common physical means, will not be the same for different people, since they depend not only on the present physiological state but on the stock of memories in the mind of each individual. But inasmuch as the appearances of Jesus were vouchsafed to groups such as the five hundred and more of 1 Cor. 15:6, who may, like Paul, never have known Jesus personally, the agreement between what each person experienced could have been minimal yet sufficient for all to say that they had seen a vaguely-conceived risen Jesus. Furthermore, the nonconformist is mistrusted, and so every individual, whatever he may inwardly feel and believe, may try to give the impression that he believes what those around him seem to believe—a phenomenon made familiar by Hans Andersen's story of the Emperor's New Clothes. These conditions prevail not only in crowds—where every member is ready to sink his private view in deference to what he takes to be the general opinion, as soon as he thinks he has ascertained it—but wherever people feel that their actions may be subjected to public scrutiny. And with early Christianity we are dealing with a social phenomenon where unbelief is a cardinal crime (Jn. 3:18 and 36) for which whole communities are to be most frightfully punished (Mt. 10:14f). "He that doubteth is like the surge of the sea driven by the wind and tossed" (James 1:6).

On all this, as on so many other matters, Cheyne and Black's old (and as good as forgotten) *Encyclopaedia Biblica* is still helpful. Schmiedel, writing there (col. 4083) gave numerous examples of collective visions, and commented that "in circumstances of general excitement and highly strung expectation, visions are contagious . . . and others easily perceive that which at first had been seen only by one." Guignebert found that "in the history of religious enthusiasm nothing appears more contagious than visions." He added: "Even in our times the Roman Catholic Church has to be cautious in the matter of apparitions of the Virgin, the reality of which is readily attested by enthusiastic groups of people" (1935, p. 518). Many for whom these recent appearances to crowds carry no conviction nevertheless suppose that Paul's specification of a large audience authenticates his record of one of the appearances of the risen Jesus.

iii. The New Testament Evidence as a Whole and the Synoptic Burial Narratives

What we have in the New Testament, apropos of the resurrection, is different layers of a tradition that is in course of developing. The earliest Christians will simply have asserted that Christ died and was raised, in the kind of preaching formula that Paul quotes. The next stage will have been to offer supporting evidence by listing appearances, and this is represented in the Pauline passage which, as Elliott notes, "does no more than provide a list". Such visions are quite in accordance with religious psychology. Isaiah (6:1ff) was called to God's service by a vision of the Lord. Initiations into the pagan mystery religions involved "a personal meeting with the God", and Isis afforded "comfort through visions" (Witt 1971, pp. 153, 189). Paul himself records that he and others were prone to supernatural visions (2 Cor. 12:1–4; cf. Coloss. 2:18).

The next stage was to give actual descriptions (not mere listings) of the appearances, as in the canonical gospels. Finally, in the apocryphal Gospel of Peter, there is a description of the resurrection itself: Jesus is actually seen emerging from the tomb. Here we have the "climax" and, virtually, the "terminus" of what Leslie Houlden calls the "'happenedness' concerning the resurrection", enabling us to see "all that there is to see". All that remained to do, he adds wryly, was "to set about locating the site of the Resurrection and build a church on it"; and that was accomplished two centuries later (1993, p. 61).

These stages are summarized by Fuller (pp. 28–29, 66–67) who shows that, in the course of the development, the claims about the resurrection become different sorts of claims. The theologian John Hick admits that the earliest references simply allege Jesus to be risen, and that the gospels elaborate this message into a catena of incompatible stories characterized by "progressive degeneration from history to legend", so that we cannot tell whether he did actually emerge from his grave, or whether this was merely an idea based on "a series of visions" of him "as a glorified figure of exalted majesty" (1985, pp. 171, 175ff). In other words, the stories of the appearances (the stage represented in the gospels) do not record events on which the resurrection faith was based, but are clumsy attempts to justify this faith by allegations of underlying events.

An important predispositioning factor was that the earliest Christian thinking on the resurrection occurred within the context of Jewish apocalyptic thought: soon the end would come, the dead would be resurrected and judged, and the wicked punished. As Leslie Houlden says, "in its origins the resurrection faith was part and parcel of a conviction that the last days, as foreseen in apocalyptic, were in process of realization and soon to be consummated" (1986, p. 152). Whatever it was that these early Christians saw, they interpreted it in the framework of resurrection faith as known to them.

The so-called 'Easter event' is often taken as what has ironically been called a kind of theological equivalent to the Big Bang: once granted, it is thought to account for nearly everything that followed. Against this, it is appropriate to keep in mind that, because early Christianity was so diverse, not all strands of it posited a resurrection at all. Bart Ehrman instances the recently discovered Coptic Gospel of Thomas which has only sayings of Jesus - no stories about him, "no birth, no baptism, no miracles, no travels, no trials, no death, no resurrection" (2003, p. 55). According to this document, salvation has nothing to do with Jesus's death and resurrection, but is accorded to those who can correctly interpret the enigmatic sayings of which this gospel consists: "Whoever finds the interpretation of these sayings will not experience death" (saying 1). Many today, says Ehrman, have difficulty in accepting Jesus's resurrection and in regarding his death as an atonement, but call themselves Christians because they try to follow his teachings. "Maybe", then, "there were early Christians who agreed with them" (p. 58).

There were certainly Christians in Corinth in the 50s who did not believe that they would be resurrected. Paul objects to them that, if they really hold that "there is no resurrection of the dead", then they will have to deny that Jesus himself rose, the basic article of the Christian faith (1 Cor. 15:12). They may have been beholden to Hellenistic ideas about the immortality of the soul rather than the resurrection of the body. At any rate, Paul expects them, from their standpoint, to ask, incredulously, "in what kind of body" the dead would be raised. He dismisses this as a silly question, and declares that man's animal body will be raised as a "spiritual body". If the kind of traditions represented in the gospels either concerning what Jesus himself had said on the subject ("When they shall rise from the dead . . . they are as angels in heaven": Mk. 10:25 and parallels) or concerning the nature of his own resurrected body had been known to them, such a question would surely not arise, and if it nevertheless did, Paul would surely have pointed to such traditions by way of answer, had he known of them.

Now that I have surveyed the New Testament material, I can appropriately ask: Is it likely that Jesus was buried in a particular tomb at all? Many have thought that probably the body was thrown into a common grave for criminals, so that, after a few days, nobody could have recognized the remains, even if they had been looking for them. (Allison 2005, p. 307, quotes Loisy's argument that this is what happened.) It is an old apologetic plea that, not only was there a tomb, but also that, if it had not been demonstrably empty, the Jewish authorities would have silenced the apostles' preaching simply by producing the body. But according to the New Testament itself, the apostles did not go public with their preaching of the resurrection until Peter's Pentecost sermon (Acts 2:14ff), a full fifty days after Easter, by which time any remains would have been unidentifiable. Not that we can trust the New Testament here, for this speech, and others in Acts, although addressed to and, we are told, enthusiastically embraced by orthodox Jews of Jerusalem, nevertheless rely on the Greek translation of the Old Testament for proof texts in cases where the Hebrew original is so different that it would not support the argument. We really cannot believe, with Acts, that thousands of Jerusalem Jews turned Christian in response to obvious distortions of their own scriptures. Peter's first sermon to them is said to convert three thousand, and his second another two thousand (Acts 2:41; 4:4). As we saw (above p. 74), these speeches must have been concocted in a Hellenistic Christian community remote from Jerusalem—a community which ascribed its own understanding of the Jewish scriptures to the Jerusalem Jews.

If Jesus was not buried, the story of his burial by Joseph of Arimathea is legendary. It is certainly not without its difficulties. Some have argued that it must nevertheless be authentic, since no Christian would have fabricated a tradition which made Jesus receive burial from some outsider, instead of from one of his own supporters. But according to the earliest gospel, his male disciples have deserted him, so that—if a man is to bury him—it must be the work of an outsider. Joseph is not known apart from the incident where he asks Pilate if he may have the body. Mark's Greek represents him as "a respected councillor" (15:43, not as a member of *the* council of Jerusalem, the Sanhedrin. He may have belonged to some local council elsewhere). That he was "looking for the kingdom of God" suggests that he shared Messianic expectations of other Jews. He would naturally wish Jesus to be buried before nightfall, for the law stipulates that a criminal's body should not remain overnight on the gibbet (Deuteronomy 21:23). According to the previous verse in Mark, he had an additional motive for acting quickly, for the sabbath will commence at 6:00 P.M. (In Jewish reckoning, a day runs from evening to evening, not from one midnight to the next.); and the implication seems to be that he would not be able to do on the sabbath what he had in mind to do. However, according to Mark's preceding Passion narrative, the day of Jesus's death and of Joseph's approach to Pilate was the passover, and, as Nineham observes, "the prohibitions with regard to passover were pretty nearly as strict as those relating to the Sabbath". He thinks that the burial story reached Mark "from a cycle of tradition which knew of *no chronological* tie-up between the crucifixion and the Passover" (1963, p. 433), and that Mark has simply incorporated it without adapting it to his Passion chronology. Moreover, since Mark delays Joseph's approach to Pilate until "evening had come" (that is, 6:00 P.M.), the sabbath had in fact already begun. The evangelist chooses this hour for the first incident in his burial narrative because, throughout chapter 15, he is imposing an artificial time scheme on the principal events, making them occur at three-hourly intervals. Thus Jesus is delivered to Pilate "as soon as it was morning", and is crucified "at the third hour" (9:00 A.M.); from the sixth to the ninth hour darkness covers the land, and at the ninth hour (3:00 P.M.) Jesus utters his last cry and dies. Finally, "when evening had come", Joseph seeks permission to take the body from the cross.

Clearly, this time scheme leaves Joseph with no opportunity of completing his task before the sabbath begins. Mark nevertheless represents him, after his approach to Pilate, as embarking on the yet further errand of "buying a linen cloth" before he proceeds to take the body down, wrap it in this shroud, and place it in "a tomb which had been hewn out of a rock" (perhaps an echo of Isaiah 22:16, which refers to a grave "carved in the rock"). Mark is here presumably reproducing the story as he found it in some earlier tradition, where there will have been no three-hour intervals, where Joseph could therefore have approached Pilate before evening, with sufficient time for all the operations alleged.

How quickly traditions about Jesus grew and changed can be seen from the ways in which Matthew and Luke have adapted this account. Luke took Mark's phrase "a respected councillor" to mean that Joseph was a member of the Sanhedrin; and so he is at pains to explain that he was "a good and righteous man" who had not consented to "the purpose and deed" of his Sanhedrin colleagues (23:50f). Matthew supposed that Mark's "looking for the kingdom" meant that Joseph was expecting it to be brought by Jesus, and was therefore "a disciple of Jesus" (27:57). He was also a "rich" man, who buried him not just in "a tomb hewn from a rock", but "in his own new tomb, which he had himself hewn from the rock". Joseph's wealth is perhaps intended to link the burial with that of the suffering servant of Yahweh, who had his grave made "with a rich man in his death" (Isaiah 53:9). Luke also locates the burial in a 'new' tomb, "where no one had ever yet been laid". This, says Evans (1990, p. 882) is "the language of hagiography". It may however be merely an attempt by Luke to establish that the body could not have been mixed up with others—a possibility which Mark's account had not excluded.

Mark emphasizes that there was no anointing of the body, for he motivates the visit of the women to the tomb on Sunday morning by ascribing this purpose to them—to anoint a body that had lain for a day and two nights in a hot climate, although they had no idea how they would be able even to enter the tomb (16:3), since they had seen that it was sealed by a large stone.

The fourth gospel gives a very different account of the burial, but I have shown that already Matthew and Luke make significant changes to Mark's narrative. Evans says that the burial pericope "provides a necessary transition from the crucifixion to the discovery of the empty tomb", and that, apart from that, its purpose "could be to assert that the corpse of Jesus was not left on the cross to rot, as could happen, nor thrown into a common fosse with those of other criminals" (p. 880). And Beare regards Joseph's part in the burial as "the first element" in a legend which grew and grew, "bringing him to Glastonbury in Britain, carrying with him the Holy Grail, and founding the first Christian church in the country" (1981, p. 538).

In his recent thorough account of the discussion concerning Joseph, W.J. Lyons of Bristol University records (2004, p. 31) Loisy's statement of 1908 that "all the details of the story . . . are conceived in view of the discovery of the empty tomb." Lyons adds that this "once lonely questioning of the historical existence of Joseph has now become a widely held view, especially among those associated with the Jesus Seminar", whose verdict he quotes (pp. 29f) as: "The burial is a fiction because it goes with the empty tomb story, which is the central fiction in Mark's passion narrative." He also notes J.D. Crossan's view that Jesus's body "was dealt with by the Romans, and that Mark created Joseph in order to resolve the problem created by his lack of knowledge as to its whereabouts" (p. 47). Lyons himself takes a less sceptical view, arguing that Mark did not create Joseph, but the story about him reached him from earlier tradition (p. 49). Joseph, Lyons says, is not required in order to supply continuity between Jesus's death, burial, and resurrection; the women who witness the death and the burial, and then the empty tomb, suffice for that. He thinks that Mark's portrayal of this pious Jew fits well with Mark's overall tendency to include a number of characters exhibiting the sort of exemplary behaviour that contrasts with his very negative portrait of the twelve disciples (amply documented in chapter 5 of the present book). Thus "the inclusion of the positive description of Joseph is typical of a significant Markan motif" (p. 52).

Many exegetes who have not accepted the resurrection have admitted the discovery of the empty tomb as a historical fact, and so have felt obliged to account in some way for its emptiness. Hence, said Guignebert, "much ingenuity has been wasted in an attempt to establish the probability of the removal of the body either by the Jews, or by Joseph of Arimathea who, having provisionally deposited the body near Calvary, would come to remove it in order to give it a final burial place elsewhere; or by one of the women; or by some disciple without the knowledge of the others". It would, he added, be a waste of time to discuss these and other hypotheses with similar aim, "since the discovery of the empty tomb seems improbable" (1935, p. 499).

iv. Recent Defenders of the Traditional Doctrine

That the historical evidence for Jesus's resurrection is less than fully adequate is now very widely admitted, even by apologists. Fr. O'Collins, for instance, allows that belief that Jesus rose depends only to some extent on historical knowledge, and requires also "the grace of an interior divine illumination" and "a loving commitment and a trusting hope which . . . enters into a personal relationship with Christ" (2003, p. 31).

Today the most prominent British advocate of Jesus's resurrection is N.T. Wright, the indefatigable bishop of Durham, author of more than forty books. He has set out his case in a lengthy 2003 book, in a lecture at Roanoke, Virginia of 16th March, 2007 (of which I have been sent a cassette recording), in a further lecture at Cambridge, England, on 15th May, 2007 (at which I was present), and in his most recent book, issued late in 2007. The arguments are substantially unchanged in all four.

Wright is well aware that he is challenging a "broad consensus" that the gospel resurrection stories are "late inventions" (2003, pp. 7, 588). Like O'Collins he allows that the historical evidence is not in itself absolutely conclusive; but he finds it nevertheless very strong, in that Jesus's tomb was known to be empty, and his disciples saw him alive, and not as a mere ghost, after his crucifixion, these two facts together being sufficient to justify the Easter faith. Both, says Wright, are necessary for this: the encounters with the risen one are alone insufficient, and would have been dismissed as hallucinations, since ghostly visions of the recent dead were, then as now, not uncommon; and the empty tomb alone is insufficient, as tomb robbery was common in the ancient world.

In his Roanoke lecture Wright found it arbitrary to specify elements in the resurrection narratives that are earlier than others, and did not allow that they consist of traditions which developed and changed over a period of time. In his 2003 book he does, however, acknowledge that "Luke used Mark", but nonetheless "tells the story in very much his own way", and that Matthew is "probably" also dependent on Mark (pp. 589, 679). What he consistently stresses is that, in his view, however late they were actually written down, all these accounts go back to very early oral tradition, earlier than Paul's writings of the 50s. Hence he draws uncritically from them all, and so is unrestrained by Evans's caveat (cf. above p. 123), and unperturbed by what he calls "surface discrepancies" between them. Indeed, these, for him, argue for authenticity in showing that the evangelists did not write in collusion, and in illustrating the way in which discrepant accounts of an event can be given by intelligent witnesses of it. In his 2007 book he refers in this connection to a 1946 confrontation at Cambridge between Karl Popper and Ludwig Wittgenstein, in front of a distinguished audience, at which tempers became somewhat frayed, and Wittgenstein picked up a poker and waved it about. Subsequently there was disagreement over "the precise details" of what happened on the occasion, "but nobody doubts that the meeting took place". According to Wright, "we have in the four gospels, together with Acts and Paul, a first-century equivalent of the varying accounts of Wittgenstein's poker". In both cases, "even if our eyewitnesses disagree in detail, something must have happened" (pp. 43f, 46). Bart Ehrman's questions form a sufficient riposte to this commonly made suggestion that the discrepancies in the relevant accounts pertain only to trivialities:

> Who actually went to the tomb? Was it Mary Magdalene alone or Mary with a group of women? If other women, which ones and how many were there? When they arrived, was the stone rolled away from the tomb or not? Did they see one man there in the tomb, or two men, or two angels? What did the person(s) in the tomb tell the women (or woman) to do? Did the women do it or not? What were the disciples supposed to do? Were they to go to Galilee or were they told not to leave Jerusalem? Did they go or stay? Did Jesus appear to them? When and how many times? Did Jesus then ascend to heaven on the day of his resurrection, or did he do so forty days later? (2006b, pp.147f)

Wright specifies four features of the gospel accounts which, in his view, show that their material must be very early:

> 1. Up to this point, all four evangelists have drawn heavily on Old Testament material as evidence that Jesus's death and burial occurred 'according to scriptures'. But their resurrection narratives make practically no use of such material, and this suggests that these stories "go back to very, very early oral tradition, which had been formed, and set firmly in the memory of different storytellers before there had been any time for biblical reflection" (2007, pp. 64f).

But it is surely obvious that this contrast between the non-use of the Old Testament in the resurrection stories and extensive use of it elsewhere is due to the fact that, while there is much in the Old Testament about suffering and death, it says very little about resurrection, which came into Jewish thinking only at a quite late stage—and even then, the references are to a final general resurrection of the dead, and not to the resurrection of some one individual prior to that final event. Wright himself is well aware of this (p. 56).[8] While Acts makes it clear that preachers in the early church did appeal to Old Testament passages to argue for Jesus's resurrection, these are, as Evans has stressed, "plainly forced into service and made to bear a sense other than the original" (1970, p. 12). That they are even laughably irrelevant has long been clear (cf. below, p. 252 for a striking example given by Reimarus). Admittedly, the evangelists, and Matthew in particular, are capable of adducing, at many points in their overall narratives, quite unpromising Old Testament excerpts in support of their claims, but I have already recorded Elliott's observation that "the resurrection seems to have baffled them", and in the whole of the New Testament "no adequate Old Testament quotation is ever produced." The best that the gospels can do is the pericope where Matthew makes Jesus prophesy to the scribes and Pharisees, while he is still ministering in Galilee, that "as Jonah was three days and three nights in the belly of the whale, so shall the Son of man be three days and three nights in the heart of the earth" (12:40). This does not even accord with the resurrection accounts, for death on Friday and reappearances on Sunday morning cannot be made to yield three nights in the tomb. It is, then, unsurprising that these accounts can do no more than claim that Jesus's resurrection is foretold in the Old Testament, and are unable to quote anything to that effect from it. Thus in Luke's story of the walk to Emmaus, the risen Jesus, "beginning from Moses and from all the prophets, interpreted . . . in all the scriptures the things concerning himself" (24:27), but gave no indication of what it was to which he could have been referring.

> 2. Women are the first witnesses at the tomb, even though women were not regarded as credible witnesses in the ancient world, and were so "apologetically embarrassing" that, even by the time of Paul, they have been "quietly dropped" (2007, p. 66).

One might note that Paul's account is not only devoid of women witnesses, but also makes no mention of a tomb, empty or otherwise. Wright nevertheless insists that "Bultmann and his followers are quite wrong to say that Paul knows nothing of the empty tomb" (2003, p. 626). Paul's account is admitted to be earlier than those of the gospels, and if we then not unreasonably take the traditions he records as earlier than those which came to be represented in the gospels, we can, with numerous exegetes, see both the tomb and the visitations of the women as later fictions— especially since reliance on women witnesses follows from the story-line of the earlier of the gospel narratives, which represent the male disciples as fleeing at Jesus's arrest, with no suggestion that they did other than remain in concealment, leaving only the women followers available to inspect the tomb (cf. Schmiedel's argument, pp. 124f above. He also saw (cf. above, p. 138) no reason to suppose that Paul would have been too embarrassed by women witnesses to mention them).

> 3. No biblical texts predicted that a resurrected man would have a body that is normal enough for him to be mistaken for a gardener, yet is sufficiently transformed to enable him to pass through locked doors and also sometimes not to be recognized (2007, p. 66).

But these features—the non-recognition motif, and the body that is normal for some purposes but not for others are rather a source of difficulty (cf. above, pp. 119f, 125f), and certainly not anything that betokens an early date.

> 4. If these stories were late, they would certainly have included mention of "the future Christian hope" (2007, p. 67), the final resurrection of all God's people, as do other New Testament references to Jesus's resurrection.

I cannot see why such mention would be required in (supposedly) historical accounts, whether early or late, of the actual resurrection events, while it is quite intelligible that preaching to the post-resurrection churches, as in the rest of the New Testament, should spell out what Jesus's resurrection means to their members. One might, of course, expect a historical account to *conclude* with some indication of its significance; and this is what we actually find in the solemn conclusion at the end of Chapter 20 of the fourth gospel: not indeed a reference to a final resurrection of God's people, as the fourth evangelist has all but abandoned earlier Christian eschatological ideas (cf. below, pp. 274ff), but certainly a clear indication of the Christian hope: "These signs", says the evangelist here, "are written that ye may believe that Jesus is the Christ, the Son of God, and that believing ye may have life in his name" (20:31. The NEB renders the final clause as: "that through this faith you may possess eternal life by his name").

Wright also finds it significant that Jesus's tomb was never venerated in the early days of Christianity (p. 73). One can retort that the absence in the early epistles of attention to holy places of any kind in Jerusalem is not supportive of the gospels' overall story. Paul spent the first three years of his Christian life before even briefly visiting Jerusalem (Gal. 1:17f), and in all the early epistles Jerusalem is never mentioned in connection with Jesus, nor is there any mention of Calvary. Wright seems to suppose that, if there had been a tomb containing Jesus's remains, it would have been venerated, so that the lack of veneration suggests that it was empty—this in spite of the fact that, in later centuries, Christians mounted Crusade after Crusade to recover the 'holy sepulchre' (which Helena, the mother of the emperor Constantine, claimed to have discovered in the fourth century) in the full knowledge that there was no body there.

In the same context Wright claims that the emphasis in the early church on "the first day of the week" is inexplicable from the Jewish context, and implies that "something striking really did happen then".

What it implies is that something striking was believed to have happened then, not that it really did happen. The gospels and Acts show the early Christians in serious conflict with Jewish orthodoxy; and so they would want to have their own day, as well as their own places, of prayer, and would not share either of these with those whom Matthew repeatedly calls "the hypocrites". From similar motives Islam has come to distinguish itself from both Jews and Christians in the same manner. Against the view that it was Jesus's resurrection that made Sunday the day on which Christians met to worship him, Guignebert suggested that it was the reverse that happened, namely that the resurrection was fixed on Sunday because that was the day on which the faithful gathered together. Once for any reason the first day of the week had been selected for that purpose, it would naturally be regarded as "the Lord's day or, if you prefer, the risen Lord's day" because it was the day on which Christians honoured him and his resurrection, not because it was the day on which he had supposedly risen—although it could easily come to be supposed that this "day of the Lord" was in fact the day of his resurrection. In this way, Sunday will have been "the first detail of Holy Week to be fixed, indeed it determined all the others" in this week from Palm Sunday to Easter Sunday, including the day of the death; for "there is scarcely any probability that the fixing of the death of Jesus on the Friday depends on a reminiscence". It depends rather on supposed "prophetic references" about three days in the tomb (1935, pp. 423, 533).

The gospels themselves show a development apropos of how long was spent in the tomb before the Sunday resurrection. In Mark Jesus is represented as thrice foretelling that he will rise "after three days" (8:31; 9:31; 10:34). The other two synoptic gospels pointedly alter this to "on the third day". We may note that, according to Plutarch's *De Iside et Osiride*, the festival of Osiris—a god widely worshipped in the classical world—was spread over three days, his death being mourned on the first, and his resurrection celebrated on the night of the third with the joyful shout "Osiris has been found". Here, as in the Christian case, the original idea was surely that the resurrection followed the death after a short interval, which was later made precise.

Wright urges that the disciples would not have suffered and died for a belief that was not firmly anchored in fact. This is a very weak point. Readiness to die for beliefs without inquiry into the evidence supporting them is by no means uncommon, and is not even restricted to devotees of religious creeds. Nazism and Communism supply plentiful examples, and such readiness testifies to the strength, rather than to the accuracy, of the underlying beliefs. It has been evinced by orthodox

Jews and by Christian heretics, as much as by mainstream Christians (all of whom regarded belief as a virtue and as the key to salvation). In Islam it now occurs on an almost daily basis. If Wright is referring to Jesus's twelve companions, it must be asked how many he supposes to have died as martyrs. In Acts' account of the early Church, only three of the surviving eleven (after Judas's death), namely Peter, James and his brother John, are anything more than names.

Altogether, Wright speaks as though the gospels provide four quite full accounts of the resurrection events. In fact, as we saw, Mark records no actual appearances, and Matthew adds a single appearance to the women fleeing from the tomb and a single appearance to the disciples in Galilee. Wright acknowledges that "Mark's eight verse ending does not . . . bring the risen Jesus on stage"; but he claims that there are "powerful reasons" for proposing that he wrote "a fuller ending that is now lost" (2003, pp. 608, 619). As R.T. France notes in his recent massive commentary on Mark, the majority of current interpreters do not take this view, and although he himself does, he allows that Mark does not in any way suggest that the silence of the women about their experiences at the tomb was only temporary, so that "it must be admitted that, by writing 16:8, Mark seems to have made things difficult for himself" if he intended to add a sequel (2002, pp. 670, 684). As we saw, many exegetes argue that 16:8 is meant to explain why hitherto no one knew about such a tomb, and betrays that the entire episode of the women finding it is inauthentic. Of the three synoptic evangelists only Luke writes in any fullness of the appearances, which he deliberately and pointedly restricts to Jerusalem. There remains the multiple material of the closing chapters of the fourth gospel, and we have seen how difficult it is to defend either their trustworthiness or that of this gospel as a whole.

Matthew has some strange special material of his own in his accounts both of Jesus's death and of his resurrection. All three synoptic gospels allege an unnatural darkening of the sun at his death, and Mark and Matthew declare that the veil of the temple was rent, but Matthew alone supplements these with further miracles which include an earthquake, the splitting of rocks, the opening of graves, and the resurrection of the "saints" occupying them (27:45ff), who, however, did not emerge from their miraculously opened graves until after Jesus's resurrection, when they are said to have entered the city and appeared to many (verse 53). This seems to be a clumsy attempt to harmonize a story of their resurrection at the time of Jesus's death with the tradition, preserved in Acts 26:23, that he was the first to rise (cf. 1 Cor. 15:20, 23). Martin Werner noted that these miraculous signs include clear motifs of an apocalyptic picture of the end of the world. The idea, then, was to suggest that the death of Jesus heralded the last days, in accordance with the expectations expressed in Jewish apocalypses (1957, p. 33). Wright is a little embarrassed by this material. He does not want any "cheap and cheerful rationalistic dismissal" of it, but agrees that it "points towards . . . the theological meaning Matthew is working towards: that with the combined events of Jesus's death and resurrection the new age, for which Israel had been longing, has begun" (2003, pp. 635f).

Since Wright allows that the historical evidence is not in itself absolutely compelling, it is appropriate next to examine the component of his belief in Jesus's resurrection that is not rational in the ordinary sense of the word. He complains that doubters are beholden to an "arrogant rationalism" which fails to acknowledge that there is another and a more profound kind of knowledge than that which results from historical or scientific enquiry. He deplores the "2,000 years of sneering scepticism against the Christian witness", and points out that "post-Enlightenment left-brain rationality alone does not prompt the most important decisions we take in life." He adds that, to understand Jesus's resurrection, we need "a different kind of knowing", a "higher" kind, which "brings history and faith together" and which requires "the whole personal engagement and involvement for which the best shorthand is love" (cf. his 2007 book, p. 84).

For Wright, this different kind of knowing is unique in two respects. First, as we have just seen, it requires "the whole personal engagement of the knower". Second, it immerses itself much more fully in the entity that is being known. Love is "the deepest mode of knowing because it is love that, while completely engaging with the reality that is other than itself, affirms and celebrates that other than self reality. This is the point at which much modernist epistemology breaks down" (2007, p. 85).

What is here claimed is not merely that there is knowledge of different entities, with closer scrutiny and more emotional involvement in some cases than in others. Obviously, our attitudes towards other people carry what the sociologist Andreski calls "a much greater emotional loading" than our attitude towards things, so that we are much more upset when we find that we have misjudged a person or group than when we have to revise our feelings about the nature of some material object (1972, p. 37). Wright is claiming far more than this, namely that there is—in the wording of John Macquarrie, who makes a similar claim—a knowing which "involves the whole person" of the knower, as against the "more detached and observational kind of knowing" to which "positivistic prohibitions" would fain restrict us (Macquarrie 1998, pp. 81f, 87, 97).

To illustrate this supposedly superior form of knowing Wright refers to the appended chapter of the fourth gospel—not, some of us will think, an in any way reliable source. There, the risen Jesus asks Peter: "Do you love me?" Peter replies affirmatively, thus repudiating his earlier denial of Jesus. For Wright, this affirmation of love in the face of the risen Jesus illustrates—I quote from his Roanoke lecture—"the refashioning of how we know things, corresponding to the refashioning of reality in God's new creation", Jesus's resurrection being "the defining central prototypical event of the new creation, the world which is born with Jesus". In this context Wright endorses Wittgenstein's statement that "it is love that believes the resurrection."

It is of course true that many human decisions are not based on "left-brain rationality", but this gives no justification to Wrights's far-reaching psychological theorizing. People act from instinct, from impulse, from custom and habit, and from imitation of others, as much as from reflection. The function of reason is to show us how to obtain what we desire, and the driving force behind the behaviour is still the desire. While the reasoning process guides us towards our goal, the goal must exert some kind of attraction before this process can be brought into play. This was perfectly well understood by philosophers of the Enlightenment who are so often accused of underestimating the efficacy of non-rational factors. Thus Locke says that, were it not for desires or fears, there would be nothing to direct thoughts or prevent them from wandering in endless reverie (*An Essay Concerning Human Understanding*, Book 2, Chapter 7, sections 2–3); and Hume noted that "reason, being cool and disengaged, is no motive to action, and directs only the impulse received from appetite or inclination by showing us the means of attaining happiness or avoiding misery" (*An Inquiry Concerning the Principles of Morals,* section 9, end of Appendix 1). Thinking is a process which requires some motive, and unfortunately the motive can interfere with the results, in that powerful emotions can prompt a minimum of reflection on which action is then based. Hitler believed—'with his whole being' one might say in order to indicate the strength of his conviction—that the salvation of Germany depended on the elimination of the Jews, although he in fact knew next to nothing of the effect of racial character. Unfortunately he was in a position of power which enabled him to act on this belief. In more abstract reasoning emotion is often left with considerable scope, and ideas can become so attenuated as to consist of little more than words with strong emotional colouring. It is difficult to understand in any other way Wright's statement in the Roanoke lecture that Jesus's resurrection is "the centre not only of history but also of epistemology", that is "not only of what we know about the past, but how we know anything at all". Such capacious propositions have not infrequently come from religious persons who regard Christianity as the acme of religion, as when, in 1917, William Temple "declared that, without the doctrine of the Trinity, 'the universe is completely unintelligible'" (Kent 1992, p. 83).

If, as I believe, knowledge is all of a piece, we have to bring all our theories into direct relation with one another, contradictions and incoherence being ruled out. But if there is more than one kind of knowledge, this restriction need not hamper us. The theory that there are independent forms of knowledge, that there is more than one meaningful way of studying the world, and that science is only one of these, is of course a psychological theory, and needs justification. But what we are offered is mostly nothing more than asseveration. Typical in this respect is the Catholic New Testament scholar Luke T. Johnson, who declares that, if Christians live by "the logic" of their "myth vision of reality", they are "able to challenge the intellectual idolatry of the Enlightenment", which demands "the fearful contraction of the mind to what the mind can grasp and control", instead of following "the lead of the imagination", which would enable them to "insist on the superiority of myth to history" (2003, pp. 306, 308).

Wright's position differs from this, for he does not admit to myth in the matter. What he seems to suggest is that, as it is generally admitted that there are "different types of knowing", it is not arbitrary to posit a further and superior type. What he has in mind as the already acknowledged different types are historical knowledge and scientific knowledge. He obviously regards them as independent of each other, and supposes that this gives him some ground for positing a third type, one which includes but transcends them: "Faith in Jesus risen from the dead *transcends but includes* what we call history and what we call science" (2007, p. 83. Wright's italics). But science and history are not in fact independent. History, he says, acquaints us with "the unrepeatable", whereas science studies "the repeatable" (p. 75). I agree that Socrates drank a particular potion of hemlock only once and died only once. The events were not repeated. But we believe that they occurred not only on the basis of a few old documents, but also because it is a scientific fact that hemlock contains a poisonous ingredient that can be extracted and administered with lethal effect. Similarly, there can be no ground for inferring a historical ancient salt lake from the present distribution of the New Red sandstone, with its lack of fossils, its deposits of salt, and its ripple-marked surfaces with reptilian footprints, except on the basis of such generalizations as: fish cannot live in water of a certain degree of salinity; soft sand on the shores of extensive waters is moulded by the waves and often retains traces of the animals that prowl across it; and when waters created by inland drainage dry up, they leave deposits of salt. Altogether, it is only scientific (generalized) knowledge of forces which mould the surface of the Earth that enables the geologist to trace its history back to Cambrian times. The differences between history and science do not make them independent of each other, and so do nothing to justify positing a yet further form of knowledge which "transcends" them both.

Wright tries to illustrate the kind of knowing he stresses so much by appealing, quite unjustly, to the story of doubting Thomas in Chapter 20 of John's gospel. Thomas initially, "like a good historian, wants to see and touch". But when Jesus invites him to touch his body, he "transcends" this kind of knowing, and "passes into a higher and richer one" which brings history and faith together, addressing Jesus as "my lord and my God" (2007, pp. 81f). But there is in fact no 'transcending' here, for Jesus responds by complaining that Thomas reached this faith only "because thou hast seen me"; whereas "blessed are they that have not seen, and yet have believed" (20:29). Thomas does not here transcend empirical knowledge, but is simply made to voice the high Christology of the fourth gospel (cf. above, p. 128). Again, in his comments on the episode with Peter in the following chapter of John, we find Wright saying that the love he distinguishes as shorthand for the superior kind of knowing is "love in the full Johannine sense of agape" (p. 84). But we saw above (p. 50) that Johannine love means loving other Johannine Christians, and that those outside this circle are described in the harshest terms.

The rhetorical elements in Wright's two lectures are present also in his books, as when he asks: "What if the resurrection . . . should turn out to be, in the twenty-first century as in the first, the most socially, culturally, and politically explosive force imaginable, blasting its way through the sealed tombs and locked doors of modern epistemology?" It has in fact, he claims, made the world "a different place", and those who believe in it are "committed to living in this different world, this newly envisioned universe of discourse, imagination and action" (2003, pp. 713f). In the 2007 book he reiterates this designation of the resurrection as "the defining event of the *new* creation, the world which is being born with Jesus" (p. 84). In the penultimate chapter he rises to the following peroration:

> In the resurrection one is given the beginning of a new knowing, a new epistemology, a new coming-to-speech, the Word born afresh after the death of all human knowing and speech, all human hope and love, after the silent rest of the seventh-day sabbatical in the tomb. (pp. 252f)

And here as elsewhere, he deplores the "arrogant rationalism" of the Enlightenment, and its failure to recognize that "love is the deepest mode of knowing", which requires "the refashioning of epistemology" (pp. 81, 84f).

Against all this, I would note that it has long been recognized that love has its roots—parenthood, sex, friendship—in the animal world, and I see no reason to believe that its human manifestations require any major epistemological reorientation.

In his very substantial 2005 book on the resurrection, Dale C. Allison Jr. is severely critical of Wright, and "remains unconvinced . . . that his apologetical moves really amount to evidence that demands the verdict he so relentlessly summons us to return" (p. 347). Among his criticisms, Allison makes the not irrelevant point that Wright is predisposed to accept that Jesus was raised because of his overall very positive assessment of Jesus and his ministry. Those who maintain that we know very little about him, or who find him to be "a profoundly ambiguous character", will not so readily conduct their reasoning "with the implicit, large, and controverted assumption that Jesus is someone who *should* have been raised from the dead" (p. 349).

Allison's own conclusion is that, "when the mundane historical work is done, the results are disappointingly scanty, and severely circumscribed" (p. 350). But he ends with an appeal to emotion, saying that "religious or theological warrant need not be empirical warrant or strictly historical warrant" (p. 342), for "true religion . . . involves realms of human experience and conviction that cannot depend on or be undone by the sorts of historical doubts" raised by the New Testament evidence: "All I have to do is to look up at the night sky or look into the face of my neighbour, and I know that there is more to life and faith than this" (p. 352).

Allison's account reveals one reason why belief in Jesus's quite literal resurrection remains, as he puts it, "congenial" to him as to many Christians, namely because this resurrection constitutes an initial indication, indeed promise, that all the dead will in fact rise. (Cf. 1 Cor. 15:20; Christ has been raised as "the first fruits of them that are asleep"); and he finds this idea, that there will be a life beyond this one, essential if one is to continue to believe in a good God. He adduces a number of theologians who have observed that, for the great majority of mankind, life is irredeemably bleak, and who argue that "the heartbreaks and horrors and injustices of this age cannot be squared with the doctrine of a consoling Providence . . . unless there is something more than death and extinction." Otherwise, God must be thought of as treating so many of his creatures like garbage, casting them into nothingness without anything good ever happening to them (pp. 217f). For John Polkinghorne, who resigned his Cambridge chair in theoretical physics in order to become an ordained minister of the Church of England, one does not even need this premiss, that the human condition is so often wretched, to reach a reassuring conclusion about divine intentions. For him it is simply because God is steadfast in his love for his creation that he has shown, by resurrecting Jesus, that he intends to give it and us a destiny beyond death. In this sense, he says, Jesus's resurrection is "the beginning of the vindication of God" (1992, p. 89. Cf. below, p. 270, for a similar argument by Dunn).

How difficult it is to envisage a plausible survival after death is well illustrated by Polkinghorne himself elsewhere (2002, pp. 43–55). He points out that, since we now know the great extent to which our psychological processes are bound up with our bodily physiology, we can no longer think of the soul in the manner of Plato or Descartes as a separate spiritual entity which, at the death of the body, can float off to an independent existence. Instead of speaking of my 'soul' in that traditional sense, we must understand this word to refer to "the real me", "the complex, dynamic information-bearing pattern in which the matter of our bodies at any one time is organized." This pattern will be dissolved at my death as my body decays. Nevertheless, if I am to achieve immortality, the immortal me must bear some resemblance to, and have some continuity with, the me that exists now, and not be an entirely different entity having the same name. Hence we may tentatively suppose that, at my death, the everlastingly faithful God will hold the pattern that is me "perfectly preserved in the divine memory, and then re-embody it in the ultimate divine eschatological act of resurrection at the last day." In the interval between my death and my resurrection, my 'soul' will, then, exist in a disembodied intermediate state, "held in the divine memory", and may even experience some "redemptive transformation" in that state because of its "closer contact and interaction with the reality of God". In sum, Polkinghorne is saying that the human soul consists in an "information-bearing pattern" that can be extracted from our present earthly bodies and reinstated in a further resurrected body, which of course will not be of perishable flesh and blood, but more like the body of the glorified Jesus, whose resurrection is "the foretaste and guarantee" of what we may expect not only for ourselves, but for all creation, which will be similarly renewed at the eschaton—not as a second, totally new creation *ex nihilo,* but as "the redeemed transformation of the old creation", just as my resurrected self will have some continuity with my present self. Polkinghorne observes that if the present natural laws continue to operate indefinitely, the world will be destroyed after some billions of years. But "reflections on the faithfulness of the Creator" can lead us to believe that he is not bound to maintain natural laws unchanged, and will not only ultimately reinstate human personhood, but will do so within the transformed material creation, for it is not only human beings that really concern God forever: "There is a destiny for *matter* as well as for men and women."

Polkinghorne allows that there is "an element of speculation" in all this, but denies that it is "an exercise in fantasy". He concludes:

> I believe that scientific insight and theological understanding can be combined to enable us to embrace a credible hope . . . , a hope whose substance has already been manifested in the resurrection of our Lord Jesus Christ and whose reliability is founded on the faithfulness of the God of Abraham, Isaac and Jacob.

The final seven words of this quotation are from those of God to Moses in the burning bush, and are quoted by Jesus when he rebukes the Sadducees who denied that the dead would rise: "I am the God of Abraham, and the God of Isaac and the God of Jacob. He is not the God of the dead, but of the living" (Mk. 12:26f and parallels). They are in turn quoted in the 1995 Report of the Doctrine Commission of the General Synod of the Church of England, entitled *The Mystery of Salvation,* published by Church House. It shows that views like those of Polkinghorne are more widespread than one might expect. Like him, it argues that "if today we are to continue to use language about the soul, we may perhaps best understand it as the 'information-bearing pattern' of the body"—'pattern' being an appropriate word because the essence of a pattern is "the web of relationships in which the parts are organised" (pp. 12, 191). The Report goes on—again in agreement with Polkinghorne—to state that, although death "dissolves the embodiment of that pattern", the "person whose that pattern is is 'remembered' by God, who in love holds that unique being in his care." And for "some" Christians this in itself adequately characterizes their sharing in the life of heaven, while "others" insist that more is involved, namely "an appropriate bodiliness" (p. 191)—presumably the kind of re-embodiment suggested by Polkinghorne.

Wright has some ground in common with all this—unsurprisingly, as he, with Polkinghorne, is one of the clergy who authored the Report from which I have just quoted. He offers the following paraphrase as not "too much of a caricature" of Polkinghorne's view: "God will download our software into his hardware until the time when he gives us new hardware to run the software again" (2007, p. 175). Wright likes to speak not of 'life after death', but rather of "life *after* life after death" (p. 163), on the ground that the dead are not really lifeless, but in a state of "restful happiness" (p. 183). When Christ returns to Earth, they will be raised, and both they and those who had not yet died will have their bodies transformed as he renews the whole of creation in "the newly embodied life *after* 'life after death'" (p. 210), "no longer subject to sickness, injury, decay and death" (pp. 171f). Jesus "will be personally present" as "the agent and model" of the transformation which "Easter has foreshadowed" (p. 148). He will not abolish the present creation and translate the redeemed ones to somewhere in the sky, but will come as judge to "set the world right once and for all" (p. 150). This "must necessarily involve the elimination of all that distorts God's good and lovely creation" (p. 192). But those who have persistently refused to turn from wickedness will not be tortured. They will continue to exist, but "as creatures that have ceased to bear the divine image at all" (p. 195). The redeemed ones, for their part, will not be somewhere in the sky, bored stiff by eternally singing God's praises, or "lounging around playing harps". In the redeemed creation "there will be work to do, and we shall relish doing it" (p.173).

Wright adduces numerous texts in order to establish that this is in accordance with New Testament teaching. He is well aware that many Christians, laymen and clergy, in mainstream and in other churches, will not agree.

Wright's conviction—it may fairly be called an obsession—that Jesus's resurrection is of fundamental significance to the modern world has long been well represented in theology. Karl Barth, whose stance against liberal theology Wright greatly admires, voiced it in 1941, when he declared that "the enterprise of Adolf Hitler . . . is the enterprise of an evil spirit, which is apparently allowed its freedom for a time in order to test our faith in the resurrection of Jesus Christ" (quoted from Barth's *A Letter to Great Britain from Switzerland* by Alan Wilkinson, 1986, p. 202). Such writing testifies indeed to the writer's courage, and hence to the strength of his conviction. Nazi forces could easily have occupied

Switzerland in 1941, and were expected to launch such an attack. But it also requires us to believe that the 'God of love' was allowing an 'enterprise' involving the killing of millions in order to put the resilience of a particular Christian belief to the test. Barth was no doubt beholden to biblical ideas (prominent, for instance, in the book of Job) that God inflicts suffering as a test of faith. He added that the war should be fought purely "in the name of Jesus Christ", with no thought of the problems of post-war reconstruction; for the kingdom of Christ will come without our assistance.

Although Barth is a repulsively extreme case, the resurrection remains central in Christian thinking, and the theologian J.G. Crossley is surely correct to suggest that Wright owes much of his publishing success to his saying what is congenial to "a Christian-dominated scholarly community." It is this, says Crossley, that has "allowed his views of the bodily resurrection to be published as a major book in the study of Christian origins and to gain praise from some of the most famous scholars in the field", who, for all their reservations, do not impugn his views on this matter (2006, pp. 25f). Crossley illustrates this by quoting from James Dunn's review which, although critical, finishes .with the words: "But in the end what Christian heart could fail to rejoice at such a trenchant defence of Christianity's central claim regarding Jesus?"

The latest book I have seen on the resurrection—by the Jewish Hungarian-born scholar Geza Vermes ("the greatest Jesus scholar of his generation" according to the *Sunday Telegraph,* as quoted on the cover of his book)—gives Wright but a single passing reference as representing the opposite extreme to the scepticism of Strauss (2008, p. 104). Vermes himself finds that "not even a credulous non-believer is likely to be persuaded" by the New Testament stories of the empty tomb and the visions, which do not satisfy "the minimum requirements of a legal or scientific enquiry." If, then, we "cannot offer an explanation for the physical resurrection of Jesus", we can at least do so for the birth and survival of Christianity, in that he rose "in the hearts of his disciples". Their conviction of "the spiritual presence of the living Jesus accounts for the resurgence of the Jesus movement after the crucifixion" (pp. 142, 149, 152).

v. Recent Reinterpreters of the Traditional Doctrine

The way in which a sacred text is defended can often be seen to pass through three stages which are familiar to students of mythology, and which are exemplified, for instance, in the history of interpretations of

Homer (summarized by Hatch, 1895, pp. 51–60). First, his verses were taken for inspired utterances of undying wisdom. But as some of them, if taken as they stood, were morally unacceptable, it began to be said that, on balance, what is good predominates over what is evil. When this defence proved insufficient, hidden meanings were found underlying their plain statements. It is only when a story seems incompatible with ideas or principles of the commentators, and yet is part of a sacred or semi-sacred tradition which cannot simply be discarded, that there is any need of such interpretation. It is the last resource of those still interested in keeping alive the religious traditions.

This third stage of interpretation is much in evidence in current Christian statements about the resurrection. I give examples in my 2004 book of those who, for instance, regard it as "poetic symbol" of something or other, often of love. Such a position is no novelty: William Temple, then Archbishop of York, wrote in 1937 that, while he himself accepted "as historical facts" both Jesus's virgin birth and his resurrection, he nevertheless "fully recognise[d] the position of those who sincerely affirm the reality of Our Lord's Incarnation without accepting one or both of these events as actual historical occurrences" and who instead regard the records as "parables" rather than history, as "a presentation of spiritual truth in narrative form" (quoted in Kent 1992, p. 181). What has happened since 1937 is that such reinterpretation has both proliferated and become so vague that Archbishop Carnley has been moved to complain of the "very significant number of theologians who are content to treat the resurrection with a degree of ambivalence or lack of candour which makes it somewhat difficult to discern any clear outline of the exact position that they espouse" (1987, p. 12). The breadth of the spectrum of opinion on the matter is evident in Barton and Stanton's 1994 symposium entitled *The Resurrection,* with nineteen contributors. In the view of one of them (Michael Goulder, a theologian but not a theist), "it would be helpful if Christian scholars would . . . tell their churches that the tale of the resurrection of Jesus has no dependable basis, and is not worthy of serious consideration." The reviewer of this symposium in *Theology* (Volume 98, 1995, p. 305) has hinted that it would be nice if some of the other eighteen were to indicate with equal clarity where they stand, "for it is not always easy to know".

What this symposium does make clear is that today many Christian scholars have come to admit that the New Testament accounts cannot be reconciled with each other; nor is it felt allowable to play one of them off against the others (such as Paul's against those of the gospels, or Mark's against the revision and expansion of it by Matthew or Luke).

Robert Morgan finds this "a dangerous game in which Christian belief is eroded". Hence some other basis than these accounts must be sought if belief in the resurrection is to be sustained. Accordingly, some of the contributors, instead of reinterpreting the texts, either frankly designate God's vindication of Jesus in the resurrection as "a mystery, like God's identification with Jesus in the incarnation" (Robert Morgan, p.12 of his contribution); "a divine act" that is "not intelligible, imaginable", or "reproducible" in narrative form, as other events are (Francis Watson, p. 101 of the article he contributes); or they regard it as a justified inference from some doctrinal proposition—what Stephen Barton calls reading the gospel accounts "in the light of a resurrection hermeneutic" (p. 54). In this sense, Graham Stanton finds that, whether the disciples experienced genuine visions or mere hallucinations "can be settled only on the basis of wider considerations that are theological, rather than historical or psychological" (pp. 82f). Stanton's predecessor at Cambridge, C.F.D. Moule, did not contribute to this symposium, but illustrated what this can mean by claiming that Jesus's "unique degree of unity with the will of God" effected his resurrection; "for it seems consistent with all we know of God" that "perfect goodness of character cannot be held by death" (1965a, p. 17). Pheme Perkins likewise thinks that an inference from doctrine is required: "Only those who are convinced that a special revelation of God occurred in the life and teaching of Jesus of Nazareth can be persuaded that God raised Jesus of Nazareth from the dead" (1994, p. 442).

Returning to Barton and Stanton's 1994 symposium, we find Maurice Wiles sensibly noting that, although "doctrinal reasons" for belief in Jesus's resurrection have been alleged because of "the indecisiveness of the historical evidence" and its "many legendary characteristics", we need nevertheless "to be very wary of doctrinal arguments that claim to determine for us facts for which we otherwise lack sufficient evidence"; for doctrinal propositions "have their own distinctive kind of inconclusiveness" (pp .118–120). But he himself can finally do no more than "suggest" that "various lines of constructive possibility for a theological treatment of resurrection still lie open" (p. 125). One might add that 'doctrinal reasons' are no more than expressions of theological or religious needs, and these cannot answer historical questions.

While, then, apologists sometimes try to vindicate belief in Jesus's resurrection by appealing to some doctrinal premiss, they also commonly complain that rejection of this belief is often itself based on doctrine, as an inference from the anti-religious premiss that "the idea of miracle is empty and indefensible". If, says Rowan Williams, "we don't take this for granted, we may be less inclined to be completely sceptical" (2007, pp. 47f). But as he well knows, scepticism concerning both the resurrection and the virgin birth (which, he complains, is often "written off" in the same way, p.75) has a much stronger basis than this (cf. above, apropos of Strauss, pp. 66f). Williams himself—inevitably as theologian—is much beholden to inferences from doctrines as the basis for his convictions; as when he declares that, notwithstanding "contradictions of detail", the gospels "tell us what God wants us to know"; and that "ultimately, Christians believe in eternal life not because they believe something about themselves as human (that they have an immortal element in them)", nor because of psychical or other "evidence for survival", but "because they believe in something about God", namely that God is "trustworthy", totally committed to what he has made and loved and so "will not let us go even on the far side of death" (pp. 125, 143f).

With this we are back to the kind of argument we met from Allison, Polkinghorne, and others in the previous section of this chapter. But some of my quotations have illustrated the kind of vagueness in theological statements of which Archbishop Carnley complained. An even better illustration is provided by the arguments of David Jenkins, formerly bishop of Durham. For him, the "pictorial" or "mythological" language of the New Testament is such that "Jesus Christ points decisively to ultimate reality" (1976, pp. 87, 121; 1967, p. 22). Elsewhere—in a brief 1986 article—he says that "the ultimate reality" is God, further defined as "the creative possibilities within all present realities", meaning possibilities of improving present situations; and also as "the promise of a final reconciliation between facts (what is) and value (what is worthwhile)", in other words the assurance that such improvements can be achieved. It is hard to see how inferences can be drawn from the premisses that God is a reality, a possibility, and an assurance—"a presence who is also an absence and a promise". Jenkins seems fascinated by the word 'possibility', for it occurs also, apropos of the resurrection, in his statement that "a series of experiences" convinced apostles that, after Jesus's death and burial, "the very life and power and purpose and personality which was in him was actually continuing both in the sphere of God and in the sphere of history, so that he was a risen and living presence and possibility."[9] This is what a critic has called the bishop's "sophisticated reinterpretation of the resurrection" (M.J. Harris 1985, p. 31). The unsophisticated view pictures Jesus as coming to life in his tomb, emerging from it, and then conversing with his friends. But as the New Testament accounts include contradictions, and are unsubstantiated by external evidence, and as we are today in any case disinclined to believe that anyone can return to life after death, many apologists prefer to describe the supposed events in words which suggest no such concrete images. This is easily done, as we habitually represent many realities in our minds in this way. We may speak, for instance, of 'scientific progress', 'world opinion' or 'juvenile crime', and may well not have specific images in mind. But if error is to be avoided, there must be a continual return to concrete ideas as a check on any process of reasoning with such words.[10]

If, however, it is desired to make a questionable proposition look plausible, then this conversion of the words into more concrete conceptions must be discouraged. This is not difficult, as the task of conversion is too laborious to be undertaken readily, even if it is recognized as advisable. Hence the many 'sophisticated' interpretations of the proposition 'Jesus rose from the dead'.

It is equally unhelpful to regard the resurrection, with Bultmann, as not a historical event, but nevertheless an important one (cf. above, p. 74, and also below, pp. 297f, for Dunn's criticism of Bultmann's "demythologizing" of the resurrection). All such vague talk results from an irresistible tendency, often encouraged by a university education in the humanities, to confuse words and ideas, so that people come to suppose that they are thinking, when really they are doing no more than making up sentences. In normal communication there is never any doubt as to the distinction between the *word* 'cow', an *idea* of a cow, and the *real* cow. By an 'idea', I mean some kind of mental representation of some thing or process or set of things which can be profitably manipulated and experimented with in the imagination, just as real things and processes can be manipulated with the aid of our hands and eyes. But in philosophical and theological discussions there is sometimes little sign of such ideas. The writers seem to suppose that a word is an idea, that the manipulation of words in the imagination is as useful as the manipulation of genuine ideas. Their emotions become linked to these words, and they suppose that the words denote things which really exist. The impossibility of representing these things by any real ideas suggests their 'transcendent' character.

The emotional element is often decisive. Marcus Borg implies as much when he finds that "Christianity seems clearly to 'work'" as "a means or vehicle by which people experience 'the sacred'"; it has an "ability to mediate the sacred" quite independently of "the historical accuracy of any of its claims" (1994, pp. 193, 199n30). In other words: the sense of exaltation generated by Christian beliefs is independent of any historical basis they might have. Hence Borg is not disturbed to note that today "most Jesus scholars do not think Jesus was born of a virgin, or that he ascended into heaven in a visible way, or that there is a literal second coming." He does not mean that this is to deny the resurrection—only to make it "not a historical event in the ordinary sense of the word" (pp. 183, 196n2).

The sociologist Steve Bruce, surveying the overall present-day British religious scene, sees "an increasingly secular people gradually losing faith in the specific teachings of the Christian tradition, but retaining a fondness for vague religious affirmations" (1995, p. 51). Similar vagueness is widespread in other subjects too: freedom of ideas and of expression is all too often degraded into licence to talk at random and make phrases. Words are a common substitute in thought for things, especially for thoughts of complicated things; and as they have no natural affinity with the things they denote, they are most unreliable representatives. The fact that many vast and complex things can be just as easily represented in our thoughts by means of short words as the most simple concrete object is more often a source of error than an aid to the imagination. In the concrete branches of science, words and phrases are kept in constant touch with real things, so that nonsense is excluded or easily detected. But in other subjects—in, for instance, literary criticism, and indeed in the humanities generally—what is propounded sometimes has no contact with reality and can serve only to be verbally repeated in various combinations.

A complete contrast to any such meanderings was the outspokenness of Strauss in his final book of 1872, where he found it greatly to Christianity's discredit that it is based so fundamentally on the resurrection. Jesus, he says, could have done and taught what he liked, it would all, however sublime, have been forgotten but for this "delusion about his resurrection" (1997, Volume 1, pp. 83). He finds that Christianity survives among educated nations only by dint of the corrections which secular reasoning has introduced into it (p. 73). He also asks with what right we refuse to acknowledge the obvious facts of death by positing the persistence of a part of our being of which there is, in any case, no ascertainable trace (pp. 143f). Strauss insists on the physical basis of mind—mental capacities develop and decline with the body (p. 150). He does not find it humiliating to be related to the gorilla (cf. Volume 2, pp. 4f), and observes that the fossil record gives strong support to Darwin's theory, from which man cannot be arbitrarily exempted. All this suggests that Strauss thought that the dogmas of the church would not survive the discoveries of the nineteenth century. But he was mistaken, and religion was destined to take on a new lease of life in the twentieth.

Like many others, Hans Frei does not much like this final book by Strauss. But he does allow that it displays "that stubborn and courageous honesty which had been his life-long hall mark", and also that it "can still serve as an enduring warning to the 'hermeneutical' arts of those theologians who invariably find a modern 'understanding' ready to hand with which to 'interpret' Christianity so that it is guaranteed *a priori* against every threat that it might be an anachronistic superannuated outlook" (1985, p. 225).

It is presumably because belief in Jesus's resurrection is so central to Christian doctrine and yet so hard to justify that the appetite for discussion of it continues to be well-nigh insatiable. A 2006 SPCK symposium on the subject, edited by R.B. Stewart, is devoted mainly to dialogue between N.T. Wright and J.D. Crossan who, the editor tells us (p. 74), understands Jesus's resurrection as a metaphor for his continued presence in the church, and who holds that there was no tomb, since Jesus was never properly buried. One contributor (Gary R. Habermas) records that he has tracked "well over two thousand scholarly publications on the resurrection", which have appeared since 1975 in German, French, and English, written by "a wide range of critical scholars" (p. 78). But altogether, far more continues to be written on all aspects of the New Testament than can be profitably read, and the endless discussion of the resurrection is but an extreme case of a more general phenomenon that has occasioned some malaise even among theologians. In a 1975 Festschrift for Christopher Evans, U. Simon "questioned whether the endless production of New Testament commentaries and related monographs has added anything substantial to our knowledge of Jesus. . . . There is certainly something ridiculous in the fact that a fairly small collection of writings evokes so much learned comment with so little result." In the same symposium Maurice Wiles asked, in similar vein: "Do not many New Testament interpreters find themselves more or less forced into putting forward far-fetched interpretations in the desperate hope of saying something new?" (in Morna Hooker et al. 1975, pp. 116, 162). And Ernst Haenchen shook his head sadly at the way in which interpretations of the Passion were becoming "ever bolder and ever more surprising" (1980, p. 526). The New Testament is indeed a small collection, not an inexhaustible source for meaningful originality.

5

The Gospel of Mark: History or Dogma?

i. William Wrede's Epoch-Making Book

a. The Role of the Disciples

William (sic) Wrede, born in the district of Hannover and a student at Leipzig and Göttingen, was from 1893 until his death Professor of New Testament at Breslau. At least his name is still familiar from Albert Schweitzer's famous *Von Reimarus zu Wrede,* a history of life-of-Jesus research published in the very year of Wrede's premature death (1906), and known in the English-speaking world from the catching title of its translation, *The Quest of the Historical Jesus.* Here Schweitzer, although radical enough himself, stamps Wrede as the exponent of extreme scepticism. Wrede has certainly not endeared himself to traditionally-minded theologians. "Indistinguishable from the shallowest of freethinkers" was the 1939 verdict of one of them, quoted by Georg Strecker, a New Testament scholar appreciative of Wrede's work (1960, p. 67). Wrede himself pleaded, in his own defence, that we cannot change the gospels, but must take them as they are. He would have been devoid of sympathy with present-day efforts to turn awkward doctrines in them into vague and barely intelligible philosophemes. His standpoint was: "Blessed are the unpretentious in speech, for they shall be understood" (1907, p. 25). The Finnish New Testament scholar Heikki Räisänen finds him an outstanding representative of the healthy tradition of "calling a spade a spade" (1987, p. 11).

When Strauss argued that much in the canonical gospels is unacceptable as history, his critics tried to discredit him by attacking his belief that Matthew was the oldest of them. Once that position had been assigned to Mark (which Matthew and Luke had adapted and expanded), it was held that Mark can be read as a straightforward and reliable account, and that Strauss's thesis that all the gospels are myth-ridden falls to the ground. It was to this position that Wrede's 1901 book on *The Messianic Secret in the Gospels* constituted a reply. Räisänen, who covers the same ground in his 1990 book (to which I am deeply indebted), holds that modern Markan study begins with Wrede's book, and "no student of the gospels can bypass it" (p. 38).

Wrede begins from the position that a document, even a canonical one, alleging that something happened is not decisive evidence that it did happen, and that it is too often forgotten that all the gospels were written by Christians who could look at the life of Jesus only with the eyes of their own time, and who described it on the basis of what was believed in the Christian communities for which they wrote, with the needs of those communities in mind. Hence we must first ask "what the narrator in his own time intended to say to his readers" before we can address the task of reconstructing the life of Jesus from the texts (Here and subsequently I quote the English translation, 1971, pp. 5f). But these provide only the barest of frameworks, a deal of which is widely admitted to be incredible:

> No critical theologian believes Mark's report on the baptism of Jesus, the raising of Jairus's daughter, the miraculous feedings, the walking of Jesus on the water, the transfiguration, or the conversation of the angel with the women at the tomb, in the sense in which he records them. If the theologian sees facts *behind* such information, he is nevertheless compelled to grant that they have undergone a very substantial transformation and distortion, whether in the mind of Mark or otherwise. (pp. 9f)

In consequence, many a Markan commentary "suffers from psychological 'suppositionitis' which amounts to a sort of historical guesswork", the result of which is a proliferation of interpretations to suit every taste (p. 6). Things have perhaps not, in this respect, changed a great deal since 1901. At any rate, the New Testament scholar E.P. Sanders could still say, in 1985, that it is "amazing" that so many of his colleagues "write books about Jesus in which they discover that he agrees with their own version of Christianity" (p. 330).

Räisänen follows Wrede by illustrating the problems involved in taking Mark's account of the ministry as history. At 4:11–12 disciples are said to have been given the secret or "mystery" of the kingdom of God— that is, God's plan of salvation through Jesus (cf. Coloss. 2:2f: Christ is "the mystery of God")—in contrast to outsiders, who are not meant to understand Jesus's teaching and whom he does not want to save (I shall return to this strange passage). But Jesus at once goes on to complain of their incomprehension (4:13), and has to give them additional instruction (4:14–20, 34). Nevertheless, they still lack faith (4:40) and do not understand who he is (4:41). He sends them out to exorcise (6:7), and on their mission they not only do this, but also preach a doctrine of repentance, cure the sick, and teach (6:12–13, 30). When they return, they still do not understand what they can expect of him (6:35–37) and do not understand his feeding of the five thousand because their hearts were "hardened" (6:52). (Commentators explain that, for the ancients, the heart was the seat of understanding and that the Greek noun *pōrōsis* [petrification] and the corresponding verb [used here] came to mean 'obtuseness', 'intellectual blindness': cf. NEB: "their minds were closed".) The situation here is that "straightway" after the feeding they are in difficulty, rowing on the lake against a strong wind. He sees their distress, walks on the water towards them, tells them not to be afraid and enters their boat, whereupon "the wind ceased: and they were sore amazed in themselves; for they understood not concerning the loaves." Wrede commented (p. 104): this can only mean that, in spite of that earlier incident, they still had not noticed that he possessed miraculous powers—even though, according to the text, they had, on that earlier occasion, witnessed that with only five loaves and two fishes they had sated the hunger of five thousand, and had then collected twelve baskets of left-overs. Matthew realized that such obtuseness is not to be believed, and so the parallel passage in his gospel to Mk. 6:52 makes them acknowledge Jesus as "truly the Son of God" (14:33). Matthew did not notice that this emendation makes Peter's later 'confession' that Jesus is "the Son of the living God" no longer the unexpected stroke of divinely inspired genius that Jesus there declares it to be (Mt. 16:16–18). In this instance as so often, adapting a document so as to dispose of one problem simply creates another.

In Mark's next chapter Jesus declares that "there is nothing from without the man that going into him can defile him". The disciples fail to realize that he is thereby declaring all foods to be clean and are rebuked for their dullness (7:18–19). Then, although they have already been present at the miraculous feeding of the five thousand, they have no idea how he will be able to supply food to another crowd in a desert place (8:4). Even when he then repeats the miracle, they still do not understand him and are accordingly rebuked (8:17, 21). Räisänen asks, appositely: "What on earth did these simpletons preach and teach when Jesus sent them out (Chapter 6)?" (1990, p. 18). Wrede's comment is: "Disciples of the kind presented to us here by Mark are not real figures—disciples who never become any wiser about Jesus after all the wonderful things they see about him—confidants who have no confidence in him and who stand over against him fearfully as before an uncanny enigma" (p. 103).

How thoroughly stupid Mark will have the disciples be is illustrated when Jesus tells them, at a time when they are short of bread, to "beware of the leaven of the Pharisees and the leaven of Herod" (8:14f). They think he is warning them not to fetch leaven for bread from these people, for they reply: "We have no bread" (Cf. the parallel passage in Matthew where it is said that it took a little time before they realized that Jesus was not referring to "the leaven of bread", 16:12). The implication of the passage is that they suppose Jesus to be telling them to bake or buy bread, but in either case to beware of Pharisaic or Herodian attempts to poison it. Even some recent commentators can note that this is so, with barely a hint that it is ridiculous of Mark to impute such thinking to the disciples (as when Moule says that they "solemnly take Jesus's proverbial words literally, thinking, since they have forgotten to bring sandwiches, that they are being warned against accepting poisoned food from others": 1965b, p. 62). Jesus interprets their reply ("We have no bread") as implying that, although they have witnessed the two miraculous feedings, they do not trust him to supply bread. He rebukes them for this, and then catechizes them:

> When I brake the five loaves among the five thousand, how many baskets (*kophinous*) full of broken pieces took ye up? They say unto him, Twelve. And when the seven among the four thousand, how many basketfuls (*spuridōn*) of broken pieces took ye up? And they say unto him, Seven. And he said unto them, Do ye not yet understand? (8:19–21)

All but the most conservative commentators agree that this conversation could not have taken place. That Mark has earlier recorded two miraculous feedings, with much the same vocabulary and sequence of events in each case, is usually attributed to the existence, before he wrote, of a tradition of one such feeding in slightly different written forms, which he took to refer to different incidents (cf. above, p. 65). If so, then Jesus's words here referring to two incidents cannot be authentic. That the words are Markan composition is obvious from the fact that they presuppose the Markan written form of both incidents: the baskets were *kophinoi* at 6:43 and *spurides* at 8:8, and the same distinction is made here at 8:19–21. Wrede not only notes this, but is particularly scathing about the whole pericope of which these three verses form the conclusion: in their hardness of heart the disciples have forgotten both miraculous feedings completely, yet they are represented as being able to recall them so as to answer Jesus's questions accurately. And as for their supposing that he is telling them not to fetch leaven from Herod, how is it, Wrede asks, that nobody seems to notice that such nonsense can be read in our oldest gospel? (pp. 104–05). He later answers this his own question by noting the way in which long-standing honoured traditions can dull critical sensitivity: "If Mark's gospel were to come to light for the first time today from some tomb . . . many of the features belonging to it would be recognized without the slightest difficulty" (p. 148). Familiarity with our own traditions makes them seem reasonable, or at any rate inhibits the instant disbelief with which we respond to doctrines not our own.

If we read this Markan pericope without demurring, Matthew and Luke were more circumspect. Matthew makes Jesus's words about leaven a warning against false teaching, and as Herod had no teaching, the disciples finally understand Jesus to be telling them to "beware of the teaching of the Pharisees *and Sadducees*" (Mt. 16:12). Luke deletes the whole conversation about bread and, in a different context, interprets "the leaven of the Pharisees" as "hypocrisy" (Lk. 12:1).

Returning to Mark, we find that at 8:29 Peter recognizes Jesus as "the Christ". How he achieved this insight after all the previous incomprehension is not explained. Jesus then tells his disciples that "the Son of man [he himself] must suffer many things and be rejected by the elders and the chief priests and the scribes, and be killed and after three days rise again". This teaching is given quite "openly" or "plainly" to the disciples (8:32). Peter, however, does not accept that these events must happen, rebukes Jesus for saying that they must, and is in turn rebuked by him. Jesus repeats his teaching at 9:31, but the disciples "understood not the saying". Wrede finds this very strange (p. 94). They have already heard him say the same thing "openly", and Peter then understood it sufficiently to protest against it. Matthew and Luke sensed the difficulty; for Matthew replaces "they understood not the saying" with "they were exceeding sorry" (Mt. 17:23); and although Luke retains their incomprehension, he attributes it to divine intention: "They understood not the saying and it was concealed from them, that they should not perceive it" (Lk. 9:45).

At Mk. 10:32–34 Jesus foretells his Passion and resurrection for a third time, and in even greater detail:

> And he took again the twelve, and began to tell them the things that were to happen unto him, saying, Behold, we go up to Jerusalem; and the Son of

man shall be delivered unto the *chief priests and the scribes: and they shall condemn him to death and shall deliver him unto the* Gentiles: and they shall mock him, and shall spit upon him, and shall scourge him, and shall kill him; and after three days he shall rise again (The italicized words are omitted in the Lucan parallel, Lk. 18:31–34).

This time Mark does not say that the disciples either protested or failed to understand—for the good reason that the following pericope (where the sons of Zebedee declare themselves able to drink the cup which Jesus will drink, 10:35–45) presupposes that they had understood. Only Luke, who omits this incident with the Zebedees, has a statement about the disciples' incomprehension (18:34) analogous to the previous cases.

Wrede insists that all three of these predictions of the Passion and resurrection are unhistorical. The detail, particularly in the third of them, corresponding so precisely to subsequent events, makes them look like later Christian creations, for which there was an obvious motive: If Jesus died to save us, any idea that he might have been surprised by his death had to be repelled, and so the tradition about his life had to be "corrected" so as to include his foreknowledge of his death, just as it had to be corrected in other ways, for example by making him foretell that the Christian community would be persecuted (pp. 88–89). Luke goes so far as to correct Mark so as to bring this third Passion prediction into line with his own account of the Passion, where the Sanhedrin does not condemn Jesus, but sends him on to Pilate without first passing any sentence: so he makes Jesus foretell only that "the Son of man shall be delivered up unto the Gentiles" (18:32), thus omitting Mark's references to the Jewish authorities (italicized in the Markan passage quoted above).

Wrede (pp. 82ff) finds a further indication that the predictions are unhistorical in the later behaviour of the disciples. They abandon Jesus at his arrest (Mk. 14:50) and (in the appendix to Mark's final chapter) do not believe the women's report of his resurrection (16: 11–13). Luke represents two of them as totally unprepared for Jesus's death (24:20–21) and the eleven as incredulous when told of his resurrection (24:11). It really does not look as though he had prepared them by the "plain" speaking ascribed to him at Mk.8:31 which Peter understood well enough to protest against, nor by the detailed forecast of 10:32–34, which is perfectly clear and where it is not said that they failed to understand. In sum, the predictions present two problems (additionally to ascribing to Jesus detailed foreknowledge in harmony with the different requirements of different Passion narratives): first, it is unintelligible that the disciples do not understand such plain language; and second, their failure to understand is not consistently alleged, yet their later behaviour implies that they were completely taken by surprise by what subsequently happened. Three of them (Peter, James, and John) had seen Jesus in heavenly glory conversing with Elijah and Moses at his transfiguration, and had heard the heavenly voice calling him "my beloved Son" (9:2–7). Yet they were reduced to despair at his arrest and crucifixion.

Wrede insists that Mark was not out to denigrate the disciples (p. 106). In his view, Mark thought it natural for them to behave as they do during Jesus's lifetime, and supposed that it was only his appearances to them after his resurrection that made them aware of his true status. Wrede points out (p. 166) that this cause of their changed attitude is explicit in Luke, where the risen one opens their minds to the meaning of all that is "written in the law of Moses, the prophets and the psalms concerning me" (24:44–45). Wrede also adduces Philippians 2:6ff (Jesus "emptied himself" of divinity when he humbly became a man), Romans 1:4 (he "was declared to be Son of God with power" by his resurrection) and Acts 2:32 and 36 (Peter tells the "men of Israel" that "this Jesus whom ye crucified" God raised up and made "both Lord and Christ"). All three passages, he says (p. 218), are evidence that the oldest Christian belief of which we have any knowledge was that Jesus became the Messiah only at his resurrection. Whether in fact he did or did not "give himself out as Messiah" in the time of his earthly life Wrede does not claim to know (p. 230; cf. pp. 209, 223, where he says that this question is still not settled). What he does feel able to assert is that those who had accompanied Jesus did in actual historical fact alter their views about him as a result of their experiences of his appearances to them after his resurrection (p. 234). But the extent of their earlier, real historical misunderstanding has been exaggerated into something quite incredible in Mark because he was writing in a situation where Christians had not been able to continue to believe that Jesus had lived inconspicuously. They could no longer accept that he became Son of God only at his resurrection, but came to think that he had been this from the first, and hence that he had worked impressive miracles and had behaved generally in an authoritarian way. Such stories about him were clumsily worked by Mark into some sort of consistency with the older ideas by representing the plainest manifestations of his power and authority as not understood even by his closest associates until after the resurrection. In so far as they did earlier understand him—as when Peter confesses him to be the Christ—they are told to reveal this truth to nobody (8:30). Similarly, those who witness his transfiguration are told, immediately afterwards, to "tell no man what things they have seen, save when the Son of man should have risen from the dead" (9:9). And so it was supposed that he had kept his true status secret from the general public until then.

The secrecy motif will occupy us in the next section of this chapter. Here, we can note that, for Wrede, the secrecy is a "transitional idea", a bridge between two clashing Christologies, a residual effect of the view that the resurrection was the beginning of the messiahship at a time when the life of Jesus "was already being filled materially with messianic content" (p. 229. For Wrede, 'messianic' means anything that suggested that Jesus had supernatural power and authority). It is a transitional idea also in the sense that it was soon dropped: "That Jesus, if he had been messiah, would have shown and revealed himself as such was too natural an idea for it to remain long suppressed" (p. 244). And so, by the time of the fourth gospel, he is depicted as openly "manifesting his glory" with a stupendous public miracle at the wedding feast in Cana at the very commencement of his ministry (Jn. 2:11).

We saw that in Mark the very disciples who so often understand nothing, are said to have been given the secret, in contrast to outsiders, who are deliberately kept in the dark:

> Unto you is given the mystery of the kingdom of God: but unto them that are without all things are done in parables: that seeing they may see and not perceive; and hearing they may hear, and not understand; lest haply they should turn again and it should be forgiven them. (4:11f)

Wrede (p. 58) and others have noted that the Greek rendered here as "unto you is given the mystery" actually has the verb in the perfect tense, implying that the secret 'has been given' to the elite, already and once and for all, not that they gradually grasp what it is all about in the course of their discipleship. Moreover, Jesus here states quite plainly that

1. he speaks to outsiders only in parables, and
2. these are meant to be unintelligible so as to deprive all but the chosen few of any chance of salvation.

For Wrede (p. 62), the procedure here ascribed to him is both cruel and purposeless: to set out to prevent people from being forgiven is cruel; and why bother to address them at all if one deliberately makes what one says unintelligible? He further noted that it is not true that, in the rest of the gospel, Jesus speaks to the multitude only in parables, nor, when he does use them, that they are not clear. To take but one example, the parable of the wicked husbandmen, addressed to his enemies, is perfectly well understood by them (12:12).

The phrases "that seeing they may see and not perceive", and so forth, clearly derive from Isaiah 6:9–10, which is worded differently in the Hebrew text, the Greek translation of it known as the Septuagint or LXX, and the Aramaic version—the Targum read in synagogues as an interpretive translation of the original. Meagher has noted that

> the differences are slight in wording, but powerful in implication. The Hebrew text has God charge Isaiah with the task of taunting the people and making them unresponsive at the same time, so as to prevent their understanding and salvation. The LXX softens this dreadful instruction by changing a taunt to a prediction and assigning the responsibility for their dull rejection of the way of healing to themselves rather than to Isaiah's carrying out of God's orders. The Targum takes the Hebrew original to a still gentler form, in which God seems to be sending Isaiah on an errand of mercy, but with the sad awareness that they have closed themselves off from response and forgiveness. The shift in language is minor; the shift in theological implication is enormous. (1979, p. 117)

The wording may have reached Mark in something like the Targum form, for he has "lest it should be forgiven them", and only the Targum mentions forgiveness: the Hebrew and the Greek have "lest they be healed". Nevertheless, Mark's wording is "not the Targum's gentle exasperation", but is "bent back toward the darker meaning of the original Hebrew", which seems to have been occasioned by desperate anger at the failure of Isaiah's mission. According to Mark, then, "what happens is happening in parables *so that* those who are outside may be left in the dark and excluded from repentance and forgiveness . . . Jesus is teaching in parables as a strategy of deliberate obfuscation in order to prevent the outsiders from seeing, repenting and being forgiven" (*Ibid.*, pp. 120–21).

Matthew and Luke understood very well the cruel predestinarian doctrine Mark here ascribes to Jesus, for each does his best to mitigate it.

Mt.13:13–15 makes the unintelligible parables a punishment for an already existing blindness in the audience, and quotes Isaiah from the LXX accordingly. Luke 8:9–10 omits Mark's "lest they should turn again and be forgiven" but adds words like it to the interpretation of the parable of the sower that follows so as to make not God but the Devil the one who wants those who hear the word to persist in their unbelief:

Mk.4:15	*Lk.8:12*
And straitway cometh Satan and taketh away the word which hath been sown in them.	Then cometh the devil, and taketh away the word from their heart, *that they may not believe and be saved.*

As I have already pointed out, it is not in fact the case that Jesus's parables in Mark are unintelligible and are not understood. He speaks to the scribes "in parables" at 3:23, and there is no suggestion that they are perplexed. As we saw, the parable of the wicked husbandmen is well understood, and there are numerous other examples. He teaches the multitude "as he was wont" (10:1) and "the common people heard him gladly" (12:37). They would hardly have responded in this way to unintelligible riddles. At 7:14 he calls the multitude to hear him "and understand". Meagher (p. 87) says that the overall picture in Mark is that "the crowds see and hear quite well, while the inner circle has difficulties"—nearly the opposite of the policy strangely advanced at 4:10–12.

At 4:33 Jesus "spake the word" to the people with many parables, "as they were able to hear it". This is obviously intended as helpful: he is adapting what he has to say to their capacity to understand him. Moreover, 'speaking the word' is a standard phrase for clear, straightforward imparting of the Christian message, as when Christians in foreign parts "spoke the word" to gentiles (Acts 11:19), or when Jesus himself "spoke the word" in Capernaum (Mk. 2:2). Yet in the very next verse following 4:33 Mark says

> And without a parable spake he not unto them: but privately to his own disciples he expounded all things.

So 'the word' spoken to the crowds is after all insufficiently clear, and elucidation is vouchsafed only to the disciples. Taking verses 33 and 34 together we have sheer countersense—"missionary preaching which must later be decoded for the chosen inner circle!" (Räisänen 1990, p. 106). One cannot, Raisanen says (p. 54), get round this countersense by making more or less plausible conjectures as to why a historical Jesus might possibly have wished to avoid publicity. Such conjectures do not answer Wrede's question of how the tension between concealment and openness, characteristic of Mark's account, is to be explained.

This fourth chapter of Mark's gospel clearly puts together incompatible traditions. Commentators have long been aware that it is in this sense composite. After Jesus has been introduced as the sole speaker for the rest of the chapter with the words "and he said unto them" (verse 11), this formula is quite unnecessarily repeated at verses 13, 21, 24, 26, and 30, indicating that the evangelist has here joined together Jesuine utterances that were originally independent units. Moreover, the setting at the beginning of the chapter is public: Jesus is teaching the crowds from a boat. At verse 10 he is alone with his disciples, but verse 33 suggests that the parables he has been speaking were after all addressed not to them, but to the crowd, and this is confirmed by verse 36. "The private bypath with the closer disciples seems clearly to have been an afterthought, imperfectly carved out of public territory by a somewhat clumsy redactor" (Meagher, pp. 89f).

How did Mark come to write such a muddle? The answer seems to be that he requires the disciples to play more than one role. As Wrede was aware (p. 231), it is they who vouch for Jesus's teaching, and Mark's Christian community has to hold to them as the sole guarantors of it. Räisänen agrees that at 4:11f and 34 "the community's own teaching is traced back to a special enlightenment which all outsiders lack" (p. 112). When, contrariwise, the disciples fail to understand Jesus, this is, for Wrede, as we saw, because Mark also holds that their eyes were opened only at the resurrection. Räisänen objects to this that the disciples did in fact come to understand Jesus's true nature earlier than this—when Peter declared "Thou art the Christ" (8:29). For Räisänen (p. 127), this was a turning point (against Wrede, who held that the disciples' lack of understanding remained the same); for after 8:29, although the disciples still cannot grasp the necessity of Jesus's Passion and resurrection, there are at least no more questions like 4:41 ("Who is this that even the wind and the sea obey him?") or rebukes like 7:18 ("Are ye so without understanding also?"). In Raisanen's view, the disciples' incomprehension is meant to "underline the difficulties that Jesus's teaching presents for its hearers" (p. 118), reflecting the experience of Christians of Mark's day that their missionary preaching found little acceptance and that converts were few. When, on the other hand, Jesus preaches successfully to the crowds, as he often does, he is, for Mark, "the great preacher of the gospel, the archetype of the Christian missionary". Hence "the mission experience of Mark's congregation provides a key" to the puzzles of Chapter 4 (pp. 138f). Both these commentators agree that the confusion arises because "on the one hand Mark is telling a story of what happened when Jesus of Nazareth was active in Galilee and Jerusalem", and "on the other hand he is projecting the story of his own Christian congregation on to the same screen". As a result, "the disciples function . . . at one point mainly as historical followers of Jesus, at another mainly as representatives of a later community" (Räisänen, p. 19).

If we now turn from the role of the disciples to that of the outsiders, we find that Jesus's supposed activity in deliberately hardening or blinding them can be explained in the same way. Missionary preachers—Christian and other—have repeatedly found it impossible to get their message across to the obdurate, that however good their sermon, few accept it. Such preachers can console themselves with the thought that God wishes it to be so, that he has determined in advance that an elect will be saved, and has made the rest unreceptive to the truth. The Isaiah passage alluded to at Mk. 4:12 originated as an attempt to explain in this very way the failures of Isaiah's mission. Such predestinarian thinking has repeatedly—in Islam and elsewhere, as well as in Christianity—been inconsistently combined with complaints that outsiders remain outside only because of their own perversity. The two positions are sustained with equal vehemence by Paul when he tries, in Romans, to explain why most Jews refuse to turn Christian: God has actually dulled their faculties (11:7), he "hath mercy on whom he will, and whom he will he hardeneth" (9:18); yet they are to be blamed for abiding by the old covenant, and will be "grafted in" if only they will drop their unbelief (11: 23).

b. The Secret of Jesus's Status as Son of God

It is not only Jesus's teaching but also his exalted status as Son of God that has to be concealed if the church's conviction that he had behaved supernaturally throughout his whole life is to be combined with the older view that he had lived inconspicuously.

Wrede writes of the "Messianic secret" rather than the 'Son of God' secret, but he uses either 'Messiah' or 'Son of God' to denote Jesus's supernatural status. To avoid circumlocution we can follow him, and speak of Jesus achieving the status of Messiah at his resurrection, or alternatively of his having been Messiah from the first.

As we saw, on the few occasions when disciples discern Jesus's true status—as when they see his majesty at his transfiguration—they are told to keep this knowledge secret "until the Son of man should have risen from the dead" (9:9). Wrede finds the key to Mark in this passage: during Jesus's earthly life his messiahship "is absolutely a secret . . . No one apart from his confidants is supposed to learn about it; with the resurrection, however, its disclosure ensues" (p. 68).

Of course, the *supernatural* beings in Mark know the truth about Jesus from the first. The demons, or "unclean spirits" he casts out from people address him as "Son of the most high God" (5:7; cf. 3:11). So if his true status is to remain hidden, they must keep silence about it. Accordingly, he tells them not to make it known (1:25; 3:12). But this instruction is futile. The crowd has already heard the demons addressing him as "the Holy One of God", and has marvelled at his power over them (1:27). How can there be any secrecy if demons are heard shouting out who he is? Mark, says Wrede (p. 133), "seems very quickly to forget his own presuppositions".

In curing the Gerasene demoniac, Jesus does not simply dislodge the "legion" of demons, but allows their request to be transferred to a herd of two thousand pigs, which promptly rush down into the sea and are drowned. The swineherds then report this to all and sundry "in the city and in the country", so that people come to the scene—Jesus is still there with his cured patient—and, having been told what had happened by eyewitnesses, they "beseech him to depart from their borders" (5:17)— "a commendably restrained response to two thousand drowned pigs" (Meagher, p. 73). We are not told whether the demons also perished. That is of no interest to the narrator. He needs the pigs and their demented behaviour only as visible evidence that the demons have in fact left the man.

Not only do the demons already know who Jesus is, but also his power to work stupendous miracles would tend to betray his status to all who witnessed them. This problem Mark deals with in the same way— by making him order silence, in these cases about what he has done, sometimes even when such an order is quite senseless, as the miracle has already become public. Thus he restores Jairus's daughter to life in the presence only of Peter, James and John, and "charged them much (RSV "strictly") that no man should know it" (5:43), even though the house where he has done this was already full of mourners who knew that the girl was dead (Wrede, pp. 50–51). The prohibition could not possibly be implemented, but "Mark does not notice this" and has "only a limited capacity for transposing himself into the historical situation with which he is dealing" (p. 133). Likewise, Jesus repeatedly commands sick people—the reference is not here to cases of demonic possession—to keep the fact of their healing secret, yet performs the cures in the full glare of publicity. It will not do to say that public healings begin only after injunctions to silence cease; for already at 2:1ff there is a cure before everyone's eyes, while miracles that are to be kept secret occur much later (p. 17). He even tells the cured Gerasene demoniac to tell his friends "how great things the Lord hath done for thee". The man complied, published the whole matter in the Decapolis, "and all men did marvel" (5:19–20). Thus the instruction to be silent is sometimes senseless, and sometimes entirely lacking, and sometimes the precise opposite is actually enjoined.

Miracles apart, there is much in Jesus's behaviour and in people's reaction to him that is incompatible with the idea that his status went unrecognized until the resurrection. "At the entry into Jerusalem he permits himself to be feted as Messiah, the blind man of Jericho calls him 'Son of David' (10:47), and before the High Priest he acknowledges in plain terms that he is Son of God (14:62)" (p. 70). Wrede finds such contradiction of the idea of secrecy inevitable, in that, if Mark's Jesus had really kept himself and his powers strictly concealed, then his life would hardly have been worth relating. To demonstrate that he was God's son, he had to be shown as acting with appropriate powers (pp. 125–26).

Wrede's conclusion is that "Mark no longer has a real view of the historical life of Jesus" (p. 129), whose person he conceives "dogmatically" as the bearer of supernatural dignity. Mark did not, in Wrede's view (p. 145), originate the idea that Jesus kept his status secret during his ministry. He thinks that the clumsiness and inconsistency with which this motif is handled in Mark excludes this. It was, in his view, taken from pre-Markan tradition, and arose as an attempt to reconcile the earliest view of Jesus's ministry (as having been unmessianic and unspectacular) with later stories which credited him with pre-resurrection behaviour displaying supernatural powers. If we allow that the old idea is more likely to represent the truth than the later stories, it would follow that the historical Jesus did not in fact give himself out as Messiah, although, as we saw, Wrede did not claim to have established that this is the case. What he does claim to have shown is that "Mark is very far removed from the actual life of Jesus and is dominated by views of a dogmatic kind" (p. 145). His Jesus acts with divine power and knows the future. His actions are not humanly motivated but derive from divine decree. "In this sense the Gospel of Mark belongs to the history of dogma" (p. 131), and so is a good deal closer to the fourth gospel than is commonly supposed (p. 145).

Finally, Wrede shows how Matthew did his best to avoid some of Mark's absurdities. "Prohibitions to the demons are lacking. . . . The story of Jairus's daughter contains neither the prohibition nor the feature of the three confidants. On the contrary, in the concluding verse (Mt. 9:26) we read: 'And the report of this went through all that district'" (pp.

152–53). After the second prophecy of the Passion it is not said that the disciples did not understand (see above, p. 183). Clearly, Matthew found Mark's picture of them "no longer tolerable" (p. 160). He made them much more consistently "the guarantors and representatives of Jesus's teaching and of the true understanding of his person" (p. 163), thus reflecting "the general view that the church has of them" (p. 164). Luke remains closer to Mark, and can retain their incomprehension because he so much stresses that their eyes were opened only after the resurrection (p. 179; cf. Lk. 24:25–27; 44f).

Wrede is quite unimpressed by what he calls the "much-lauded concreteness" of Mark, so often taken as an indication of its historical accuracy. He quotes, as a particularly characteristic passage, 7:24f:

> And from thence he arose and went away into the borders of Tyre and Sidon. And he entered into a house, and would have no man know it: yet he could not be hid. But straightway a woman whose little daughter had an unclean spirit, having heard of him, came and fell down at his feet . . .

He comments that one might in the same fairy-tale manner tell of a disguised Spanish prince journeying into French territory, where he went into a house because he did not wish to be recognized, but a poor woman heard of it and sought him out (p. 142). Precisely in the passages he has adduced in his book, there is "a strong lack of concreteness", and merely "a brief hasty word of Jesus's or someone else's and a short remark on the impression it made". Throughout the gospel the scene changes rapidly, and does so even within individual incidents; and who is being addressed or dealt with fluctuates likewise, with "the people or the disciples now appearing and now withdrawing". Moreover, the "psychological and other motivations which would be the pre-condition for giving palpable shape to the events are lacking . . . because they were not thought of at all". In any case, concreteness would not mean authenticity: "A document can have a strongly secondary and indeed even quite apocryphal character and yet display a great deal of concreteness" (p. 143).

Although Wrede writes clearly, his book is not easy to read, as the abundant detail is confusing. Räisänen gives a very lucid summary, and a comprehensive account of alternative proposals that have been made to explain the data. He himself agrees that the secrecy motif is one of several in Mark, and that others are inconsistent with it. Jesus is killed because of his Christological claims (14:61), so there can be no secrecy here. Hence although the disciples so often grasp so little, his opponents *must* understand what his claims are: "An apparently absurd story world therefore results: while those close to Jesus understand nothing, those vehemently opposed to him grasp everything that matters!" (1990, p. 229), and do so well before the Passion narrative (2:7; 12:12, etc.). Again, the disciples are not always uncomprehending, as they have to function as teachers of others (6:7ff) and also as reliable mediators of Christian truth for the future. And Jesus himself at times "acts as the proto-missionary, proclaiming the gospel and teaching the word" quite openly and publicly (pp. 213, 247).

One can see what it was in Wrede that infuriated the theologians of Oxford. T.W. Manson said that the "Wredestrasse" is the road to nowhere (quoted by Telford, 1995, p. 29); and William Sanday, although known for introducing German critical scholarship to England, was appalled at the "arrogance" of interpreting such exalted documents as the gospels on the basis of mere "common sense" (quoted by Tuckett in his editorial introduction to the 1983 symposium on *The Messianic Secret*, p. 24n23). Against such criticism, Wrede held that "for logical thinking there can be no middle position between inspired writings and historical documents", even though claims of "partial inspiration" are commonly made (1897, p. 69 of Morgan's 1973 translation). He never wavered from his insistence in this 1897 essay that study of the New Testament, like every other science, must have its goal entirely within itself and should on no account set out to help systematic theologians accommodate themselves to the results of treating the canonical books as others are treated by historians. Problems raised by the texts should not be glossed over, for "clear recognition of a problem is always a positive gain for historical understanding" (*Ibid.*, p. 97).

Later Oxfordians, notably R.H. Lightfoot and D.E. Nineham who has followed him, have been more circumspect than Sanday, and have accepted that the view which Wrede was opposing—that Mark is a straightforward unadorned transcript of Jesus's life—is untenable. Lightfoot closed his 1934 Bampton Lectures with the words:

> It seems, then, that the form of the earthly no less than of the heavenly Christ is for the most part hidden from us. For all the inestimable value of the gospels, they yield us little more than a whisper of his voice; we trace in them but the outskirts of his ways. (1935, p. 225)

As a result, "a storm of protest broke over the theological scene in England, where Wrede had never been taken seriously" (Beare 1970, p. 69). In Germany, as Tuckett notes (1983, p. 12) there has long been "a greater willingness to accept some, if not all of Wrede's evidence as indicating the existence of secondary elements in the tradition." The 1962 entry on him in the encyclopaedia *Die Religion in Geschichte und Gegenwart* acknowledged that his "critical destruction of the psychologizing life-of-Jesus theology which based itself on Mark's gospel" has been "fundamental" to more recent research.

I began this chapter with mention of Schweitzer's assessment. The reader of Wrede's book, he says (1954, p. 329), "cannot help feeling that here no quarter is given". He maintained (as we shall see in Chapter 8 below) that the secrecy motif is not, as Wrede supposed, a construction of the early church, but is rooted in the actual behaviour of the historical Jesus, who thought he could induce God to bring about the kingdom and the end of the world by sacrificing himself on the cross, after which he would be changed into a supernatural Messiah who would come down from the clouds as the kingdom arrived. Since Schweitzer's Jesus regarded the Messiah as supernatural, he of course did not think himself to be the Messiah during his earthly existence. But he cherished the conviction that he would be exalted *post mortem,* and kept it secret, telling his disciples also to do so once they had become aware of it. All that they and the general public really needed to know was that the kingdom will be coming soon (Schweitzer, English translation 2000, p. xxxviii).

In the second (1913) and later German editions of his book, Schweitzer even claimed: "Either Jesus did not exist, or he was just as Mark and Matthew, understood literally, depict him" (2000, p. 406). This was meant not to endorse every detail in these gospels, but to accept what Schweitzer understood to be their overall burden. I have noted (above, p. 2) that the present bishop of Durham, N.T. Wright, allows that the question at issue between Schweitzer and Wrede (whom, in that context, he quaintly describes as a "Dutchman"!) is still debated today. He himself, as we shall see, although sharply critical of Schweitzer, owes a good deal to him, but is totally out of sympathy with Wrede and with Räisänen's partial endorsement of him—he writes of their "sterile positivism" (1992, p. 25). Räisänen, for his part, is repelled by the bishop's "passionate and polemical conservatism" (2000, p. 128), and by his dismissive caricature of Wrede's book (Wright 1992a, pp. 104, 391). Wright, like Schweitzer, will occupy us in Chapter 8 below.

ii. Mark and Community Tradition: K.L. Schmidt and Form-Criticism

In 1919 K.L. Schmidt gave Markan studies a new direction with his book on the 'Framework' of the story of Jesus, where he raised the question of the stages through which traditions about Jesus had passed before their inclusion in the gospels. He showed that Mark's account of the Galilean ministry is merely a series of separate, short single stories (pericopes); and he argued that each of these had been transmitted, originally orally, in the preaching and teaching of early Christian communities. Each story was designed to represent a point of doctrinal interest to these early Christians, the miracle stories, for instance, showing how great Jesus's powers were. The stories seldom indicated where or when he spoke or acted as he did, as that was not doctrinally important. He adds that, as Christianity originated as a cult, these stories must be understood in the light of their setting within the cult, in the practices of public worship (1919, p. vi). In other words, the main purpose of the anecdotes was not to preserve the history of Jesus, but to strengthen the life of the church. Nineham, who is greatly indebted to Schmidt and his successors, explains more fully what was involved. The people passing on the stories were "preachers and teachers, speaking at meetings for public worship or addressing groups of catechumens and the like". They would tailor what they said to the particular needs of a given audience: if a lesson in good-neighbourliness was required, the parable of the good Samaritan could be recited; if there was some doubt whether to pay taxes to the Romans, what we now have at Mk. 12:13–17 would be suitable. "Consequently, the order in which the incidents were recounted would vary from church to church, in accordance with local needs; and there would be no compelling motive for preserving, or even remembering, the order in which they actually occurred during Our Lord's lifetime" (1963, p. 22).

Schmidt (pp. 63ff) takes the story of the healing of the leper as typical of a Markan pericope: "And there cometh to him a leper, beseeching him" (1:40). There is no indication of time or place. Of the cured leper, it is said that he "went out" (verse 45)—from what (a synagogue or a house?) is not indicated. The story is quite independent of the anecdotes that precede and follow it. My quotation of its initial words shows that it is linked to what precedes it only by the simplest of all links—the word 'and', quite often the only linkage between Markan pericopes. Links elsewhere are almost as simple; for example 'and' combined with 'again' ("and he went forth again"; "and he entered again into the synagogue"; "and again he began to teach"); or "immediately", rendered "straightway" in the RV ("and straightway he entered into the synagogue . . . And straightway there was in the synagogue a man with an unclean spirit"). The feeding of the four thousand is introduced with the quite unspecific "in those days" (8:1).

Schmidt shows that Matthew and Luke obviously felt that this was not good enough and so introduced references to time or place so as to bind individual pericopes together. Thus Matthew makes the leper come to Jesus as he came down from the mountain after the Sermon on the Mount (Mt. 8:1–2). Luke does not indicate the time but provides a place: "And it came to pass, while he was in one of the cities, a man full of leprosy . . ." (Lk. 5:12). Variations between different manuscripts of Mark also show a tendency to localize the stories. There was a conflict of interests here: on the one hand a certain antiquarian desire to be assured of the where and the when; on the other the cultic practice which fastened only on a story in itself, apart from any context (p. 77).

As Mark's material paid so little regard to chronology or topography, he could not arrange it so as to give a true itinery in truly chronological sequence. There is no historical reason why, for instance, the section about the cleansing of a leper—those six verses in Chapter 1 are independent of the context on either side—should occur at this point in the narrative rather than at any other (p. 76). And the same is true of many other pericopes. Schmidt is referring here only to the account of the ministry. He does not dispute that Mark's Passion narrative is continuous and replete with indications of time and place: "The passion narrative will have been read out in public worship as a continuous lection. Only as a whole could it give the answer to a question that repeatedly surfaced in the missionary period of the church, namely: how could Jesus be brought to the cross by the people graced with his signs and wonders?" (p. 305).

Sometimes the very nature of a story requires some indication of locality. A tale involving a boat must have a sea or sea-shore setting. A heathen person is essential to Mk. 7:24–30, so this story must be sited in heathen territory: "And from thence he arose and went away into the borders of Tyre and Sidon" (verse 24). But there is nothing precise: Jesus would fain remain concealed in "a house", but a heathen woman extracts a miracle from him. That is all (pp. 198–99). The link with the preceding story is also tenuous: the 'from thence' in "from thence he arose" seems to mean from "the house" of verse 17, which is as vague as many another Markan setting—"the mountain" or hill-country, "the shore" (of the lake of Galilee), a "lonely place" or "the synagogue".

Some stories require a reference to time. The call of the disciples naturally comes early in the ministry. Synagogue preaching and sabbath-breaking behaviour must take place on the sabbath. The setting in the cornfields on the sabbath (Mk. 2:23) is necessitated by the story thus introduced, and provides the basis on which the Pharisees take Jesus to task because his disciples do what they say is forbidden on the sabbath (plucking ears of corn). But, as usual, precise details are lacking. We are not told on what sabbath or in what neighbourhood. Such questions, says Schmidt (p. 89) must not be asked of an individual anecdote which is not linked to the preceding or following one chronologically, but only thematically, in that it is one of a series which portray Jesus responding to hostile criticism. As Mark's material did not give him any true chronology of Jesus's deeds, he (or a predecessor on whose writing he drew) was reduced to grouping them in this way, that is, by their themes—a series of parables in Chapter 4 and of miracles in Chapter 5. Mk.2:1 to 3:6, which includes the cornfield episode, comprises five stories where Jesus, in conflict with opponents, says something of importance for the gospel message; for instance, "the Son of man hath power on earth to forgive sins" (2:10); "I came not to call the righteous, but sinners" (2:17).

Returning to the cornfield episode, we see that it must be set at harvest-time (April to mid-June). Schmidt observes that only here, in this pericope, is a season specified, apart from the setting of the Passion at a roughly similar season (passover). It has often been supposed that this entitles us to infer that, for Mark, the whole ministry lasted but a single year. For Schmidt no such inference is justified. Mark has put individual anecdotes into a series, giving no indication of in what year or years the different events of the ministry occurred. It is pure chance that one of the anecdotes required a spring setting. Others may equally well have occurred at some other springtime or at another time in some other year. Schmidt begins his book (pp. 1–17) with an amusing account of the often heated attempts to come to terms with the contradiction between the supposed one-year ministry of the synoptics and the Johannine chronology of apparently three years (indicated by John's references to three passovers). Catholic commentators had struggled to harmonize the two, as any admission of contradiction would militate against the reliability of the gospels. Protestants, on the other hand, were willing to give up the fourth gospel as historically worthless, but clung all the more to the synoptic outline of Jesus's life as a historically accurate sequence. Schmidt holds (p. 91) that there is in fact no synoptic chronology of the ministry with which the Johannine narrative can conflict, and that Mark in fact gives no indication of how long the ministry lasted. When, for instance, he groups together in successive narratives the stilling of the storm, the cure of the Gerasene demoniac, the raising of Jairus's daughter and the cure of the woman with the issue of blood (4:35–5:43), he does so because they all tell of acts of divine power and all require or happen to have had a setting on or near the sea (pp. 150–51). There is no reason to suppose that they really occurred in succession or even in the same year.

Schmidt also notes (p. 92) that in the cornfield episode nothing is said that motivates the appearance of Jesus's opponents, the Pharisees, at 2:24. Nineham takes up this point, saying: "It is idle to ask what the Pharisees were doing in the middle of a cornfield on a sabbath day; the process of oral tradition has formalized the stories." Hence there is "a considerable element of truth" in the judgement that "Scribes or Pharisees appear and disappear just as the compiler requires them", as "part of the stage-property and scenery, like 'the house' and 'the mountain'" (1963, p. 107). In the same way Jesus is repeatedly able to 'call the people' to be his audience. Those responsible for the anecdotes collected by Mark had no difficulty in supposing that there was a multitude at hand, ready to be summoned when Jesus wants to make some public statement. Thus, although in the context he has been addressing only his disciples, he summons the multitude to hear his views on the costs and rewards of discipleship (8:34). Schmidt notes (p. 221) that Mt. 16:24 wisely makes him here address only the disciples.

Because Mark had no knowledge of the real order in which the events of Jesus's ministry occurred, he sometimes puts disparate sayings together simply because a word or phrase is common to them, although their meanings are not at all cognate. Schmidt instances (p. 233ff) Mk. 9:36–50:

> Whosoever shall receive one of such little children in my name . . .
>
> We saw one casting out devils in thy name . . .
>
> Whoever gives you a cup of water in (the) name, because ye are of Christ . . .

These sayings about the 'name' are followed by two about 'fire': in hell "the fire is not quenched. For everyone shall be salted with fire". This mention of salt leads to the addition of two further sayings where it functions as the connecting catchword: "Salt is good, but if the salt have lost its savour, wherewith will ye season it? Have salt in yourselves and be at peace with one another."

Schmidt called his book 'The Framework of the Story of Jesus', and he holds that this framework consists of short generalizing summaries of Jesus's behaviour which he calls "Sammelberichte" (summary statements), frames in which the individual anecdotes are placed. They are quite general in their wording and so they do not allow, any more than do the anecdotes, any chronological inferences (p. 13). Some ease the transition to the next pericope (p. 33), others bear no relation to what follows. Examples from Mark are:

> And he went into their synagogues throughout all Galilee, preaching and casting out devils. (1:39)

> And he went forth again by the seaside; and all the multitude resorted unto him. (2:13, followed by the call of Levi with which it has no connection)

A somewhat longer summary is given at 3:7–12, emphasizing Jesus's very extensive success (p. 106): he withdrew to "the sea" but is followed by a great multitude from Galilee, Judea, Jerusalem, Idumea, and elsewhere, who were "hearing what great things he did", for "he had healed many".

Schmidt regards these summaries as in the main Mark's own compositions (p. 160)—younger therefore than the individual anecdotes. These latter cannot be traced back to any precise point of origin (p. 105), but will have been repeated again and again in the oral tradition; whereas the summaries are artificial constructions of a particular writer. C.H. Dodd, who criticized Schmidt in an influential article in 1932, nevertheless allowed that "the main stuff of the gospel is reducible to short narrative units and the framework is superimposed on these units." He also allowed that the Markan order of the ministry's events "is in large measure . . . the result of the Evangelist's own work, rather than directly traditional."

R.H. Lightfoot did much to introduce the work of Wrede, Schmidt, and their successors into Britain. In his Bampton lectures of 1934 he showed that Westcott's statement of 1851—"St. Mark is essentially a transcript from life"—is quite unacceptable, and he called Sanday's condemnation of Wrede "regrettable" (1935, pp. 16f). He found it no longer possible to maintain the patristic view that Mark was put together from statements by Peter: We now see it as "a compilation of materials of different date, origin, character and purpose, many of which may have had a considerable history—whether oral or literary or both—before they were finally inserted into this gospel, at least a large part of the book being formed from anonymous traditions which had long been current in the church" (p. 25). In a later book, he outlines Schmidt's arguments concerning the topographical and chronological vagueness of Mark, and he follows him in stressing that the little stories served the interests and reflected the concerns of the early church. In them, "the Lord Himself is always central, either in word or act, or in both: frequently enemies seek to oppose or provoke Him; if the disciples are present, they are seldom more than lay-figures." What is emphasized is "the immense impression made by the Lord. . . . We read again and again of the astonishment, bewilderment and fear produced by the mighty works and by the teaching." And in all the stories of conflict with opponents "the sympathy of the reader with the Lord's position is assumed" (1952, p. 11).

Lightfoot is here making the point that each of the individual stories in Mark has its "Sitz im Leben", its 'setting in the life' of the church, in that it expresses interests that are related to faith; and it is to these interests, not to historical concerns, that it owes its formulation and preservation.

The attempt to trace gospel pericopes to one or other of the literary forms to which preachers would naturally resort (such as miracle stories, conflict stories, or stories inculcating some moral point) has become known as 'form-criticism'. Nineham, who follows Lightfoot, stresses that

> If the form-critics have shown anything, they have shown the essential importance of the factor they call *Sitz im Leben* in the preservation of the material included in our gospels: that is to say, no such material is likely to have survived for long unless it was relevant to *something* in the life, worship, beliefs and interests of the earliest communities. (1977, p. 14)

For instance, Christians and their Jewish opponents will have argued about whether it was necessary to keep the sabbath. For this reason the Christians will have narrated stories in which Jesus defends, against Jewish critics, the practice of the later church of not keeping it (Mk. 2:27–28). In his book Schmidt does not often raise the question whether such stories are historically accurate accounts of Jesus's words and deeds—in a later essay he gives, as we shall see, a surprisingly conservative answer to it. But many of his followers have held that the relevant behaviour was simply ascribed to Jesus in order to justify the church's practice. Käsemann, for instance, says that, as it was religious, not historical interests that the individual sayings and stories served, the overwhelming mass of the tradition "cannot be accepted as authentic". The "preaching about Jesus" came almost entirely to supplant his own preaching, "as can be seen most clearly of all in the completely unhistorical Gospel of John" (1964, p. 59).

In their recent study of the synoptic gospels, Sanders and Davies offer some criticisms of the form critics, but agree that they were right to say that "in the gospels one can see individual and originally independent units. The pericopes do not flow along smoothly in chronological order." There is a 'rounding off', in that each one has a marked beginning and end, and "one does not run on to the next as would be the case if they originated as part of a coherent and consecutive narrative". It follows that "the individual pericopes can and in fact must be studied apart from their present settings if one is to get behind the gospels as we have them to earlier situations"—whether these are to be found in the actual life of Jesus or, as the more sceptical hold, only in the early church (1989, p. 134). The artificiality of some of the present settings is evident from comparison of the gospels: "The parable of the Lost Sheep in Matthew is addressed to the disciples, as admonition, but in Luke to the Pharisees, as rebuke" (p. 339). That the various parts of the synoptics are self-enclosed can be illustrated from the way in which Jesus's opponents vary early and late in the narrative: the synoptics "make no connection between the Pharisees, who are depicted as opposing Jesus in Galilee, and the chief priests, who were instrumental in his trial and execution in Judea" (p. 135). At Mk. 3:6 the Herodians and the Pharisees plot to have him killed, and Mark reintroduces them at 12:13 where they try to trap him with a question. But "when it comes to the arrest and the trial, neither Pharisee nor Herodian appears" (p. 149) , nor in the equivalent narratives in the other two synoptics. After the point in the narrative represented by Mk. 12:13, the Pharisees actually appear again only in a narrative unique to Matthew where, with the chief priests, they ask Pilate, after the execution, for a guard to the tomb (Mt. 27:62).

Schmidt emphasized that it follows from his investigation that no biography of Jesus can be constructed from the synoptics (p. 317). So many commentators have allowed that Mark leaves gaps in his record of Jesus's life, but have assumed that what he does narrate is given in proper temporal sequence. In fact, says Schmidt, there is not even this relative coherence, and the whole collapses into individual stories. Mark's outline is not a row of pearls, arranged at a distance from each other but nevertheless in a chronological line, so that one could interpolate, now here and now there, other pearls—further incidents—as Matthew and Luke do, with no impairing of true chronology. Rather is it a heap of pearls, with no linear arrangement, even if now and then a few of them do belong chronologically together (p. 281).

It has by now become customary to say that 'the gospels are no biographies', but Nineham wonders how often the full implications of the statement have been faced. A 'life of Jesus', he says, could be written "only if the writer has exact information about the order in which the various episodes in the subject's career occurred and a sufficiently detailed knowledge of them to be able to show for what reasons he felt and acted and developed as he did" (1977, p. 22). Such information is simply not forthcoming. Yet biographies continue to appear. People have had a long time to fill in the gaps left by the gospel records and, as E.P. Sanders notes (1993, p. 76), "an apparently endless amount of energy and inventiveness to use in the endeavour".

In an essay of 1923 Schmidt designated the gospels as unpretentious writings for ordinary folk, not "Hochliteratur" (cultured literature) but popular "Kleinliteratur", and not biography but "cultic legend" emanating from the life of a religious community (pp. 76, 89). He compared the synoptics, particularly Mark, with collections of the German tales of Faust and Eulenspiegel, in that the earliest compilers did not, as did the later ones, obtrude their own ideas and manipulate the material to make it exemplify some overall interpretation, but put the individual items together almost higgledy-piggledy (p. 92). We are apt to assume that a biography written by an individual author is more reliable than a collection of anecdotes about the person in question; and Schmidt grants that this is true if we are comparing what a modern historian writes about someone to a collection of tales about him. But he holds that in antiquity there was no sharp distinction between historiography and rhetoric: the historian or biographer was something of a poet who aimed at literary effectiveness, whereas the collector of popular tales—then as now—intruded his own thinking far less (pp. 80–81). Schmidt thus suggests that a collection based on community tradition has a certain reliability which may be lacking in more pretentious literary performances: "That the people as community became the vehicle and creator of the tradition makes its content secure" (p. 124), that is, gives it a firm and, it is implied, reliable foundation. He allows that an early Christian community will have felt edified and strengthened as a group by its stories of Jesus, just as the legends of the saints owe their origin to the cult of the saints and in turn promote this cult (p. 100). A certain tendentiousness and lack of detachment towards the material is, then, undeniably present. But he holds that it is less distortive than when the collection is reworked and given the stamp of an individual mind—as when Mark's collection was reworked by Matthew and Luke. The "fidelity to the material which characterizes all popular tradition" (p. 131) is thereby lost, whereas in the oldest layers of the gospels "the smell of Palestinian earth" is still distinct (p. 128).

This whole idea that folk-traditions are reliable because free from individual, self-conscious shaping is not sustainable. The idea has a certain superficial plausibility mainly because it is seldom known where given oral traditions, ancient or modern, originated, and precisely who invented them. But such stories, circulating by word of mouth, although generally anonymous vary constantly in particular details from one telling to another; and such variations are good evidence against credibility. In a number of books (such as *The Vanishing Hitchhiker,* 1981, and *The Mexican Pet,* 1986, both published by Norton in New York and London), the folklorist J.H. Brunvand has collected and commented on numerous supposedly recent and believable happenings - "urban legends" told repeatedly even in today's highly technological world. He distinguishes two kinds of variations: adaptations to make a given story fit local conditions (such as circumstantial details of name, place, time and situation) and introduction of new elements (new characters or additions to the plot) which aim at explaining the story or making it in other respects more plausible. There is also normally an appeal to source authorities—it all is said to have happened to, for instance, a friend of a friend of the storyteller. Such stories, says Brunvand, can survive if they possess a strong basic story-appeal, a foundation in actual belief (in that such things are acceptable as possible occurrences), and a meaningful message or moral—often something appropriate to the desires and anxieties of the society in which the stories circulate. To find acceptance they need not be true, but merely believable: "The truth never stands in the way of a good story." It is not possible to retain much faith in the truth of community tradition once one has read Brunvand's books.

Recent studies of Mark, while endorsing Schmidt's estimate of its non-literary quality, are more reluctant to adduce this as evidence of reliability. Reiser finds Mark's syntax and style comparable to that of Hellenistic folk-literature, below the level of literary forms of the 'koine' (the 'common' [universal] Greek of the Graeco-Roman world of the time). This lowly type of writing, Reiser adds, was regarded by the educated with a contempt comparable to what cultured Germans have felt for the German 'chapbooks' (pamphlets of tales and tracts hawked by pedlars) (1984, p. 35). Bryan observes that students with just about enough knowledge of Greek to cope with the gospels will find, say, Plutarch or Philo hard going, but will have little difficulty with the type of contemporary narrative prose designed for popular consumption, such as Chariton's *Callirhoe* (a romantic novel probably from the midfirst century A.D.). Bryan includes a selection from such popular material in the original Greek at the end of his book so that his readers can ascertain this for themselves. He concludes that Mark wrote in "a genuine popular literary style", and notes that Origen and other Christian apologists found themselves obliged to defend such simplicity against criticism (1993, pp. 17, 53f).

All this is of interest in view of attempts that have been made—because Mark does not hold up as history—to interpret its details as forming subtle and ingenious literary patterns with symbolic significance, as mysterious signals with hidden meanings for the reader to decipher. The kind of 'training' purveyed in the literature departments of our universities has produced a climate in which scholars delight in the necessary display of ingenuity. Meagher has countered all such make-believe by giving a detailed demonstration that Mark is "the product of a rather ordinarily clumsy writer, probably working on materials that had come to him in ordinarily clumsy form" (1979, p. 58). Räisänen too insists that Mark is not an example of the kind of sophisticated literature where (if indeed anywhere!) one might be entitled to assume subtle verbal links and associations, or recondite connections between distant passages. He adds that, if it is hard to imagine a theologian who would hide a sophisticated network of associations in such lowly garb, it is "harder still to imagine a *readership* in Mark's time and culture that would have understood such a message." Moreover, "even such relatively well-educated readers as Matthew and Luke obviously missed the alleged symbolic contents, interpreting Mark in a straightforward way as an historical account of the words and deeds of the Lord. Nor were they blamed for this until modern critics entered the stage" (1990, pp. 22–23).

6

Q, the Sayings Gospel

So far I have covered sections of Matthew and Luke which are at variance with each other and are also unrepresented in Mark, namely the birth and infancy accounts and the stories of post-resurrection appearances. But Matthew and Luke do have a great deal of material in common, and not all of it is drawn from Mark, for they share some 230 verses of non-Markan material. If, as is widely agreed, neither of these two evangelists knew the work of the other—we have seen how violently their accounts can clash—then this shared non-Markan material was presumably drawn from a source common to them both—a Greek document known now as Q (= Quelle, German for 'source'), not extant but reconstructable from this non-Markan overlap between the two extant gospels.

A few scholars (notably M.D. Goulder and M. Goodacre) explain the overlap without positing Q at all, by supposing that Luke took the relevant material from Matthew. But the majority accept that these two wrote independently of each other, both drawing on Q as one of their sources.[1]

There is strong evidence that Q existed in written form, not merely as oral tradition; for about half of it is verbally identical in Matthew and in Luke, and differences in the other half can be explained as due to the one or the other evangelist—sometimes both—adapting the source so as to improve it stylistically or theologically. That Matthew has adapted Q (as well as he has Mark) in order to serve his own distinctive ends is betrayed by the fact that words and phrases that appear in his reworking of his Markan source, as well as in material found only in him, are also found in his version of the Q material; for example, repeated references to 'righteousness'. (This noun occurs seven times in the gospel, and the adjective 'righteous' seventeen times.) As a result of twenty years of work by members of the International Q project, a critical text of the whole of Q (edited by J.M. Robinson et al., 2001) has now been reconstructed by identifying and discounting such redactional traits. Luke seems on the whole to have done less editing of Q than Matthew, and so scholars cite Q texts by their Lucan position. Thus Q 10:12 = either Lk. 10:12 as it now stands, or this verse from which a primitive Q text has been reconstructed.

Further reasons for supposing that Q existed in written form are given by Kloppenborg: 1. It contains a number of unusual and peculiar phrases; in oral transmission these would surely have been replaced by more common expressions in at least one of the synoptic versions. 2. There is considerable agreement between Matthew and Luke in the sequence of the units when there is no logical reason for them to occur in that particular order.[2] 3. There is doubling of some Markan and Q material: an incident in Mark may be included by Matthew or Luke (or both) both in the Markan sequence and in what appears to be its relative position in Q.[3] If Q traditions had been oral, they could easily have been conflated with the single Markan version. Finally, Q is without the mnemonic devices—important in Homer and in rabbinic traditions—which would be required as an oral basis for verbatim or near-verbatim agreements, and there is no evidence for mnemonic practice in the Christianity of the time.

The original language of Q was Greek. There is no evidence that any New Testament books are written in a Greek that was translated from Aramaic.[4]

Q does not emphasize Jesus's capacity to work miracles in the way that Mark does. It includes a dialogue with the Devil in which he declines to authenticate himself as "Son of God" by working them (cf. below, p. 237), and has only two miracle stories (a healing and an exorcism) and a general statement concerning Jesus's miraculous powers. This latter has a striking parallel in one of the Qumran Dead Sea Scrolls, in that both do not merely echo Isaiah 61:1f ("the Lord hath anointed me to preach good tidings unto the meek . . . , to bind up the brokenhearted . . . , to comfort all that mourn"), but also expand it by adding a reference to raising of the dead. The Qumran passage reads:

> He will heal the wounded, give life to the dead, and preach good news to the poor.

The Q passage begins by echoing Isaiah 35:4–6 ("the blind receive their sight, and the lame walk, the lepers are cleansed and the deaf hear": cf. above, p. 69), but then adds the expansion of Isaiah 61:

The dead are raised and the poor have good tidings preached to them (Q 7:22).

G.J. Brooke claims that, in the whole of Jewish literature between the Bible and the Mishnah, it is only in this Qumran passage and here in Q that Isaiah 61 is expanded with a statement about the raising of the dead. "The details of the similarities", he says, "are too great to be brushed aside" (2000, p. 24). There seems to be a common tradition underlying both texts, which each has adapted in its own way. Although in the Qumran passage the antecedent of the 'he' who works the miracles is God, and he is the one who normally raises the dead, he is not the one whom one might expect to preach the good news. That is normally done by a messenger or agent. The speaker in Isaiah 61 is in fact an anointed prophet, and the Qumran text also mentions "the Messiah whom heaven and earth obey" who can be understood as a prophet like Elijah, who was credited with raising the dead during his historical career. Hence the idea may well be that both the raising of the dead and the preaching were effected by an agent (Collins 1997, pp. 88f, 158). In Q, the agent is of course Jesus.

Most of Q comprises Jesus's sayings, and when it was first isolated from its setting in Matthew and Luke it was hailed as a record of his authentic voice, proclaiming an unselfish ethic and largely, if not completely, free from the miracle and myth encumbering him in the canonical gospels. "Once William Wrede had removed Mark from the status of a historically accurate report on which the quest of the historical Jesus could confidently build, it was to Q to which critical scholarship . . . naturally turned" (J.M. Robinson 2001, p. 35). The contrast between Q and Mark, which has one miracle after another during the Galilean ministry and few teachings there, is particularly striking.

Mark does have its own version of some of the traditions represented in Q, and one instance of this is that both speak of John the Baptist. Many scholars hold that, although influence of Q on Mark cannot be excluded, it is more likely that Mark had independent access to Q-type material. Mark's use of Q is, then, still a minority view. Nevertheless, this whole question is a debate which is "becoming increasingly acrimonious" (Schmidt, in Labahn and Schmidt 2001, p. 15). Q used to be dated at ca. 50, but more recently ca. 70 has been thought more plausible; and if it was in fact composed as late as this, Mark's use of it becomes less probable (cf. J.M. Robinson 2001, p. 52).

In associating Jesus with John the Baptist, Q unambiguously sets Jesus's life in the Palestine of the first century A.D.; for John is known from Josephus to have been executed by Herod Antipas, ruler of Galilee, some time before the year 34 (Joan Taylor 1997, p. 257). The places Q assigns to Jesus's activities are also Galilean. Moreover, Q is thoroughly Jewish in its theological orientation (for example, toward the Jewish law) and so, unlike Mark, was not written at any great ideological distance from the situations it purports to describe.

What Q does not affirm about Jesus is as instructive as what it does. It certainly does not regard his death as redemptive and does not explicitly mention either his crucifixion or his resurrection.[5] It never calls him "Christ" (Messiah) and does not name any of the 'disciples' who 'followed' him. Q also has no allusion to Eucharist, nor indeed to any social or cultic practices which would separate its group from mainstream Judaism. In these respects the Jesus of Q differs both from the Jesus of the gospels, and from the Jesus of Paul, who was "delivered up for our trespasses", "put foward" by God "as an expiation by his blood", and "raised for our justification" (Rom. 3:25; 4:25).

Admittedly, Q may have been more extensive than the non-Markan passages common to Matthew and Luke, as they have a certain amount of further similar material that they do not share. We know that they both omitted some material from their Markan source, and they could have done the same in their use of Q, so that some Q passages may be preserved by only one of them.

Nevertheless, Q as it can be reconstructed from these two evangelists is a substantial document, and so the fact that it makes no mention of Pilate, nor of Jesus's Passion, crucifixion, or resurrection is surely significant. Such additions as one finds in Matthew and Luke to the Markan Passion narrative are quite different from each other (hence presumably no part of Q), and are followed by a return to the Markan order and substance. Furthermore, in Mark Jesus repeatedly predicts his Passion; but in Matthew and Luke such predictions are either taken over from Mark, or are peculiar to the one or the other gospel, and so form no part of Q—unless we can assume that, in all these cases, only one of the two evangelists is here preserving Q material. If the extent to which Matthew and Luke assimilated Mark is any guide to how they treated Q, then it would appear that they omitted very little of it; for Matthew retains some ninety percent of Mark, Luke admittedly less, but probably because he omits a Markan pericope in order to retain a parallel version of the same pericope from Q. This, says Tuckett, "suggests that Luke may have had a higher regard for Q than for Mark, and this in turn makes it less likely that Luke has made wholesale omissions from Q" (1996, p. 94).

It used to be said that, as a document consisting of sayings, with no mention of the Passion or resurrection, Q cannot be regarded as a gospel. But in 1945 the Coptic Gospel of Thomas was discovered (known earlier only from fragments in the original Greek), consisting of 114 of Jesus's sayings—about one third of them have parallels in Q— with no indication of where or under what circumstances he spoke them. It has no narrative framework, no birth or childhood stories, and no account of a public ministry (hence no baptism and no miracles). There is criticism of the Pharisees and one mention of John the Baptist (saying 46), but no suggestion of contact between him and Jesus. There is nothing about a trial, and the only allusion to Jesus's death comes in saying 55: "He who shall not hate his father and mother cannot be my disciple, and (he who does not) hate his brethren and sisters and take up his cross like me shall not be worthy of me". There is no mention of a resurrection. Some now date the Greek original underlying this Coptic text to the final quarter of the first century; others argue for a date in the first forty years of the second century.

Underlying Q are Jewish 'Wisdom' traditions. The Jewish Wisdom literature is extremely varied. In some passages Wisdom figures as a primordial being who, in the Wisdom of Solomon from the Old Testament apocrypha, sits beside God's throne as his consort (9:4), and, according to Proverbs 8:22–31, participates with him in the creation of the world. When she sought an abode on Earth, mankind refused to accept her, whereupon she returned in despair to heaven (1 Enoch 42:1f). As Tuckett notes, these ideas were "heavily exploited in early Christianity where the texts concerned were applied to Jesus" (1996, p. 169). Metzger and Coogan's 1993 *Oxford Companion to the Bible* states (art. 'Jesus Christ', p. 362) that the "Christology of pre-existence and incarnation" (according to which Christ existed in heaven before his birth on Earth) is "generally agreed" to "have developed from the identification of Jesus with the wisdom of God". In the Pauline and deutero-Pauline letters we find that Jewish statements about Wisdom are made about Jesus: Christ is "the power of God and the Wisdom of God" (1 Cor. 1:24). In him "are hid all the treasures of Wisdom and knowledge" (Coloss. 2:3). Like Wisdom, he assisted God in the creation of all things (1 Cor. 8:6)—an idea spelled out in the Christological hymn of Colossians 1:15–20. And like the Jewish Wisdom figure, he sought acceptance on Earth, but was rejected, and returned to heaven.

Wisdom traditions underlie Q, but not in the same way; for in Q Jesus is not identified with Wisdom, but both he and John the Baptist are represented as messengers sent by Wisdom (Q 7:34f) to preach the need for repentance before an imminent and final judgment. But they were ignored or rejected by their Jewish audience.

This coming judgment is to be effected by "the Son of man", a strange term clearly designating a supernatural figure:

> Be ye also ready: for in an hour that ye think not the Son of man cometh. (Q 12:40)

> I say unto you, Everyone who shall confess me before men, him shall the Son of man also confess before the angels of God: But he that denieth me in the presence of men shall be denied in the presence of the angels of God. (Q 12:8f)

The term 'Son of man' can not only designate this apocalyptic figure who will exercise a key role in the coming judgment; it is also a Semitic idiom for 'human being' which can be used as a self reference, as an alternative to the pronoun 'I' or 'me'. In Q this ambiguity is exploited, in that the term is used in both senses. It can designate the speaker, Jesus, who is now on Earth as a human being; for example:

> The Son of man is rejected by the present generation because "he is come eating and drinking", in contrast to the abstemiousness of John the Baptist. (Q 7:34)

> The foxes have holes and the birds of the heavens have nests; but the Son of man hath not where to lay his head. (Q 9:58)

> Blessed are ye when men shall hate you . . . for the Son of man's sake. (Q 6:22)

The first two of these three sayings seem strangely discordant. If a man lives as a vagrant, he is not likely to "come eating and drinking", nor, as this Q saying continues, to be a glutton and a friend of tax collectors. The second of the three sayings, whatever its appropriateness in Q may have been as the statement of a wandering, charismatic teacher, does not fit Jesus's circumstances in its context in Matthew, where "the settlement at Capernaum implies that Jesus had at least some kind of roof over his head, and the narrative mentions 'the house'" (Beare 1981, p. 213). Nevertheless it is true that all of these 'Son of man' sayings are "primarily concerned with hostility, suffering and rejection" (Tuckett, p. 266). When Jesus speaks of the Son of man in the other sense—that of a supernatural figure—he must mean either some soon to come apocalyptic personage, or himself who will return to Earth as judge in the form of this personage. Tuckett, with other commentators, holds that this latter is what is meant, that "the intention of Q's composition as a whole is to identify the 'coming one' . . . with Jesus who will 'come' as Son of man" (p . 119). Tuckett shows that the idea of a figure of the past being kept in heaven to reappear at the end-time in some capacity was a widespread one; and in Q Jesus's role in the final judgment is not dissimilar to that ascribed to the Son of man figure in 1 Enoch - a heavenly individual of very exalted status who will occupy us in Chapter 8 below. Thus the Son of man sayings in Q, taken as a whole, show a pattern of suffering for Jesus on Earth followed by "a vindication and retribution in the divine court"—all this being "remarkably similar" to the storyline of Chapters 2 and 5 of the Wisdom of Solomon and to Chapter 62 of 1 Enoch: in all three cases, "the one presently experiencing hostility and rejection will play a key role in deciding the fate of his erstwhile 'opponents'" (Tuckett, p. 275).

Q adopts the 'deuteronomistic' portrait of Israel's history as having consisted of persistent disobedience to Yahweh, accompanied by persecution of his messengers, the prophets. The community represented in Q saw itself in this tradition, as followers of a Jesus who called Israel to repentance and who as such are persecuted. Hence the Jesus of Q is made to add to his "Blessed are ye when men shall hate you . . . for the Son of man's sake" the words: "for in the same manner did their fathers unto the prophets". Wisdom traditions are invoked for the same purpose. Proverbs 1:20–23 represents Wisdom as warning against the doom consequent on rejecting her message; and in Q (11:49) Wisdom figures as the agent who sends out prophets who are persecuted. In fact, however, hostility to the Q preachers may not have extended to actual persecution. They may well just have been facing audiences who simply would not listen, and meeting with what Tuckett calls "the archetypal modern response to Christian preaching: apathy!" (p. 323).

Jesus himself may have suffered the usual fate of Wisdom's envoys— rejection and perhaps worse. This is not spelled out, and is the nearest Q comes to hinting that he may have died a martyr's death. It has been held to explain why there is no Passion narrative in Q. In the deuteronomistic tradition that Israel always persecuted its prophets; his death would be understood not as salvific, but as evidence of Israel's continuing impenitance (Jacobson 1992, p. 74). It is not simply a matter of Q being silent about salvific implications, but of a different explanation of suffering— as being the normal lot of the envoys of God or Wisdom.

Many students of Q, struck by its silence on Jesus's death and resurrection, agree that it would not have been produced by people who summarized their position as followers of Jesus with credal formulas like

Paul's in 1 Cor. I5:3f (Christ died for our sins and rose again). When Q was first isolated from Matthew and Luke, many regarded it as 'catechetical support' or 'parenetic' (morally exhortative) supplementation of the 'Easter kerygma'. As long as the latter was considered to be the essential element of any Christian preaching, it was hardly possible to regard Q otherwise. But not all early Christian movements were based on the 'Easter kerygma'. The Gospel of Thomas does not seem to consider Jesus's death and resurrection as significant for salvation, but, as we saw (above p. 152), understood it to come through interpreting the secret sayings of Jesus which it records.

Many attempts have been made to divide Q into chronological layers, with a developing Christology. The earliest layer is usually taken to consist of those sayings where Jesus advocates liberation from social constraints: one should break with family ties (Q 9:57–60), beg unashamedly (Q 11:9–13), and not worry about what to eat or wear (Q 12:22–31). Burton Mack believes that this is the nearest to the historical Jesus that Q allows us to get (1993, p. 203) and that the life-style here advocated is close to the behaviour of Cynics in the Hellenistic tradition of popular philosophy. They criticized conventional values and were known for fearless, carefree attitudes.

This Cynic analogy has been challenged by (among others) Tuckett, who holds that many of the sayings in this supposed earliest layer of Q were directions for itinerant missionaries. They gave up all their security not, as did the Cynics, in order to live a life of austerity as a means of achieving lasting contentment, but in order to proclaim their urgent message that the kingdom of God is at hand. As the judgemental theme is so prominent in Q, Tuckett and others hold that it was present from the first, and not just added as a second layer, as Mack and others have proposed.

Jesus certainly lays harsh conditions on the Q missionaries who are to go out to preach the imminent arrival of the kingdom. They are to leave home and family behind, and even to hate their father and mother (Q 14:26). Clearly, these itinerant missionaries are to depend on the hospitality of those whom they convert; and these their supporters of course are not required to renounce family and property. Homelessness and poverty result for the missionaries only when they and their mission are rejected. Thus it is itinerancy—not homelessness and other associated deprivations—that the missionaries must welcome. Arguing in this way, Tuckett (p. 367) holds that their strange wandering existence is not to be taken as reflecting the ideals of the Cynic philosophers of the time, but is rather a concomitant of the urgency of their message that the judgment is imminent. Eschatology dominates the Q preaching, and the itinerancy adopted by some Q Christians "should be seen in the same light" (p. 390).

J.S. Kloppenborg Verbin observes that reducing the historical Jesus to a Cynic-like personage has naturally provoked "muscular opposition", motivated in part by "theological rather than merely historiographic interests" (2000, pp. 422f), in that such a Jesus is even less "amenable to Christological discourse" than a Jesus who mistakenly foretold the imminence of an end-of-the world judgment (p. 440). Yet criticism of the Cynic estimate of Jesus can be independent of theological bias, and Kloppenborg himself does not accept it, finding it wrong to suppose that apocalyptic prophecy cannot originally have co-existed with sayings of a different type (p. I50). He does divide Q into chronological layers, but insists that this is a purely literary analysis, and does not imply that what he has distinguished as the earliest compositional layer includes all that is historically authentic about Jesus, making all that is present only in later layers necessarily inauthentic. Kloppenborg's earliest layer is "a collection of sapiental speeches and admonitions"— a "formative element subsequently augmented by the addition and interpolation of apophthegms [pithy sayings] and prophetic words which pronounced doom over impenitent Israel". But to say that these are "secondary" is *"not* to imply anything about the ultimate tradition-historical provenance of any of the sayings". He concludes:

> It is indeed possible, indeed probable that some of the materials from the secondary compositional phase are dominical [derive from Jesus] or at least very old, and that some of the formative elements are, from the standpoint of authenticity or tradition-history, relatively young. Tradition-history is not convertible with *literary history,* and it is the latter which we are treating here. (1987, pp. 244f; italics here, and in the previous quotation, are original.)

Tuckett allows that Kloppenborg "makes a strong case for the existence of some secondary additions modifying earlier traditions". Nevertheless, he himself prefers a "simpler model" than Kloppenborg's division of the text into multiple layers, namely one Q-editor "taking up and using (possibly a variety of) earlier materials" (pp. 71, 74). Certainly one cannot avoid positing some "secondary additions". Perhaps the most striking of them is the way in which, immediately after expressing pain and anger because Galilean towns had rejected his message (Q 10:13–15), Jesus thanks God for hiding "these things from sages and the learned" and disclosing them only to "children" (Q 10:21, presumably the Q community). Jacobson notes that this completely contradicts the overall deuteronomistic perspective of Q, which has no place for *thanksgiving* for Israel's unbelief. Jesus then adds: "Everything has been entrusted to me by my Father and no one knows the Son except the Father, nor [does anyone know] the Father except the Son, and to whomsoever the Son chooses to reveal himself" (Q 10:22). Here, even Israel's knowledge of God is denied, such knowledge being restricted to the Son and those who receive his message. This can only be "the expression of a radically sectarian group whose alienation from their own people exceeds anything found elsewhere in Q". Instead of pain and anger, we have here "the attitude of a self-satisfied conventicle, . . . convinced that it alone has access to the truth and that all others vainly grope in the darkness" (Jacobson 1992, pp. 149, 151),

If we take Q as a whole, as it now stands, we can infer that the community responsible for it cultivated the memory of a Jesus as their founder figure, an authoritative teacher who should be obeyed. They urged their fellow Jews who had earlier rejected his message to change their ways and accept it as a last chance to avoid the doom that would otherwise soon overtake them. Q has numerous such apocalyptic sayings, and evangelical commentators avoid embarrassment at this suggestion of imminent catastrophe by depriving these sayings of their references to time. Richard Valantasis, for instance, does grant that they seem to imply that "God will soon release a cosmic wrath in order to separate the good from the bad as a preparation for establishing his permanent reign on earth". Yet he holds that they "have a universal significance", applicable to "anyone at any time who picks up the collection of sayings to read them. . . . That universality makes sayings collections perpetually relevant" (2005, pp. 44–46).

Although there is a good deal of Wisdom-inspired legend in Q's portrait of Jesus, the specific references to the places and to the relatively recent time of his activities, and the theological orientation which fits the scene of Judaism, make it reasonable to accept that the whole is based on the life of an actual itinerant Galilean preacher of the 20s or 30s, although it is surely hazardous to try and decide which details are really authentic.

As I noted in the Introduction (above, p. 15), in the gospels the Galilean preacher of Q has been given some features of the Jesus of the early epistles, namely a salvific death and resurrection; and these have been set not in an unspecified past, as in the early epistles, but in a historical context consonant with the date of the Galilean preaching. Movement towards dating the earthly life of the Pauline Jesus in a relatively recent past is intelligible even without the influence of Q on later Christians; for Paul's Jesus came to Earth "when the time had fully come" (Gal. 4:4), and this soon developed in Pauline-type communities into the more specific statement that he had lived "at the end of the times" (Hebrews 9:26; 1 Peter 1:20). Even if this originally meant no more than that his first coming had inaugurated the final epoch (however long) of history (the epoch that would culminate in his return as judge), it would in time be taken to mean that he had lived in the recent past. And to post-Pauline and post-Q Christians of the late first century, familiar as they were with crucifixion as a Roman punishment, his death by crucifixion—already attested by Paul, but not given any historical context in his nor in other early epistles—would have suggested death at Roman hands, and hence during the Roman occupation of Judea from A.D. 6. From such a premiss, coupled with the Q datum of Jesus as a contemporary of John the Baptist, Pilate would naturally come to mind as his murderer; for he was particularly detested by the Jews, and is indeed the only one of the prefects who governed Judea between A.D. 6 and 41 to be discussed in any detail by the two principal Jewish writers of the first century, Philo and Josephus.

Another factor prompting the gospels' assigning of Jesus's life to the early first century is that it will have been known that Paul and his fellow apostles experienced their visions of the risen Jesus about the year 30; and so the evangelists naturally assumed that the crucifixion and resurrection had occurred shortly before. This, as we saw, was not expressly alleged by Paul, but it would seem plausible enough to evangelists writing outside Palestine, after earlier events there had been obscured from their view by the devastating war with Rome from A.D. 66. (Ellegård makes this point in his carefully argued article of 1993.) It was also easier to cope with deviant Christologies if Jesus's life could confidently be placed in specific historical circumstances. Gnosticism was describing Christ's redemptive work in mystical and quite unhistorical terms; and the so-called Docetes regarded flesh as sinful, and suffering and pain as incompatible with the divine nature, which was not subject to change. Hence they supposed that Jesus did not have a real human body, but lived on Earth as a phantom, incapable of suffering. Against all such ideas it was helpful to be able to point to a quite definite historical situation in which Jesus had lived and suffered. It was in order to confute the Docetes that Ignatius of Antioch—the earliest Christian writer outside the canon to link Jesus with Pontius Pilate—insisted that he was truly born from a human mother, the virgin Mary, that he was dependent on food and drink like any other man, and was "truly nailed to the cross" in the days of "Pontius Pilate and Herod the Tetrarch". As I noted above (p. 11), he reiterates this dating in three of his epistles with an emphasis that suggests that not all Christians were then agreed on the matter.

Once Pilate had been introduced to give the crucifixion a historical setting, most of the rest of the gospels' Passion story was prompted by musing on what was taken for prophecy in the Old Testament. "The details and individual scenes of the narrative do not rest on historical memory, but were developed on the basis of allegorical interpretations of Scripture" (Koester 1990, p. 224). The behaviour of Judas may serve as an example. Passages in the Psalms spoke of the righteous man as treated with brutal insolence by a close friend; and at Jn. 13:18 Jesus actually quotes Psalm 41:9 ("he that eateth my bread lifted up his heel against me") as "scripture" to be "fulfilled" by Judas. 1 Corinthians had represented the crucifixion as effected by supernatural powers, the *archontes* (Satan and his acolytes), to whom God, not man, had delivered Jesus.[6] In the gospels, Judas is introduced as a human intermediary; but as a residue from the original conception, Satan is said to have impelled him: "And Satan entered into Judas" (Lk. 22:3; cf. Jn. 13:27).[7]

Finally, I would stress that my overall thesis—that the gospels represent a fusion of elements in two originally independent streams of tradition—does not depend on the existence of Q as the source of the life of Jesus stream; for Q-type material is present already in Mark, and so existed earlier, and may derive from some source resembling Q rather than from Q. Moreover, Matthew presumably did not just invent his non-Markan sayings material, but drew it from tradition of some kind (Q or other). Hence my claim that the gospels fuse ideas represented in the early epistles with life-of-Jesus material independent of them is not invalidated even if Q is eliminated by supposing, as some few scholars do, that Luke had read Matthew. This, however, seems to me unlikely, and I find, with many others, that the Q hypothesis makes better sense of the non-Markan material common to these two evangelists.

7

The Prelude to Jesus's Public Ministry

i. Jesus and John the Baptist

The historical Baptist was a preacher with a following of his own—the gospels repeatedly make mention of his "disciples". Joan Taylor's recent study finds that they were not more cohesive as a group than were the disciples of other teachers of the time, and did not form a 'Baptist sect', out of line with mainstream Judaism (1997, pp. 29, 105). The gospels make him into a proto-Christian, preparing the way for Jesus the Messiah and of no significance in his own right. This is done most blatantly in the fourth gospel, which stresses already in its prologue that he was not the light of the world, but was merely sent to bear witness of it (1:8). In fact, however, the Baptist and his disciples seem to have been quite orthodox Jews, advocating the careful following of the Jewish law as the way of righteousness in expectation of an imminent judgment. They probably did not persist as a group for very long; at any rate, they are unmentioned in the Talmud. Nor were they particularly prominent in early Christianity, for neither Paul, who makes it clear that Christianity was a baptist sect, nor the authors of other New Testament epistles ever mention John.

It is the Paul of Acts—very different from the real Paul of the epistles—who knows something of the Baptist. Acts 19:1–7 mentions some dozen Christians who had been immersed "into John's baptism", and so were unaware that true baptism imparts holy spirit. Paul then baptized them "into the name of the Lord Jesus", "the Holy Ghost came upon them and they spake with tongues and prophesied." Paul took Christianity to gentiles, and as a result there are, as Larry Hurtado notes, "certain phenomenological analogies between the significance and role of Jesus in early Christian baptism and the significance and role of the deities of the pagan mysteries. As in the pagan rites, in which the initiates were assured of the power of the deity into whose rites they were entering, so early Christian baptism seems to have involved coming under the power of Jesus as the divinely-appointed Lord" (1999, pp. 82f).[1] The baptism of John will have been quite irrelevant to such gentile communities; for John "wished to point people towards a renewed commitment to Torah" (Joan Taylor, p. 8).

Our information about the historical Baptist comes only from the gospels and from the Jewish historian Josephus who, around A.D. 93–94, mentioned him as "a pious man" who exhorted the Jews to "come together for baptism" which was to "purify the body when the soul had previously been cleansed by righteous conduct". When "everybody turned to him", the Tetrarch Herod Antipas feared that his "so extensive influence over the people might lead to an uprising", and had him put to death (*The Antiquities* of *the Jews,* 18:5, 2 = paragraphs 16–19). This passage is almost certainly genuine. It is true that elsewhere Christian scribes have retouched Josephus's text. But if this passage had been interpolated by a scribe familiar with the gospels, then its account of the motives for John's imprisonment and execution would not be (as they in fact are) entirely different from those specified in the gospel version of these events (Schürer 1973, p. 346n). This is Josephus's only mention of the Baptist, whom he does not in any way link with Jesus.

In what follows I shall first give Mark's account of each relevant incident and then discuss alternative or additional matter in the other gospels.

At Malachi 3:1 Yahweh speaks of a "messenger" who "shall prepare the way before me". Possibly Elijah is meant, for at 4:5 Yahweh promises: "I will send you Elijah the prophet before the great and terrible day of the Lord come". This book, placed as the final one of the Old Testament in the Christian Bible, was written about 460 B.C., when Judah was a Persian province, and complains of laxity in ritual observances, and of immorality and unbelief among the people. Evil-doers prosper to such an extent that doubts have come to be expressed about God's justice. But Malachi gives an assurance at 3:1 that, after his "messenger", Yahweh himself will "suddenly come to his temple", purify unworthy priests, and condemn all who have "turned aside from mine ordinances" (3:7). Those who repent will be saved, but the wicked burned as in a furnace, and the righteous will tread on their ashes (4:1–3). This judgment is clearly regarded as imminent, as a threat to Malachi's contemporaries. Mark, however, identifies the "messenger" as John the Baptist, and makes him herald, not God but Jesus by changing

Yahweh's statement that "he shall prepare the way before *me*" to "he shall prepare *thy* way" where the possessive pronoun refers to "Jesus Christ the Son of God" in the preceding verse (Mk. 1:1f).

The other passage quoted here by Mark is from the second division of the book of Isaiah. What is genuinely Isaianic in its first division is set in Jerusalem in the Assyrian period (eighth century B.C.) and frequently mentions Isaiah by name. The second division (from Chapter 40) does not once refer to him, is set in Babylon two centuries later, and promises the Jews prompt release from captivity there because of the rising power of Persia; for Chapter 40 begins with: "Comfort ye, my people"; the iniquity which had led to their exile is forgiven. The historical Isaiah could hardly have undertaken to comfort his people about an exile which was not to befall them until more than a century later.

The Hebrew text continues with a passage which, as Joan Taylor observes (1997, p. 25), in literal translation reads: "A voice is calling in the wilderness prepare (the) way of Yahweh". She adds: if the quotation of what the voice says begins after the participle 'is calling', then we can punctuate:

A voice is calling: 'In the wilderness prepare the way . . .'

The caller is, then, not in the wilderness, but a voice (somewhere not specified) is saying that in the wilderness a way is to be prepared. That this is what is meant is strongly suggested by the second half of this verse: "Make straight in the desert a highway for our God" (40:3). However, the Greek (Septuagint) version presupposes a different punctuation, namely:

A voice is calling in the wilderness 'Prepare the way of Yahweh'.

This places the caller in the wilderness. The synoptic gospels all follow the Septuagint here; and so Mark is enabled to make the passage into a prophecy of the Baptist's preaching in the desert. The Septuagint has 'the Lord' to render the divine name Yahweh, but for Mark it is a path for Jesus that is to be prepared; and so, instead of continuing with the Septuagint's "make straight the paths of our God", Mark writes "make his paths straight" where 'his' refers back to 'Lord', taken to mean Jesus. Mark's composite quotation from Malachi and Isaiah (the whole of which he erroneously attributes to Isaiah) thus reads:

> Behold I send my messenger before thy face,
> Who shall prepare thy way;
> The voice of one crying in the wilderness,
> Make ye ready the way of the Lord,
> Make his paths straight.

The original meaning of Isaiah 40—that a highway is to be prepared, in the desert between Babylon and Palestine, through which God is to lead his people back home from their captivity - has been completely disregarded, and a wilderness preacher, sent to prepare the way for Jesus, extracted from it. The Qumran sectaries, who survived until the Romans destroyed their settlement in A.D. 68, followed the Hebrew text, and (punctuating it as I have suggested) took it, equally arbitrarily, to mean their own retreat into the desert from a Jerusalem given over to wickedness: "Prepare in the desert Yahweh's way" (Details in Anderson 1976, p. 69).

Josephus does not specify where the Baptist was active, and Mark's siting of his activities in "the wilderness" has some theological significance. The many—both positive and negative—associations of such a place are listed in the relevant article in Metzger and Coogan's 1993 *Companion to the Bible*. It is the traditional haunt of evil spirits, and in New Testament times was believed to be the place of encounter between heavenly and infernal powers. But it is also the place where some Jews of this time expected the Messiah to appear. The idea was that the age of salvation would correspond to the early history of Israel, and a number of Messianic fanatics felt that they were called, as the second Moses or Joshua, to bring things to a head in the wilderness (cf. Schürer, pp. 463f). The association of wilderness and Messiah is alluded to when Jesus warns against "false Christs" and against their supporters who say: "Lo, here is the Christ. . . . Behold, he is in the wilderness" (Mt. 24:23–26). The Baptist, then, is appropriately located there because he combats evil and heralds the Messiah. Matthew (3:3) and Luke (3:4) follow Mark in quoting "Isaiah the prophet" apropos of the 'voice in the wilderness' calling for the way of the Lord to be prepared. They do not, however, also give the Malachi passage about the 'messenger' in this context, and so avoid Mark's error in ascribing it, with the rest, to Isaiah. This correction was doubtless deliberate. They reserve the Malachi quotation for its position in Q, where it appeared in a speech by Jesus about the Baptist. He is said there to be "more than a prophet", indeed the man "of whom it is written, Behold I send my messenger before thy face who shall prepare thy way before thee" (Mt. 11:9f = Lk. 7:26f). As in Mark, the Old Testament passage has been adapted to make it serviceable. Instead of Malachi's 'I, Yahweh, will send a messenger who will prepare for my coming judgment', Q has 'I, Yahweh send my messenger (John) who shall prepare *thy* (Jesus's) way'. The passage thus becomes an address by God to his Messiah.

Returning now to the quotation from Isaiah, we find that, unlike Matthew, Luke allows it to run on so as to include the two verses which follow the reference to the voice in the wilderness, which are thus also represented as a prophecy of the Baptist's preaching. The second of these two verses, which in the Septuagint reads "all flesh shall see the salvation of God" is, then, quoted by Luke (3:6), and will have been particularly welcome to him, as he is much more concerned than Matthew to emphasize the universality of salvation.

Mark continues, saying "even as" Isaiah prophesied, "John came who baptized in the wilderness and preached the baptism of repentance unto remission of sins" (1:2, 4). Forgiveness of sins is no mean function, and at 2:5–7 it is implied that, in the Jewish view, God alone can forgive them, and that it is blasphemous of Jesus to claim to do so. Mark, then, although clearly anxious to subordinate John (as Jesus's forerunner), nevertheless assigns to him a function which even in Jesus is considered excessive. Matthew was obviously not prepared to credit the Baptist with such powers, and assigned to Jesus the function of "saving his people from their sins" (1:21) by the sacrificial shedding of his blood in death. And so he studiously deleted the phrase 'unto remission of sins' from the Markan account of the Baptist's activities—he mentions (3:6 and 11) the 'repentance' specified by Mark, but not the forgiveness—and inserted it into the report of Jesus's words at the Last Supper. In Mk. 14:24 this reads: "This is my blood of the covenant, which is shed for many." To this Matthew (26:28) adds "unto remission of sins". Beare (1981, p. 509) observes that "almost certainly, this was done with the conscious intention of teaching that the forgiveness of sins is not given in baptism, but is effected by Christ's offering of his life in sacrifice." Once again, we see how one evangelist 'edits' the work of another in the interests of his own theology.

Mark next notes that "John was clothed with camel's hair and had a leathern girdle about his loins" (1:6). Zechariah 13:4 reveals that a "hairy mantle" was the conventional garb of a prophet, and John's clothing is clearly modelled on that of Elijah (described at 2 Kings 1:8 and margin as "a man with a garment of hair" and "girt with a girdle of leather about his loins"). As we saw, the final verses of the book of Malachi (possibly added to it later) interpret the 'messenger' of 3:1 as

Elijah who will return to Earth: "Behold I will send you Elijah the prophet before the great and terrible day of the Lord come" (4:5). By New Testament times the returning Elijah had come to be regarded as the forerunner of Messiah: "The scribes say that Elijah must first come" (Mk. 9:11). Mark, who makes the Baptist this forerunner, does not actually say that he is Elijah, but merely implies it. After the Baptist's death, Mark's Jesus says (9:13) that Elijah has already come, but again does not expressly say that the Baptist was he. This reticence seems to be occasioned by one of the artificial features which Mark has imposed on his material, namely the so-called 'Messianic secret' (which occupied us in Chapter 5 above), in accordance with which Jesus's true status is not understood by people who come into contact with him. If Mark's Jesus had proclaimed that John was Elijah, forerunner of the Messiah, then his own status as Messiah would have been disclosed. Matthew dispenses with the Messianic secret, and so is able to adapt Mk. 9:13 so as to make the identification of the Baptist with Elijah explicit: he represents Jesus's audience as understanding that "he spake unto them of John the Baptist" (17:13); and at 11:14 Matthew makes Jesus declare, with an explicitness unique in the New Testament, that John is Elijah.

Mark next devotes two sentences to the substance of the Baptist's preaching. I quote them together with the parallel passage in Matthew, which derives from Q. (The agreements here of Matthew and Luke against Mark are too numerous and substantial for the passage to be independent reworking, by those two evangelists, of Markan material):

Mark 1:7-8	*Matthew:* 3: 11 *(cf. Luke* 3: 16)
There cometh after me he that is mightier than I, the latchet of whose shoes I am not worthy to stoop down and unloose. I baptized you with water: but he shall baptize you with Holy Ghost.	I indeed baptize you with water unto repentance: but he that cometh after me is mightier than I, whose shoes I am not worthy to bear: he shall baptize you with Holy Ghost and with fire.

The idea that the spirit of Yahweh will be poured out immediately before the end of the world and the final judgment is stated in Joel (2:28–31):

> And it shall come to pass afterward that I will pour out my spirit upon all flesh . . . The sun shall be turned into darkness, and the moon into blood, before the great and terrible day of the Lord come.

The addition in Matthew and in Luke, from the Q source, of the words "and with fire" to Mark's account make it quite clear that the coming one is to effect this final judgment. He will pour a river of fire onto the wicked, but God's spirit, and all the blessings that go with it, onto God's people. The context in Q in which this is set shows that these events were expected to happen soon:

> Even now is the axe laid unto the root of the trees: every tree therefore that bringeth not forth good fruit is hewn down and cast into the fire . . . The fan [of the coming one] is in his hand, and he will thoroughly cleanse his threshing floor, and he will gather his wheat into the garner, but the chaff he will burn up with unquenchable fire. (Mt. 3:10–12 = Lk. 3:9, 17)

Clearly, says Tuckett, one is here "in the thought world of Jewish eschatology, with a vivid expectation of an imminent End culminating in some kind of judging process", this being a recurring theme in Q: "divine intervention is imminent and positive response is demanded" (1996, p. 115).

For Q, then, if not for Mark, the coming one will simply judge, not give any further opportunity for repentance and salvation. John's call is the last opportunity, and only those who submit, with proper contrition, to his 'baptism of repentance' will belong to the 'wheat' soon to be gathered into the heavenly barn. Hence this baptism must not be allowed to unworthy persons, who would thereby be saved from the wrath to come. Here it is of interest to see how the Q material is manipulated differently by Matthew and by Luke. In Luke it is "the multitude" who are turned away as unworthy, as an "offspring of vipers" (Lk. 3:7). Matthew, however, makes John's audience consist of "Pharisees and Sadducees" (3:7), obviously thinking that they, rather than an indiscriminate multitude, deserve such strong abuse. Matthew can, for the most part—23:2f is a very unusual exception—see little good in Pharisees, and in an extended passage, expanded from Q, of his Chapter 23 makes Jesus denounce them as "hypocrites" and "serpents", even though they are his neighbours, neighbours being people who, according to his own teaching in this same gospel, are to be loved (5:43; 19:19).

As we saw in Chapter 1 above, the reason for Matthew's polemic is not that the historical Pharisees were in fact wicked, but that he was writing in a post-A.D. 70 situation where they were the dominant party in Judaism, and Christian propagandists were competing with them in trying to attract followers. Thus at 23:15—a verse without parallel in the gospels—he maks Jesus address scribes and Pharisees as "hypocrites for ye compass sea and land to make one proselyte; and when he is become so, ye make him twofold more a son of hell than yourselves." Such behaviour, although offensive to Matthew, was surely not in fact 'hypocritical', for its practitioners believed sincerely enough in the faith they were promulgating. But the point I am making here is that hostility is always more violent against rivals than against outsiders. A man will object particularly strongly to someone making proselytes if thereby potential proselytes are diverted from himself. The Antichrist for Luther was not Mohammed, Buddha, Confucius or Aristotle, but the Pope.

Who then, is this mightier, coming one, so superior to John, who will effect the final judgment? Surely not Yahweh himself, for his superiority to any mortal, even to a prophet such as John, was so obvious to any Jew that it would have seemed blasphemous for John to stress that he was unworthy to carry God's shoes. The evangelists and Q—at any rate Q as represented in Matthew and Luke—wish us to think that Jesus is meant; and the early church was quite unequivocal about this, so that, in Acts, Paul is made to say to certain disciples at Ephesus that "John baptized with the baptism of repentance, saying unto the people that they should believe on him which should come after him, that is on Jesus" (19:4). It is however, far from certain that this was the original implication of the relevant traditions. If John's call to repentance was the last opportunity, there is no room for a subsequent ministry by Jesus. Hence some commentators suppose that, at a pre-Q stage, the mightier coming one meant, if not God, then at least some supernatural personage who would shortly bring the world to an end. If this is so, it confirms the impression given by Josephus that the historical Baptist had no connection with Jesus.

After Mark's very brief account of the Baptist's preaching, Jesus is introduced: he "came from Nazareth of Galilee and was baptized of John in the Jordan" (1:9). We have seen that Matthew was not prepared to allow John to forgive sins and reserved this power for Jesus: and so we are not surprised to find this evangelist—in contrast to Mark—making John so conscious of Jesus's superiority that he hesitates to baptize him, and says, incredulously: "I have need to be baptized of thee, and comest thou to me?" How he could have come to know of Jesus's superiority is not explained; and if he did know of it, it is strange that he should later inquire of Jesus: "Art thou he that cometh, or look we for another?" (11:3). However, Jesus overrules his modesty in Chapter 3, and tells him to proceed with the baptism "to fulfill all righteousness" (verse 15)—a phrase which suggests that this baptism is ordained by God.

Luke changes Mark's account even further, and "avoids saying that Jesus submitted to John's baptism by using a passive verb: 'During a general baptism of the people, when Jesus too *had been baptized'* (3:21). Thus he does not need to say by whom! And just in case readers might assume John was responsible, Luke precedes this story by telling us that John the Baptist was already in prison by this time" (Elliott 1982, p. 24).

What happened at Jesus's baptism also depends on which gospel one reads. Mark has it that as he came out of the water, "he saw the heavens rent asunder and the Spirit as a dove descending upon him: and a voice came out of the heavens, Thou art my beloved Son, in thee I am well pleased" (1:10f). The scene presupposes the ancient idea that 'the heavens' form a solid canopy, which must be opened ("torn asunder") if the spirit of God is to 'descend'. Matthew changes the voice so as to make it an announcement, in the third person, not just to Jesus, but a public theophany. "The heavens were opened"—it is not just that 'Jesus saw' this happening, as in Mark, although some manuscripts read "the heavens were opened *to him"* (two final words retained in the RV but not in the RSV and NEB)—and the voice does not just address him personally with "thou art my beloved Son", but makes a general statement to all and sundry: "This is my beloved Son" (3:16f). Luke who, as we saw, does not portray the actual baptism, nevertheless wished to retain the reference to the opening of the heavens and the descent of the spirit; and so he says that these things occurred after the baptism, when Jesus was at prayer (3:21f).

Most manuscripts of Luke represent the words of the voice from heaven as identical with those given in Mark: "Thou art my beloved Son. In thee I am well pleased". But in one early Greek manuscript of Luke and several Latin ones, the voice says, instead of the second of these two statements: "Today I have begotten thee". This quotes Psalm 2:7, where the speaker is possibly an Israelite king affirming his claim to his throne against rebel princes: "The Lord said unto me, Thou art my Son, this day have I begotten thee." Early Christians took this as an address by the Father to Jesus the Son, in other words as a proof text of his Messianic sonship (as at Hebrews 1:5 and Acts 13:33 where, however, it is adduced as relevant to his resurrection, not his baptism). The text of Luke which quotes the Psalm may well—in spite of its poor manuscript attestation—be the original reading; for when the Fathers (such as Justin, Origen, Augustine) quote this verse from Luke, they almost always give it in this form. Moreover, Luke assimilates so much of Mark that it is surprising that he should deviate here from the Markan account unless he did so deliberately. If, then, the poorly attested reading is original, scribes must have replaced it with one that aligns the wording with that of Mark; and their motive could well have been to delete any suggestion that Jesus was not Son of God from the first, but was only adopted as his son at some stage in his life—at his incarnation, or resurrection, or, as here, at his baptism: *"today* I have begotten thee" could—so scribes may well have feared—be interpreted in this way. There were certainly Christian groups in the second and third centuries who had such an 'adoptionist' view of Christ, maintaining that he was not divine, but had been adopted by God as his son at some stage. And wording which might be adduced to bolster such 'heresy' should not be allowed to remain in the text.

This verse (Lk. 3:22) is among those discussed in detail by Ehrman in his 1993 book which shows the effect of early Christological controversies on the text of the New Testament. He concludes that, during the earliest period of its transmission, the text "was in a state of flux" and "came to be more or less standardized in some regions by the fourth century and subject to fairly rigid control (by comparison) only in the Byzantine period" (p. 28). He adds in a note that this is the view of a wide range of scholars.

In the fourth gospel the revelation of Jesus's sonship is directed neither to Jesus himself, as in Mark, nor to all witnesses of his baptism, as in Matthew, but to the Baptist, who twice confesses that he did not earlier know who Jesus was. The event has occurred before the narrative begins—note in this connection the past tense in the following quotation of the relevant passage (Jn. 1:29–34)—so that the evangelist (going in this respect even further than Luke) is able to omit the actual baptism scene:

> (29) On the morrow he seeth Jesus coming unto him, and saith, Behold the Lamb of God, which taketh away the sin of the world! (30) This is he of whom I said, After me cometh a man which is become before me: for he was before me. (31) And I knew him not: but that he should be made manifest in Israel, for this cause came I baptizing with water. (32) And John bare witness, saying, I have beheld the Spirit descending as a dove out of heaven; and it abode upon him. (33) And I knew him not: but he that sent me to baptize with water, he said unto me, Upon whomsoever thou shalt see the Spirit descending, and abiding upon him, the same is he that baptizeth with the Holy Spirit. (34) And I have seen, and have borne witness that this is the Son of God.

The Christological title 'Lamb of God' (verse 29) is absent from the other three gospels. Here, in the fourth, the Baptist is represented (verse 30) as knowing even Jesus's pre-existence (that he existed as a supernatural being before he was born on Earth). This doctrine is not stated in the other gospels (and certainly not even hinted at by the Baptist there), and commentators agree that it is even quite foreign to Luke (Fitzmyer, p. 197). The fourth evangelist, however, takes a different view and represents Jesus (at 17:5) as reminding God of the splendour they had experienced together before the world was created. In the earliest (pre-gospel) Christian documents, Jesus's pre-existence is simply alleged. Here, in the fourth gospel, he himself is represented as stating it. This can only be a relatively late development, reflecting the theology of the Johannine community.

The first three gospels agree in affirming that, immediately after his baptism, Jesus went into the wilderness, where he was tempted by the Devil, that he and John never met again, and that by the time he began his ministry John had been imprisoned. The fourth gospel contradicts this and represents the two men as both at work baptizing people before John's imprisonment (3:22–24). Here, then, Jesus baptizes (although the first three gospels give no hint that he ever did so), and John continues to baptize, even though the sole purpose of his baptism, namely to manifest Jesus to Israel (1:31) is already accomplished. The point of all this is that it enables the evangelist to bring out Jesus's superiority: "Jesus was making and baptizing more disciples than John" (4:1). It is what Fitzmyer, in another connection, has called parallelism involving one-upmanship (see above, p. 91).

We saw earlier that already Matthew took exception to John's baptism being "for remission of sins". If, as in the fourth gospel, Jesus is "the Lamb of God which taketh away the sin of the world", then John's baptism can have but a modest function, and he is accordingly completely self-effacing, his final statement being that Jesus must increase and he himself decrease (3:30). After this we hear no more of him. "His death is not even mentioned [as it is in the other gospels], so unimportant is his person" (Wink 1968, p. 95). His sole function is to be a 'witness' to Jesus's Messiahship. As Joan Taylor notes, this characterization of the Baptist results in an illogical story; for if he really recognized that Jesus was so much his superior, why did he not stop immersing people and become Jesus's disciple? (p. 296). He not only repudiates any claim to be himself the Christ (and even calls upon his own disciples to take cognizance of this denial; 3:28), but declares too that he is neither Elijah, nor even a prophet, but merely the voice in the wilderness (1:19–23), "sent before the Christ" (3:28), but certainly not in order to proclaim him as judge at the end of the world; for one of the most striking differences between the fourth gospel and the other three is that it is practically devoid of apocalyptic ideas. Its Jesus does not preach an immediate and catastrophic end of the world.

Luke was likewise writing in a situation where the final judgment had failed to materialize, in spite of the predictions in Mark and Matthew that it was imminent. And therefore in some passages he adapts Markan material so as to delete any implication of a prompt end to the present dispensation. Thus Jesus's proclamation at Mk. 1:15 ("the time is fulfilled and the kingdom of God is at hand: repent ye and believe in the gospel") becomes in the Lucan parallel (4:15) what Fitzmyer calls "a bland narrative statement about Jesus's preaching in synagogues and being praised by all the people" (p. 232). Luke also makes Jesus tell the parable of the pounds, inherited from Q, for the purpose of correcting any idea that "the kingdom of God was immediately to appear" (Lk. 19:11, unrepresented in the parallel account of Mt. 25:14ff). And he sometimes rephrases words of Jesus so as to make them guides to everyday living, rather than pointers to some catastrophe. The best-known example is Lk. 9:23: "If any man would come after me, let him deny himself, and take up his cross daily, and follow me", where 'daily' has been added to the Markan material (Mk. 8:34).

This concern to avoid implication of immediate catastrophe influences what Luke has to say about the Baptist, whose declaration at Mt. 3:2 ("The kingdom of heaven is at hand") has no equivalent in Luke. In a passage with no canonical parallel, Luke makes the Baptist give moral advice (tax collectors are not to demand more money than is due, soldiers are to be content with their pay) which suggests that ordinary everyday life will continue and not shortly be brought to a catastrophic close (Lk. 3:10–14). Even more significantly, Luke has retained nothing of the Baptist's role as Elijah and suppresses Mark's hints on this matter. Mk. 9:9–13, where Elijah is said to have come, and Mk. 1:6, where John is represented as dressed as Elijah, are absent from Luke. Yet he retains some Q passages which predict a prompt end, as when he allows the Baptist to preach about the axe which already lies at the root of the trees and to declare that the winnowing fan of judgment has already been taken up. Again, Lk. 10:9, 11 states that "the kingdom of God is come nigh", and Lk. 21:32 that "this generation shall not pass away till all things be accomplished." Wilson has shown that this gospel alternates between affirming and denying the proximity of Jesus's return, his *parousia*. He attributes this clash to the evangelist's concern to combat two extremes which its delay had already provoked, namely scepticism as to whether it would ever occur at all, and a fervent renewal of apocalypticism, with false Messiahs coming forward (1973, pp. 67ff).

Only the Q source (hence Matthew and Luke, but not Mark) tell that, during his imprisonment, the Baptist sent his disciples to ask Jesus whether he was "the coming one" (Mt. 11:2–6 = Lk. 7:18f)—presumably the one who will "baptize with holy spirit and with fire". Jesus replies by alluding to his own miraculous curative powers and his preaching to the poor, which fulfil the expectations of Isaianic prophecies (Isaiah 29:18f.; 35:5f.; 61:1). This does not at all certificate him as the one who will baptize with fire, although we are obviously meant to infer that the miracles and the preaching mark him out as the person expected by the Baptist. Jesus himself is here represented as allowing that his ministry does not correspond with the picture the Baptist had drawn up; for he adds: "Blessed is he who shall find none occasion of stumbling in me". In the fourth gospel the Baptist of course makes no such inquiry, for there his acceptance of Jesus's exalted status remains unwavering.

That Jesus and the Baptist were close to each other is certainly what the gospels argue. The Baptist's message "Repent ye, for the kingdom of heaven is at hand" (Mt. 3:2) is stated by Jesus as his own message, with these same words in Matthew's next chapter (4:17). The most puzzling statement about the relationship of the two men is the Q passage Lk. 16:16, with an equivalent at Mt. 11:12f. I quote Joan Taylor's rendering (p. 309) of the former:

> The Law and the prophets [missing verb] until (*mechri*) John; since then (*apo tote*) the good news of the kingdom of God is told, and everyone breaks into it violently.

The missing verb can only be guessed at: it could be 'prophesied' as in Matthew's equivalent passage: "For all the prophets and the law prophesied until John" (11:13). The word 'until' (*mechri*) could be understood so as to include or exclude John from the proclamation of the kingdom; but Matthew's verse 12, "from the days of John the Baptist until now", seems to include him in the eschatological age, in the time of fulfilment alongside Jesus. Tuckett notes that the problems of this Q verse "are legion and the debate it has engendered is enormous." He agrees, however, that "within the context of Q, it would seem that John must definitely be included in the new era"—an era "characterised by the phrase 'kingdom of God'" and "one in which the preachers of the kingdom are suffering some kind of violence". The belief the passage expresses is that "the final establishment of God's kingdom will be consummated in the near future", while the present in itself is already "in part an era of eschatological fulfilment" (1996, pp. 135, 137).

Jesus's closeness to the Baptist is relevant apropos of the question of the origin of the so called Lord's prayer. If in a previous chapter we saw that Mary's Magnificat may not be hers at all, and may have referred originally to the Baptist, we may note here that there is some indication that the Lord's prayer may derive from him. Elliott thinks that the introduction to it at Lk. 11:1 betrays as much:

> There the disciples ask Jesus to teach them to pray *as John taught his disciples.* Now, as Jews, Jesus' disciples would know *how* to pray—and, in fact, in several places in the gospels Jesus assumes that they will pray. What is meant in Luke 11:1 is that the disciples of Jesus ask for the special prayer that John is known to have used. From this Baptist background, therefore, came the so-called Lord's prayer. (p. 28)

Matthew (6:9ff) does not preface the prayer with any statement that it is 'just as' or 'exactly as' (the Greek *kathōs* could mean either) John taught his disciples, and it is easier to envisage that Matthew dropped such a tradition than that Luke invented it. Joan Taylor agrees that Luke's wording "does not necessarily suggest that Jesus should teach his disciples a prayer different from that taught by John to his", and so it could be that the disciples of Jesus "wanted exactly the same prayer" (pp. 151f).

Did the historical Baptist ever meet Jesus? Josephus does not suggest that he did. The account of the collaboration of the two men in the fourth gospel is prompted by theological motives and in many respects at variance with what is said on the subject in the other three. As Scobie notes (1964, p. 149) these three "give us no sayings of John which are directly applied to Jesus". And Brown thinks that "the idea that he was preparing the way for the Messiah whom he identified as Jesus (Jn. 3:28 most explicitly) is a Christian adaptation of the Baptist's own thought that he was preparing the way for God". Brown adds that, "as part of this Christian reinterpretation, the Baptist was attributed the role of Elijah through an exegesis of Malachi . . . combined with Isaiah 40:3, with Jesus seen as the Lord whose coming was thus heralded" (1979, pp. 283–84).

Jesus's baptism by John has nevertheless repeatedly been classed among the best attested data of his life. The argument is that, since evangelists later than Mark found the sinless Jesus's submission to John's "baptism for the remission of sins" embarrassing, and tried to explain it or cover it up, Mark's statement on the matter cannot be a Christian invention. However, what embarrassed later Christians need not have embarrassed him. Justin Martyr, writing about A.D. 150, betrays that it was the Jewish notion that the Messiah would be unknown as such to himself and others until Elijah as his forerunner should anoint him;[2] and Morna Hooker concedes (1983, p. 80) that Mark, who implies that the Baptist is Elijah, may have been influenced by a tradition of this kind. Apart from this possibility, if Jesus was to be brought into contact with John, baptism would have to be involved, as it is clear from Josephus that the principal thing known about John was that he baptized. Mark could unthinkingly have made Jesus come to him for baptism because opportunity was thereby provided to introduce the heavenly voice proclaiming Jesus's supernatural status as God's son. It is this supernatural aspect of the proceedings which Mark stresses, not the actual baptism (which is dismissed in half a dozen words), and he obviously did not pause to ask himself whether the baptism could be taken to put Jesus's sinlessness in question. In the earliest Christian tradition of which there is a record, the resurrection was the moment when his true status as "Son of God in power according to a spirit of holiness" was revealed (Rom. 1:4). But Christians came in time to think that he must always have been what he was at that moment disclosed to be; and so, as Brown observes (p. 181), the revelation of who he is was brought back first to his baptism and, later still, in the infancy narratives, to his conception. Furthermore, early Christian communities, believing as they did that baptism imparted the Spirit, could not unnaturally suppose that Jesus himself had received it at baptism "as a dove descending upon him" (Mk. 1:10). Hence Haenchen can say that Mark's account is based "not on an old historical tradition, but on the projection of early Christian experience onto the life of Jesus" (1968, p. 62). When baptism had become a universal Christian practice, the belief could naturally arise that Jesus had commended and consecrated it by his own example. The American New Testament scholar H.J. Cadbury said:

> All the gospels indicate that Jesus was baptized with water and at that event the Spirit came upon him. This was regarded as the normal experience of Christians, and was possibly transferred from Christian experience to Jesus rather than *vice versa*. (1937, p. 21)

Enslin puts in question not only the historicity of the role of the Spirit at Jesus's baptism, but also that of his baptism itself, saying that "reading farther and farther back" of an important rite "is invariably the case in a religion which takes itself seriously as one of revelation. What is now under God's blessing must always so have been." He finds a parallel to such thinking in the standpoint of the priestly material of the Pentateuch, dating from the exile or after, but ascribing current religious law and ritual to the initiative of Moses, hundreds of years earlier (1975, pp. 5, 9).

ii. The Temptation

After his account of Jesus's baptism, Mark continues:

> And straightway the Spirit driveth him forth into the wilderness. And he was in the wilderness forty days, tempted of Satan; and he was with the wild beasts; and the angels ministered unto him. (1:12f)

Satan is an old Hebrew word meaning 'adversary', and was at first a common noun designating an opponent in war or in a lawsuit. It came to be the proper name of one of Yahweh's specialist angels, whose function was to thwart and punish evil doers; and only gradually did increased powers come to be ascribed to this angel, who eventually was represented as opposed even to Yahweh himself.[3]

Mark makes no reference to fasting or hunger, which are integral to the version of the temptation episode preserved by Matthew and Luke. On the contrary, the 'ministry' of the angels (which the tense of the Greek verb shows to have been continuous) could only have consisted in supplying food, as angels fed Elijah (1 Kings 19:3–8) when he was in the wilderness for forty days. Altogether, forty is a suspiciously sacred number. Moses fasted forty days and nights on Sinai (Exodus 34:28; Deuteronomy 9:9), and Israel spent forty years being tested by God in the wilderness (Deuteronomy 8:2). We recall too that, according to Acts 1:3, Jesus's resurrection appearances lasted for forty days.

Mark's statement that during the forty days Jesus "was with the wild beasts" is agreed, even by conservative commentators, to be 'an imaginative element' in the narrative. The beasts may have affinity with Satan, in that they are the associates of demons, as is already suggested in the Old Testament: Isaiah links "wild beasts of the desert" with "satyrs" (13:21; cf. the Septuagint of Isaiah 34:11–15, where "devils shall meet with satyrs" and both are associated with animals). Although Mark, unlike Matthew and Luke, does not state wherein Jesus's temptation consisted, the wilderness is the traditional haunt of evil spirits, and the background to Mark's story is "the current belief that the Messiah was the divine agent for the overthrow of Satan and all his powers, and that therefore a tremendous battle, or trial of strength, between him and Satan would form an integral element in the last days" (Nineham 1963, p. 63).

Belief in angels and demons is generally considered to have entered Jewish religious thinking from Zoroastrianism from the time of the Babylonian exile. By New Testament times, the Jews were so conscious of evil that they repudiated the Old Testament view that Satan and other supernatural powers were subservient to God, and supposed instead that these demonic forces had seized control of the world. In the apocalyptic literature of this time, Satan's dethronement was anticipated as a cosmic event, to be effected, in Christian understanding, by Jesus, who showed that he had the capacity to do so by facing up to him from the first, and then by giving his disciples "authority to cast out devils" (Mk. 3:15) and "authority over the unclean spirits" (6:7). At Mk. 1: 24 one of these actually asks him: "Art thou come to destroy us?"

However, Mark's reference to the temptation is strangely brief, and does not state that Jesus, already at this point, won a victory over Satan. Evans observes: a single sentence in which Jesus is spoken of not as the active assailant, but only as the passive object of Satan's trial, is hardly an effective way of saying that the Son of God is victorious over him. "Since no temptations are specified, victory over them cannot be expressed" (1968, p. 14).

Matthew and Luke give the temptation story not as a narrative, but as a dialogue between Jesus and the Devil, in which the two speakers contrive to settle disputed points by regaling each other with Old Testament quotations. No witnesses are present, and those who regard the exchanges as authentic have to suppose that, on some 'holy occasion', Jesus confided their content to his disciples. Against authenticity is, first, that all the quotations agree with the Greek (Septuagint) text, not with the Hebrew, suggesting that the dialogue was drawn up in a Greek-speaking Christian environment, not in a Palestinian one; and, second, that none of the quotations are really to the point. They appear relevant only because they have been made to bear a meaning alien to their Old Testament context. As we shall see, what the evangelists are here giving us is a learned dispute in the manner of the rabbis of the time, who characteristically argued in this way, ignoring what words of scripture meant in their Old Testament contexts. We have seen Matthew doing this in his comments on Jesus's birth and infancy, but here it is Jesus himself who is made to follow this same method.

The words of Jesus in these two accounts of Matthew and Luke are practically identical, and derive from Q, which, we recall, was essentially a collection of Jesus's sayings, with minimal indication of the circumstances in which they were spoken. Kloppenborg, among others, favours the suggestion that this temptation episode is a late addition to

Q which shows Q to be moving from a sayings collection to the pattern of a typical biography of the Greek and Roman kind, where it is not unusual for the hero's story to begin with some kind of testing (1987, pp. 248ff, 262). In addition to its narrative form, the episode has further features that are otherwise unusual in Q: only here is the tempter called *diabolos* (elsewhere in Q he is Beelzebub or Satan); and it is only here in Q that Jesus says nothing except to quote scripture.

If the words of Jesus in this episode derive from Q, the two narrative frames, differing from each other, represent the work of the respective evangelist, with also some assimilation of the brief Markan material. The first four verses are as follows:

Matthew 4:1–4

(1) Then was Jesus led up of the Spirit into the wilderness to be tempted of the devil.

(2) And when he had fasted forty days and forty nights, he afterward hungered.

(3) And the tempter came and said unto him, If thou art the Son of God, command that these stones become bread.

(4) But he answered and said, It is written, Man shall not live by bread alone, but by every word that proceedeth out of the mouth of God.

Luke 4:1–4

(1) And Jesus, full of the Holy Spirit, returned from the Jordan, and was led by the Spirit in the wilderness (2) during forty days being tempted of the devil.

And he did eat nothing in those days: and when they were completed he hungered.

(3) And the devil said unto him, If thou art the Son of God command this stone that it become bread.

(4) And Jesus answered unto him, It is written, Man shall not live by bread alone.

Here, and elsewhere in the Q temptation narrative, the translations read "the Son of God", whereas in fact there is no 'the' in the Greek, and 'a Son of God' would be a more appropriate rendering. We notice that Mark's reference to wild beasts has been dropped, but not his mention of the wilderness and the forty days. Matthew adds "and forty nights", thus pressing the parallel with Moses's fast of "forty days and forty nights" on the wilderness mountain. New altogether compared with Mark is Jesus's fasting, leading to his hunger which gives the Devil occasion to tempt him. According to Matthew, there was no tempting during the forty-day fast, but only subsequently, as an attempt to exploit Jesus's hunger. This was presumably the situation as presented in Q. Luke rather clumsily retains (verse 2) Mark's idea that the tempting was spread over forty days, yet also follows Q in restricting it to the Devil's later approach initiated by Jesus's hunger after this period (cf. Schramm 1971, p. 36). Luke also has (verse 3) "this stone" (singular) and the singular of "bread" in the Greek (in other words, 'command this stone that it become a loaf'), instead of the corresponding plurals, as in Matthew. The inference is that Matthew retained these from Q, but Luke changed them "in the interest of plausibility . . . Since Jesus is alone, the changing of one stone to a loaf would satisfy his need and reduce the grotesque image of a desert full of loaves" (Fitzmyer, p. 515). This small detail shows how rationally and deliberately a sacred writer can go to work in 'editing' his material.

Jesus responds (verse 4 of both accounts) with words from Deuteronomy 8:2–3, where the people of Israel are being reminded that, although God afflicted them by letting them hunger in the wilderness, he then provided food of a miraculous kind:

> He humbled thee, and suffered thee to hunger, and fed thee with manna . . . that he might make thee know that man doth not live by bread only, but by everything that proceedeth out of the mouth of the Lord.

The reminder is thus intended to show that life depends not only on material sustenance, but on reliance on God; and the Deuteronomist's point is: even where a natural food supply is wanting, God can sustain those who trust him with miraculous food. The point the evangelists are making, however, is: it is not permissible to sustain life miraculously because God can keep man alive by other means. As Haenchen has noted, the evangelists (and their predecessor, the compiler of Q) can make Jesus use the Old Testament passage only because they are following not its sense but its wording in the manner of rabbinic exegesis (1968, p. 67).

Two of the three items of the temptation episode, as given in Q, do seem, as we shall see, to suggest that working miracles implies an improper lack of trust in God, and hence can be read as a reply to the charge that Jesus was a magician, as polemic against a view of him that might well be suggested by the Markan miracle stories. There are few references to miracles in Q, and the Q passage "if I by the Spirit of God cast out devils, then is the kingdom of God come upon you" (Q 11:20) makes the exorcisms signs of the inbreaking kingdom, rather than of Jesus's divine sonship. Räisänen observes that Mark's strangely curtailed version of the temptation story could be due to his having suppressed the sort of miracle critique discernible in its Q version. Whatever Mark knew about the temptation he "must have mutilated: 1:12f is an almost unintelligible excerpt" (1990, p. 218n).

Returning now to the Q account, we find that the two further temptations are given in reverse order in the two gospels, and I quote next what Matthew gives as the second, with its Lucan parallel, where it figures as the third. Here it is likely that Matthew has preserved the Q ordering, while Luke departs from it in order to close thescene with Jesus on the pinnacle of the temple, as an effective climax to the whole.

Matthew 4:5–7

(5) Then the devil taketh him into the holy city; and he set him on the pinnacle of the temple (6) and saith unto him, If thou art the Son of God, cast thyself down: for it is written, He shall give his angels charge concerning thee: And on their hands they shall bear thee up, Lest haply thou dash thy foot against a stone. (7) Jesus said unto him, Again it is written, Thou shalt not tempt the Lord thy God.

Luke 4:9–12

9) And he led him to Jerusalem and set him on the pinnacle of the temple and said unto him, If thou art the Son of God, cast thyself down from hence: (10) for it is written, He shall give his angels charge concerning thee, to guard thee; (11) and, On their hands they shall bear thee up, Lest haply thou dash thy foot against a stone. (12) And Jesus answering said unto him, It is said, Thou shalt not tempt the Lord thy God.

Whereas in the first temptation Jesus, being hungry, might be supposed to be willing to supply himself with food, he is given no motive that would lead him towards succumbing to this further temptation. Some commentators have tried to make good this deficiency by supposing that he is being asked to give an exhibition miracle, a public display of God's care for him, thus authenticating himself as Messiah. But no public is said to be present to be impressed by such a demonstration. The Devil does not say: do this so that people will believe in you, nor does Jesus's answer imply that this is what was meant.

The Devil here quotes a Psalm which, in a series of images, represents God's protection of the Israelite who has "made him his refuge". In one image this protection is pictured as aid to a traveller walking along rough and rocky paths: the angels will hold him up to keep him from tripping over a stone. The Devil wisely omits the phrase (italicized below) which refers to these paths so that he can apply the passage to the quite different situation of jumping from a height:

For he shall give his angels charge over thee,
To keep thee in all thy ways.
They shall bear thee up in their hands,
Lest thou dash thy foot against a stone. (Psalm 91:11–12)

If Jesus were to object that, as the Psalm does not promise protection to those who jump from a height, he cannot feel any inclination to do so, the whole story—which presupposes that he is meritoriously resisting what he feels as a real temptation—would be ruined. And so instead of objecting to the Devil's distortion of scripture, he replies in the same vein with Deuteronomy 6:16: "Ye shall not tempt the Lord your God, as ye tempted him in Massah". This alludes to the situation described in Exodus 17: 2ff, where the Israelites, thirsting in the desert, doubt God's willingness to preserve them. They are here said to "tempt" the Lord, instead of trusting in him, and he responds by miraculously supplying water from a rock. But if the people here 'tempt' God by *not believing* that he will save them, the exact opposite is implied by Jesus's use of the verse from Deuteronomy; for he says that he will not tempt God by *believing* that God will come to his rescue.

We pass on to what in Matthew is the third and final temptation, and in Luke the second:

Matthew 4:8–11	*Luke 4:5–8*
(8) Again, the devil taketh him unto an exceeding high mountain, and sheweth him all the kingdoms of the world, and the glory of them;	(5) And he led him up, and shewed him all the kingdoms of the world in a moment of time.
(9) and he said unto him, All these things I will give thee, if thou wilt fall down and worship me.	(6) And the devil said unto him, To thee will I give all this authority, and the glory of them: for it hath been delivered unto me; and to whomsoever I will I give it.
(10) Then saith Jesus unto him, Get thee hence, Satan; for it is written, Thou shalt worship the Lord thy God, and him only shalt thou serve.	(7) If thou therefore wilt worship before me, it shall all be thine.
(11) Then the devil leaveth him; and behold, angels came and ministered unto him.	(8) And Jesus answered and said unto him, It is written, Thou shalt worship the Lord thy God, and him only shalt thou serve . . .
	(13) And when the devil had completed every temptation, he departed from him for a season.

Matthew's final verse introduces the angels of Mark's brief narrative—Luke omits them altogether—but adapts them to the situation he has constructed. They do not, as in Mark, minister to Jesus during the whole forty days, but are appropriate and acceptable heavenly ministers to him at the end of his three trials.

A mountain from which "all the kingdoms of the world" (Matthew's verse 8) are visible can only be mythical. This is possibly why Luke deleted it, making the Devil simply 'lead Jesus up', that is, into the air, for a bird's eye view. In Matthew the view from the mountain discloses not only all kingdoms, but also "the glory of them". This was obviously too much for Luke, who transfers this phrase from the narrator (Matthew's verse 8) to the Devil (Luke's verse 6), leaving the pronoun 'them' with no antecedent in the Devil's speech: the antecedent ("all the kingdoms of the world") has been left (verse 5) with the narrator. The Devil's next sentence in Luke's verse 6 is altogether unrepresented in Matthew (occurring neither as narrative nor as dialogue there), and expresses very clearly the belief, common in New Testament times, that the world is in the power not of God but of the Devil. Jesus is made to repudiate him at the end of this temptation with Deuteronomy 6: 13–14, where Israel is forbidden to worship the gods of other peoples, not the Devil, who was unknown to the author of Deuteronomy.

Early in the twentieth century J.M. Robertson suggested how this story, where the Devil offers all the kingdoms of the world in return for worship, could have originated. He was stressing the effects of pagan art on Christian believers. Paintings or sculpture, originally representing some event, historical or imaginary, coming to the eyes of those who know nothing of the real subject represented, may be freshly interpreted by such people in accordance with their own prepossessions. (Strauss, we saw, argued that Christian interpretation of Old Testament texts originated in a similar way.) Robertson quotes (1910, p. 318) a story (recorded by Evemeros) of the young Jupiter, led by Pan to "the mountain which is called the pillar of heaven; whereupon he ascended it and contemplated the lands afar; and there in that mountain he raises an altar to Coelus (or Heaven). On that altar Jupiter first sacrificed; and in that place he looked up to heaven". In a picture or sculpture representing this story, Pan would be given horns, hoofs, and tail, and would stand beside the divine youth at the altar. Christians who saw such a picture would take Pan for the Devil and suppose that, standing by the young divinity at the altar on a mountain top, he was asking to be worshipped in return for the kingdoms of the Earth to which he was pointing. This would give rise to a narrative where the Devil takes Jesus to an "exceeding high mountain" and tempts him.

Since Robertson, the view that ideas were transmitted to early Christianity by pictures has been taken up (without reference to him) by Toynbee, who stressed the importance of visual representations in conveying ideas among illiterate people (1939, pp. 508–518). Robert Graves believed that some Greek myths themselves originated from misinterpretations of a sacred picture or dramatic rite. He called such a process "iconotrophy", and declared that "examples of it can be found in every body of sacred literature which sets the seal upon a radical reform of ancient beliefs" (1958, p. 21).

It has long been noted that, in the whole temptation dialogue, the real meaning of the Old Testament quotations is completely distorted. Jesus and Satan, says Beare, are not in the least interested in the original setting of a text, and "the use of Scripture . . . on both parts is like nothing so much as the way in which a pair of rabbis would proceed in a disputation. . . . This debate is the creation of someone who was trained in the methods of the rabbinical schools" (1981, p. 111).

The kind of curiosity which led to the formation of infancy stories could well have led to such learned expansion of a bare tradition that Jesus had confronted Satan. Once it had come to be said that this had happened, people wanted to know what had transpired on the occasion. On this view, the whole story is a legend about Jesus's confrontation with the forces of evil, based on fairy-tale motifs and arbitrary interpretation of Jewish scripture. "All three incidents", says Haenchen, "collapse when deprived of the quotations wrongly interpreted in the manner of rabbinic dispute" (1968, p. 71).

The temptation episode has evoked many over-subtle interpretations. Some have supposed that the dialogue is based on what went on in Jesus's own mind. Dodd, for instance, argues that gaining power by "doing homage to the devil" means "in realistic terms, exploiting the latent forces of violence to wrest from Rome the liberation of his people"; and that Jesus did go into the wilderness after receiving the spirit at his baptism in order to ponder whether his vocation as Messiah implied that he should act in this manner (1971, p. 123). Alternatively, it is supposed that he wrestled with such questions not once but throughout his ministry, so that the biblical story is "a commentary by the later Church, couched in mythological imagery", on temptations with which he "must often have had to contend" when he wondered how best to assert his authority (So Gilmour, art, 'Jesus Christ' in Grant and Rowley 1963). But we are in fact told nothing of such psychological processes in the text. For Joseph Ratzinger (the present Pope Benedict XVI) the "deep point" of the temptation story is to remind us that the Devil can quote scripture, that "scriptural exegesis can become a tool of the Antichrist", as when "the alleged findings of scholarly exegesis have been used to put together the most dreadful books that destroy the figure of Jesus and dismantle the faith" (2007, p. 35. On p. 229 he illustrates what he has in mind when he indignantly repudiates the suggestion that the discourses of the fourth gospel are no more than "Jesus poems", put together by people "claiming to be acting under the guidance of the Paraclete").[4]

Jesus's temptation is not mentioned in the fourth gospel, even though the Devil is by no means ignored in it, and even though Jesus there thrice refers to "the prince of this world" (Jn. 12:31, 14:30, 16:11), obviously meaning the Devil and assigning to him the function of ruler he performs in one of the passages from the Q dialogue. The fourth evangelist characteristically omits details which might be taken to depress Jesus's dignity—these include the scene describing his baptism, his prayer in Gethsemane and his forsaken cry from the cross (Mk. 15:34 = Mt. 27:46)—and makes him stoutly declare that the prince of this world "has nothing in me" (14:30), that is, has no power over me.

There are no references elsewhere in the New Testament to the temptation situations as given in the synoptics. In the epistle to the Hebrews we are indeed told that Jesus was tempted (2: 18)—not, however, on a specific occasion in the wilderness, but "in every way" (or "at all points"), *kata panta* (4:15). The idea is that this supernatural personage (1:2f), if he was to help mankind, and thus "succour them that are tempted", must have lowered himself so as to become completely human, and in no way above the weaknesses of the flesh. The tempting and the "suffering" which went with it (2:18) are soteriological requirements, necessitated by his function as saviour, not reflections of the supposedly historical experiences recorded in the synoptics.

Morna Hooker observes that, if the ideas in Mark's temptation. narrative seem "fanciful", this is "because we no longer think, as Mark and his contemporaries did, of a world dominated by demons" (1983, p. 15). Quite so. For Beare, not only the demons but also the Devil is "a mythological conception" which we cannot accept "without falling victim to superstition" (1981, pp. 107–08). Once again we see modern theologians quietly setting aside what has been taught as literal truth for hundreds of years, but is no longer acceptable to educated audiences of today.[5] Such antiquated ideas are not normally simply dismissed, but are made acceptable by reinterpretation, as when Caird grants that "the devil is a mythological figure", but holds that "myth . . . is a pictorial way of expressing truths" (1963, p. 79). Fitzmyer claims that the "theological import" of the temptation scenes is "in the long run of greater importance than any salvaging of their historicity" (p. 510). So much in the gospel narratives is now treated in this way: Morna Hooker writes, even of the Passion, that "in terms of historical verisimilitude, many of Mark's scenes creak". Yet of course they have great "significance for Christian believers" (p. 92). The 'theological import' and the 'significance' of the narratives used to be founded on their historical truth. It is not easy to see what remains—apart from pious fantasies—once this has been ceded. Allison's verdict is surely just: the temptation narrative is "in no way the record of a historical event", but evidences "the first long strides toward uninhibited creativity that later led to, among other things, the canonical infancy stories and, still later, the apocryphal gospels" (1997, p. 62).

8

Jesus as Apocalyptic Prophet

i. The Transition from Prophecy to Apocalyptic Thinking

Looking forward to a happier future formed the core of the Jews' religious ideas from very early times, and the original idea was that it was the nation that would enjoy it. The older prophets hoped that the nation would be morally purified, that its enemies would be destroyed and that it would be governed by a just, wise, and powerful king. Later, the future hope was extended from the nation to the world, and with this enlargement there is combined a far more decided reference to the individual. This change was doubtless caused by the breaking down of the tribal barriers and the absorption of the nation in a large empire (first the Greek and then the Roman). In the older days religion could still be a national, not an individual matter. The tribe would expect its god to succour it in matters which concerned the well-being of all, such as the growth of its crops or its fortunes in war. But when the nation ceased to exist as an independent unit, the deity could no longer be a tribal appurtenance, and, as the god and ruler of all mankind, he would be regarded as favouring particular individuals rather than a particular tribe. As individuals were dying all the time, and as the virtuous were no less mortal than the wicked, the hope of a blessed future could no longer remain in the form of an expectation of earthly bliss, from which the dead would have been excluded. It had to become a belief in individual resurrection after death. While the belief related only to Israel as a nation there was no need for it to be supramundane. The nation would always be there to benefit from its fulfilment. But once the expectation had been transferred from the nation to the individual, it was necessary to provide for the virtuous dead.

Another consequence of the absorption of the nation in a large empire was the birth of ideas that the whole existing world would be destroyed by a miraculous act and that God would inaugurate his kingdom with a universal judgment of the living and dead. These ideas are expressed in Jewish apocalypses which succeeded the prophetic literature. 'Apocalypse' means 'revelation', and apocalypses purport to be supernatural revelations imparted by men of God. The prophets had promised the nation delivery from political and moral ills, and had prophesied fighting and great affliction before this would occur, but nothing in the way of supernatural catastrophe. The apocalypses, however, foretell a deliverance preceded by the whole natural order passing away. For instance the 'Apocalypse of Weeks' (1 Enoch 93:1–10, followed by 91:12-17 in the Ethiopic text) tells that, in the eschatological finale, "the world will be written down for destruction" (91:14), after which there will be a great judgment: the old heaven will be taken away and a new one revealed. Collins (2003, p. 72) thinks that this apocalypse is probably the first Jewish document to envisage the end of the world in a literal sense. The book of Enoch in which it is embedded is composite (its different sections deriving from the second century B.C. and later) and of course pseudepigraphic. But the New Testament epistle of Jude (verse 14) quotes a verse from a different section of it as authoritative prophecy from "Enoch, the seventh in descent from Adam".

It is not difficult to see how this apocalyptic type of writing sprang from the changed world situation of the Jews. When the early prophets were active, the world they knew consisted of God's people, a number of small neighbours (Edom, Moab, Phoenicia), and the two great powers of Egypt and Assyria at opposite ends of the geographical horizon. The Jews could measure their strength with the small kingdoms, and even the two large ones were so countered by one another that Israel could turn to the one for protection from the other. But with the rise of Alexander the Great's empire, which extended from Greece to Persia, and later with the even more extensive Roman dominion, the Jews found themselves facing a situation where some of them began to think that only a cosmic act of God would have the power to break the vast and totally corrupt empires oppressing them. However, even at the beginning of our era, the old hope of a glorious future for the nation was still alive, so that the ideas of these later times were a mixture of conflicting expectations. Old ideas survived alongside newer ones, as always.

ii. From Reimarus to Schweitzer
a. Hermann Samuel Reimarus (1694–1768)

Eschatology is teaching concerning the last things—the transformation of the existing world order and its replacement by a new one, concomitant with the resurrection of the dead and the Last Judgment. According to Albert Schweitzer (1954, p. 23), the first scholar to "grasp the fact that the world of thought in which Jesus moved was essentially eschatological" was Reimarus, a teacher of Hebrew and oriental languages at a Hamburg grammar school. As a deist, he based his belief in God on evidence to be obtained from reason, and did not accept that sacred literature provided revelation in any sense. His views are embodied in his lengthy *Schutzschrift für vernünftige Verehrer Gottes* (Defence of Reasonable Worshippers of God), a prolix and repetitious work with involved sentence constructions which present any translator with a difficult task. Perhaps he would have made the work easier for the reader, had he intended it for publication. But, as a man of peace, he withheld it, knowing full well that, at that time, dispassionate discussion of its contentions was not to be expected.

When Reimarus died in 1768, he left his manuscript in the hands of his son and his daughter. G.E. Lessing, who was then in Hamburg as consultant dramatic critic of the recently founded theatre there, knew the family, and realized that the manuscript was too long and unwieldy to be publishable in full, quite apart from censorship problems. But in 1769 he became librarian to the Duke of Brunswick at Wolfenbüttel, and in that capacity he was able, between 1774 and 1778, to publish, free from censorship, what he called "Fragments" from the work—anonymously, from consideration for the family of the deceased author. That this was Reimarus was early guessed, but not officially known until his son acknowledged it in 1814 and presented the rest of the work to the Hamburg city library. By then the public had lost interest. But in the 1770s Lessing's 'Fragments'—particularly the longest and most inflammatory of them all—evoked such a furore that the Duke ruled that in future Lessing's publications on religion should be subject to the censor.

Prominent in the outcry of the 1770s was J.M. Goeze, chief pastor of Hamburg's best-known church, who insisted that the Bible's infallibility was not hypothesis but indisputable fact. He was abusive both to the unnamed author of the Fragments and to Lessing, who, he said, was capable of understanding only the religion of the deists. To deny, with them, validity to any revelation was of course to reject the whole apparatus of established Christianity and hence to question the need for a professional class of clergy to administer it. Reimarus himself certainly owed a good deal to English and French deists of the earlier eighteenth century.

The following account is based on G.W. Buchanan's 1970 Introduction to, and English translation of, the longest of the Fragments, headed 'The Goal of Jesus and his Disciples', and on Strauss's appreciative essay on Reimarus of 1861. Both had access to the whole manuscript, although it was not published in full until 1872, when G. Alexander issued it in two volumes at Wiesbaden. Strauss devotes most of his long essay to Reimarus's criticisms of the Old Testament, but sections 23–37 cover the New Testament, and the final section 38 gives his assessment of Reimarus's achievement.

Reimarus was convinced that those parts of the Old Testament written before the Babylonian captivity actually deny that there will be life after death. It is true that, in the pre-exile period, there was no notion of a judgment of the dead, or of belief that they would enjoy God's presence. Belief in the resurrection of the faithful did not become prominent in the Jewish world until it helped to sustain the Maccabean martyrs in the second century B.C. The first six books of the Old Testament were of course written much earlier, and Reimarus's criticism of them is so severe that one could almost suppose that one was reading Colenso.[1] Witness the following passage on the exodus from Egypt and the conquest of the promised land:

> The author makes all the beasts of Pharaoh die three times, one time after another, so that none was left over, and there always are new ones present again in his rich imagination, ready to be killed anew.... On the other hand, the Israelites took all their cattle with them on the way so that no hoof is left behind; yet when he wants to create a miracle, there is none there, so that they suffer hunger every moment and it is necessary to rain meat. He can make thirty times a hundred thousand men with wives, pregnant women, children, sucklings, with old, sick, lame and blind; with tents and baggage, wagons and tools, with 300,000 cattle and 600,000 sheep pass through the dried up bed of the sea, which must have been at least a German mile [7,500 metres, or 4.7 English miles] wide, whose ground was impracticable: here because of moss and slime, there because of sand or coral shrubs ... in pitch darkness of night, in three hours safe and sound.... He makes the sun stand still for twenty-four hours in order to provide light for the Israelites who were winning.... He blows and screams down the firmest walls, although he was not able to scream away or make the terrible iron chariots stand still ... (p. 118. This and further unexplained page references are to Buchanan's translation).

Schweitzer remarked that in such passages Reimarus exposed all the impossibilities of the narrative, but of course did not realize that the Pentateuch is a composite work, a combination of at least four major documents of different provenance and age, so that the separation of those sources, as effected by later critics, would explain the perplexities of the text (1954, p. 15).

For Reimarus, says Buchanan (p. 4), "the primary goal of the Israelites was not religious but political, aggressive, and military. They wanted to take the land away from the Canaanites." Reimarus obviously held that, as they wished to justify their seizure of land already occupied by another tribe, they found it expedient to write books in which they represented God as saying that he has given it to them. The legacy of this still burdens us. James Barr observes that "the situation in the present-day Middle East sufficiently demonstrates the result that follows when ancient ideologies of war, people and land are allowed to survive and grow without adequate ethical evaluation", and are given this allowance because of "the simple confidence that, if God has commanded something, that fact must override and blanket out all other ethical considerations" (1993, p. 220).

As for Christian doctrine, Reimarus asked: by what justice could a good God demand sacrifice, especially the sacrifice of his own son? And "he doubted that children baptized before the age of understanding were by that magical act classified among the small minority of those whom God loved, whereas the overwhelming majority of mankind, who had not been so treated, were damned" (Buchanan, pp. 3f).

The longest 'Fragment' has come to be regarded as something of a first step in modern life-of-Jesus research. It begins by noting that his message was no more than "repent, for the kingdom of heaven has come near" (Mt. 4:17), "repent and believe in the gospel" (Mk. 1:15). 'Gospel' does not, Reimarus says, here mean the complex specifics of modern Christian doctrine (p. 44), but only this joyful message that the kingdom is near, and that Jesus himself would soon inaugurate it. His forerunner John the Baptist had given the same message: "Repent ye, for the kingdom of heaven is at hand" (Mt. 3:2). Repentance, a necessary preparation, entails "a change of mind toward sincere love of God and neighbour" (p. 40).

As for the kingdom itself, since neither Jesus nor his forerunner explained what it meant, they obviously understood it in the well-known customary Jewish way, as a secular kingdom that will free the nation from oppression (p. 77). Jews were not expecting a "saviour who would blot out the sins of the whole world through his suffering and dying", but someone who would "save the people of Israel from its secular servitude" (p. 79). Reimarus adduces, as evidence for this, the disappointment the disciples expressed when Jesus was killed and such hopes came to nothing: "We hoped that it was he which should redeem Israel" (Lk. 24:21). Not only did Jesus not teach that he was an atoning sacrifice, but also he had no intention of founding a new religion; for he insisted that the whole Jewish law be kept (Mt. 5:17f). His message was innovative only to the extent that he regarded himself as the coming one who would establish the kingdom. This obviously correct view has recently been endorsed by Allison (cf. below, pp. 280f).

The doctrine of the trinity was also not taught by Jesus. "I and the Father are one" (Jn. 10:30) does not, says Reimarus (p. 59), mean that he is God, but expresses "simply the powerful kind of love he had toward the Father and that the Father had toward him" (cf. above p. 44). The way the terms Father, son, and holy spirit are used in the New Testament does not suggest that these three are one. The voice, presumably of the Father, from heaven at Jesus's baptism which designates him as "son" (Mk 1:11) meant only that he was "beloved of God": ordinary men were called "sons of God" in this sense (p. 46. It is quite true, as many have pointed out, that in the scriptures a 'son of God' may be an angel, an Israelite king, or simply an Israelite, or a particularly pious one). The spirit which Jesus saw descend upon him on this occasion (Mk. 1:10) implies no more than that he was gifted. In the New Testament, to possess the spirit means to have, often extraordinary, gifts. The other mention in the gospels of the three all together occurs at Mt. 28:19, where the risen Jesus tells the disciples to baptize all the nations "into the name of the Father, and of the Son, and of the Holy Ghost". Apart from the fact that this incident presupposes the resurrection and so, for Reimarus, cannot be historical, the wording is at variance with the baptismal practice of the early church; for it is quite clear from the Paulines and from Acts that baptism was administered "in the name of Jesus" (pp. 66f), not with the three-fold formula. If Mt. 28:19 had actually been spoken by Jesus, it is unintelligible that Peter should have been reluctant to go anywhere near the pagan Cornelius, and needed a special revelatory vision to convince him that to do so was allowable (Acts, Chapter 10), and equally unintelligible that he failed to appeal to these dominical words at the subsequent Jerusalem meeting which called him to account for his behaviour (pp. 62f). Altogether, baptism became important only after Jesus's death. When he sent the apostles out as missionaries (Mt. 10:7f), he did not tell them to baptize, but "to proclaim that the kingdom of heaven had come near, and to heal the sick, cleanse the lepers, awaken the dead and drive out the devil" (p. 63).

In Reimarus's view, Jesus hoped he would soon be supported by an uprising of the people against Roman rule. In this connection he mentions Jesus's commands to keep silence about his miracles, even in circumstances where they could not but become known—a feature of Mark which Wrede was to find of great significance. Reimarus interprets these senseless commands as evidence of Jesus's desire "to make the people even more curious" (p. 90), and so increase his following, and thereby make an uprising more likely. This interpretation, although quite unconvincing, does show that Reimarus recognized these commands to silence as a problem feature of the narratives—particularly problematic since on other occasions Jesus enjoins the exact opposite, namely that his miracles be made known. When the disciples of the imprisoned Baptist come to him, inquiring who he is, he replies by declaring, thus publicly, that his miracles certificate him: "Tell John what you have seen and heard: the blind again receive their sight, the lame walk . . ." (p. 91). Elsewhere, as Strauss notes (1861, p. 352), Reimarus said that if Jesus could perform such powerful miracles, why did he not get the poor Baptist freed from prison? It is clear from Acts that release from captivity by means of supernatural help was no problem in those early days.

Hoping, then, for an uprising, Jesus made a triumphal entry into Jerusalem so as to be hailed as king. But he counted too much on the people's acclaim, was betrayed, deserted and killed, dying in despair with a cry that God had forsaken him, since his hopes had come to nothing (pp. 90–95). In the immediate aftermath, "the apostles were overcome only by anxiety and fear that they also might be persecuted." But as in the event nothing untoward happened, they quickly plucked up courage, and decided on a course of action that would continue to give them the renown they had enjoyed as Jesus's disciples (pp. 126–28). They proclaimed that he had first to suffer to atone for mankind's sins, and that only then would he enter into his glory. They could argue in this way because a small number of the Jews themselves did not expect, as Messiah, a secular ruler who would free them from slavery, but believed the Messiah would come twice—once as poor and suffering, but then, later, from the clouds of heaven, with power. As Strauss pointed out (1861, p. 363), pre-Christian Jews were not in fact expecting a suffering Messiah, and the statements of Trypho the Jew in Justin Martyr's Dialogue (of the mid-second century A.D.), to which Reimarus appeals (p. 105), are not evidence for any such Jewish belief in pre-Christian times. Nevertheless, the idea that the saviour might be a supernatural personage is certainly pre-Christian. Reimarus points to the vision of Daniel (7:13): "Behold, with the clouds of heaven there came one like unto a son of man." Here, this figure in human form is a personification of the Jewish "saints" who will receive "dominion, glory and a kingdom" after the destruction of the oppressive world signified in the narrative by various "beasts" (7:17). In later Jewish apocalyptic literature, however, Daniel's words were understood not as a personification, but as a reference to a specific supernatural personage, *"the* son of man", who would come down from the clouds in judgment as ruler of God's kingdom. The apostles, says Reimarus, "made use of this system" (p. 106), which "came in handy" to them (p. 129). And so they stole and hid Jesus's body quite soon after his burial, pretended that he had risen from his grave, had gone to heaven, and would come again as "son of man". They waited, however—so we learn from Acts—a full fifty days before making any public declaration that he was risen. By then, the body, even if found, could not be identified, and "they could say all the more boldly that they had seen him here and there, that he had been with them, spoken with them, and eaten with them; and finally that he had left them and gone to heaven so that he might soon return again and more gloriously" (p. 130. This 'soon' is important, as we shall see). Schweitzer picked up this point about the disciples' delay, saying: "That it was only after a lapse of weeks that they came forward with the 'Easter message' is a problem which has been given far too little attention in the studies of the resurrection" (2000, p. 477).

It remains only for Reimarus to note that the gospel accounts of the resurrection—in themselves hopelessly contradictory—would be more convincing if they showed that God had allowed the risen one to be seen by those who had condemned him (p. 138) and not just by his followers. He found his estimate of the resurrection as a fraud confirmed also by the feeble way in which, in Acts, the apostles 'prove' it by twisting and distorting Old Testament passages. Can we really believe, he asks (p. 101), citing one of the many examples, that "I will give you the sure good deeds of David" says the same as "I will awaken Jesus of Nazareth from the dead that he may never again return to the grave?" (Isaiah 55:3; Acts 13:34). Modern commentators (notably Haenchen in his commentary on Acts) have observed that Acts has to quote the passage from Isaiah from the Septuagint, as the Hebrew wording would obviously not be to the point, and that even the Septuagint rendering has to be trimmed to make it appear relevant.

Reimarus is justifiably dismissive of the 'fulfilment' passages in the gospels as well as of those in Acts, and not only of those adduced concerning the resurrection. Matthew, he says, repeatedly and more often than the other evangelists, claims that certain events happened so that what had been said by a prophet "might be fulfilled". But in every case the event bears no relation at all to what the Old Testament passage means in its context, and all such citations are "mere distortions of scripture" (pp. 103f). He mentions, as a signal example from Matthew's infancy narrative, "Out of Egypt I have called my son", which does not refer to Christ at all (p. 120; cf. above, p. 97); and if very many people choose to accept that it does, this does not mean that "their choice was made logically or with reflection" (p. 124).

It is clear from all this that, in Reimarus's view, the new, post-crucifixion estimate of Jesus has been worked into the text of the gospels by the evangelists themselves. This could easily be done because they did not write until "thirty to sixty years after the death of Jesus . . ., in a language which a Jew in Palestine could not understand, at a time when the Jewish nation and republic was in the greatest confusion and trouble"—a clear allusion to the Jewish War with Rome and its aftermath—"and when very few who had known Jesus were still alive" (p. 119). Strauss notes (1861, pp. 340f) that Reimarus elsewhere states that the evangelists were geographically dispersed in widely different locations. This is presumably why they did not collude and bring their separate accounts of the resurrection into any sort of agreement. Each one of the four imposed in his own way the new ideas of the apostles and disciples on to his material—but only to some extent; for Jesus's original ideas and message are still discernible in the gospels, however much they present the new system of a suffering and spiritual saviour in Jesus's own words—for instance in his repeated predictions of his Passion and resurrection, which are unhistorical. If they were genuine, the disciples would not have been disconsolate after his death (pp. 81f).

Reimarus is a little confused at this point. Earlier he had insisted on distinguishing the evangelists, as historians, from the apostles, as the theologians, saying that, in reconstructing Jesus's teaching we must be guided by the evangelists, not by what is taught by apostles such as Paul in epistles, or by Peter and Paul in their speeches in Acts. Here, in this later passage, he again makes this distinction between evangelists and apostles; yet as he wishes to retain the view that the evangelists were eyewitnesses (or at least had their information from eyewitnesses), he here declares that they also "belong to the number of the disciples and apostles of Jesus" (p. 180), thus blurring the distinction.

Now the apostles' new view of Jesus entailed that his return on the clouds would happen soon. If they had represented it as something for the remote future, "people would have laughed at them"; and so Jesus is made to declare (Mt. 24:30ff) that he will return in glory "before this generation, or those living at his time, had entirely passed away" (pp.106f), and that "there be some standing here", as his audience, who will witness it all (Mt. 16:27f). Reimarus stresses that the text says: before the passing of this "generation", a word which means a specific span of time or the people alive within that span—as when Matthew writes of "fourteen generations" in his genealogy of Jesus, or when Jesus himself speaks of "this evil and adulterous generation". It cannot be made to mean something which would free him from the delusion of having prophesied his prompt return—as when exegetes pretend that 'generation' here means 'the Jewish people', who will never 'pass away' to falsify the prophecy (p. 108). Moreover, the New Testament epistles, the book of Revelation, and the early Fathers, all believed in Jesus's early return, and modern theologians dismiss this material only "because it is not useful to their purposes". 2 Peter 3:8–10 tries to dispel anxiety at the delay of the return by saying that, in God's time, a thousand years is as one day. Reimarus retorts that "the coming was not defined according to the days of God", but according to the days of the lives of Jesus's audience, "standing here" by him (pp. 114f). Evangelical apologists of today still maintain that, in the relevant New Testament passages, 'soon' means soon "in God's time, not in ours" (art. 'Second Coming of Christ' in Elwell 1996).

In sum, the resurrection and the second coming soon after Jesus's death are, says Reimarus, "the pillars on which Christianity and the new system of the apostles is built" (p. 115); and they cannot be made solid even by any number of miracles (p. 117). Testimony afforded by miracles is altogether questionable; it is not difficult to contrive them if one is dealing with people who are accustomed to them and inclined to believe in them (p. 132). And the gospels' record of them is late, written many years after their supposed occurrence. Strauss (1861, pp. 263f) points to the significance of Reimarus's insistence that we do not possess revelations directly from God, but from people who say that they are from God. This, then, is human testimony, and must be scrutinized in the way such testimony is normally considered.

That Jesus was a political Messiah, a would-be social reformer, has often been advocated since Reimarus, as Bammel shows in his informative study of 1984. Whether or not it is feasible to regard Jesus's speeches about the Son of man coming soon with cosmic catastrophe as secondary material imposed on an entirely different message, political or other, the fact remains that such apocalyptic ideas are represented not only in the gospels, but also in the epistles and in the writings of the early Fathers. This should surely give pause to those who wish our lives and policies today to be based on an acceptance of the Bible as a reliable revelation.

Strauss concludes his assessment of Reimarus by implying that all too often it is supposed that Christianity is either a fraud or a divine revelation—as if these were the only alternatives—and that, since it is clearly, *pace* Reimarus, not a fraud, the other alternative is established as the truth. As I show in my 1999 book, C.S. Lewis is a striking example of the persistence of this attitude. We saw in Chapter 2 above that Strauss found it absurd to suppose Christianity to have been built on conscious fraud, and that, in his estimation, the eighteenth century altogether had shown too little awareness that so much of sacred literature consists of pure, honest myth, sincerely believed by its proponents. Reimarus, he says, is nearly always right in what of Christian doctrine he denies; but what he replaces it with is equally often erroneous (pp. 269f). In much the same sense Schweitzer declared (1954, p. 24) that although Reimarus's solution to the perplexities of the text is wrong, the observations from which he proceeded are "beyond question right".

Strauss was well aware of the prominence in the synoptic gospels of the eschatological speeches to which Reimarus had drawn attention. Referring to Mark 13, Matthew 24 and 25, and Luke 17 and 21, Strauss says (section 115 of the 1840 edition of his first *Life*) that Jesus predicted that he would come on the clouds of heaven to close the present period of the world, and by a general judgment open the future age; and that all this was to occur "shortly", within the term of the contemporary generation (Mt. 24:29, 34). Earlier in this book (section 66) he declares:

> Anyone who shrinks from adopting this view of the Messianic background of Jesus's plans, because he fears by so doing to make Jesus a visionary enthusiast, must remember how exactly these hopes corresponded to the long-cherished Messianic expectations of the Jews; and how easily, on the supernaturalistic assumptions of the period, and among a people which preserved so strict an isolation as the Jews, an ideal which was in itself fantastic . . . could take possession of the mind even of one who was not inclined to fanaticism.

The question remains: did Jesus actually speak in this way? In his second *Life* Strauss finds that "we cannot tell whether his followers, in the troubles and distress after his first departure, may not have consoled themselves by putting into his mouth prophecies of this kind" (1879, Volume 1, 331).

Schweitzer quotes in full the passage I have given here from section 66 of Strauss's first *Life,* and comments that, when one reads his treatment of eschatology, "one sometimes almost seems to be reading Johannes Weiss" (1954, pp. 92f.). Weiss's famous book will occupy us shortly.

b. Franz Overbeck (1837–1905), Johannes Weiss, (1863–1914), and William Wrede (1859–1906)

Overbeck lectured on the New Testament and church history from a chair of theology specially set up in Basel by a party of liberal reformers. He wrote later than the so-called 'Tübingen School', a group of German New Testament scholars founded by Strauss's teacher, F.C. Baur, who held that his pupil's work needed to be supplemented by ascertaining the different 'tendencies' which various New Testament books followed. Instead of thus discriminating the documents, Strauss, he complained, "takes the gospels all together and always refutes one with the other" (quoted by Horton Harris, 1973, p. 101). Nevertheless, he made Strauss's work the basis of his own; for to seek out the 'tendencies' which dominate the narratives presupposes that they are not to be taken at their face value as straightforward historical reports.

Baur died in 1860, when Overbeck had only just completed his student studies. The one thing he owed to Baur, he said, was the principle of a purely historical interpretation of the Bible, independent of all credal presuppositions, and concerned solely with establishing the truth.

This principle is very evident in Overbeck's 1873 booklet *Über die Cbristlichkeit unserer heutigen Theologie* ('On the Christian-ness of Our Contemporary Theology'). It was reissued in 1903 with an introduction and an epilogue, and this second edition was reprinted in 1974. He here denies that a "theological" view of the New Testament has any justification at all; for "Christianity came into the world with the proclamation of the world's imminent destruction", allowing no more for a Christian theology than for an earthly history (p. 27). "There cannot be a more world-negating faith than that of the earliest Christians, expecting the prompt return of Christ and the end of the world in its present form" (p. 85). He mentions Strauss's 1872 remark that Jesus's teaching is of no avail in regard to domestic and family life, and agrees that, if we are seeking helpful ideas about "the fundamental pillars of all human morality", namely the family and social organization, then we must look elsewhere (pp. 89f). Christianity could develop a "theology" only when its original expectations had proved to be erroneous, when, that is, "it wished to make itself possible in a world that it actually disavows" (p.

33). It managed to survive the non-fulfilment of its original outlook only by adopting "a more ideal form" of it, namely an ascetic ideal of life. Neither the hermit nor the monk or nun needed to accommodate him- or herself to the world, any more than did the original Christians with their expectation that the world would soon be destroyed. Hence the rise of monasticism in the third century constituted "a true metamorphosis of the original Christian ideas" (pp. 86f.).

Overbeck wrote when apologists were defending the historical accuracy of the gospels, and liberals were making notable concessions to sceptics. He held that both alike were beholden to the same delusion: the apologists thought they could defend traditional Christianity by scientific, especially historical means; their liberal opponents supposed that, after disintegrating it by their criticisms, they could rebuild it by the same historical means (p. 73). For Overbeck, "every theology which binds its teachers with credal confessions forfeits its scientific character" (p. 124); and if liberal theology makes a serious attempt to be independent of creed, it will need "to reflect on the extent to which it can still call its efforts Christian" (pp. 108f).

Overbeck continued in office until he retired at the age of sixty; and in the 1903 epilogue to his booklet he expressed deep gratitude to Basel for such tolerance which, he was convinced, would not have been extended to him in Germany. Here I am concerned to note that—almost twenty years before Johannes Weiss—he clearly stated that the earliest Christianity was based on eschatological ideas that proved to be false. John O'Neill's informative chapter on him, in his 1991 survey of theologians from Lessing to Bultmann, recognizes his clear perception that "Christianity began as a movement looking forward to the end of our sort of human history and the coming of the Kingdom of God". O'Neill adds: "Although there are still some scholars who try to deny this conclusion, they do not, in my view, make a very convincing case." What leaves O'Neill dissatisfied is Overbeck's "absolute dichotomy between Faith and Knowledge" (1991, pp. 187f). Of course, for one who holds that scholarship and religion are mutually destructive, the latter can be based only on faith. Not that Overbeck himself had faith. "His only theological function was to pronounce the Last Judgement on Christianity" (O'Neill, p. 179).

In 1892 Johannes Weiss, who was then a Professor of New Testament at Göttingen, published a book of a mere sixty-seven pages entitled, in the English translation of 1971 (to which my page numbers refer), *Jesus' Proclamation of the Kingdom of God*.[2] Nineham finds it "something of a mystery" that "this short but extremely important book was not translated into English for nearly eighty years." He adds: "The suspicion that this may have been due to defensiveness is hard to resist" (2000, p. 490n27). Bultmann called the book "epoch-making" (1960, p. 12), and Schweitzer declared that its every sentence "is a vindication, a rehabilitation of Reimarus as a historical thinker" (1954, p. 23)—although the book in fact makes no mention of him. Schweitzer saw in it the third significant stage in the development of life-of-Jesus research. The first was the insistence by Strauss that Jesus had lived as a human personage, without supernatural powers. The second was the recognition by "the Tübingen school" that the synoptic gospels and John are incompatible. "Now came the third: *either* eschatological *or* non-eschatological" (p. 237). *The Oxford Dictionary of the Christian Church,* in its third edition of 1997, calls Weiss's book "the first attempt at a consistent eschatological interpretation of the Gospel, defending the thesis that the central purpose of Christ's mission was to proclaim the imminence of a transcendental Kingdom of God, in which He himself was to be manifested as the Messiah."

Weiss wrote when the current view was that the kingdom means the rule of God in the hearts of mankind, the exercise of the moral life in society. He allowed that modern man may well think of the kingdom in this way, as some inward, psychological state, an ethical ideal, but he argued that this is not, according to the New Testament, how Jesus thought of it. The editors of the English translation note (p. 26) that, before Weiss, "the Kingdom of God was equated—if not with social progress and/or individual religious experience—with the church, especially the 'dead in Christ', now in heaven".

Against this, Weiss argues (p. 65) that "according to the oldest report", Jesus appeared in Galilee with the message "repent, for the kingdom of God is at hand" (Mk. 1:15). Q, he says, records the same message (Mt. 10:7 = Lk. 10:9, 11). Hence "Jesus' activity is governed by the strong and unwavering feeling that the messianic time is imminent" (p. 129). If he sometimes speaks of the kingdom as already present, it is because at such moments he is carried away with enthusiasm, since by dint of his exorcisms he seems to be so victorious over Satan's kingdom (p. 78). But fundamentally, the kingdom is not yet come. He puts into the mouths of his disciples the prayer 'thy kingdom come'—not 'may it grow bigger than it already is' (p. 73). Neither they nor anyone else, not even Jesus himself, can establish it: that will be the work of God alone, and will result from his supernatural intervention (pp. 82, 129). But before this could happen, "an enormous obstacle, the guilt of the people", had to be removed (p. 87), and hence the need for repentance.

After some initial optimism, Jesus came to believe that the people's guilt would not be obliterated in his own lifetime, but that he would first fall victim to the hatred of his opponents (p. 87). Indeed, he seized upon the idea that his death itself should be "the sin offering for the people" (p. 88), the "ransom" for them (Mk.. 10:45), without which they would be destined for destruction.

After his death, he will return, so he believed, on the clouds of heaven as the "Son of man" and establish his kingdom. He knew that in this present life he was no more than a teacher, but he was confident that, in the kingdom, as the apocalyptic figure "the Son of man" (on whom cf. above, p. 212), he would be the Messiah, the king (pp. 115f), the judge (p. 127). He will return as this within the lifetime of the generation which had rejected him. When this happens, God will destroy this old world, ruled as it is by the Devil, and create a new one. Weiss stresses the universality of these events (they will encompass the whole world), their suddenness, and their destructiveness. He refers here to Mk. 13:24f and Rev. 6:12–17, saying: "The sun will be darkened, the moon will no longer give its light, and the stars will fall from the heavens" (pp. 92f). He adds that the Jewish author of 4 Ezra had already expressed "the standard idea" that "the age is hastening swiftly to its end".[3] And he stresses that "Jesus' consciousness of the *nearness* of the Kingdom is a feature that cannot be disposed of" (pp. 91, 130f. Italics original). In the second, 1900, edition of his book, he goes into more detail concerning the source of Jesus's notion of the kingdom in late Jewish apocalypticism. Since Weiss's time, the discovery of the Dead Sea Scrolls, which were composed before and during the time of Jesus, has given us documents with strong eschatological expectations.[4] But as Allison notes, quite apart from this only recently available material, portions of 1 Enoch, some of the Jewish *Sibylline Oracles,* and the *Testament of Moses* have long been known to have been in circulation in Jesus's day;[5] and the decades after him "saw the appearance of 2 Baruch and the *Apocalypse of Abraham*".[6] Hence "eschatology was indeed flourishing in his day" (2003, p. 145).

Weiss can use the language of 'transformation' *(palingenesis)* with reference to individual persons: those who are saved will be 'transformed' to be like the angels (Mk. 12:25); but the world, he says, will be destroyed (pp. 94f, 130). Yet he also speaks of the 'transformation' of the world (p. 96). He refers in this connection to Mt. 19:28 and posits some continuity between this age and the age to come, in that "the land of Palestine will arise in a new and glorious splendor, forming the centre of the new Kingdom" (p. 130), the rule of God, which will bring release from all affliction of body and soul, and deliverance from all enemies and oppressors (pp. 102f).

Either before or after the world's destruction—it is not clear which—comes the judgment (pp. 96f). Weiss adduces Mk. 9:43: "If thy hand cause thee to stumble, cut it off: it is good for thee to enter into life maimed, rather than, having two hands, go into hell, into the unquenchable fire". These words show that the way to life, or to the kingdom, "leads through the Judgment", in which the resurrected dead will also participate. According to Mt. 25:31f, "all the nations pass before the judgment throne of the Son of man" (p. 98). Those who are condemned will either be annihilated (Mk. 8:35) or tormented eternally (Mt. 25:41,46; Mk. 9:48; Lk. 16:23f). To which of these two prospects Jesus inclined "cannot be said with certainty" (p. 99). The harshness of Jesus's ethical demands is a natural consequence of the need to prepare for the coming of the kingdom. The righteousness he enjoins is "the condition for the future enjoyment" of it (p. 134)—the kingdom itself being "the highest religious Good" (p. 132). He knew that, so long as people "continue in their former relationships, they will not be able to succeed in the 'seeking of the Kingdom' which he demands" (p. 111). This accounts for what have often been called the 'hard sayings' which commentators try to erode away (pp. 107f), such as the condemnation of riches (it is "easier for a camel to go through a needle's eye than for a rich man to enter into the kingdom of God", Mk. 10:25) and, even worse, the injunction to hate one's parents, wife and children (Lk. 14:26, toned down in the equivalent at Mt. 10:37). The summons to repentance means turning away from all worldly ties and treasures. Clearly, then, "our modern Protestant ethic" is more relaxed, and "does not represent a simple application of the teaching of Jesus" (p. 113)—a teaching dependent on a religious attitude which we cannot share, which indeed "has something strange about it for our modern way of thinking" (p. 128). "We no longer pray 'may grace come and this world pass away', but pass our lives in the joyful confidence that *this* world will evermore become the showplace of the people of God" (p. 135).

To this, Weiss adds: "We do not await a Kingdom of God which is to come down from heaven to earth and abolish this world, but we do hope to be gathered with the church of Jesus Christ into the heavenly Kingdom. In this sense we, too, can feel and say, as did the Christians of old, 'Thy Kingdom come'." Theologians now, as in Weiss's day, are most anxious that we should be able to go on using the old formulas, however much we change their meaning. He supposes that, if we reinterpret this particular formula in the way he suggests, then "we will at least approximate Jesus' attitude in a different sense" (pp. 135f). But this is in reality no 'approximation', but is far removed from what he thinks Jesus believed.

As already indicated, there are passages in the synoptics which imply that the kingdom is in some sense present. Apologists have gladly seized on them as annulling those which specify cosmic disturbance. In this manner C.H. Dodd spoke of "realized eschatology", in the sense that the kingdom has already fully come with Jesus's ministry, death and resurrection. One passage which he adduced is the pericope where Pharisees accuse Jesus of casting out devils only by virtue of his alliance with "Beelzebub, the prince of the devils". He retorts that his exorcisms no more prove alliance with Satan than does the same activity on the part of Pharisaic exorcists; and he adds: "But if I by the spirit of God cast out devils, then is the kingdom of God come upon you" (Mt. 12:24–28). Dodd and others take this to mean that, in his view, the kingdom was fully present in his own actions. But if this is so, why should not the successes of the Jewish exorcists be good evidence that the kingdom has long been there? Their skills, although admitted in this passage, and not condemned as Satanic, are, it seems, to count for nothing, while similar skills on his part are to be taken as establishing his exalted status. Moreover, the 'you' upon whom the kingdom is supposedly come are his critics, the Pharisees, not the people he healed, so that his words must be a warning to them: the kingdom is now bearing down upon them, and if they continue to reject him, they will regret it in the immediate future when God—so he supposed—will intervene and set up his kingdom. Sanders points to the parallel with Mk. 8:38: "For whosoever shall be ashamed of me and of my words in this adulterous and sinful generation, the Son of man also shall be ashamed of him when he cometh in the glory of his Father with the holy angels". Here too a present positive response to Jesus is of crucial importance, but the kingdom is put in the future; individual commitment now will determine who will enter it when it arrives (1993b, p. 61).

But I must return to Weiss. He seems a little embarrassed by Mt. 12:28 and other passages which, he allows, suggest that the kingdom is in some sense already present (p. 67). He finds that Mark and Matthew are "moving toward identifying the Kingdom of God with the contemporary church" (p. 69), and hence they sometimes move away from Jesus's conception of it. He also discusses Mt. 21:31 ("the publicans and the harlots go into the kingdom of God" before the Jewish leaders), and says that this means not that they are already within the kingdom, but that "they have a head start, . . . they are travelling toward it" (p. 69).

Then there is Mt. 11:12: "From the days of John the Baptist until now the kingdom of heaven suffereth violence, and men of violence take it by force". Weiss takes this to mean only that "since the days of John, there has dawned a movement of passionate longing for the Kingdom" (p. 70). Finally, at Lk. 17:21 (unrepresented in the other gospels) Jesus tells the Pharisees that the kingdom of God is "among you" ("in the midst of you", RSV. Most scholars agree that *entos* here means 'among', not 'within'). Weiss recognizes this as, from his standpoint, a "difficult saying" (p. 91), but does not really elucidate it. To do so, we may note that Jesus surely does not mean that the kingdom is present in the unbelieving Pharisees, but in himself: hence he will bring it again, and finally, when he returns at his second coming. The verses that follow do in fact say that "the Son of man" will come in the future with destructive cosmic signs; hence verse 21 is not to be taken as meaning that Jesus has finally brought the kingdom in his own lifetime. Presumably Weiss could afford to regard this verse as one of the passages in which Jesus is overcome with enthusiasm at his success in routing the earthly kingdom of Satan.

This whole problem is still very much discussed today. Sanders reflects the opinion of many in allowing that, while the New Testament does not use the term 'kingdom of God' in a uniform sense, most of the sayings place it *"up there,* in heaven, where people will enter after death, and *in the future,* when God brings the kingdom to earth and separates the sheep from the goats" (1993a, p. 176).

I shall revert to this whole question in a later section of this chapter; but here I wish to point to the comments of Weiss's English translators that, to suppose—as we shall see many still do—that Jesus's "references to the future coming of the kingdom were 'only symbolic' or 'stylistic' ... leaves unexplained why he should have wished to obscure his 'real' message that the Kingdom had already arrived by speaking of its coming in the future" (pp. 44f). They add (p. 48): "It is remarkable that so many different theories have been advanced" to explain this, and that "none of them has gained general support". There can be little doubt, they say, that "Jesus regarded certain preliminary and preparatory eschatological phenomena as present or being realized. Elijah had appeared [Mt. 17:12]; the final campaign against Satan's household was under way; the preaching of repentance in prospect of the nearness of the Judgment and the Kingdom had begun. But did Jesus also believe that the Kingdom of God had come?"

That Jesus believed no such thing is the position that was taken by William Wrede in lectures of 1894 on 'Jesus's Preaching of the kingdom of God', published posthumously in 1907 in a volume which collects various of his essays and studies. He is very supportive of Weiss, whose book had only recently been published. Like Reimarus, he observed that, as Jesus never explains what he means by the kingdom, he must have taken for granted that his audiences knew what he was talking about; and so they had their own specific ideas of the kingdom. Wrede knew, as did Reimarus, that in most of the Hebrew Bible, the hope of the individual was not for life after death, but for a long life on Earth, and for prosperity and offspring in the context of a prosperous nation. But, differing here from Reimarus, he insisted that late Jewish expectations were no longer in this sense political. From Maccabean times the kingdom had come more and more to be regarded as something heavenly, supernatural - a purely future kingdom which God himself would bring about (1907, p. 92). Wrede of course comes to terms with the gospel passages which exercised Weiss in that they represent the kingdom as already in some sense present. Mt. 12:28, he says, means that there are two kingdoms, God's and Satan's, and so if Jesus impairs Satan's he enhances God's. But the final end which Satan's kingdom will suffer has not yet occurred (p. 99). And Lk. 17:21 must be interpreted from its context (pp. 110f), as I have suggested above.

An important point for Wrede is that it is often overlooked that Jesus (and Paul too) never speak of his *second* coming, only of his coming. This suggests that he had not come to Earth as Messiah, but in lowliness, and would come on the clouds as Messiah—shortly, but only in the future. Only in the later church did his earthly ministry come to be regarded as having been as Messianic as his future coming would be. His earthly preaching did but prepare the kingdom. To claim that it was then already present would be to make his future coming in glory into a mere appendix (pp. 104f).

Above all, Wrede does not want the problem which Jesus's view of the kingdom poses for the modern Christian to be evaded. It was an eschatological view, bearing no resemblance to modern ideas of the kingdom as a timeless communion of the soul with God (pp. 92f). Historical inquiry must be beholden to the facts it uncovers, not to pre-existing conclusions (pp. 125f).

Finally, it is relevant to note that in later works, including later editions of his 1892 book, Weiss himself gives considerable encouragement to allowing New Testament words to be reinterpreted in modern theology, while he still insisted on not giving out any reinterpretation as the meaning of the original. In this way he distinguished the 'historical' from the 'theological' task. As proclaimed by Jesus, the kingdom of God is a supramundane future reality; but as interpreted in mid-nineteenth-century Protestant theology (for example by Albrecht Ritschl) it is a community of morally acting people. Clearly, Jesus's idea of it is of no help with regard to modern ethical problems, whereas Ritschl's is, and hence is useful "theologically" and better for modern Christianity. The translators of his 1892 book sum up Weiss's position, as expressed in his later works, in their Introduction:

> Weiss was perfectly willing to accept the results of honest historical scholarship, whatever they might be. He was not prepared, however, to insist that the church in subsequent ages had to adhere to interpretations which were identical with those held by Jesus. He was ready to allow a radical hiatus to exist between Jesus's teachings and those of subsequent Christians. Indeed, he could see no alternative to that position. The plain meaning of the New Testament texts, as even the earliest Christian exegetes (e.g. Clement of Alexandria and Origen) had recognized, was utterly inapplicable in any literal sense to succeeding ages. (p. 21)

Heikki Räisänen has welcomed Weiss's position as an early example of the kind of "symbolic" theology which, he implies, is the only way in which a Christianity that is intellectually acceptable can survive: New Testament words such as kingdom of God, resurrection, redemption, even Christ or God, are to be taken as "evocative and challenging symbols" and not restricted to what they mean in their New Testament context (1995, pp. 136f).

Weiss is my first example in this book of a higher critic who, while allowing that ideas prominent in the New Testament are flawed and erroneous, was not thereby alienated from Christianity. Reimarus's thinking led him from the first to deism, and so away from Christianity, and Strauss and Overbeck finally repudiated it. Something very similar to Weiss's standpoint was affirmed by Schweitzer, to whom I turn next. He too saw that the synoptic Jesus was concerned with an eschatological kingdom, and hence had to be reinterpreted if he was to be a guide on modern ethical or other issues. This position has never been as widely endorsed as the view that, somehow or other, the New Testament words in themselves, without reinterpretation, can be taken to mean something acceptable today.

c. Albert Schweitzer (1875–1965)

Schweitzer is well known as theologian, physician and organist. He took a medical degree in 1911, and in 1913 gave up his academic career to care for the natives of French Equatorial Africa at the hospital of Lambaréné. He was awarded the Nobel Peace Prize in 1952.

In his famous *Von Reimarus zu Wrede* (1906) he outlines the various reconstructions of Jesus's biography that have been made since the late eighteenth century, and gives his own theory as to what kind of person Jesus was. An English translation was published in 1910, under the title *The Quest of the Historical Jesus,* and the publisher, A.and C.Black, issued a third edition of it in 1954. All three are based on the original German edition, even though in 1913 a second German edition had appeared, with the new title *Geschichte der Leben Jesu Forschung* (History of Life-of-Jesus Research). It had two additional chapters on the historicity of Jesus, which a number of scholars had called in question in the previous decade, a further chapter on other developments between 1907 and 1912, and an expanded conclusion. Two chapters of the original were also enlarged and revised.

Subsequent German editions made few changes to this second one of 1913; and an English translation of the whole, based on the ninth German edition of 1984 was at last published (by SCM, and edited by John Bowden) in 2000. My account refers to the more widely available earlier translation—to its third edition of 1954—except where the 2000 version substantially differs from it.

In the second and later German editions, some notable concessions are made. It is admitted that all our information about Jesus comes from Christian sources, as the sparse pagan and Jewish notices of him are clearly dependent on Christian tradition. They all "go back to one source, . . . Christianity itself, and there are no data available in Jewish or Gentile secular history which could be used as controls" (2000, p. 402). Tacitus's reference, in the early second century, to the crucifixion of "Christ" under Pilate at best establishes that the second century church believed in that event (p. 360). Not that one can expect "the crucifixion of a Galilean who had no political importance" to have attracted pagan attention at an early date.

In this context, Schweitzer even allows that Christianity must reckon with the possibility that it will have to surrender the historicity of Jesus altogether, and must have, in readiness for such a contingency, "a metaphysic, that is, a basic view of the nature and significance of being which is entirely independent of history and of knowledge transmitted from the past" (2000, p. 402). He says too that, although he holds that the gospel Jesus did exist, it must nevertheless be admitted that there are things about him which may well be found morally and religiously offensive: his ethical teaching is impaired by its constant appeal to the prospect of heavenly rewards as incentives for good behaviour, and by "Jewish particularistic ideas". It is also "shot through with ideas of predestination" (p. 404), and above all is inextricably linked with his conviction that the whole world is shortly to be brought to a catastrophic end: "The relation of his moral claims to the expected future is absolutely basic in the gospels" (p. 454).

Schweitzer contributed a new introduction to the third, 1954, English edition of *The Quest,* and he there summarizes the views argued in the book. First, he sets aside Luke, as later than Mark and Matthew, and also John, as incompatible with all three synoptics (p. v). Whereas Matthew is generally regarded as an adaptation of Mark, supplemented with non-Markan material, he accepts the portrayal of Jesus's ministry in both gospels as basically reliable (p. vi) and thinks it of little account which of the two is "a trifle older" than the other, although "Matthew's fulness gives it greater importance" (p. xi). In fact he relies heavily on material available only in Matthew.

Schweitzer focusses on Jesus's teaching about the kingdom of God that is to be finally established. (Matthew calls it 'the kingdom of heaven', reflecting Jewish reluctance to use the name God.) He holds that Jesus, and many of his contemporaries, believed that this kingdom would come soon, but only after a period of cosmic tribulation which would bring the world to an end. It is certainly true that "ancient Jewish sources regularly depict the birth of a better world as accompanied by terrible labor pains", and "the sort of disasters catalogued in Mark 13 can be found in many documents, Jewish and Christian" (Allison 2003, p. 154). From Matthew's tenth chapter Schweitzer infers that Jesus believed that this tribulation would happen during his ministry in Galilee; for he there sends out his disciples to preach that "the kingdom of heaven is at hand" (verse 7), and tells them: "Ye shall not have gone through the cities of Israel till the Son of man be come" (verse 23—a saying represented only in Matthew). As we saw, the Messiah-Son of man is a supernatural personage who is to come down from the clouds at the end of time (Mt. 24:29–31); and as Jesus repeatedly refers to himself as the Son of man, he obviously, says Schweitzer, expected to be changed into this personage and "to be recognized as such when the Kingdom of God arrives" (p. viii). That this will happen before all the existing generation has died is the doctrine of Jesus in a number of passages in both Mark and Matthew; but only from the tenth chapter of Matthew can Schweitzer infer that he believed that the kingdom would come in a matter of weeks.

When Jesus sends the disciples out to preach the imminence of the kingdom, he prophesies that they will suffer persecution—as part, says

Schweitzer, of the final cosmic tribulation—yet in the sequel they return to him from their mission without mishap. (Their safe return is merely presupposed by Matthew, but is actually stated by Mark, at 6:30.) Nor has the Son of man appeared. Schweitzer claims that Jesus must have said the words attributed to him by Matthew when he sent them out; for no evangelist would invent a speech containing such prophecies and then go on to provide the evidence that they were not fulfilled and that Jesus had been mistaken. Nor, in Schweitzer's view, would the evangelist have committed Jesus to these prophecies had he been writing some fifty or sixty years after his death, by which time they would have clearly been falsified. In this way Schweitzer can argue for a pre–A.D. 70 date for this gospel. In this interpretation of Matthew's Chapter 10 he has been eagerly followed by J.A.T. Robinson (1976, pp. 24f).

Matthew's Chapter 10 certainly presents commentators with problems. In Schweitzer's interpretation of it, Jesus envisaged the disciples making a hasty tour of cities, rushing from one to another with their brief proclamation that the kingdom is at hand. He thinks that Jesus urged such haste by telling them to take only a minimum of money and equipment: "Get you no gold, nor silver, nor brass in your purses; no wallet for your journey, neither two coats, nor shoes nor staff" (verses 9–10). The underlying idea, Schweitzer says, is that they will need so little because the end of the world is so near. But in the text, Jesus gives a quite different reason for his injunction: they are to travel light because "the labourer is worthy of his food", in other words because they have the right to claim support from those they convert. When they enter a city or village, they are to take accommodation from a "worthy" resident (they are to lodge with the pious, not with persons of ill repute, or who are hostile to Christianity); and they are to stay in these lodgings for the whole period of their missionary activity in the area (verse 11), presumably to avoid provoking rivalry or jealousy between families competing for their favour. The evangelist obviously has in mind not missionaries who rush from one place to another from fear that the end of the world would come quickly, but rather preachers who stay in an area long enough to found a Christian community there. This will obviously take some time, for Jesus warns them that they will be delivered up to councils, scourged in synagogues, and brought before governors. When they are thus persecuted in one city, they are to flee into the next (verse 23). Clearly, he is not envisaging a universal persecution, or one of whole Christian communities, but harassment of individual missionaries who, if not safe in one town, can reckon to be unmolested, at least for a time, in another. If Matthew was writing near the end of the century, when sporadic persecution of Christians had begun to be a real possibility, it is quite intelligible that a ruling to preachers not to court martyrdom, but to move on when harassed, should have been put into Jesus's mouth.

Jesus's whole speech in Matthew's Chapter 10 cannot, *pace* Schweitzer, be accepted as a discourse actually delivered by him, since it is a compilation of units of different provenance. After first recording the equivalent words in Mark (Mk. 6:7–11), where there is no mention of danger from persecution, Matthew adds warnings which, in Mark, were spoken by Jesus much later in his career (just before his betrayal and arrest). These warnings told the disciples to expect persecution—presumably after his death—from governors and kings (pagans) as well as from (Jewish) synagogues and councils. Matthew has calmly taken this material from the apocalypse in Mark's Passion narrative and inserted it into his chapter 10 (Mt. 10: 17–22 = Mk. 13:9–13), into the Galilean mission speech, so that it no longer refers to what will happen to the early churches only after Jesus's death, but indicates a danger hanging over the disciples from the very beginning of the Christian mission, and will not come only from Jews: "Before governors and kings shall ye be brought for my sake, for a testimony to them *and to the Gentiles*". The words I have italicized have been added to the source (Mk. 13:9).

J.M. Robinson notes that, even when Schweitzer wrote, it was normally recognized that, in Matthew's Chapter 10, not only has "material from the Markan apocalypse been interpolated into the Mission Instructions of Mark and Q", but also that "these were conflated both with each other and with other Q and special Matthean material" (2001, p. 31). Commentators understand the whole resulting discourse as a compilation of rulings on matters of importance to Christian preachers at the end of the first century, put into Jesus's mouth as an address to the missionaries he dispatched, and thereby made into a paradigm of missionary behaviour. If verse 23 means merely that the end will come before the new faith has gained a hold in all the Jewish cities, he is not there being made to say anything that a Jewish-Christian writer of the late first century would have felt as inappropriate. And in the second half of the discourse (verses 24–42), there is, as Luz (1995, p. 76) notes, no indication that the sayings are meant as applicable only to the situation of the historical Jesus. On the contrary, "the disciples are paradigmatic for, or representative of, the Matthean community" (p. 92).

Davies and Allison note in their commentary on Matthew that Schweitzer's conclusions "have been contradicted on all sides" (1991, p. 196). They note too that, although Matthew's text in Chapter 10 goes beyond the historical situation of the twelve to include that of missionaries of his own day, such passing from the past to the present without explicitly noting the fact need not occasion surprise, as "the phenomenon . . . occurs elsewhere in early Christian literature" (pp. 179f). Matthew's wording does at least suggest this transition. He begins with an address to the twelve, warning them that individual private houses may not accept their message (10:13). But he goes on to foretell what is better understood as persecution of Christian missionaries generally, who will incur universal hatred (verses 21f), presumably in their attempts to convert the wider world; and from verse 26 his repeated injunction "fear not" is accompanied by consolatory assurances, such as "he that loseth his life for my sake shall find it" (verse 39).

The disciples, then, returned to Jesus unharmed, and the end did not come. Schweitzer believed that Jesus's disappointment at this non-fulfilment led him to revise his view of the tribulation which he thought must precede the end; that he reflected on Chapter 53 of Isaiah, which speaks of the servant of God who gives his life for others; and on this basis he came to think that, if he alone suffered and died, God would spare mankind any general tribulation and would inaugurate the kingdom (1954, p. ix).

Schweitzer resents the application to Jesus of what he calls "the petty standards of . . . psychology" (p. 309)—overlooking the fact that, if we cannot apply these, we cannot investigate history at all. Yet here, in spite of his veto on psychology, he claims to trace the development in Jesus's thinking which led him to suppose that he alone needed to suffer and die. Nineham has justly observed (1977, pp. 126f) that this "detailed reconstruction of the development of Jesus' outlook and expectations . . . goes far beyond the evidence, and it is ironic that the very scholar who repeatedly pricked the bubble of the allegedly 'assured results' claimed by his predecessors, and whose survey showed the impossibility of writing a life of Jesus or tracing his 'development', should have thought himself able to trace that development in some detail, and should have claimed that the view he championed rested on a 'scientifically unassailable basis'."

Schweitzer's position really makes sense only if Matthew is taken as based on eyewitness testimony. The discourse of its Chapter 10 is, in his estimation, "historical as a whole and down to the smallest detail" (1954, p. 361). J.M. Robinson records that he "simply dismissed as absurd efforts to dismantle it into its sources" (2001, p. 31). He held that both Matthew and Mark originated in Palestine around A.D. 70, and rest on a common source which, "as well as the special material in Matthew, go back to men who were present during the ministry of Jesus. They have . . . a clear conception of the order of events and give a reliable report of the speeches of Jesus" (quoted from Schweitzer, 1968, p. 71, by Nineham, 2000, p. xxi). The work of K.L. Schmidt and other 'form critics', as detailed in Chapter 5 above, has shown that this is simply not true. And, as Nineham notes, "Wrede had much stronger grounds than Schweitzer appreciated for his contention that even the earliest evangelists—and indeed the pre-gospel tradition—were as much interested in theological interpretation as in accurate chronicling" (2000, p. xxi).

Nineham adds that, nevertheless, Schweitzer's view that Jesus's eschatology "was broadly that of contemporary Jewish expectations has, on the whole, withstood subsequent attempts to play up the originality of Jesus and show that eschatological ideas were radically transformed as they passed through his mind." Dunn, commenting on the work of Weiss and Schweitzer, goes so far as to allow that "in a very real and important sense almost all historical Jesus research since then has been an attempt to escape from or at least to soften [their] evaluation of Jesus" (2006, p. 345). There is, he adds, a natural temptation not to face the challenge which they "still pose to twentieth-century theology" and to resort instead to "a neo-Liberalism which stresses only that strand in Jesus's teaching which is most easily translatable into modern terms" (pp. 351f). But this temptation must be resisted, for not only "can there be no doubt that apocalyptic eschatology had an integral part in first-century Christianity" (p. 365), but also Jesus's own expectation of the future kingdom was "apocalyptic in character", and he "thought the end was imminent." "It is not possible to excise such a well rooted strand without seriously distorting the Jesus-tradition" (pp. 349f). But where does this leave Christianity? Nineham sees that, to come to terms with the fact that the founder was strongly influenced by such ideas is still "one of the central problems of contemporary Christianity" (2000, p. xxiii). Dunn seems unworried by the delusions of 'the founder', and is content to affirm that "apocalyptic eschatology has a valid and important place within Christianity", in that it sees God as concerned about the world and as decisively "operating 'behind the scenes'." It also sees history as "having a purpose" (cf. p. 300 below) and teaches us that "the suffering of the present is in some sense [sic] a necessary preparation for and antecedent to the greater, richer future of God" (2006, pp. 369f). Christians should both retain the "hope of God's imminent [sic] intervention and the enthusiasm it brings", yet at the same time, "restrain it from becoming detailed" and "too dependent on a particular fulfilment of that hope" (pp. 370f).

T.W. Manson commented that "in spite of the moving eloquence with which the story is told by Schweitzer, there is no escape from the fact that its hero was a deluded fanatic" (1956, p. 216). The 'eloquence' at times amounts to vague and mystical language that serves the purpose of obscuring the unorthodoxy of Schweitzer's views. He does not say plainly that Jesus was deluded, but rather that his behaviour rested on "considerations lying outside the history" ('outside history' would be a better translation), on "dogmatic eschatological considerations" (1954, pp. 351, 357). Eschatology means theories about the end of the world, how it will come about, and what circumstances will attend it. That Jesus was beholden to eschatological considerations must mean that he was actuated by a belief in the coming of the kingdom, or by the conviction that he was the Messiah who would inaugurate it. But instead of putting the matter plainly, Schweitzer says: "Eschatology is simply 'dogmatic history'—history as moulded by theological beliefs—which breaks in upon the natural course of history and abrogates it" (p. 349). He means simply that Jesus's behaviour was determined by his religious ideas, just as anybody's behaviour is determined by their own beliefs as much as by the "natural course" of events. It is as if, for Schweitzer, theological beliefs are an objective force, outside history. Thus he says, apropos of Jesus's identification of John the Baptist with Elijah (Mt. 11:14), that here, in Jesus's thought, "Messianic doctrine forces its way into history and simply abolishes the historic aspect of the events" (p. 373).

Instead, then, of saying plainly that Jesus was deluded, Schweitzer writes of "the largeness, the startling originality, the self-contradictoriness and the terrible irony" in his thought (p. 208). He even makes a virtue of the inconsistencies and incredibilities of the gospel portraits by claiming that Jesus is a supreme personality whom we really cannot expect to understand. The "chaotic confusion" of the narratives "ought to have suggested the thought that the events had been thrown into this confusion by the volcanic force of an incalculable personality" (p. 349). John Bowden, editor of the 2000 translation of the revised German edition of Schweitzer's book, claims (p. vii) that his prose is "clear" and "matter-of-fact", and that it is the translator of the original German edition who has rendered it in "a kind of bombastic, end-of-the-nineteenth-century style." But I cannot see that the somewhat revised translation Bowden is editing puts matters more plainly. As an example, "the volcanic force of an incalculable personality" has been changed to "the volcanic force of an unfathomable self-awareness" (2000, p. 315).

In spite of his rhetoric, Schweitzer does stress that his findings give no encouragement to conventional Christian beliefs: "Those who are fond of talking about negative theology can find their account here. . . . There is nothing more negative than the result of the critical study of the life of Jesus" (1954, p. 396). His readers cannot but notice that his book is silent on the empty tomb stories and the resurrection, quite apart from the way it construes the ideas which governed Jesus's ministry. In the second and later German editions he is very scornful about the ambiguous way in which, even at that time, the resurrection was treated in critical accounts: "The art of preserving credit on all sides by indistinct statements which will comply with every change of wind is becoming more and more highly rated, and is practised with ever-growing virtuosity" (2000, p. 477). Yet, in spite of his negative results, he finds that "Jesus means something for our time because a mighty spiritual force streams forth from Him"—a fact which "can neither be shaken nor confirmed by any historical discovery", and which forms "the solid foundation of Christianity" (1954, p. 397).

In the chapters added to the second and later German editions of this famous book, Schweitzer presses this argument that religion needs to be in essence independent of historical fact, since even the best historical scholarship may in time have to be revised, thus making any faith based on it vulnerable. In his view, philosophy should form the basis of religion, and he appealed in this connection to the German metaphysical tradition, and in particular to Schopenhauer's view of the primacy of the will as a transcendent reality at the basis of self-consciousness.[7] Consciousness, Schweitzer held, can furnish unmediated, immediate certainties, whereas propositions concerning past events rest on testimony that is no longer directly available, and so are no more than hypotheses. He censured the theologians of the late nineteenth century who had broken with German metaphysics and—in his view, foolishly—based their faith on what they took for the 'assured results' of historical criticism.

This was written at a time (1913) when some New Testament scholars were reaching results which, if assured, were by no means reassuring. Wrede, we saw, refused to accept even Mark, the earliest of the canonical four, as historically accurate, and set it aside as no more than a record of what an early Christian community happened to believe. Even more alarmingly, Arthur Drews in Germany and John M. Robertson in England were, among others, maintaining that there had been no historical Jesus at all.[8] Schweitzer did not accept that they had made out a convincing case, but as I have indicated he allowed that Christianity must reckon with the possibility of having to give up the historicity of Jesus, and must have a metaphysic in readiness for such a contingency, so as to base religion on mind, not on history.

The implication of all this is that what we learn from our consciousness of our thoughts and feelings is not fallible in the way in which what we learn from observation of the external world is fallible. Against such a claim, the British empirical tradition in philosophy—typified in Alexander Bain's insistence in his famous *The Emotions and the Will* (London, 1859, p. 556) that "there is a very large amount of fallibility, fallacy and falsehood in both the one and the other"—has been one long drawn out protest.

In spite of all his metaphysics, Schweitzer does not want to dispense entirely with Jesus, and thinks that, if he be allotted a place as merely one element in religion, then the danger of narrowing it to a purely historical basis will have been avoided (2000, p. 407). What matters about Jesus, he says, is that he attempted to impose his will on his situation, believing that his action in sacrificing himself would bring about the kingdom. Modern people seem to lack such strongly developed willpower, and Jesus's function today can lie in this, that "as a powerful influence" he can bring the hopes and the longings inherent in us "to heights and a clarity we would not achieve if dependent on our own devices and without the influence of his personality" (p. 482). The limitations of his outlook fall away "once his will as such is transposed into our own world-view" (p. 485).

Schweitzer is pleading for what he calls an "ethical eschatology" as the "equivalent" of Jesus's late Jewish eschatology (p. 483). He concludes, appropriately enough from his premises, by conceding that our relation to Jesus is "ultimately of a mystical kind" (p. 486). We are to establish community with him by sharing his will to "put the kingdom of God above all else"—although what this phrase means to us (if anything at all) is not what it meant for him.

Allison (2005, pp. 121, 125) shows that, although some described Schweitzer's book as "blasphemous", others found his eschatological Jesus—who "at least imagined himself to be somebody"—preferable to the Jesus of liberal theology, who was often no more than a decent chap who went about doing good (Acts 10:38). Allison himself reluctantly accepts that Jesus was deluded—"a Jesus without eschatological error would certainly make my life easier" (p. 133)—and reconciles himself to him by understanding "biblical eschatology to be akin to Platonism. Both are mythological ways of directing us beyond this world, to a larger reality about which we cannot speak literally because it transcends our mundane minds" (p. 147).

Many who have accepted that Jesus was a failed end-time prophet have likewise found it possible, on some basis or other, to remain within

Christianity. Andrew Furlong, who was Anglican Dean of Clonmacnoise, Ireland, is a rare exception. He wrote: "I would feel inclined to apply the term 'crackpot' to anyone who came to my front door to tell me that it was their religious belief that the world was about to end"; and he confesses that he sometimes thinks of Jesus in this way, although he still believes in God (2003, pp. 185f). His book describes how his bishop had him brought to a heresy trial—a "medieval way" of solving the situation (p. 67)—and why he felt it right to terminate the trial, before a verdict was reached, by resigning his appointment.

More common is to deny that Jesus expected an imminent catastrophic end to the world. William Temple, Archbishop of Canterbury from 1942 until his death in 1944, thought that he would have to consider renouncing Christianity if he believed that Jesus held any such views. John Kent notes in his biography of Temple that "many radical New Testament critics of the early twentieth century shared the opinion that one could not take Jesus seriously if his theology turned on a literal Second Coming, and many, like Temple, solved the problem by reading the evidence to mean that Jesus rejected such a view" (1992, p. 42). A number of New Testament scholars still do read the evidence this way, as I have already indicated, and as we shall further be seeing.

iii. The Fourth Gospel and Later

There were two obvious ways in which Christians could cope with the failure of the 'end-events' to occur. They could suppose either that the events (suitably reinterpreted) were being realized in the present, or that the end would come at some indefinite future. Acts takes this latter course, and allows for a period between Jesus's resurrection and his second coming, during which the church exists and grows. One is reminded of Loisy's famous remark: "Jesus announced the kingdom, and it was the church that came." The former course was taken by the fourth gospel. It holds that the blessings of the coming age are available here and now to those who have faith in Jesus. Although in this gospel he does declare that there will be a future judgment, he at the same time is made to correct this doctrine by saying that the reference is not really to the future at all: "The hour cometh, *and now is*, when the dead will hear the voice of the Son of God" (5:25; cf. 4:23: "The hour cometh, and now is, when the true worshippers shall worship the Father in spirit and truth"). Whereas in the other gospels Jesus refers repeatedly to the kingdom of God, and to its imminent appearance, in the fourth gospel this kingdom is mentioned only at 3:3 and 5, where he says to Nicodemus: "except a man be born anew . . . of water and the spirit, he cannot enter into the kingdom of God."[9] And this kingdom is not represented as an imminent and drastic re-ordering of the world. Instead, the stress is on a new quality of life, gained here and now, by being "born anew" or "from above" (*anōthen*), regenerated through faith in Jesus. "I give my own sheep eternal life" (10:27f), a life which can be enjoyed at once through coming to belief in him, and of a quality quite different from the everyday life we all know. "He that heareth my word and believeth him that sent me hath eternal life . . . and hath passed out of death into life" (5:24). At 17:3 he addresses God with words which expressly equate knowledge of God and of himself with eternal life: "This is life eternal, that they should know thee the only true God, and him whom thou didst send, even Jesus Christ."

John's story of the raising of Lazarus (recorded only in this gospel) is instructive in this connection. Jesus there assures the sister of the deceased that "your brother will rise again" (11:23). She takes this as meaning that "he will rise again in the resurrection at the last day". To make Jesus's audience misunderstand his words, by construing them in what seems to be their obvious sense, is what Lindars calls one of the fourth gospel's "favourite tricks" (1972, p. 53). It is not documented in the other three, and it serves the function of enabling Jesus, by his correcting of the misunderstanding, to enunciate the theology of the fourth gospel. Here, in the Lazarus story, he counters the woman's reference to a general resurrection at the end of time by declaring: "I am the resurrection and the life; he that believeth on me, though he die, yet shall he live, and whosoever liveth and believeth on me shall never die" (11:25f). Dodd agrees that here "the evangelist appears to be explicitly contrasting the popular eschatology of Judaism and primitive Christianity with the doctrine which he wishes to propound" (1970, p.147). Barrett sums up John's position nicely, saying that he does not expressly deny that there will be a "last day" when those who believe in Jesus will be "raised" (Jn. 6:39f, 44, 54). He "may have recognized that apocalyptic language was unavoidable" because established in the tradition, and that "to give it up would falsify the Christian faith." So he "retains it and reworks it" (1975, pp. 73f). Alternatively, many agree with Bultmann that the text of this gospel has been expanded by a later redactor, and that he is responsible for introducing the old, futuristic eschatology (for example at 5:28f), and also the reference to the eucharist at 6:51b–59: "Except ye eat the flesh of the Son of man and drink his blood, ye have not life in yourselves" (verse 53).

All this makes it obvious that we cannot expect any allusion in John to the eschatological discourses that are prominent in the other gospels. These discourses are replaced by farewell addresses in which Jesus reveals that what is to come is not cosmic catastrophe and final judgment, but a "paraclete", a counsellor, comfortor or advocate, who will replace him in the form of the Holy Spirit. He assures his disciples that he will not, in dying, leave them to be "orphans"; at his request the Father will give them "another Comforter" (*paraclēton*), who will be with them for ever as "the Spirit of truth" (14:16–18). All believers in him will have this Spirit after he has been "glorified" (7:39)—crucified and raised from the dead. He himself actually imparts it to the disciples by breathing on them when he appears to them after his resurrection (20:22). In the farewell addresses before his death he had told them that this Spirit "shall teach you all things" and also "bring to your remembrance all that I said unto you" (14:26). There are "many things" which at this stage he cannot say because they "could not bear them", but "when the Spirit of truth is come, he will guide you into all the truth . . . and declare unto you all the things that are to come" (16:12f). His guidance will consist of new words of Jesus, presumably for new times and new problems. In this sense the Spirit "will bear witness of me" (15:26). None of this is represented in the other gospels. Jesus's imparting of the Spirit by breathing on the disciples on Easter morning is a sophisticated—commentators say a 'profound'—exploitation of the story of the creation of man, made into "a living soul" when "the Lord God breathed into his nostrils the breath of life" (Genesis 2:7). The evangelist's idea is that, in a similar way, the disciples had their whole being transformed; and this has become one basis for the claims of many modern 'charismatic' believers to be speaking infallible words of the Spirit-paraclete.

I noted in my chapter on the resurrection that the contradiction between the fourth gospel and Acts here is striking. In Acts the Spirit comes to the disciples (by then 120 in number) like a mighty wind from heaven, and only at Pentecost, fifty days after Easter, whereas the fourth gospel combines Easter and Whitsun into a single incident.

Altogether, Acts and John exemplify two extremes of early Christian Christology. Acts has it that Jesus received his high status after his death, whereas, for John, he possessed it from all eternity. For Acts, it was only after his resurrection, when he was taken up to heaven, that "God made him both Lord and Messiah" (2:36). But John's view is that he existed in heaven in communion with God before Earth was even created, and that, as a man on Earth, he could recall this past relationship with the

Father, reminding him of "the glory I had with thee before the world was made" (17:5). He not only recalls this 'glory', but expects to resume it after he has laid down his earthly life: "I have power to lay it [my life] down; and I have power to take it again" (10:18). His death, then, will be entirely voluntary (cf. above, p. 48), and his whole earthly life is but a brief interlude in a supernatural existence. Even J.D.G. Dunn, anxious to posit a modicum of unity in the manifold traditions included in the New Testament,[10] and confident that "Christianity has nothing to fear from scholarship" (1985a, p. 103), recognizes that the fourth gospel abandons Acts' idea of "a divine sonship given or enhanced by resurrection, and presents Jesus . . . as conscious of his divine pre-existence as Son of God in heaven with the Father prior to his being sent into the world" (1989, p. 59). He summarizes: for Mark "the beginning of the Christ event" is Jesus's baptism, for Matthew and Luke it is his conception by Mary, "whereas John sets it before creation itself" (2006, p. 243). It is "not easy to see" how these views can be harmonized, and we "should simply accept that these are all different attempts to express the character and significance of Jesus' relationship with God" (1989, p. 60).

Some of the Fathers certainly found the doctrine of the gospel of John more congenial than the eschatology of the synoptics. Justin Martyr, writing in the mid-second century, could still accept the synoptics' position unequivocally, but a generation later Clement of Alexandria transmuted it into what Henry Chadwick calls "a Johannine existentialism". Chadwick finds it "characteristic that the gospel saying 'Watch, for you know not in what hour the Son of man comes' has become for Clement a warning about the enervating effects of lying too long in bed" (1966, pp. 101f. He refers here to Clement's *Paedagogus* or 'Tutor', ii, 77–82, "where the New Testament exhortations to watch with loins girded are interpreted as part of a discussion of discipline in regard to sleep"). Chadwick notes also that in the third century Origen found that it was only simple believers who took Christ's second coming literally, instead of embracing a spiritual and symbolic meaning of the doctrine, namely either "the universal expansion of the Church throughout the world . . . or the inward coming of Christ to the soul" (p. 77).

We shall see later in this chapter that there are still many attempts to supply alternatives to the literal understanding of the relevant passages, and that what the English translators of Johannes Weiss noted in 1971 (cf. above, p. 262) is still true, namely that none of these alternatives commands anything like general assent.

iv. An Appraisal of Relevant Passages

According to Hans Frei, only "a few devoted souls" still believe, with Strauss and Schweitzer, that Jesus died "a deluded fanatic" (1985, p. 238). Certainly, notable scholars regard the relevant gospel pronouncements as not spoken by Jesus, but as ascribed to him by the early church, or as not meaning what they say, but something innocuous. Nevertheless, other scholars have continued to show that there is massive support in New Testament texts for what Ehrman calls Schweitzer's "basic emphases" (1999, p. 127).[11] The following are among the passages Ehrman himself adduces (pp. 129f). We have met some of them already, but it is worthwhile to put them together to show the wide extent they cover in the synoptics. Their stress on the need for watchfulness and vigilance would make no sense if a prompt catastrophe were not envisaged:

From Mark:

Whosoever shall be ashamed of me and of my words in this adulterous and sinful generation, the Son of man also shall be ashamed of him, when he cometh in the glory of his Father with the holy angels. . . . Verily I say unto you, There be some here of them that stand by, which shall in no wise taste of death, till they see the kingdom of God come with power. (8:38–9:1)

But in those days, after that tribulation, the sun shall be darkened, and the moon shall not give her light and the stars shall be falling from heaven, and the powers that are in the heavens shall be shaken. And then shall they see the Son of man coming in clouds with great glory. And then shall he send forth the angels, and shall gather together his elect from the four winds, from the uttermost part of the earth to the uttermost part of heaven. . . . Verily I say unto you, This generation shall not pass away, until all these things be accomplished. (13:24–27, 30)

From Q:

For as the lightning, when it lighteth out of the one part under the heaven, shineth unto the other part under heaven; so shall the Son of man be in his day. . . . And as it came to pass in the days of Noah, even so shall it be also in the days of the Son of man. They ate, they drank, they married, they were given in marriage, until the day that Noah entered into the ark, and the flood came and destroyed them all. . . . After the same manner shall it be in the day that the Son of man is revealed. (Lk. 17:24, 26–27, 30; Mt. 24:27, 37–39)

Be ye also ready: for in an hour that ye think not the Son of man cometh. (Lk. 12:40; Mt. 24:44)

From the material special to Matthew:

As therefore the tares are gathered up and burned with fire; so shall it be in the end of the world. The Son of man shall send forth his angels, and they shall gather out of his kingdom all things that cause stumbling, and them that do iniquity, And shall cast them into the furnace of fire: there shall be the weeping and gnashing of teeth. Then shall the righteous shine forth as the sun in the kingdom of their Father. (13:40–43)

From the material special to Luke:

But take heed to yourselves, lest haply your hearts be overcharged with surfeiting, and drunkenness, and cares of this life, and that day come upon you suddenly as a snare. For so shall it come upon all them that dwell on the face of all the earth. But watch ye at every season, making supplication, that ye may prevail to escape all these things that shall come to pass, and to stand before the Son of man. (21:34–36)

All six of these passages make mention of "the Son of man" who is to come as judge. Jesus is not expressly identified with him here. From the point of view of the evangelists, the two were only potentially identical: Jesus was not yet the heavenly Son of man, but would soon be returning to Earth in that capacity. For this reason, then, he is made to speak of the Son of man in the third person, as if the reference were to someone other than himself. Sanders, among others, holds that, quite possibly, he did think that the coming Son of man would be someone else and did not identify himself with this personage (1993, p. 248). In that case it is the evangelists, or their Christian sources, that have done so.

In other passages Jesus, as we saw, uses the term 'Son of man' to mean himself as a man now on Earth. Thus "the Son of man has nowhere to lay his head" (Mt. 8:20; Lk. 9:58); and "the Son of man" will be killed and will rise again after three days (Mk. 8:31). All such sayings are quite separate from those in which he predicts his parousia, his final coming in glory as Son of man with his angels. These latter in no way suggest that he is already on Earth, and must first die, be resurrected and elevated to heaven before he comes as judge. A reasonable inference is that his resurrection and his parousia were originally independent traditions; that logia, familiar in Jewish apocalyptic thinking about the final coming of the Son of man, have been ascribed (rightly or wrongly) to someone who was believed to have died and risen again. The evangelists' identification of the two is not surprising: if he had risen from the grave and had joined God, he could reasonably be equated with the Son of man who was to come down from heaven.

We saw (above, p. 252) that this apocalyptic use of the term 'Son of man' derives ultimately from the book of Daniel. The earliest extant Jewish evidence for such interpretation and re-use of the relevant passages in Daniel is found in the 'Parables' or 'Similitudes' of 1 Enoch, which form chapters 37–71 of that composite work. The 'Son of man' is introduced at 46:3f, and will cast down kings and the mighty from their seats. At 48:10 and 52:4 he seems to be equated with the Messiah (the Lord's 'Anointed'); and he will be seated as judge on the throne of his glory (62:5; 69:29). Collins (1992, p. 459) dates this work at around A.D. 50—prior to the fall of Jerusalem in A.D. 70, which passes unmentioned in it, and earlier than Matthew, which is clearly influenced by it, or by some earlier Jewish document with similar ideas. Mt. 25:31 introduces a vision of the Last Judgment strikingly similar to that given in 1 Enoch 40ff. Enoch says that "the Lord of the Spirits seated the Elect one"—another title for the Son of man, for the two designations are juxtaposed in 62:1, 5—"on the throne of his glory" (61:8). Matthew reads: "When the Son of man shall come in his glory . . ., then shall he sit on the throne of his glory." Both writers go on to describe how the righteous are vindicated and the rest punished. In 1 Enoch angels "cast them into the burning furnace" (54:6), and the righteous enjoy the spectacle of their torment (62:11f). This book repeatedly refers to the Son of man seated "on the throne of his glory". Similarly, at Mt. 19:28 Jesus foretells that "in the regeneration, when the Son of man shall sit on the throne of his glory", the twelve disciples will share in his authority: "Ye also shall sit upon twelve thrones, judging the twelve tribes of Israel." The twelve tribes had, in fact, long since ceased to exist: ten of them did not survive the deportations of Sargon in the eighth century B.C. (Beare 1981, *ad. loc.*, p. 399). And this view of the twelve disciples is quite different from that which was to make eleven of them founders of the 'apostolic tradition' on which the teaching and organization of the church was supposedly based (cf. Mt. 28:19f: "Go ye therefore and make disciples of all the nations . . . teaching them to observe all things whatsoever I commanded you"; and Acts 1:8: "Ye shall be my witnesses . . . unto the uttermost part of the earth").

But my point in the present context is that, with these 'Son of man' passages in the synoptics, we are dealing with expectations already cherished in Judaism. As Allison observes, "in most respects the eschatology of Jesus must be regarded as conventional. The nearness of the consummation, the coming of judgment, and belief in the general resurrection were all things handed to him by his tradition. What was new was the connection he made with his own time and place" (2003, p. 163). Elsewhere, Allison asks: "Do we really have suitable reasons, other than saving our theology, for holding that, when the Jesus tradition speaks about the Son of man coming on the clouds of heaven, this was not meant literally?" (1998, p. 159).

We saw that, according to Mt. 12:28 and Lk. 11:20 the kingdom has to some extent already been initiated in Jesus's own ministry: "If I by the Spirit of God cast out devils, then is the kingdom of God come upon you". At Lk. 17:21 it is even said to be "in the midst of you" (RSV), presumably in Jesus's person. Many scholars speak in this connection of 'inaugurated eschatology': the unfolding of the final scenario has already begun. In the coming kingdom the demonic powers controlling the world will be overthrown, and disease and death abolished; but Jesus is already casting out demons, healing the sick, and raising the dead. "These", says Ehrman, "were not simply acts of kindness. They were parables of the Kingdom" (1999, p. 180).

Although the defeat of Satan has begun (Mk. 3:27; Lk. 10:18), the present world is still largely controlled by evil forces. It follows that those who prosper in it are empowered by such forces. This belief accounts for the disparagement of rich persons, a feature which we saw to be particularly prominent in Luke (cf. above, p. 40). They will fare badly at the judgment:

> Woe unto you that are rich . . . Woe to you that are full now, for ye shall hunger. (Lk.6:24f.)

That riches are obtained evilly is, in most passages, simply assumed, but is expressly stated in Chapter 5 of the epistle of James.

There are repeated references in the gospels to eschatological reverses of this kind: the last will be first (Mk. 10:31), the humble will be exalted (Lk. 14:11). Such passages show that Jesus's apocalyptic ideas are not evidenced only in references to the Son of man. At the Last Supper he declares: "I will no more drink again of the fruit of the vine until that day when I drink it new in the kingdom of God" (Mk. 14:25). And in the epistles the Son of man is never mentioned, yet they are charged with keen eschatological expectations. Paul believed that the end would come in the lifetime of his addressees, indeed in his own lifetime. He distinguishes those who have died ("fallen asleep") from those of us "who are alive, who are left" when Christ comes again (1 Thess. 4:15), and adds that, when this occurs, "the dead in Christ shall rise first; then we that are alive, that are left, shall together with them be caught up in the clouds"—'raptured', in the terminology of modern fundamentalists—"to meet the Lord in the air." Elsewhere he declares that, because "the appointed time has grown very short", those who have wives should "from now on live as though they had none; for the form of this world is passing away" (1 Cor. 7:29–31, RSV). Attempts are still made to interpret this as meaning no more than: the present state of affairs will not last—with no implication of anything supernatural. But the idea that Christ's coming will shortly bring the world to an end is far too common in the epistles for this to be the case. Representative passages include:

> Now salvation is nearer to us than when we first believed. The night is far spent and the day is at hand. (Rom. 13:11f)
>
> We upon whom the ends of the ages are come. (1 Cor. 10:11)
>
> The day of the Lord cometh as a thief in the night. When they are saying, Peace and safety, then sudden destruction cometh upon them . . . and they shall in no wise escape. (1 Thess.5:2f.)
>
> For yet a very little while, he that cometh shall come. (Hebrews 10:37)
>
> The coming of the Lord is at hand. (James 5:8)
>
> The end of all things is at hand. (1 Peter 4:7)
>
> It is the last hour. (1 Jn. 2:18)

Nineham comments: "It would not be too much to say that a great many early Christians, including St. Paul, lived with their ear permanently cocked for the sound of the last trumpet" (1976, pp. 141f).

The early church, after Jesus's lifetime, longed for his return. And he himself is placed, historically, between these ecclesiastical expectations and those of his forerunner, John the Baptist, who was equally concerned with the eschaton, and whose message he did not disavow but, as we saw, repeated as his own. The Baptist, so Q tells, warned people "to flee from the wrath to come", claimed that "even now is the axe laid up to the root of the trees", and foretold a "coming one" who would baptize "with fire". With such a forerunner, and with such thinking in the early church, it would surely be likely, even without the additional evidence in the synoptics, that Jesus himself had similar views. Wrede pressed this point in 1897, saying that if we suppose (as many then did, and today still do) that "Jesus spoke of a present and worldly development of the kingdom, and thought of it as an ethical community growing on earth", this would have clashed with Jewish apocalyptic ideas then current, and so would "have struck the disciples as an innovation." But in that case it is quite remarkable that his view "is what was lost in the following period from Paul onwards", and that what was then accepted was "a concept of the kingdom . . . more in line with that of late Judaism" (Wrede in Morgan 1973, p. 97).

The early Christians' idea that history had only a short time to run, and that Jesus would soon bring about a totally new and transcendent state of affairs, may seem strange to us, but at the time it was a significant factor in making Christianity popular; for, as Nineham says (1976, p. 143), it was "good news indeed to many":

> To the slave, for example—and many early Christians were slaves—it meant that the days of his slavery were numbered; he would soon be redeemed indeed! For the Jewish Christian it meant that the domination of his people by the hated pagans would not last much longer; to those oppressed by ills of any other kind, natural or supernatural, it meant light at the end of the tunnel. Whatever distresses the Christians suffered from, they would soon be swallowed up in what St. Paul called 'an eternal glory which outweighs them far'. (2 Cor. 4:17, NEB)

As the expectations were not fulfilled, they are toned down in some of the later New Testament documents (cf. above, p. 274). Mk. 14:62 has it that the persons there addressed "shall see the Son of man sitting at the right hand of power, and coming with the clouds of heaven". But at Lk. 22:69 the same audience is told merely that "from henceforth shall the Son of man be seated at the right hand of the power of God." Again, Mk. 9:1 promises that some persons then alive will see "the kingdom of God come with power", whereas Lk. 9:27 has deleted the words 'with power'. Luke's non-Markan material includes a passage that is equally instructive in this regard. At 19:11 (unique to this gospel) Jesus is represented as telling a parable in order to stop his disciples from supposing that "the kingdom of God was immediately to appear" (cf. Acts 1:6f, where, in his risen state, he reproves them for asking "dost thou at this time restore the kingdom to Israel?").

In spite of some muting of earlier expectations, Mark's statement that "this generation shall not pass away until all these things be accomplished" is retained both by Luke (21:32) and by Matthew (24:34). Beare, commenting on the latter passage, says it is no use pretending that the reference is not to the end of the world: "It must be recognized that the entire apocalyptic framework of early Christian preaching is shattered beyond any hope of rescue" (1981, p. 473). Matthew and

Luke, then, continued to believe that the end would come in their own lifetime, even if they had given up the belief that it would occur in the days of Jesus's companions.

Mk. 13:10 states that, before the end, "the gospel must first be preached unto all the nations." I suggested (above, p. 26), following Telford, that Mark wrote this because the hope that the fall of Jerusalem in A.D. 70 would herald Jesus's second coming had, in the meantime, proved to be false, so that missionary activity had to be continued. Some commentators, however, infer from this verse that the end was, after all, not expected as imminent in the evangelist's time. But are the two ideas (extensive missionizing and a prompt end) really incompatible? It seems not, as Paul held them both. He expected, as we saw, an imminent end, yet had embarked upon and completed a great missionary tour "from Jerusalem and round about even unto Illyricum" (Rom. 15:19), and intended to go on to Rome, and thence even to Spain, for further preaching (verses 24, 28).

The latest of the New Testament's twenty-seven books, 2 Peter, finds it necessary to counteract "mockers" (3:3) who taunt the faithful by pointing out that a whole generation has died off, yet Jesus has not returned, and life goes on normally. When we come to the apocryphal Coptic Gospel of Thomas we find actual disparagement of an eschatological understanding of Jesus. At saying 18 he castigates the disciples for being concerned about the end; and he spurns their question about when the kingdom will come, since "the kingdom of the Father is spread out upon the earth and people do not see it" (saying 113). For these gnostic sayings, "the Kingdom of God is not a future reality that will come to earth in a cataclysmic break in history at the end of the age", but "a salvation from within, available now to all who know who they really are and whence they have come" (Ehrman 1999, p. 131). Allison agrees that this gospel "both knows and disparages an eschatological understanding of Jesus" (2003, p. 143).

To summarize the development, the apocalyptic message begins to be muted by the end of the century, and in the fourth gospel it has virtually disappeared. Then it begins to be explicitly rejected. Christians, says Ehrman, had to take stock of the fact that Jesus was wrong in saying that the end would come, and "changed his message accordingly. You can hardly blame them" (1999, p. 134).

Ehrman concludes that the real historical Jesus is "a far cry from the Jesus many people in our society may well know." They may think of him as "a proponent of 'family values'", whereas in fact "he urged his followers to abandon their homes and forsake families for the sake of the

Kingdom that was soon to arrive." He did not "encourage people to pursue fulfilling careers" or to "work for a just society for the long haul: for him, there wasn't going to be a long haul. The end of the world as we know it was already at hand" (1999, p. 244). According to Q (reconstructed from Lk. 14:26 and Mt. 10:37 by J.M. Robinson et al.) Jesus declared: the one who "does not hate father and mother cannot be my disciple", and the one who "does not hate son and daughter cannot be my disciple" (2001, p. 137). On the same page, these editors of Q point to parallels from Mark and from the Gospel of Thomas:

> There is no man that hath left house or brothers or sisters or mother or father or children or lands, for my sake and for the gospel's sake, But he shall receive a hundredfold ... houses [etc.] ... and in the world to come eternal life. (Mk. 10:29f)

> Jesus says: Whoever will not hate one's father and one's mother will not be able to become a disciple of mine. And whoever will not hate one's brothers and one's sisters and will not take up one's cross, as I do, will not be worthy of me. (Gos. Thom. 55)

Parents, siblings, spouses, even one's children are, then, of no importance in comparison with the coming kingdom. And those who accept Jesus's message will be at odds with their families:

> Do you think that I have come to hurl peace on earth? I did not come to hurl peace but a sword. For I have come to divide son against father and daughter against her mother and daughter-in-law against her mother-in-law.

This is again the reconstruction of Robinson et al. (p. 127), from Lk. 12:51, 53 and Mt. 10:34f, and they again quote parallels from Mark and Thomas. Ehrman justly comments that "these 'anti-family' traditions are too widely attested in our sources to be ignored" (2000, p. 246). The gospels nowhere suggest that Jesus supplied guidance for improving the social structure of the time. He was not a social reformer, but obviously assumed that, if better circumstances were to come, they would be brought about by God himself.

Ehrman is aware that "some people, possibly lots of people", once they know that Jesus suffered apocalyptic delusions, would "claim he can no longer be relevant." He brushes this aside with the observation: "That claim can probably be disputed on theological grounds", with which, in his book, he is not concerned (1999, p. 244). We shall be considering them.

v. Recent Attempts to Cope with the Texts
a. Sundry Proposals

There is no doubt that many of the passages quoted in the previous section of this chapter are among those which "many Christian scholars would like to see vanish" (Sanders, 1993a, p. 178). The brothers R.P.C. and A.T. Hanson, both then bishops in the Church of England, admitted that "today this belief in an imminent *Parousia* is an embarrassment to intelligent Christians. . . . An event that has been just round the corner for a thousand years is a non-event" (1980, p. 196).

Recent theories about the compositional history of Q have done much to encourage the view that apocalyptic ideas have been foisted upon a historical Jesus who in fact did not think in that way at all. Although Q is replete with apocalyptic sayings, these are said by some scholars not to be original, but added as a secondary development before Q reached Matthew and Luke. The original Q is held to portray Jesus as a teacher of subversive wisdom, uttering provocative statements in criticism of existing social conventions in the manner of the Cynic philosophers. Even Q itself is not extant, but has to be reconstructed from non-Markan material common to Matthew and Luke; and to divide it into multiple editions, specifying which are earlier and later, must be to some extent speculative. Moreover, the mixture of Cynic-like and apocalyptic sayings does not mean that they were necessarily originally separate layers. It was, says F.G. Downing, "a very eclectic age", in which greatly diverse material could be combined (2000, pp. 126f). Even if the two were separate layers in the *literary* history of Q, it would not follow that the apocalyptic material was *historically* secondary (cf. above, p. 215).

Keith Ward does not deny that the gospels are "problematic . . . in their clearly expressed belief in the imminent end of the world." But he thinks that whether Jesus is to be regarded as "a deluded eschatological prophet" or as "a human being consciously united to God in knowledge, will and feeling in quite a unique way" will be determined "not by objective historical evidence alone, but by whether one has an experience of forgiveness of sins and new life in the Spirit, through the proclamation of Jesus as a living mediator of God within the community of faith" (1992, p. 12). Such 'experience' can only be personal, individual and subjective, and if it is allowed to decide the issue, there is no more that can be said. Ward's reference here to "the community of faith" shows that he is aware that such personal experience is more impressive in a situation of communal worship, where it is visibly shared by others.

This merely means that it is easy to believe what one's chosen associates believe, and is true of assemblies of Marxists, Fascists, Hindus, and atheists, without making any of their beliefs better founded. I have remarked (above, p. 8) on the psychological fact that united expressions of an emotion tend to increase the intensity of the emotion in each individual.

Bultmann likewise does not deny that Jesus's preaching was "mythological", that its "dominant concept" is the reign of God, soon to be initiated by a "cosmic catastrophe which will do away with all conditions of the present world as it is", and that this expectation "turned out to be an illusion" (1968, pp. 3, 22). Yet he believed that a "deeper meaning" underlies all this (1960, p. 18), and that, when Jesus says that the end of the world is imminent, this really means that none of us knows what the future will bring, so that it behoves us "to be open to God's future which is really imminent for everyone of us." God's future is "a judgment on all men who have bound themselves to this world" (1960, pp. 31f); and this judgment itself consists in their failure to realize "the emptiness of the human situation" (p. 26) so that they are unable to attain to what Bultmann elsewhere calls "authentic life" (cf. above, p. 74)—what used to be called 'salvation'.

Bultmann links his method of exegesis with the philosophy of Heidegger and claims that it is appropriate to interpret the New Testament mythology "existentially" since both the Bible and the existentialists are concerned with human existence (1960, pp. 45, 55, 57). Only man, he adds, exists at all, for the existentialists have explained that other beings "are not 'existing' but only 'extant' (vorhanden)", whereas man is a "historical" being, meaning that "every man has his own history. Always his present comes out of his past and leads into his future" (p. 56). Since animals learn from experience one might suppose that their present comes out of their past and leads into their future. But this is evidently not the view of existentialists.

How all this is to be connected with New Testament exegesis is not easy to understand. The idea seems to be that (1) human existence is something special, and (2) the New Testament appeals to this special something: "Christian preaching is *kerygma,* that is, a proclamation addressed not to the theoretical reason, but to the hearer as self" (p. 36). This means that when the Christian interprets the Bible, he must relate what it says to his own self, his own aspirations, beliefs and fears. When, for instance, the Bible says that God created the world, this must not be taken to mean what it says, but rather something about the personal relation between the believer and his God. "Only such statements about God are legitimate as express the existential relation between God and man. Statements which speak of God's actions as cosmic events are illegitimate." Hence to say that God is creator "can only be a personal confession that I understand myself to be a creature which owes its existence to God. It cannot be made as a neutral statement, but only as thanksgiving and surrender" (p. 69). A 'neutral statement' seems to mean a detached, objective statement about some process in the world not primarily or exclusively connected with my own personal existence. Here, then, we have the key. To understand scripture aright we must give it the relevance to ourselves which it appears to lack. "To hear the scriptures as the Word of God means to hear them as a word which is addressed to me, as *kerygma,* as a proclamation. Then my understanding is not a neutral one, but rather my response to a call" (p. 71). In this way, Jesus's second coming can be understood symbolically to mean that Christ 'comes to me' in my decision to accept him and his rule.

John Macquarrie (Emeritus Professor of Divinity at Oxford) understandably finds this "blatantly individualist" and complains that, "not only in his treatment of eschatology, but in his work as a whole, Bultmann . . . sometimes appears as a rather old-fashioned evangelical preacher, concerned with individual decision and individual salvation" (2003, pp. 107f). In one frank passage Bultmann himself admits that it is because the Bible does not stand up to historical criticism that he has to introduce his emotional approach to it in order to make it religiously useful:

> It is precisely the mythological description of Jesus Christ in the New Testament which makes it clear that the figure and work of Jesus Christ must be understood in a manner which is beyond the categories by which the objective historian understands world-history, if the figure and work of Jesus Christ are to be understood as the divine work of redemption. (1960, p. 80)

Others, not finding philosophical jargon about being and existence helpful, have faced up to Jesus's eschatological preaching quite differently. We have already met Dodd's "realized eschatology" (above, p. 261). But it left him the task of disposing of passages not amenable to this interpretation. He suggests that the disciples, under the influence of traditional Jewish apocalyptic ideas, may simply have given their master's words "a twist away from their original intention" (1971, p. 114). Robert Funk has recently said, similarly, that "they had not understood the subtleties of Jesus' position . . . and so reverted to the standard orthodox scenario once he had departed from the scene" (1996, p. 164). For Dodd, even their new 'twist' of Jesus's words is not to be understood literally. The Great Assize when the Son of man will come in his glory and separate sheep from goats is, he says, not meant as a forthcoming event to which a date might be assigned, but is a symbol for "the reality to which the spirit of man awakes when it is done with past, present and future" (1971, p. 115).

Hoskyns likewise, in his *Cambridge Sermons,* held that "our Lord's eschatological language . . . was mainly symbolical" (Quoted approvingly by Glasson 1980, p. 14). J.A.T. Robinson's interpretation furnishes an example of what this 'symbol' has been taken to mean. He discusses it in connection with Adam's "Fall" which he calls a myth, but "none the less profoundly true for that", in that the Fall is "a way of giving theological expression to our existential condition rather than a once-and-for-all 'event'" (1973, p. 21). Obviously, without a 'Fall' of some sort, man would not be naturally depraved, there would be no need for a 'redemption', and the work of Christ would have been superfluous. The parousia or second coming is likewise "not a once-and-for-all event in the historical future, whether near or remote, but part of a myth designed to clarify what it means—as well as what it will mean - to see all things 'new' in the kingdom of God. It asserts that the reality depicted by the Fall, the truth of all things 'in Adam', is not the only or the final truth about the cosmic scene" (p. 117). John Kent comments appropriately that "this approach . . . is to be found in many other writers", and amounts to "a means of saving traditional language from complete disuse" (1982, p. 112). The traditional formulas are firmly embedded in the creeds and in the liturgies, and so cannot be relinquished, however radically they are reinterpreted.

Quite often the unwelcome passages are simply set aside as of no great significance. John Fenton allows that Mark repeatedly expresses the expectation that the kingdom will come soon—he refers to 1:15; 9:1; 13:30 and 14:62—whereas in fact it did not, and "it is not altogether adequate or honest to say that it may even now come soon." It is "almost impossible", he adds, to take over this aspect of Jesus's message and preach it today. Nevertheless, "we can still learn from his teaching the way of life that God requires" (2001, pp. 25f). This would mean that the 'hard sayings' do not express merely a temporary ethic, a preparation for the advent of the kingdom in the first century A.D., but constitute a permanent guide to human behaviour. Or, alternatively, that one can select maxims which seem acceptable from the whole. But such selection would have to be justified.

Leander Keck supposes that God's "vindication" of Jesus through resurrection provides a solution to the perplexities of the apocalyptic sayings. Keck recognizes that these sayings are substantial in number and that it is unrealistic to suppose that all of them have been "fed into the Jesus tradition from the reservoir of Jewish apocalyptic thought" (2000, p. 169). He is aware that "according to Mark, Jesus assured his disciples twice that what he expected would be actualized in their lifetime (Mk. 9:1; 13:30)", and that God would "act soon" (pp. 108f). He admits that Jesus's expectations were not fulfilled (p. 111); but nevertheless his disciples "came to believe that he was vindicated by resurrection that transformed him; for them, this was a sign that the new age broke in with him, although nothing else had changed visibly." Keck stresses the transformation: "although it was *Jesus* whom God vivified and vindicated by his resurrection, and not only his teachings, ... the resurrected Jesus is not simply Jesus resumed", but transformed:

> The strange stories of his appearances can be understood as narrative precipitates of the conviction that the same Jesus is now fundamentally 'different'. He is for them transformed into a mode of existence that *still* assures and presages the future when the new age will be fully actualized. ... Resurrecting Jesus means validating indefinitely the one whose life was lived out of the future, even if what occurred turned out not to be what he expected. (p. 110)

Keck's wording about what the disciples "came to believe", about their "conviction", and about what the post-crucifixion Jesus was "for them", leaves it unclear whether he himself accepts the historicity of the resurrection, or regards it as possibly no more than a belief of the disciples. It is also unclear how, in either case, Jesus's "teachings" can thereby be "vindicated" or "validated". He had certain beliefs about the future, and the disciples came to have others. The fact that, in both cases, a "mode of existence" different from the present mode was involved does not harmonize them. But for Keck it suffices that the kingdom of God is "a tensive symbol" (p. 109), "an image for a different sort of reality altogether" (pp. 111f), and that this much is common to what Jesus said and what his disciples 'came to believe'.

John Dominic Crossan takes what Keck has designated the unrealistic view that Jesus's many apocalyptic sayings were ascribed to him by the early church (1991, pp. 247, 255). Although this may well be to some extent the case, the fact that the early church thought apocalyptically does not mean that Jesus himself did not. In any case, to distinguish what is authentically Jesuine in the synoptics is hazardous; and it is the gospels as they stand to which, in Christian preaching, we are urged to be beholden.

Crossan's books have sold in enormous numbers. The dust cover of this 1991 volume informs us that it is "the first comprehensive determination of who Jesus was, what he did and what he said." He believed that Jesus did indeed, as a follower of John the Baptist, begin as an apocalyptic believer, but then changed his mind. As evidence, Crossan points to two adjacent passages in Q. In the first, John is said to be "more than a prophet" (Lk. 7:26 = Mt. 11:9), and this "reads like an attempt to maintain faith in John's apocalyptic vision despite John's own execution." But two verses later, Jesus declares that: "the least in the kingdom of God is greater" than John. "Between these two assertions", says Crossan, "Jesus changed his view of John's mission and message" (pp. 236f, 259). To this, Allison (1998, p. 105) retorted that the second of these two passages "may simply show that Jesus took himself to be further along the eschatological time line than John. It certainly does not demonstrate that he had abandoned John's eschatological framework."

For his reconstruction of the true historical Jesus Crossan relies heavily on non-canonical material which he dates later than the Paulines but earlier than Mark. His reviewer A.E. Harvey notes that he appeals in this way to "no less than twelve sources, mostly extra-canonical" (1993, p. 227). These include the "Egerton Gospel" (fragments with four stories about Jesus, usually dated at A.D. 150 plus or minus twenty-five years), the Gospel of the Hebrews (not extant, but quoted by some church Fathers from the late second century), and parts of the Gospel of Peter (again, now available only in fragments). Ehrman comments that the Gospel of the Hebrews, for instance, is "never mentioned or even alluded to" until around A.D. 190, and "is seen by nearly everyone as a second-century production"; and that while the synoptics can confidently be placed in the first century, to give an early date to material which in most cases "is not quoted or even mentioned by early Christian writers until many, many decades later seems overly speculative" (1999, pp. 133f).

b. "Meta-narratives"

A more philosophical solution to the difficulties is proposed by Hans Küng. He holds that the end of the world, like its beginning, is not verbally expressible except by means of poetic images and imaginative narratives. Hence both the Genesis creation stories and the New Testament apocalyptic discourses are not to be understood literally and dismissed as erroneous—the idea of mistakenness being quite inappropriate in these contexts. The New Testament material puts into words in the only possible way "the final revelation of the rule of God" (1976, pp. 209f). However, even this exegesis does not free Jesus from error in respect of his timing of the end. Küng admits that he expected it to come soon. But has 'the final revelation of the rule of God' yet materialized? The phrase is perhaps vague enough to allow the affirmation that it has.

Richard Bauckham's arguments for the reality of Jesus's second coming, his parousia, take us even further into systematic theology. His point of departure is that secular hopes for a better world have proved totally unrealistic: "Enlightenment optimism"—some kind of dig at the Enlightenment is irresistible—and "dogmatic progressivism" have lost all credibility as prospects for the future; and so it is time for Christian hope to extricate itself from them and "recover its own source and focus in the Jesus Christ who transcends his past history, and ours, and so is still to come" (2001, p. 273). Judaism and Christianity have formulated a "grand narrative" of the origin of the world, of its history and "its final destiny in the purposes of God" (p. 266). Jesus's story remains unfinished until this "meta-narrative" is completed, until the world's origin and history is supplemented with God finally putting an end to all evil, suffering and death. This will be effected by Jesus's parousia, which is "integral to his identity" (p. 270), and is "the event which will end history"—not by destroying the world, but by cleansing it: all those, both living and dead, who survive his judgment "receive new life in the renewed creation in eternity" (p. 266).

However, the parousia "can be narrated only in symbols" (p. 270). In an earlier book, Bauckham and Trevor Hart, his colleague in theology at St. Andrews University, Scotland, explain why this is so. The parousia "cannot be an event in time and space like the other events of history, since it is the event which happens to all time and space and transforms them into eternity." But because of the limitations of our minds, we can envisage it only as an event in time and space, for example as Jesus descending, seated on clouds and attended by a vast retinue of angels (1999, p. 118). The two authors admit that their view of the future "is finally a matter of faith, rooted in and nurtured by a long tradition of Christian imagining, and belonging to the category of those things 'revealed' to faith in one way or another" (p. 175). As for the Bible's expectancy that Christians are to live "each day . . . in anticipation of the promised end", our two authors find that this does not mean that the end will come soon, but that we should earnestly set about "purifying the world through initiatives for divine justice, peace and the life to which these lead"; for the parousia is to purge the world, not destroy it. Hence "the note of urgency in Jesus's teaching reflects the fact that, no matter how much time may be left, the task is one which demands all our energy and activity" (pp. 207f). In this book, there are not many references to New Testament passages, and most of them are not to the gospels but to the book of Revelation where, we may note, "from the great winepress of God's wrath . . . blood flowed to the height of the horses' bridles" (14:20).

Ben Witherington III follows Bauckham's account to some extent. He does not deny that both Paul and Jesus "believe in such things as a future coming of the Dominion of God on earth, a future resurrection of believers and the future coming of an agent of God (Christ or the Son of Man) who will bring in a day of final redemption and judgment" (1992, p. 225). He thinks it quite wrong to suppose that the relevant texts need to be "demythologized", as if the speakers "were not trying to say anything concrete about the realities that they believed would happen at the end of human history" (p. 236). But he denies that Paul or Jesus were convinced that the end would come quickly, and interprets them to be saying no more than that it was "possibly imminent" (pp. 36, 47f). Passages which suggest immediacy can be otherwise interpreted. For instance, Mk. 9:1 (some of Jesus's audience will live to "see the kingdom of God come with power") may refer to something he thought would happen during his earthly ministry, such as his transfiguration or "any of a number of miracles or perhaps an exorcism" (p. 39). Even if it could be shown that Jesus and Paul wrongly taught that the end would come in a generation, "this in itself would not rule out that they might be right in the substance of their teaching"; for we need to take account of what we have been learning from Einstein and others about "the space-time continuum", namely that time is "dynamical. It can stretch and shrink . . ." (pp. 233f). The primary function of Jesus's "language of imminence" is "to inculcate a sort of moral earnestness in believers, so that their eyes will remain fixed upon the goal, eagerly longing for the fulfillment of God's plan for human history" (p. 48). Like Bauckham, Witherington believes that "it is God's plan ultimately to renew and redeem the world", not to destroy it. Hence "blessed be they who participate in and foreshadow that by working to clean up the environment, feed the hungry", and so on. It follows that "a proper belief in and understanding of eschatology" rules out today's North American "gospel of conspicuous consumption and wealth". It also has the great merit that "the overcoming of present evil by eschatological righteousness" can "vindicate God as righteous". He here (pp. 239f) quotes Bauckham:

"Only the hope of such a future of righteousness could make the evils of the present bearable".

c. Coping with the Romans

G.B. Caird dismisses the conclusions of Weiss and Schweitzer as "facile" (1980, p. 261) and their minds as "pedestrian" (p. 271), in that they took Jesus's statements with "flat-footed" literality. Caird supposes that by promising frightful punishment "on that day" (Lk. 10:12) or "on the day of judgment" (Mt. 10:15) to communities who do not accept his disciples or their teaching, Jesus meant no more than: the present state of affairs will not last, and if the Jews do not follow his advice and "abandon the road of aggressive nationalism", the Romans will destroy them (p. 265). Moreover, in Jesus's teaching, "the kingdom of God had arrived (Mt. 12:28) and was already being entered by the most unexpected people" (p. 43)—the harlots and tax collectors (Mt. 21:31). The Biblical writers, Caird says, "regularly used end-of-the-world language metaphorically to refer to that which they well knew was not the end of the world. . . . As with all other uses of metaphor, we have to allow for the likelihood of some literalist misinterpretation on the part of the hearer, and for the possibility of some blurring of the edges between vehicle and tenor on the part of the speaker" (p. 256). As Allison has observed, possibly this "need to treat the language as symbolic only arises because of the failure of the predictions in the first place" (1998, p. 163).

There are many statements in the Bible which put the speaker—be he Yahweh, Jesus or other—in a very unpleasant light. It is therefore important for those who are aware of this, and who nevertheless feel strong emotional attachment to the Bible, to be able to say that it need not be understood literally. The kind of training which many young people receive in the literature departments of our universities supplies them with great facility in effecting non-literal exegesis.

Caird is very much concerned to avoid ascribing unreasonable views to Biblical authors. "There are always", he says, "some naive people in any age. . . . But the writers of the Bible and its leading figures were not among them." They were not subject to the almost universal delusions of their age. "They might imagine the stars as angels and the host of heaven as a privy council around the throne of God (1 Kings 22:19: "I saw the Lord sitting on his throne, and all the hosts of heaven standing by him"). But they knew that this was only a picture" (p. 43).

Caird's method of interpretation becomes particularly clear in what he says about the New Testament epistles. Paul writes of the "cosmos", sometimes meaning not just the world in which man lives and the field of his activities, but rather the sphere of anti-godly power, of "the god of this age" who has blinded the minds of unbelievers "to prevent them from seeing the light" (2 Cor. 4:4). He writes of "the rulers *(archontes)* of this age" (1 Cor. 2:6, 8)—he uses 'this age' and 'this cosmos' interchangeably: they are equated at 1 Cor. 1:20 and 3:18f—and most commentators take the reference to be to some kind of mighty angelic powers, who include "Satan", who "disguises himself as an angel of light" (2 Cor. 11:14). Paul's wording resembles the title given in the fourth gospel to the supreme demonic being, "the ruler *(archōn)* of this cosmos" (Jn. 12:31; 16:11). These hostile forces he sometimes calls not angels or rulers, but principalities, powers, dominions, or thrones. (The empty throne, the seat of the godhead, often designated the god in the ancient world.) Ephes. 2:2 mentions "the ruler of the power of the air", and at 6: 12 the "principalities, powers and world-rulers of this darkness" are expressly said not to be "flesh and blood", but rather "spiritual hosts of wickedness in the heavenly places". But Caird supposes that, for Paul, these entities "stand . . . for the political, social, economic, and religious structures of power, Jewish and pagan, of the old world order, which Paul believed to be obsolescent" (p. 242).

Caird's comments on incidents in the gospels that seem discreditable are likewise revealing. He thinks that Jesus's words to the Syro-Phoenician woman, which imply that the gentiles are "dogs" (Mk. 7:27), "must have been spoken with a smile and in a tone of voice which invited the woman's witty reply" (p. 54).

If Caird is mildly abusive in what he says of Schweitzer, N.T. Wright, the present bishop of Durham, knows no such restraint. He begins his 1992b book by asking us to envisage "a man with wild hair and flashing eyes" who burst into a Victorian drawing room, tore the portraits from the walls "as though in a frenzy", trampled on them "with his dirty boots", and replaced them with "a stark outline of a figure, not unlike himself, with a wild visionary face". The intruder, says Wright, is Albert Schweitzer, the old portraits the nineteenth-century studies of Jesus, and the new picture Schweitzer's own substitute, "not unlike himself"!

Wright believes that Schweitzer, together with "the great majority" of later (and even of some earlier) New Testament scholars "misunderstood the nature of apocalyptic" (1996, pp. 56f); that passages in both Jewish and Christian documents about the stars falling from heaven and the Son of man coming with angels on clouds are really merely images expressing the view that God will shortly vindicate his people, and are no more meant literally than when we ourselves speak, as we might, of the fall of the Berlin wall, or the devaluation of sterling in September 1992, as "earth-shattering" (1992b, p. 55). Such metaphors apropos of these recent events of course occur in contexts where the events themselves are unambiguously being spoken of. Wright maintains that, similarly, references in apocalypses to catastrophes and to the coming of the Son of man occur in contexts which show that they are but a figurative way of designating "something like this: (a) the people of God are being opposed by pagan foes; (b) God will vindicate them soon; (c) when this happens the effect will . . . result in God's people being set in a position of authority over the rest of mankind" (p. 55). The Jewish idea, then, was that soon the pagans would be put in their place. Jesus, however, offered a new version of the way in which Israel's God was to become Lord of all the world, namely through Jesus's own work. He picked up Israel's expectation that a great turning point was imminent and "applied it to himself" (p. 100). He saw the wrath of God bearing down upon the Jews, and leading inevitably to the destruction of Jerusalem, because they proposed to fight the Romans instead of accepting his way of peace. So he determined, by means of a voluntary death, to take this wrath upon himself, believing that his death and resurrection would defeat Satan and vanquish evil. The Jews believed that the kingdom—God's universal rule—would be preceded by suffering and woe. Jesus believed that, if he took this upon himself, the kingdom would then come; his own resurrection would show that God had vindicated him and that evil was defeated. Wright has taken much of this, as he himself acknowledges (p. 101), from Schweitzer—the Schweitzer whom he so mercilessly portrays at the beginning of this same book.

Wright's vague talk about defeating evil does not inspire confidence. In his view, although evil in fact survived Jesus, his resurrection—or at any rate the church's belief in it—did show that "he had in principle [!] succeeded in his task" and had left to his followers the "further task of *implementing* what he had achieved", of becoming in their turn "Isaianic heralds, light to the world" (1996, pp. 659f, author's italics). Wright is merely restating the traditional Christian philosophy of history, according to which love will decisively triumph over evil, and in some unclarified sense has already done so in the death and resurrection of Jesus.

Wright is of course correct in pointing out that Old Testament prophets used poetic hyperbole to denote, in cosmic terms, as Amos did, the fall of the northern kingdom of Israel, or, as a passage in Isaiah does, to foretell the fall of Babylon:

> Behold the day of the Lord cometh . . . to destroy the sinners. . . . For the stars of heaven and the constellations thereof shall not give their light; the sun shall be darkened . . . and the moon shall not cause her light to shine. (Isaiah 13:9–13)

This, then, is mere imagery; but, as Collins notes, "this imagery underwent significant development in the period between the Babylonian Exile (586–539 B.C.E.) and the rise of Christianity" (2003, p. 65). As a result, statements of cosmic catastrophes were no longer meant as merely figurative, and "the end" of the world came to be understood literally, as we saw in the case of the Apocalypse of Weeks (above, p. 246). Hence Wright's interpretation that no more than imagery is involved in the Jewish and Christian material is forced. 2 Peter 3:7–12, for instance, unambiguously states that at "the day of the Lord", "the heavens that now are and the earth" will be destroyed by fire: "The heavens shall pass away with a great noise, the elements shall be dissolved with fervent heat, and the earth and the works that are therein shall be burned up"—all this to be followed by "new heavens and a new earth, wherein dwelleth righteousness". Wright can only suppose that we are dealing here with "a misunderstanding of Jewish apocalyptic language" (1992a, p. 463n)—which, however, repeatedly posits the annihilation of the world by fire (references in Russell 1971, p. 275).

vi. Finale

J.D.G. Dunn admits—what is surely undeniably the case—that "the NT presents events critical to Christian faith in language and concepts which are often outmoded and meaningless to twentieth-century man." Hence the question which "demythologizing" addresses is "whether the gospel is forever imprisoned within these first century thought forms, whether it can be re-expressed in twentieth-century terms" (1985b, pp. 300f).

Bultmann is perhaps the best-known exponent of demythologizing, and is himself best known from his view of the resurrection rather than the parousia (cf. above, p. 74). Dunn understandably finds no Christian comfort in his treatment of the former, and complains that when he talks of "the saving event of cross and resurrection it becomes fairly clear that he is talking in fact of the *proclamation* of cross and resurrection as saving event, about saving event in the here and now of existential encounter with the kerygma". And "if the phrase 'the resurrection of Jesus' is not attempting to talk about something which happened *to*

Jesus, if it merely describes the rise of the Easter faith, then it is of no more value than the mystery religions' myth of the dying and rising god" (pp. 296, 299).[12]

However, in the present context I am concerned with the parousia rather than the resurrection, and must note that attempts to free Jesus from apocalyptic ideas—either by 'demythologizing' the texts in some way or other, or by construing what they say as acceptable in itself, without reinterpretation—continue, and continue to provoke rebuttals. Marius Reiser, Professor of New Testament at Mainz (Germany), comments scornfully (2001, p. 221) on the ruling of the Jesus Seminar that the eschatological sayings, particularly those which mention judgment, are "vindictive" in a way that is "uncharacteristic of Jesus"—as if we knew, before we begin study, what is characteristic of him. Reiser refers (pp. 236f) to Q's record of "what is probably the most severe of Jesus's sayings about judgment", namely the woes over Chorazin and Bethsaida and the succeeding judgment on Capernaum (Mt. 11:21–24 = Lk. 10:13–15), spoken because the people in these places had not repented despite having witnessed his "mighty works". For Reiser, the clear implication is that he "does not want to have his miracles evaluated as sensational things that people can see and then go on living as they had before; instead, they should serve as signals calling for repentance", as necessary for entry into the kingdom which—in Mark's summary of his message—is "at hand" (Mk. 1:15).

Reiser calls a recent depiction of Jesus as a "teacher of popular wisdom", indeed any such non-apocalyptic portrayal of him, "a fantastic construction" (p. 217). He concludes his paper by reminding us that Josephus's blindness to the considerable apocalyptic trends in the Judaism of his day was deliberate, prompted by his desire to convince his upper-class Graeco-Roman audience that Jews were nice people, not people who threatened the rule and authority of Rome by belief in imminent cosmic catastrophes. Similarly, says Reiser, the non-eschatological Jesus of some of today's scholars results from their "regard for a certain upper- or middle-class public" for whom apocalyptic ideas are an "eyesore". He finds that "on the main point, Schweitzer was right" (p. 238), in that, if eschatology is deleted from Matthew and Mark, there remains "only a text cut to ribbons, which is of no good use for anything" (p. 220).

Numerous New Testament scholars express similar views. Gerd Theissen, Professor of New Testament at Heidelberg, and his colleague Annette Merz write in their handbook that "the 'non-eschatological' Jesus" seems to have more (twentieth-century) Californian than (first-century) Galilean "local colouring" (1998, p. 11). Alexander

Wedderburn, Professor of New Testament at Munich, who subscribes to "thoroughgoing agnosticism" concerning Jesus's resurrection, and even advocates "a faith that is thoroughly this-worldly", with no expectation of an afterlife, distances himself from Jesus to the extent of stressing that, "just as he was part of his own world and time and shared the assumptions and many aspects of the then prevalent world-view and mistakenly expected an imminent end of the world as we know it, so too he shared the widespread belief in another world that was still to be revealed" (1999, pp. 167, 285n385). Wedderburn is well aware that any "restructuring of the Christian faith" so as to eliminate these in his view serious delusions will not be welcome, and will present Christian ministers with problems "at the pastoral level" (p. 225). Finally, I note that the three editors of a recent volume on *The History of Apocalypticism* say in their introduction to it that "it is difficult to avoid the conclusion that modern resistance to the eschatological Jesus arises from the fact that such a Jesus is too strange and uncomfortable for modern tastes" (McGinn et al., 2003, p. xi).

Those who have read through this final chapter of my present book may well agree with the New Testament scholar Christopher Evans that "there is no greater conceptual or doctrinal mess than eschatology" (1971, p. 71). It is perhaps to Christianity's advantage that very many who today call themselves Christians know nothing of this whole mess. Ben Witherington III says:

> North America, like much of the Western world, is a society in which Jesus is virtually omnipresent, while at the same time the population is largely biblically illiterate. There is a seemingly inexhaustible fascination with Jesus, but widespread ignorance about what the Gospels and the rest of the New Testament say about him. . . . Even serious believers tend to operate with only a sketchy sense of what the Bible actually says.[13]

Leslie Houlden speaks in this connection of the "atrophy" of old doctrines, such as hell, judgment, even perhaps life after death, which "apart from pockets of increasingly eccentric traditionalists, are quietly dropped from the regular agenda." This has gone so far that "surveys now reveal not inconsiderable numbers of churchgoers who do not believe in God" (2002, p. 114).

However, 'eccentric traditionalists' fill more than minor pockets; for side by side with a great variety of scholarly appraisals, there have been, and still are, popular movements which take apocalyptic material as betokening Jesus's second coming not in New Testament times, but in their own, and as bringing with it a new and disastrous stage of God's dealings with the world. The texts have proved infinitely adaptable so that the Antichrist could be identified, in the Reformation struggles, as the Pope, and later as Napoleon, Kaiser Wilhelm, Hitler, and so on. Such exegesis has proved extraordinarily resilient, in that "repeated disappointments have not dimmed the apocalyptic fervour of fresh generations" (Dunn 2006, p. 369). And today the situation in the Middle East, or climate change and the sorry ecological condition of the planet are with equal confidence invoked as presaging the end, as foretold. "Drawing on a wide range of seemingly disparate prophetic and apocalyptic passages written over a span of several centuries under vastly different historical conditions, a succession of ingenious interpreters and popularizers have pieced together detailed and more-or-less cohesive end-time scenarios as one would patiently assemble the pieces of a jigsaw puzzle until the full picture emerges" (Boyer 2003, pp. 516f). These people have no awareness that, even within the New Testament, there have been shifts of doctrine.

A favourite text is 1 Thess. 4:17, taken to mean that just before the onset of the great tribulation, Christ's true followers will be 'raptured'—spirited away from the Earth to join him in the sky. People are very suggestible when frightened, and in a world where signs of impending disasters are frightening enough, this text, so interpreted, assures the genuine faithful that they will escape the worst. It also, as part of an overall apocalyptic outlook, provides what is felt to be a meaningful framework to the whole course of history, which otherwise seems to be depressingly devoid of any overarching meaning. Apocalyptic eschatology "sees history as having a *purpose,* a goal. It is not only *God* oriented, it is *future* oriented", and "a hope based on the belief that the forces of history are ultimately in God's control and are driving towards *his* goal" (Dunn 2006, p. 369). For the same reason, many prefer 'intelligent design', which seems to imbue the universe with purpose and meaning, to evolutionary biology, which does neither.

The millions[14] whose main concern in life is that they will be 'raptured' in this way are not going to bother themselves with higher critical studies of the relation of Paulines to gospels, the 'editing' of Mark by Matthew and Luke, or the differences between the synoptics and John, still less with such earlier key discoveries as the non-Isaianic character of Isaiah 40–55, or the origin of the book of Daniel in the second century B.C., and not in the sixth, as it claims—even though such discoveries "decisively altered our picture of what the Bible was like" (Barr 1983, pp. 106f).

Unfortunately, the confidence of these millions that the end is nigh is not harmless musing, but brings with it "profoundly dangerous baggage" in the form of "the demonizing of opponents" and "the glorification of the divine violence that will supposedly usher in the new order" (Moorhead 2003, p. 489). In such hands, sacred books, so often regarded as a blessing, can be a real curse.

9

Concluding Thoughts

Apologists continue to write (in the manner of Franklin 1994, p. 98) of the "enduring power", and so forth, of the gospels over the centuries as if this had been some spontaneous effect, not dependent on the backing of an inflexible establishment.

Until relatively recent times, the church did not have 'members': everyone was obliged to participate. J.M. Robertson summed up the historical development rather well, saying that, before the rise of criticism, we find believers "hating and burning each other in their quarrels over the meaning of their central sacrament." Then, in the eighteenth century, after the spread of science had shaken belief in miracles, they set themselves to frame explanatory lives of Jesus in which "miracles were dissolved into hallucinations or natural episodes misunderstood." This, we saw, was the situation confronting Strauss, who showed that many of the individual episodes which they had thus striven to reduce to history were but "operations of the mythopoeic faculty, proceeding on the mass of Jewish prophecy and legend under the impulse of the Messianic idea" (Robertson 1916, pp. 211f). Then Wrede undermined confidence in even the earliest of the canonical gospels, and argued that Jesus's Messiahship could well be a creation following upon the belief in his resurrection. About the same time, Schweitzer, drawing on the earlier work of Reimarus and Johannes Weiss, showed that the texts themselves, while making Jesus condemn "false prophets" in the harshest terms (Mt. 7:15 and elsewhere), represent him as speaking false prophecies and hence, according to Deuteronomy 18:22, as speaking "presumptuously".

If, after all this, we can extract some sort of historical figure from the texts, he is surely not one who may appropriately be worshipped. The historian has indeed "been far more disturbing to Christianity than the scientist" (Shaw 1983, p. 270). And in fact the hopelessness of anything like Christian orthodoxy has long been admitted by numerous knowledgeable Christian scholars. F.C. Burkitt, the Cambridge theologian who died in 1935, declared: "The old orthodoxy, regarded as a fixed system, exists no longer. . . . The whole building has collapsed. Where Gibbon saw an effete and old-fashioned building, we are confronted with a heap of ruins" (1924, p. 8). Another Cambridge New Testament man, J.S. Bezzant, who died in 1967, said that what were for centuries fundamental items of Christian doctrine have been "so shattered" that the mere recital of them has "the aspect of a malicious travesty" (1963, p. 84). John Bowden, Christian minister and, at the time, director of the religious house that published his book, admitted that he was not able to say "what remains of Jesus", only that he was still working on that question (1988, p. 206). And the estimable Heikki Räisänen, Professor of New Testament at Helsinki, finds, as we saw, that what can still be done is to use the words of the New Testament—words such as kingdom of God, resurrection, redemption, even Christ or God—as "evocative and challenging symbols" (1995, p. 136). He and others speak of the New Testament as a kind of "poetry". One cannot, but be struck by the triviality of such claims, compared with those made for theology in past times.

Not that the scholars agree on important issues. Some continue to affirm the 'relevance' of scripture in the manner of the Fathers, as when the French philosopher Paul Ricoeur claimed in 1981 that Paul's letters were no less addressed to him than to the Romans, Corinthians, and Galatians (Quoted by Prickett in Byrne and Houlden 1995, p. 152). At the other extreme, the New Testament scholar Gerd Lüdemann finds that "most of Paul", particularly his idea of God's plan for man's salvation, "belongs in the museum" (2001, pp. 221, 230). D.S. du Toit reviews a number of "influential recent images of Jesus", and notes that at many points they "seem to be at variance with each other to the point of being mutually exclusive", particularly on the question as to "whether Jesus's message was thoroughly eschatological or not" (2001, pp. 83, 98, 110). This "extreme diversity in current Jesus research" (p. 123) is in part a consequence of a similar diversity in the New Testament evidence. Houlden notes it as "a common perception" of New Testament scholars that "the New Testament writers constitute a choir of voices, harmonious indeed in their devotion and witness to Jesus, but cacophonous on almost everything else", including on "how they perceive him, what they think he stood for, . . . what really mattered about him, and how they should proceed in the light of him" (2000, pp. 33f).

As a result, some theologians have found it expedient to make their Christian faith independent of historical fact. We have already seen that

Schweitzer argued in this way. Paul Tillich too believed that "historical investigations should neither comfort nor worry theologians" (1968, p. 144), and he posited what he called "ecstatic reason" in order to overcome the crisis of relativism. 'Ecstatic reason', we are told, is "existential, a rational decision which crosses the border of mystery through a leap of faith"; and according to one of Tillich's interpreters, this "concept" is "one of his chief intellectual contributions to the twentieth century" (Details in Ericksen 1985, p. 183). Marcus Borg holds that "the core value of Christianity has to do with its ability to mediate the sacred, not with the historical accuracy of any particular claim" (cf. above, p. 175). Similarly, Jack Austin, reviewing Crossan's 1991 book, finds it "intellectually interesting" but "theologically irrelevant", since "for centuries, Christians have believed not a historical reconstruction, but a kerygmatic proclamation. The validity of the canonical witness to Christ is its character as the vehicle of the gospel, . . . not the degree to which it reproduces historical 'facts'" (1996, p. 145).

Uncertainty about the historical Jesus has even prompted the suggestion from some Christian scholars that "Christ should be replaced by God at the centre of the religious universe" (Bowden 1988, p. 173), even though belief in God is itself not without its "problems" (p. 182). The God thus accepted is—like Austin's 'kerygma'—an entity that satisfies emotional requirements, in Bowden's words, "a power at the heart of things who makes for good and who comforts, judges and absorbs what makes for bad" (p. 190). Its existence cannot be demonstrated, but it can be approached with "hope, trust and worship" (p. 194). Emotion is surely a motor force which can be directed wisely or foolishly. The way in which religiously based emotion often operates in today's world, as in the past, does not inspire confidence.

As scholars are so much at variance, it is not surprising that the basic insights of the higher critics have failed to penetrate many quarters, where they are either altogether ignored or dismissed as motivated by 'Enlightenment prejudices'. The attitude of detached superiority to their work expressed in Stephen Cox's 2006 book (which, in a most interesting way, explores the use that has been made of the Bible in literature) is quite common in the humanities. The higher criticism, he thinks, needs to be "purged of its naive scientism", and should not look askance at trying to identify "first-hand observations" (eyewitness testimony) in the gospels. He finds early dating of them quite plausible: "The question of how much of the New Testament was produced before the year 70 has no definite answer." And he does not find it "naive" to say that "authentic teachings of 'John' are embodied in the fourth gospel" (pp. 6, 253f).

Apart from the considerable number of educated laity who express such at any rate partial endorsement of the traditional views, there are thousands of clergy who see their function as maintaining them, and who address themselves to millions of laity who have no idea how to form an independent opinion on these matters, even supposing that they had the leisure, the capacity, the resources, and the inclination to do so. So long as beliefs are backed by a powerful organization of this kind, and so long as their proponents have this kind of audience, they can survive any amount of criticism. In the U.S.A. the survival rate is particularly high. According to the September 2006 issue of the American journal *The Humanist*, eighty-three percent of Americans say they believe in the virgin birth of Jesus, and eighty-seven percent believe that he was raised from the dead.

This latter belief surely goes with expectations of future life for themselves. All the higher mammals look forward to the future and work for it, but their future is short and their view narrow. Mental progress comes through a widening of the horizon, both in space and time. When man grows dissatisfied with his brief allowance of life, he must project his personal existence beyond the grave, if he is not merely to identify it with that of his race or species.

Is it in any case unrealistic to expect clergy to be *au fait* with criticism? "Current New Testament scholarship", says Nineham, "tends to be technical, and is largely purveyed in monographs on very specific topics which the clergy, at any rate, with their increased pastoral responsibilities, have neither the time to read, the money to buy, nor the background knowledge to interpret" (2000, p. xxix). One might retort that, in spite of all the current scholarly disagreements, the case against the reliability of the birth and infancy narratives has long been overwhelmingly made and very widely accepted among scholars,[1] and that the resurrection accounts have, almost to the same extent, long been shown to be unreliable,[2] yet both sets of findings are ignored by the churches. Perhaps I should not lump the virgin birth and the resurrection together, as the latter is much more central to the faith. N.T. Wright states the position well: "Take Christmas away, and in biblical terms you lose two chapters at the front of Matthew and Luke; nothing else. Take Easter away, and you won't have a New Testament; you won't have a Christianity; as Paul says: You will still be in your sins" (2007, pp. 268f). Unsurprisingly, then, many even of those who are well aware of the inadequacy of the New Testament evidence for the resurrection are unwilling to give it up altogether. Might we, then, not reasonably ask that at any rate the virgin birth be surrendered? The answer surely is that seriously to disavow even this item, firmly embedded in the creeds, would play havoc with the liturgies, also with traditional (particularly with Catholic) piety, and would alienate congregations, who do not go to 'divine service' to be told that what has been for centuries taught as Christian truth must now be abandoned. Nor will they want to hear that Jesus's outlook was strongly conditioned by bizarre apocalyptic ideas. Tom Baker, then Dean of Worcester, discussing what impact New Testament scholarship might have on liturgical revision, understandably noted that "the real problem in finding a living and relevant liturgy for today is presented by the Bible itself" (1975, p. 196). I can only conclude that the higher criticism has created an impossible situation for the churches. They cannot acknowledge it, yet their ignoring it is equally unjustified. Nor is it plausible for the churches, if they do not simply ignore biblical criticism, to counter it by claiming that the Bible is their book and must therefore be read from a deliberately theological standpoint. (We had an example of this (above p. 173) in the claim that the gospel resurrection accounts should be studied from the perspective of "a resurrection hermeneutic".) Complaints that the critics have 'taken the Bible away from the church', and insistence that it must be restored to the church on this basis, are discussed and rebutted by the Oxford Old Testament scholar John Barton. "One cannot", he says, "establish what the Bible means if one insists on reading it as necessarily conforming to what one already believes to be true - which is what a theological reading amounts to" (2007, p. 164). As with any text, one must first ascertain what it means, and only then evaluate it in relation to what one already believes. This double operation "cannot be collapsed into a single process, in which meaning is perceived and evaluated at one and the same time" (p. 159). In the case of any other text than the Bible, almost everyone, he says, agrees that one first establishes its meaning, and then asks whether what it means is true. This "elementary point" is not "the application of Enlightenment values to the text", but "simply a procedure without which we have no meaning whose truth we can even begin to assess" (p. 171).

The recent survey of church-leaving in Britain by Francis and Richter shows that, although there is a considerable variety of reasons why people stop going to church, not only "religious doubt and loss of faith" is often a significant factor, but also the feeling that "they were unable to discuss their mounting problems with Christian teaching within their churches" (2007, p. 110). Already Archbishop William Temple, who died in 1944, "recognised . . . that after more than a century of conflict, the tension between understanding the Bible as a historically conditioned text ('biblical criticism') and understanding the Bible as the God-given authority of the twentieth-century church ('revelation') could no longer be resolved: 'biblical criticism' had no more to offer to Christianity, and the authority of 'revelation' could no longer be demonstrated by the church" (Kent 1992, p. 55). Nevertheless, Catholic, Greek Orthodox, and Anglican churches can still appeal, even to those who no more than half believe their doctrines, by dint of the emotional impact of their services: the solemn music, the voice of the intoning priest, the candlelight, and so forth, can have a powerful effect even on the least susceptible, particularly in an impressive architectural setting. Guignebert noted (1968, pp. 142f) that "long and active survival of liturgy, after its dogmas have virtually perished, is a common phenomenon in the evolution of religion." Elaine Pagels who, as a historian of early Christianity, is very much aware how questionable is the "complex series of beliefs . . . formulated by fourth-century bishops into the ancient Christian creeds", nevertheless found—in a situation of personal tragedy—that her chance experience of a church service "spoke to my condition, as it has to that of millions of people throughout the ages because it simultaneously acknowledges the reality of fear, grief and death while—paradoxically—nurturing hope" (2003, p. 27). On another occasion, at a midnight service on Christmas Eve, although "knowing that we have little or no information about Jesus's birth", she was entranced with "the joy and solemnity of the festival" and felt "love and gratitude toward . . . the whole community gathered there, at hand, or elsewhere, the dead and the living" (p. 144). Such emotion inhibits any critical attitude towards the ideas associated with it, and illustrates how uniformity in a community is more easily achieved by arousing emotion, which is readily shared, even contagious, than by an appeal to reason, which leads to discussion, argument, and disagreement.

However, the creeds are still there and are still recited, and so it is not surprising that those forms of Christianity now flourish best which retain whole-hearted endorsement of them by regarding higher-critical or other questioning as a temptation from the Devil. This reliance on the traditional doctrine is often combined with emotional involvement that is quite extreme and makes for forms of worship that attract by being exciting. A good example is the ever-growing movement of Pentecostalism, which, we are told, "allows the poor, uneducated and illiterate among the people of God to have an equal voice with the educated and the literate" (Macchia 1999, pp. 12, 18). The leaders of these people feel able to speak in what they see as a non-question-begging way of what they take for ultimate truths.

A significant factor is that authoritative ruling is what many people want. Society could not cohere if all were rebels, and although some educationalists are apt to stress the value of independence and originality, the great majority of people are far better equipped to do things in a traditional manner, to follow a clear lead rather than to take the initiative. That they are content to believe what they are told is a natural consequence of man's social nature. The solitary animal faces the universe alone. His knowledge of the environment is acquired by personal experience through direct contact, and that part of the environment of which he has no direct experience remains unknown to him and without influence on his behaviour. But the member of a herd or society has additional resources. By attention to the reactions of other members of the herd, he is able to react indirectly to events which are not accessible to him through his senses. In this way his attention becomes focussed more on the actions of his fellows and less on the remainder of the environment. Thus, in the case of human societies, whenever an immediate response to the nonhuman elements is not required, there is a tendency to respond chiefly to the human ones. Instead of forming his own judgement, the individual responds to what he takes the prevailing opinion to be; and the habit thus developed may easily overwhelm tendencies to independence.

Such conformity in the majority provides the small minority in whom tendencies to independence are strongly developed with a motive for dogmatizing. Those who seek power first try to impose certain beliefs and to acquire in doing so the prestige associated with special knowledge. The willingness of millions to trust in the authority of individual leaders is particularly well illustrated in fundamentalist groups. Their evangelists enjoy far greater authority than that of bishops or other leaders in the institutional churches, or of scholars or theologians. Kathleen Boone suggests that one reason for this is that fundamentalist preachers identify what they say with what is said in the Bible, accepted as supremely authoritative on all matters of faith and conduct, so that "to question the pastor or to disagree with him is often equated to disobedience against God" (1990, p. 109). In the ancient world, the scope of such charismatic preachers to reach large audiences was much more limited. Their present-day success in winning followers on a huge scale naturally increases their own confidence, often to the point where they suppose themselves to be really inspired.

Experiences during the past century have drawn attention to the dangers inherent in human readiness to submit to authority, while it is nonetheless realized that the development of such a tendency has been an inevitable result of natural selection. Milgram, for instance, says that "some system of authority is a requirement of all communal living" (1974, p. 1). Hierarchically organized groups have great advantages over undisciplined ones in coping with the dangers of the physical environment, with threats posed by competing species, and with potential disruption from within; and in consequence a "potential for obedience" has been bred into the human organism "through the extended operation of evolutionary processes" (pp. 123–25). He nevertheless finds that these very values of loyalty, discipline, and self-sacrifice that are acclaimed in the individual "create destructive organizational engines of war and bind men to malevolent systems of authority", leaving our species "in the long run only a modest chance of survival" (p. 188).

There is a further factor. When our ideas about the immediate environment are very incomplete or erroneous, our behaviour is likely to be ill-adapted to our needs, so that we expose ourselves to some immediate unpleasantness. But in this way our attention is called to our mistake, and we may be led to rectify it. If, for instance, we believe that ether is a good fire-extinguisher, we shall be in for a rude shock when we act on this belief; and if we survive the experience, the belief will not survive with us. On the other hand, any ideas we may have formed about the nature of the universe, or about the distant future or past, are unlikely to lead to any *noticeably* inappropriate reactions on our part. Thus we may well persist in erroneous beliefs of these kinds in all our lives without experiencing the smallest surprise or disappointment.

This difference is important. It explains why even the most primitive peoples sometimes appear to have made considerable progress in the practical arts while continuing to hold quite groundless beliefs in matters that do not lend themselves to experimental control. It also explains why in our civilized societies people who are highly educated in fields where all theories are subjected to experimental tests can at the same time—to use their own phrase—'believe in the Bible'. They have never bothered with critical study of it, for erroneous views on the matter do not expose them to any obvious unpleasantness. If you try to explain to them the difficulties that lie in the way of accepting any biblical book at its face value, you have to descend into details, and they find such attention to detail trivial or pedantic. The simplest way to avoid confronting difficulties is to keep to generalities. Many people are prepared to believe—have been brought up to believe—that 'in some way', or 'in some sense' the Bible is God's revelation. And God himself, in such thinking, may be no more than a sort of something somewhere.

All this surely shows that the question: where does the work of the higher criticism leave Christianity? is part of the wider question of how behaviour is affected by ideas and emotions; and if one tries to generalize about this, one may say that an individual may be influenced by emotions (for example by desire for approval or by fear of punishment, in this world or the next), by the example, precept, or command of a leader, and by general example and contagion when certain beliefs have become widespread. Fascism, Nazism, and Communism, as well as religious beliefs of many kinds, have influenced their adherents in all these ways. The higher criticism relies too little on emotion to be effective in any of them. The number of distinct emotional states, apart from differences of degree of the relevant emotion, is small, whereas the number of distinct ideas is indefinitely large. Many persons therefore may share the same emotion, even though they may be incapable of sharing the same ideas; for a train of thought involves reminiscence and organization of memories, and different individuals, apart from differences in experience, have different capacities for both of these. This accounts for the immense difficulty of imparting, even to an attentive and selected audience, any precise ideas, whereas an orator or preacher has little difficulty in stirring an audience to anger or enthusiasm.

Controversy between persons with strong religious commitments and persons without them often involves a good deal of superficial criticism, even when religion itself is not the subject under discussion. In the debates of the nineteenth century between on the one hand Mill, Lewes, Spencer, and Huxley, and on the other such defenders of the faith as Whewell, Green, Jevons, Bradley, and Jowett, each one tries to attack some weak point in the other's exposition, not because that particular point is very important, or would not be conceded by the other party in a friendly discussion, but because the criticism is intended as a means of discrediting the opponent. Mill and Whewell argue about 'induction'; and even if they had been on the same side in the *great* debate, they might have had the same differences—only they would then have found it easy to compose them. In sum, when a writer is conscious of facing someone who is opposed to him on a major issue, there is apt to be a surplus of emotion which cannot be canalized into pure investigatory activity. Instead there is straying from the point into side-issues or irrelevancies, and arguments about what has been said by way of proving folly or inconsistency. There is a paradox here. One cannot do one's best in a vacuum, with no comment from outside: the mind works better under the stimulus of criticism and exchange of views; but comment is rarely such as to advance the subject.

In this book I have been concerned with the Christian 'revelation' rather than with belief in deity that is not linked—as, however, it commonly is—with that or with some other supposed revelation. But I am not supportive of most of the claims made for religious beliefs of any kind. Religion is often defended by pointing to the limitations of reason. It is true that human reason, in the sense of inferences from evidence, cannot solve problems when the evidence is insufficient, or the inferences too complex for even the best minds. The human brain is only to a limited extent an improvement on that of the chimpanzee, and mankind has no access to the real world different in kind from that of any other animal. But we have nothing better than our reason, such as it is, with which to investigate the world, and to invoke alternative powers or sources of knowledge is arbitrary. It is often said that the only alternative to religious belief is cynicism. But I see no reason why a realistic assessment of ourselves and our prospects should be stamped as cynical. Those who are indifferent to religion often find satisfaction in their work, which they pursue without fanaticism, and which is not infrequently useful. They try to keep in good health and protect their families from disease and accidents; but they are not overworried about death, for they are aware that, before they were born, the world went on for a long time without them, and they would not much wish to have lived in former ages. They think too that the world is likely to go on for an equally long time after they are dead, and that they have no reason to expect that it will be much better than it is now. All this is realism, not cynicism. Certain rules of life—sensible to follow because found by experience to make for contentment and good health—have nothing to do with religion, but are based on the inquiries which study man and his environment systematically with a view to reaching reliable generalizations that are confirmed in practice. Nor is ethical behaviour necessarily dependent on religion. The idea that, without belief in God, 'anything goes', is absurd; for if we are to be protected from injury and exploitation, there must be rules concerning human behaviour, and these rules, to be effective, must be enforced. Hence the need, quite independent of religious convictions, for policing and legal systems. Such sound maxims as are found in sacred books, Christian or other, were early recognized not only because they are based on social necessity, but also because social animals have some instinctive readiness to do what is good for their fellows, even though it may disadvantage the doer.[3] Moreover, it is in the interest of each individual to stress social obligations in cases where he or she is not personally involved, so that even individual egotism to this extent helps to preserve public morality.

Approval of one's fellows and fear of censure are among society's chief integrating forces. But if they are to be effective, there must exist a climate of opinion, a common attitude of approval and disapproval towards certain forms of behaviour. If this attitude is not universal or nearly so, its influence on the individual is much diminished. In a democratic community where it is permissible to put everything into question, the climate of opinion becomes unsettled; certain acts are no longer universally approved or condemned, so that the ordinary person's main motive for social behaviour is very much weakened. Awareness of this gives a certain appeal to the doctrine that moral rules must be inflexible. However, while no rules at all would make life in society totally insecure, completely inflexible ones will lead to much unnecessary suffering. The problem is to allow exceptions without breaking down the consensus on which stability depends. 'Thou shalt not kill' is a good rule, but was it wrong of some of Hitler's generals to try to blow him to pieces? This problem exists for theists and atheists alike, and illustrates the limited relevance of theism to ethical matters.

The theist may answer that he is not concerned with mere rules for social behaviour, but with a non-question-begging standard of absolute justice which needs to be anchored in God. But absolute standards mean those which can never be revised; and if many of the supposedly divinely-based precepts operative in the past were still accepted as absolutes, we should still be at the stage of heretic burning, witch hunting, Jew baiting, and capital punishment for all manner of minor offences.

When a rule is said to be absolute, what is meant is that it must always, in any circumstances, be given priority over any other considerations. Nicholas Boyle, President of Magdalene College, Cambridge, writing in *The Tablet* (19th April, 2008), accepts that we do not need God as a grounding to rules which are no more than "a competitive need for efficiency", but holds that God is needed "as soon as we start to talk about what is good", in particular if we are justifiably to allege that any moral principles are absolute. In view of what in the past has been (and in some quarters still is) justified by appeal to 'the will of God', it is perhaps not so great a disadvantage not to be able to justify absolutes. Boyle is particularly concerned, against any appeal to "Enlightenment values", to dismiss the Enlightenment as nothing other than "a Christian heresy which, because of its tendency to deist and Unitarian denials of the Incarnation, gave a theologically ungrounded aura of sanctity to the concept of 'humanity' worse still, of 'Man'." Why just 'man', he asks, and not "primates, so including the chimpanzee?" He finds that "in so far as the notion of 'human rights' gives an absolute—that is divine—status to the fact of being human, it is directly derivative from the Christian belief that God sanctified humanity by becoming human himself." "Humanity is divine because God has made it so", and only from this premiss can man be accorded more 'sanctity' than the chimpanzee. Obviously, any species may be said to have 'rights' in the sense that, if it does not stand up for itself against intruders and rivals, it will become extinct; but I am pretty sure that Professor Boyle would agree that the way in which man is at present exerting himself to the detriment of other species is deplorable. As for man's behaviour towards his own species, study of real human situations seems not to promote rigorously absolutist views of ethics. It was Macaulay, as historian, who, for instance, said apropos of the situation in England in 1687:

> A nation may be placed in such a situation that the majority must either impose disabilities or submit to them, and that what would, under ordinary circumstances, be justly condemned as persecution, may fall within the bounds of legitimate self defence.

I take this to mean that political measures draw their virtue or viciousness from the circumstances of the time, and that to say that tolerance is always and in every circumstance a good, and intolerance an evil, is to base political justice on an unconditional imperative as elusive as that on which Kant professed to base individual morality.

The conviction that lack of religious commitment leads to cynicism and selfishness underlies much of what we hear today about 'the worship of money', and the complaint is not new (cf. 1 Tim. 6:10). Lecky spoke, on the final page of his *History of the Rise and Influence of the Spirit of Rationalism in Europe* (1865) of an undefined "materialism" as a cloud hanging over rationalism, and on this basis he panegyrized the times when men could be found to sacrifice "with cheerful alacrity . . . all their material and intellectual interests to what they believed to be right." But the obsession of illusory ideals, to which all was sacrificed 'with cheerful alacrity' has brought suffering and death to millions. It was just such an obsession which, in 1914, induced many to sacrifice themselves, and the rest joined the tendency from fear of contempt and abuse. If military ideals are today largely discredited, no such discredit has fallen upon religious belief, although it is still responsible for a great deal of pain and suffering. I will not deny that religious emotion may sometimes be altruistic,[4] and may even bring about a state in which—so William James says in a famous book—"the sand and grit of the selfhood incline to disappear and tenderness to rule" (1902, pp. 255f). He says of his own religious experiences that "they all converge towards a kind of insight", the keynote of which "is invariably a reconciliation. It is as if the opposites of the world, whose contradictoriness and conflict make all our difficulties and troubles, were melted into unity" (p. 350). Elaine Pagels's experience, to which I have referred above, was obviously of this nature. But when James adds (p. 256) that "the faith state . . . carries charity with it by organic consequence", I would note that both history and present-day experience tell of another faith state which carries with it—whether or not 'by organic consequence' I cannot say— a mania for persecution and a powerful hatred for large numbers of one's fellows. The theologian John Kent rightly points out that "the spread of piety . . . is as closely linked to intolerance, cruelty and warfare as it is to any growth of charity, and charity will grow as vigorously from humanist as from Christian soil." He adds: "It is no answer to this objection to talk about the evils of Stalinism: Marxist humanism is as rare as Christian charity; it is the shortage of both that is the major problem" (1987, pp. 6f). Believers, Christian and other, who have not assimilated just criticisms of their faith—or belong to faiths where criticisms have not been allowed or, at any rate, not produced—are in danger of embracing the hatred and violence which, as J.M. Robertson noted, characterized much of pre-Enlightenment Christianity. A significant number of them are convinced that persons, and even whole nations, who do not share their views are an abomination to be wiped off the face of the Earth.[5] And they are prepared to act accordingly, with weapons of a destructive capacity which far exceeds what was available to their predecessors. It is a fearsome prospect.

Even Judaism and Christianity, which have experienced very considerable destructive criticism from within their own ranks, still include strongly intolerant elements. This has prompted Jeremy Young, an Anglican priest, to write a sustained protest against the not uncommon appraisal of Christianity as an innocent religion of peace, in contrast to Islam, assessed as a primitive, intolerant religion of violence. He comments: "Christianity is at least as capable as Islam of promoting violence and, historically, has often been less tolerant and more likely to engage in persecution than Islam" (2007, p. 193). If Zeus overdid sex, Yahweh was chronically addicted to violence, and Young shows that some of it is well represented in the New Testament: "Apocalyptic passages are especially full of visions of divine violence which are psychotic in their intensity and venom, particularly in the book of Revelation, whose visions surpass even the worst excesses of the Old Testament" (p. 101).

He instances the description of "the seven bowls of God's wrath", of which Rev. 16:3 is an example: "The second angel poured out of his bowl on the sea, and it turned into blood like that of a dead man, and every living thing in the sea died." The very death of Jesus, so basic an item in the creed, itself results from God's violence. Numerous texts—I have quoted some of them above, pp. 4f—state that "Jesus was sent to die, so that his death was both intended and required by God. . . . God's full involvement in the violence of the crucifixion is well illustrated in those medieval murals which show angels hammering the nails into Jesus' cross" (p. 5. Later, in his Chapter 7, Young dwells on the repulsiveness of various theories of the atonement).[6]

Not that religion is, or ever has been, the only major cause of social conflict and violence. These can result from any ideology harnessed with sufficient political and military power. On this basis, in our own time regimes fundamentally hostile to religion in Nazi Germany, Soviet Russia, and Communist China have inflicted enormous suffering. In a book which gives a lucid and thorough criticism of arguments for the existence of God, David Ramsay Steele nevertheless justly notes that "the history of the past one hundred years shows us that atheistic ideologies can sanctify more and bigger atrocities than Christianity or Islam ever did." Not that atheism is particularly prone to atrocities, but that "the historical rise of secular social movements coincides with the enhanced efficiency of the technological and administrative means to commit atrocities. The mass murderer Torquemada would have done as much harm as the mass murderer Mao, if only he'd had the means at his disposal" (2008, pp. xi–xii). Steele "sadly conclude[s] that atheists are morally no better than Christians or Muslims, and that the propensity of people to commit atrocities at the behest of unreasonable ideologies is independent of whether those ideologies include theism or atheism." Every species must assert itself or face extinction, but violence seems particularly endemic to man. Expressions of pain and distress in another are the usual signs of defeat, and hence pleasurable to the victor. It is biologically intelligible that some individuals in social groups inherit self-assertive tendencies, involving such infliction of pain, to an excessive degree, just as others are by nature all too ready to sacrifice themselves, having inherited strong social feelings. And it is the strongly self-assertive types who gravitate to positions of power where they can satisfy their ambitions. This again is no ground for long-term optimism concerning mankind.

Can we look to anything that holds some promise for our future, for after all there are millions of people who are as well-meaning as one can reasonably expect? When a disaster such as an earthquake befalls them for which it is impossible to blame anybody, a spirit of mutual help usually shows itself. But when anger can be directed against some kind of person, the emotion tends to find release in that way, and there develops the 'culture of blame' with which we are so familiar. But some are moving away from mutual recrimination and from exclusive positions of the past, and are trying to appreciate what is best in each other's traditions without being blind to the worst. The urbane tone of such discussions is encouraging, as is the participants' readiness to acknowledge that even cherished convictions can be questioned. It is obvious that no single faith—religious or other—will be able to become universal to the extent of excluding all others. There is, then, no sustainable alternative to co-existence, and since both religion and secularism are powerful forces in today's world, it follows that the proponents of different religions and of none need to work together as far as they can if the very serious problems that face us all are to be meaningfully confronted. This does not mean that they should blur what divides them. On the contrary, to be clear about these differences should be an important step towards realizing that they do not rule out co-operation—something even more important than education; for education may merely render someone's consciousness of his or her own interests more keen, whereas co-operation promotes sympathy and unselfish interests. Experience has repeatedly shown that, when people of radically different persuasions work together at a common task—such as performing in the same choir or orchestra, or being colleagues in the same hospital or laboratory—hostility between them is reduced, even eliminated.

In 2006 Edward O. Wilson, a humanist and a world authority on biodiversity and the development of social behaviour, published a book entitled *The Creation: An Appeal to Save Life on Earth* (New York: Norton). Its primary purpose was to save biodiversity by bringing people of all beliefs into the environmental movement, to get them to pay attention not merely to mankind and its problems, but to the rest of life on Earth, a large part of which is vanishing before our eyes. He stresses that in fact these rapid extinctions of numerous species are closely linked with mankind's problems; and, taking insects as an example, he shows that, "if they were to vanish, the terrestrial environment would soon collapse into chaos", food supplies for our own grossly overpopulated species would drastically diminish, and wars would be fought for control of the dwindling resources. "The suffering, and the tumultuous decline to dark-age barbarism would be unprecedented in human history" (pp. 34f).

In an article in the American journal *The Humanist* (November–December, 2007), Wilson tells how, with all this in mind, he has approached evangelical Christians, knowing that they have a strong ethic, even though their ideas are far removed from those of humanism. And he has succeeded in bringing them and scientists together—as representing two very powerful social forces—to discuss what they can jointly do to avert the impending crisis. He has of course not attempted to link with the very dogmatic leaders who have acquired so much power through megachurches and radio and television talk shows. He regards those unconditionally beholden to such leaders as not typical of the evangelical movement as a whole, which he has found to include a great variety of religious opinion, some of it relatively liberal. In this article, he records that, at one of the gatherings of evangelicals and scientists that he had brought about, "we were all nervous at first, but soon located the common ground that we sought. Friendships were made", and he found it "wonderful to form friendships with people that I thought would otherwise stiffen up when I got close to them."

One root, if not *the* root not only of the biodiversity problem but also of problems specific to mankind, is the continual increase in numbers of our own species, which have doubled since 1945. The urgent need to limit population has been talked about for much more than a century; and now at last it is being voiced, even shouted, in some traditionally-minded communities—as when the Catholic scholar Hans Küng notes, in criticism of Catholic policy, that "according to the most recent reports 100 million children worldwide are living a wretched life on the streets" (1994, p. xiii). The Catholic commentator Clifford Longley, writing in the Catholic journal *The Tablet* (15th March, 2008) records the Vatican's alarm at the drastic decline in the numbers of Catholics who go to confession. He comments that, if this sacrament is due for a revival, "the church must stop acting as if all is well in the related area of sexual morality"; for many Catholics have come to regard contraception as "a necessity, not a sin".

It is easy to respond to Edwards, Küng, and, others like them, with the cliché 'too little too late'. But what I have here represented them as recommending points to a direction from which we can entertain hope.

EPILOGUE

The Gospels and Eyewitnesses

i. Richard Bauckham

Richard Bauckham, Professor of New Testament studies at the University of St. Andrews, Scotland, has recently issued a book of a full five hundred pages, in which, as he himself avows, he runs counter to "almost all recent New Testament scholarship" in arguing that the texts of all four gospels "are close to the eyewitness reports of the words and deeds of Jesus" (2006, p. 240). The evangelists, he says, "were in more or less direct contact with eyewitnesses" and, in the case of John, "an eyewitness wrote it" (pp. 5f).

Bauckham is much beholden to the Swedish scholar Samuel Byrskog, who, he says, argued that "the ancient historians—such as Thucydides, Polybius, Josephus and Tacitus—were convinced that true history could be written only while events were still within living memory, and they valued as their sources the oral reports of direct experience of the events by involved participants in them". The standards set up by these historians were "historiographic best practice, to which other historians aspired or at least paid lip-service". This final phrase is surely a rather important qualification. Bauckham continues:

> Having established the key role of eyewitness testimony in ancient historiography, Byrskog argues that a similar role must have been played in the formation of the Gospel traditions and the Gospels themselves by individuals who were qualified to be both eyewitnesses and informants about the history of Jesus. (pp. 8–10f)

So because, for instance, Thucydides gave a sober account of political and military situations in which he personally was to some extent involved, the authors of miracle-ridden Christian apologetic treatises "must" have written on the same basis. Bauckham allows (p. 11) that

Byrskog has been charged with assuming, rather than demonstrating, that this was so; yet he avowedly "takes his initial bearings from Samuel Byrskog's work" (p. 384), and "follows" him (p. 479). The New Testament is surely more likely to be comparable with other sacred works of antiquity than with ancient accounts of then recent human history. In the opening chapters of Mark Jesus is addressed by the heavenly spirit as "my beloved son", is then waited on by angels in the wilderness, recognized as "the holy one of God" by the spirits of evil he defeats, cures a leper instantaneously, has the divine power of forgiving sins, and claims to be lord of the sabbath. Such writing is not comparable with Thucydides's account of the Peloponnesian War or with Tacitus's portrayal of the struggles and intrigues in the empire in the century before he himself wrote.

Bauckham also relies very heavily on what the second-century bishop Papias said, particularly of Mark, namely that "having become Peter's interpreter, he wrote down accurately everything that he remembered." I have discussed Papias repeatedly in earlier books, and will not go over that ground yet again here, particularly as—Bauckham is well aware of this—Papias's statements have been widely regarded as worthless.

Bauckham is unimpressed by Pheme Perkins's statement (2000, p. 53) that scholars today "recognize that Mark is not based on memories of the apostle Peter." As evidence of Peter's involvement he supposes that, because Peter is the first disciple to be named in Mark, and is also named again at its very end (16:7), we have here an "*inclusio* around the whole story, suggesting that Peter is the witness whose testimony includes the whole" (pp. 124f, 155). One can hardly imagine a more tenuous argument. That the prince of the apostles should be represented as having been called first is unsurprising, and that he is singled out at the end gives him—as Bauckham is himself aware (p. 170)—something of a much needed rehabilitation after his repeated denial of Jesus with curses (14:66–72). Even if one allows that the references to Peter can rank as an *inclusio* at all, one must bear in mind that *inclusio* is a stylistic device, which, no more than any other literary quality of a piece of writing, has anything to do with how close its author was to the events he depicts.

Bauckham notes that "following Mark, Luke has made sure that Simon Peter is both the first and the last disciple to be named in his gospel. . . ., thus acknowledging the interpretation of the Petrine witness of Mark's Gospel into his own work" (p. 131). Bauckham is not saying merely that Luke reproduced Mark's account, but claims that he was aware of its supposedly Petrine implications: like Mark, "Luke . . .

acknowledges Peter as the most extensive eyewitness source of his narrative" (p. 304). But a second such source, particularly for Luke, says Bauckham, were Jesus's women followers, and Luke indicates this by a second *inclusio,* within the Petrine one. For Luke "is unique among the gospels" in referring to them already in his account of the Galilean ministry (at 8:2–3); and at the end of his gospel the women at the tomb are called upon to "remember how he told you, while he was still in Galilee, that the Son of man must be handed over to sinners and be crucified, and on the third day rise again" (24:6–7). We saw (above, pp. 115f) that reference to Galilee in this passage is Luke's editorial manipulation of the Markan source—a manipulation which deliberately changed Mark's suggestion that the appearances of the risen one would occur in Galilee (and not in Jerusalem, as Luke would have it) into a mere reminder of something that Jesus had said in Galilee. Moreover, according to Luke's account, Jesus had spoken in Galilee of his forthcoming crucifixion and resurrection when he was "alone with his disciples" (9:18–23). But, for Bauckham, the passage in Chapter 24 shows that the women followers "had been in the audience of Jesus' private teaching to his disciples" (p. 130).

Bauckham adds that the implication is "surely that Luke owed some of his special traditions" to one or more of these women followers (p. 131). By this "secondary use" of the device of *inclusio,* Luke indicates that he drew information from the women as well as from Peter (p. 304).

Returning now to what Bauckham says of Mark, we find that, as more evidence that Mark was briefed by Peter, he adduces a 1925 article by C.H. Turner, reprinted in J.K. Elliott's 1993 edition of Turner's 'Notes on Marcan Usage', from which my quotations are taken. Turner observes that Mark has a number of sentences where "they" are said to be walking or moving along, and where then "he" (Jesus) is said to have done or experienced something or other. For instance:

> They came to the other side of the sea. . . . And when he was come out of the boat . . . (5:1–2)

The other two synoptics often reduce to 'he' this double construction. Thus Matthew has, simply: "And when he was come to the other side" (8:28). Turner supposed that this suggests that Peter will have given Mark this information, and that, what he actually said, as one of the twelve, will have been "*we* came to the other side, and when he . . ." Since however Mark was not himself "one of the company who went about with Jesus", he naturally, in his written account of what Peter had said, changed Peter's 'we' into 'they'. Such details, says Turner, "reinforce the conclusion that Mark's story is told as from a disciple and companion, while Matthew and Luke are less directly interested in that particular point of view" (pp. 36f, 82).

On all this we may comment that, if it were already established, as a reliable premiss, that, as Turner puts it, "the authority of St. Peter stands, as tradition has always indicated, very closely behind Mark" (p. 82), then we might well suppose that, underlying the 'they' of Mark's text was a 'we' spoken by Peter. But to introduce this mere supposition as in itself evidence "reinforcing" a premiss of Peter's involvement is to presuppose the truth of this involvement in the first place—a clear *petitio principii*. Moreover, the 'they' in Mark does not always mean the twelve (cf. Evans's remark on p. 147 above), and so does not always involve Peter at all. And that Matthew and Luke in such instances abbreviate Mark is unsurprising.

It is well known that Matthew abbreviates Mark in practically every instance in which he draws from him; and Bauckham himself notes that Matthew and Luke tell numerous Markan stories "much more concisely" (p. 342). Nevertheless, he (p. 156) accepts Turner's argument that Mark's story "is told from the perspective of a member of the Twelve, and that this must be because Mark closely reproduces the way Peter told the story." Bauckham argues in this way in spite of conceding that it has been rightly pointed out that "the Gospel has an 'omniscient' narrator who provides the overriding ideological perspective on the whole story, can tell us information not evident to the characters in the story" and "can access the mind and emotions of any character" (p. 162)—as when, for instance, Mark tells us what some scribes were thinking privately (2:6).

One of Turner's examples is:

And they came to a place which was named Gethsemane; and he saith to his disciples, Sit ye here while I pray. (Mk. 14:32, changed by Matthew to: "Then cometh Jesus with them unto a place called Gethsemane, and he saith to his disciples . . ." (26:36))

The prayers Jesus then goes on to speak are recorded by the evangelists, even though, according to their own account, no one was able to hear them, as the disciples, instead of "watching" as Jesus requested (Mk. 14:34), fell asleep. Nor could he have subsequently told them what he had prayed, as, immediately after this, they fled and left him, without returning, at his arrest. It is clearly the 'omniscient narrator' who here records the prayers for us. Bauckham counters feebly by claiming that the disciples will not have fallen asleep at once, but were "awake enough to gather the general tenor of Jesus' prayers" (p. 200).

If it was Peter who briefed Mark, he appears to have found it not worth mentioning that he had walked on the water (Mt. 14:28–31), that he would be the rock on which the church would be built, and had been entrusted with the keys of the kingdom of heaven (Mt. 16:17–19), had been advised and promised a miracle by Jesus concerning payment of the temple tax (Mt. 17:24–27), and had sought his advice concerning how often an erring brother is to be forgiven (Mt. 18:21). And did he also fail to tell Mark of his miraculous draught of fishes which first led him to follow Jesus (Lk. 5:3–9)? None of these incidents is recorded in Mark. They could of course be set aside as mythological expansions of genuine information about Peter, but such dismissal of non-Markan synoptic material would not appeal to Bauckham, who however does show some embarrassment because "notably lacking in Mark's portrayal of Peter . . . is treatment of Peter's preeminent role in the early Christian community after the resurrection . . . such as we find in Mt. 16:13–19, Lk. 22:31–32, and Jn. 21:4–19" (p. 171).

Bauckham finds that, in Mark as in Luke, not only the role of Peter but also that of the women as eyewitnesses is critical. "They see Jesus die, they see his body being laid in the tomb, they find the tomb empty." They "saw" these events, and it could hardly be clearer that appeal is being made to their role as eyewitnesses (p. 48). He adds: "It is natural to suppose that these women were well known . . . as people who remained accessible and authoritative sources of these traditions as long as they lived" (p. 51). In the same way, Turner had argued that these "holy women or one of them" were presumably one of Mark's primary authorities for "the story of the crucifixion and resurrection" (in Elliott 1993, p. 82). Many scholars would retort that Mark's narrative instead shows how purposefully he uses these women followers. Because the disciples fled at Jesus's arrest, only the women can witness his death (15:39–40) and thereby put it beyond question that he did actually die, and that his rising was truly from the dead: But Mark also wants him to die utterly alone, deserted not only by man but even by God (15:34), so that we realize what a tremendous burden he has shouldered all alone, for us. Hence the witnesses must stand "afar off" (15:40), not at the foot of the cross as in the fourth gospel. Mark also needs the women as witnesses of the burial (15:47) so that no one will be able to say that on Easter morning they went to the wrong tomb. As we saw, they are too afraid to report that they had visited the tomb and found that the body had gone—this does not make them into reporters of the resurrection!—and many commentators have suspected that this was Mark's way of accounting for the fact that so decisive a piece of evidence had been so long in gaining currency (cf. Nineham 1963, p. 447, and above, p. 117), for in the earliest period, as documented by Paul (who says nothing of any tomb let alone of women visitors to it) belief in the resurrection will have been based only on the appearances of the risen one. Mark nevertheless made sure—so this argument continues—that in spite of the women's silence, the disciples realized that they must go to Galilee (surely to found a Christian community there); for at 14:28 he had made Jesus himself prophesy that "after I am raised up, I will go before you into Galilee." This prophecy was so important to Mark that he has inserted it into a context where it does not really fit. It breaks the connection between the verses immediately before and after it, which are concerned with a quite different matter, namely whether or not the disciples will desert Jesus when the going gets rough. In sum, according to numerous exegetes, the women are made to be silent to account for the fact that no one hitherto had heard of the empty tomb. And their silence is at the same time made not to matter by means of a prophecy by Jesus which, as a prophecy by the Lord, will not have remained unfulfilled.

On this view, which has much to recommend it, what we have here is purposive fiction, not eyewitness reporting. And, as we saw (above, p. 118), the fact that the other two synoptics made such drastic changes to Mark's narrative at this point shows that they did not accept it as reliable.

Bauckham extends his claim that "the gospels themselves indicate their closeness to the testimony of the eyewitnesses" (p. 348) to the fourth gospel. He will not allow that its strange Chapter 21—called, as we saw (p. 130 above) a "Galilean fantasia" by the Archbishop of Canterbury—is a later appendix, but regards it as an "epilogue" from the evangelist's own hand which "balances" the gospel's prologue (1:1–18). "Just as the Prologue goes back in time to creation, so the Epilogue previews the future mission of the disciples, symbolized by the miraculous catch of fish" (p. 364. The fish are said to number 153, yet "the net was not rent" (21:11). Bauckham seems to be among those who regard this number as (in the mind of the writer) that of the world's peoples, to be caught in the church's net. The number does seem to be symbolical, but what it symbolizes is far from clear). Again, the last words spoken in the epilogue are Jesus's words "until I come" (21:23), "corresponding at the other end of time to the first words of the prologue: 'In the beginning'." And the correspondence goes even further. The prologue consists of 496 syllables, the epilogue of 496 words. Thus, as in Mark, we have "an *inclusio* between the beginning and the end of the gospel" (pp. 364–66)—indeed an *"inclusio* of eyewitness testimony which indicates that disciple of Jesus on whose witness the gospel in question is primarily based by making him the disciple who is mentioned both first and last in the Gospel's account of Jesus' ministry." Here, in the fourth gospel, it is "the Beloved Disciple who occupies this position, displacing Peter from the position of primary eyewitness he enjoys in Mark." Bauckham has to admit that the first disciple to be mentioned in John's gospel is in fact anonymous (1:35–40), so that he cannot there be identified as the Beloved Disciple, yet "becomes so identifiable retrospectively" (pp. 390f). Haenchen noted such identification as an example of pressing a text to say more than it in fact does (1980, p. 172. Haenchen, together with many critical scholars, recent or otherwise, is not so much as mentioned in Bauckham's book. He never there refers to Strauss, Baur, Schweitzer, Wrede, Ehrman or Räisänen; but as he is avowedly writing in defiance of so much in New Testament scholarship, this is not surprising).

Bauckham begins and ends his book with a discussion of *testimony,* which, he says, "should not be treated as credible only to the extent that it can be independently verified" (p. 5). So he will not be worried about, for instance, the fact that numerous miracles, even prodigies of raising from the dead, are separately recorded only in single gospels, each knowing nothing of the others. Nor will the absence of first-century evidence for the resurrection outside the New Testament (cf. above, p. 114), concern him, nor the manifold silences of Paul's and other early epistles concerning Jesus traditions. In any case, following Wenham (whose discussion of the matter I have criticized in my 2004 book, and also elsewhere) he claims (p. 267) that Paul is far less silent about these traditions than is generally supposed. He rightly notes that, in our everyday life, "to trust the testimony of others is simply fundamental to the kind of creatures we are." It is, for him, once again the wretched Enlightenment that has been "inclined to minimize the individual's reliance on other people" (p. 476).[1] A tradition of thinking "from Hume onward" requires that "one rely on testimony only because one has somehow been able to check the credibility of the witness, or to observe that the kind of testimony in question usually turns out to be trustworthy" (pp. 476f). Bauckham stresses that he is not pleading for uncritical credulity. But where do we draw the line? We know well enough that some people do tell stories and that others believe them.

Hume went so far as to say that the bulk of mankind has always been and will always be stupid and certainly incapable of learning the truth.

Thus, in his essay on 'The Natural History of Religion', after having written (in section 12, headed 'Doubt and Conviction') of Catholic doctrines, in particular that of the 'real presence': "It will probably become difficult to persuade some nations that any human, two-legged creature could ever embrace such principles", he added: "And it is a thousand to one but that these nations themselves shall have something full as absurd in their own creed, to which they will give a most implicit and religious assent." Such an estimate of man's capacity is scarcely optimistic—naive optimism being, according to religious writers, a pervasive weakness of the Enlightenment—but probably realistic enough.

ii. P.R. Eddy and G.A. Boyd

In 2007 Eddy and Boyd (the one a Professor of theology, the other a pastor) issued a substantial book arguing that what the synoptic gospels say of Jesus is very largely reliable. Their book is of particular relevance to this book of mine, as they are severely critical of my views—or, rather, of what they take them to be.

They say little about the fourth gospel, not because they regard it as less reliable, but because it is "so different" from the synoptics as to "require a significantly different line of consideration when assessing its historicity" (p. 14n). And they do not cover the supernatural incidents in the synoptics in any detail. "Space considerations" (in this book of more than 450 pages!) do not allow them "to assess the historicity of any particular miracle reported in the Gospels" (p. 90n), and so they write on this matter in general terms, noting that scholars with "an impoverished sense of the supernatural" naturally "find it more difficult than others to accept the miracle accounts" (p. 78). They give both the synoptics' birth and infancy narratives and their resurrection narratives no more than occasional mention. In the case of the resurrection, they are confident that N.T. Wright has done all that is necessary to vindicate it in his "landmark work" on it (pp. 89 and note, 207). Much of their book consists of what Richard Bauckham (in his recommendation of it, printed on its back cover) calls a very important discussion of "methodological issues in the study of Jesus and the Gospels"—a discussion which culminates in their rejection of what they call the "naturalistic posture . . . rooted in the assumption that the particular post-Enlightenment Eurocentric, academic perspective of a rather small tribe of Western scholars is superior to all others" and entitles this tribe to "dismiss all claims of the supernatural" and to reject as historically unreliable all texts which contain them (p. 439). In this context they even use the word "ethnocentric" apropos of this deplorable, arrogant attitude; this almost amounts to the standard insult of today: 'racist'! They endorse N.T. Wright's remark that "much of what goes on today within historical Jesus studies is 'largely the projection of an undiscussed metaphysic'" (p. 372), namely that no appeal to supernatural causes is legitimate when explaining historical events. From what we have seen Wright alleging about the necessity for epistemological reorientation because of Jesus's resurrection, he is hardly in a position to complain about metaphysical intrusions into scholarship, even if he were correct in so designating them in the case in question. (On this cf. the discussion above, pp. 66f, apropos of Strauss and Darwin.)

Our two authors write from the conviction that "a personal Creator God exists", that "God occasionally acts in the world in ways that fall outside the regular patterns of the natural order", hence that miracles "can and do occur", and that "the Jesus of history is the very revelation of the Creator God." Moreover, they themselves "have experienced . . . the reality of the risen Jesus" in their lives (p. 23).

I cannot expect much sympathy with my own work from two authors who write from such premises. They go on to distinguish (pp. 24f) three broad categories of judgement, other than their own, concerning Jesus:

1. that "the Jesus tradition is virtually—perhaps entirely—fictional."

2. that Jesus did exist but, as Bultmann argued, "the reports we have of him are so unreliable and saturated with legend . . . that we can confidently ascertain very little historical information about him."

3. that a core of historical facts about the real historical Jesus can be disclosed by research, but that he is "significantly different" from the gospel portraits of him, in that he did not, for instance, work miracles or make authoritarian claims. This third position, our authors say, "is an increasingly common view among New Testament scholars today", and they cite J.D. Crossan as a well-known example of those who subscribe to it.

Eddy and Boyd are particularly concerned to refute the standpoint of those in category 1 of these 3, and classify me as one of them, as "the leading contemporary Christ myth theorist" (p. 168n). In fact, however, I have expressly stated in my books of 1996, 1999, and 2004 that I have repudiated this theory, and now really belong in their category 2. If the reader wishes a brief statement concerning my change of position and the reasons for it—briefer than I give in those three books or in the present one—I can refer him or her to my article 'Jesus, Historicity of' in *The New Encyclopedia of Unbelief,* edited by Tom Flynn. Eddy and Boyd do mention my three post-1990 Jesus books, but have obviously assumed, merely as an inference from their titles, and against plain statements within these books, that the views I expressed in the 1970s and 1980s have remained unchanged, and that the later books offer no more than what one could call 'more of the same'. (That, we saw, was also the basis on which Professor Stanton both mis-assessed me and ignored my responses to his criticisms. Cf. pp. 14f above and notes 3 and 4 on p. 334 below).

Earl Doherty belongs unequivocally in category 1 of Eddy and Boyd's 3, and they make it easier for themselves to suggest that my ideas seem at first sight strange by repeatedly grouping me with him, even though they are in fact aware that I differ from him significantly. Doherty argues that, for Paul, the earliest witness, Jesus did not come to Earth at all, that, under the influence of the Platonic view of the universe, salvific events such as his cruxifixion were believed to have taken place in a mythical spirit-world setting. I have never espoused this view, not even in my pre-1996 Jesus books, where I did deny Jesus's historicity. Although I have always allowed that Paul believed in a Jesus who, fundamentally supernatural, had nevertheless been incarnated on Earth as a man, I agree with Doherty that, if the Jesus of the Pauline and of other early epistles and the Jesus of the gospels are really one and the same person, then it is quite remarkable that his earthly life, as represented in the gospels, is depicted to sparsely in the early documents—and even more remarkable that someone who, according to the gospels as expounded by our Archbishop of Canterbury, was something like an ancient equivalent of "a car mechanic from somewhere near Basra" (cf. above, p. 18), could, within a few decades, come to be worshipped as "the image of the invisible God" in whom "were all things created, in the heavens and upon the earth" (Coloss. 1:15f), as him "through whom are all things" (1 Cor.8:6), "in whom are all the treasures of wisdom and knowledge hidden" (Coloss. 2:3), "the effulgence of God's glory and the very image of his substance, upholding all things by the word of his power" (Hebrews 1:3). Larry Hurtado who, like Christians generally, does not dispute that this is what happened, cannot—in his 2005 book which I have discussed above—refrain from reiterating his amazement at this development, and repeatedly calls it "remarkable", "astonishing", "amazing", "extraordinary". It seems to me, as it has to others, more difficult to believe that a real human being who preached in Galilee or anywhere else could come so quickly to be so highly esteemed than that a supposed supernatural personage—in many respects similar to Adonis, Osiris, and others, and to some portrayals of the figure of Wisdom in the Jewish literature—should later be given a detailed biography. The old gods of Greece and Homer were all in due course provided with biographies. In the case of Jesus, I have since 1996 accepted that the biography was not all pure invention, but based to some extent on the life history of the itinerant Galilean preacher who figures in Q.

Eddy and Boyd find that the case I make "centres on the claim that Paul makes little or no reference to the historical Jesus" (p. 33). This is a distortion. I have expressly and repeatedly allowed that, if silence about so much of Jesus's career, as depicted in the gospels, were unique to Paul, it could possibly be explained away; whereas in fact similar silence is pervasive among Christian writers who were earlier than or writing independently of the gospels (cf. above, p. 10). And I am certainly not among those who suppose that Paul says nothing at all of a human Jesus, or that he viewed him as "a mythic deity", who "performed his saving work . . . in the heavenly realm" (p. 201). On the contrary, I have repeatedly stated that, for Paul, this pre-existent supernatural personage was incarnated as a descendant of David (Rom. 1:3), was born of a woman under the Jewish law (Gal. 4:4) and ministered to the Jews (Rom. 15:8) prior to his crucifixion on Earth. Hence I have no quarrel with Eddy and Boyd's statement that "the claim that there are no clear and specific references to the Jesus of history in Paul's writings . . . is simply incorrect" (p. 200)—although they of course mean by 'the Jesus of history' Jesus as depicted in the gospels, whereas, as they are well aware, I do not suppose that Paul's incarnated Jesus was a contemporary of Paul himself, nor that the James with whom Paul was personally acquainted was Jesus's brother, nor that Paul's colleague Cephas was the Simon Peter of the gospels and therefore known personally to Jesus as well as to Paul (cf. my detailed discussion, above, pp. 138ff).

Eddy and Boyd do allow that Paul says much less about the historical Jesus than one might expect, but they—erroneously, as we saw (above, pp. 11f)—find similar "lack of references to the Jesus tradition in Acts", whose author everyone agrees nevertheless knew of it (p. 229). They explain what they call "the elliptical manner in which Paul uses the Jesus tradition" by saying that it was then still fluid, "not yet set in fixed or unyielding forms" (pp. 229, 231).

Concerning non-Christian evidence for Jesus, our two authors make much of the reference to Christ in Tacitus and of the two brief references in Josephus. They misleadingly complain that I "debunk Josephus et al." (p. 168n), when what I in fact do is to dispute, as many have done, the validity of the inferences which apologists have drawn from these texts. As for their more direct defence of the synoptic narratives, our two authors find them based on eyewitness reports, and claim that New Testament appeals to eyewitnesses are "rather sober and modest" and "underlie the entire Jesus tradition from the start" (p. 289. I controverted this claim in 1996 (pp. 82–89) and again—in response to criticism of me by J.W. Montgomery—in 2004 (pp. 58–68), and have of course again discussed it in the present book). They add that, "building on some of the insights of Byrskog, Bauckham offers several additional lines of evidence for the presence and importance of eyewitness testimony in the early church" (p. 290). They are particularly impressed (p. 291) by what Bauckham calls "the most significant implication" of what the second-century bishop Papias said, namely that "oral traditions of the words and deeds of Jesus were attached to specific named eyewitnesses." Many have found it difficult to take Papias seriously, since what he learnt from his informants included not only what all agree to be gross legendary matter about Judas, but also that Jesus had taught the bizarre doctrine that in the millennium Christ's kingdom will be set up on Earth in material form, each vine having a thousand branches and each branch ten thousand twigs (Details in my 1996 book, pp. 71ff). Even the fourth-century bishop and Church historian Eusebius regarded Papias as "a man of very little intelligence, as is clear from his books."[2]

Our two authors also claim that the synoptics are free from serious contradictions. "The level of consistency and (at least apparent) inconsistency we find within and between them is at least on a par with what one finds in other works whose general reliability historians are willing to grant" (p. 421). In so far that this is true, it is a consequence of the literary relationship between the synoptics. Where Matthew and Luke are able to follow either of their two obvious common sources, Q and Mark—that is, for most of their narratives about the Galilean ministry and the Passion—they do so fairly closely, and such changes and additions as they make are mostly from motives that can be ascertained. It is when they are without such guidance, as in their birth and infancy and resurrection narratives, that they clash violently.

A major item in Eddy and Boyd's apology for these three gospels is that they include incidents which are too unedifying to have been invented. I have argued, following other critics, that such passages can be understood as written from motives which differ from the evangelists' supposed unitary purpose of exalting Jesus (1986, pp. 73, 148f.,

213; 2004, pp. 190–95). It would have been nice if a book that specifically sets out to target me had paid some attention to my arguments on this matter, were it only for the purpose of finding them wanting. The Harvard theologian H.J. Cadbury observed some good time ago that it is erroneous to assume that every story that did not link Jesus as closely as possible to God must have been distasteful to the gospel writers; that some incidents reflect what he called "a feeling for the humility and human kinship of the Son of man"; that "mixed motives" thus underlie the gospels, and that none of these motives can be singled out as embodying traditions which are necessarily primitive, let alone reliable.

In his impressive *The Beloved Disciple in Conflict?* (2006), the Finnish scholar Ismo Dunderberg evidences an increasing tendency in early Christian literature to authenticate a text by representing it as written by eyewitnesses of the events related.[3] While the earliest of the canonical gospels give no account of their mode of production, the fourth gospel introduces the Beloved Disciple as "a redactional fiction" to make it seem written by someone particularly close to Jesus (p. 149). Dunderberg shows that, in the Coptic Gospel of Thomas, the disciple Thomas serves the same purpose, as do other disciples in other early Christian texts. Altogether, "the more aware early Christian writers became of the diversity within early Christian traditions, the more important it became to convince their audiences that the specific branch of the tradition they were representing was the most reliable. Attribution of their writings to Jesus' disciples was one, apparently effective, means of authenticating these traditions, as can be seen by its increasing popularity" (p. 203).

Books like those of Eddy and Boyd, of Bauckham, and of N.T. Wright show that the gains made by the higher criticism are precarious to the extent that they still have to meet resolute challenges from scholars, and not only from popular writers. Hence, we cannot afford to suppose that traditional views are all over and done with, except in so far as they are promoted by the zealous ignorant.[4] Like R.M. Price, who is severely criticized by Eddy and Boyd, I welcome their book and hope that readers of mine will read theirs. I agree too with Price that one can learn much from those with whom one disagrees, even though, I would add, much of what one thereby learns is not only what one is up against, what one has to come to terms with, but also how one has oneself been misunderstood, and how careful one needs to be in stating one's case.

Notes

Introduction

1. Mark twice mentions benefits of Jesus's death without specifying them: "the Son of man came not to be ministered unto, but to minister, and to give his life a ransom for many" (10:45); and "this is my blood of the covenant, which is shed for many" (14:24). Matthew adds to this latter logion "unto remission of sins" (26:28)—words he has deleted from Mark's account of John the Baptist's activities (Mk. 1:4) so as to insert them in the Passion narrative, as more appropriate to Jesus's death than to the Baptist's preaching. If Matthew thus stressed the atonement, Luke took the opposite course. He seemed unwilling to allow any suggestion that forgiveness of sins depends on the cross, and so the logion of Mk. 10:45 is absent from his version of the incident (Lk. 22:24–27) in which Mark placed it. And Jesus's reference in Mark and Matthew's accounts of The Last Supper to his blood being "shed for many" is absent from a sufficient number of ancient manuscripts of Luke's version of the eucharistic words (22:19ff) to justify the conclusion that it was added by a later hand so as to bring Luke here into line with Mark and Matthew. The NEB does in fact relegate the words of the so-called 'longer' Lucan text (22:19b–20) to the margin.

2. The rendering of 1 Cor. 11:23 as "in the night when he was betrayed" mistranslates the Greek, which does not posit a betrayal, let alone a betrayal by Judas, whom Paul never mentions. It says only that Jesus was "given over" or "was delivered" to martyrdom—by God, for the passive voice was regularly used in the Old Testament and in early Christian literature as a *passivum divinum,* viz. to indicate that God was the agent, while avoiding having to use the divine name. Other Pauline passages (such as Rom. 4:24f) likewise show that it was the Lord who "delivered him up for our trespasses" and then "raised him for our justification". There is no suggestion that he was compromised by a third party. Cf. my remarks on the atonement. pp. 4f above. Even in the gospels, the Greek represents Judas as 'delivering Jesus up', not as 'betraying' him. Cf. below, p. 343n7.

3. For my responses to Stanton, see Wells 1996, pp. 14f, 39f, 56; and 1999, pp. 245ff. He has ignored them and repeated his same strictures in the second edition of his *The Gospels and Jesus* (2002, pp. 143–45) and in his *Jesus and Gospel* (2004, p. 128n).

4. This is clearly the basis on which Stanton wrote, in his book published in 2002 (cf. the previous note), of my 1996 book as if, in it, I had held by my earlier denial of Jesus's historicity, when in fact that standpoint is there clearly repudiated.

5. I discuss the Tacitus passage in detail in my 1982 book, pp. 16f. The Oxford theologian R.T. France, who has elsewhere described himself as "an evangelical Anglican", found this discussion "entirely convincing" (1986, p. 23).

6. The assembled Corinthian Christian community included members who "speak in tongues", that is, who speak "mysteries in the spirit" in the form of utterances which are not normal, intelligible language, but require interpretation by some listener. Paul himself practised this 'spiritual gift': "I speak in tongues more than all of you"(1 Cor. 12:10; 14:2, 13f, 18). One can readily envisage that all manner of strange ideas could arise on such a basis. Further details and discussion in Esler 1994, Chapter 3. He notes that such "ecstatic excitement" was characteristic of the early period, but seems to have died down "by the time the Pastoral Epistles were written later in the first century."

7. We need here to keep in mind the comment of the theologian John Hick, endorsed by Dale Allison (2005, p. 201n): "This was a time of excited and sometimes (from the typical twentieth-century standpoint) fantastic beliefs and practices to whose atmosphere we have a clue in the uninhibited enthusiasms of contemporary Pentecostalism and the unshakeable certainties of marginal sects expecting the imminent end of the world. In that early apocalyptic phase of the Christian movement the canons of plausibility were very different from those operating within today's mainline churches."

1 Basic Facts about the Gospels

1. Thus Ellis says in his commentary on Luke that the title 'According to Luke' originated "where a Church had two gospels and desired to distinguish them, or at the latest, when the gospels were a collected unit" (1966, p. 63). The earliest known text of this gospel (P^{75}) is as late as A.D. 175–225, and already has this title (Evans 1990, p. 5).

2. For fuller discussion see my 1999 book, pp. 11–14.

3. M.D. Goulder's recent article shows likewise that "by A.D. 100 legends were forming about Peter's sojourn in Rome (1 Peter) and his martyrdom (John 21)."

In Goulder's view, "he probably died in his bed in Jerusalem about A.D. 55" (2004, p. 377).

4. See further the article 'Emperor Worship' in Grant and Rowley 1963.

5. My account of Haenchen's interpretation draws on what I said of it in my 1982 book, where I also discuss the very instructive way in which Luke rewrote Mark's Chapter 13 (pp. 111–18).

6. Concerning the 'us' in Lk. 1:1, Fitzmyer notes that it "denotes the. people who are now affected by salvation-history . . . It includes the 'many writers' as well as 'the original eyewitnesses and ministers of the word' from whom Luke distinguishes himself in verse 2. It undoubtedly includes also Luke and other third-generation Christians, which is the sense of 'us' in verse 2" (1986, p. 293). Cf. Evans, 1990, pp. 124f.

7. The following incidents in Mark where John is named as present are absent from the fourth gospel: the call of the first disciples, the healing of Peter's mother-in-law, the appointing of the twelve, the raising of Jairus's daughter, the transfiguration, the dialogue about driving out devils (9:38); the request about sitting on thrones, the audience (13:3) of the apocalyptic discourse, and the Gethsemane scene.

8. We saw above (p. 4) that "the problem of Christology" is "how Jesus can be fully God and fully man, and yet genuinely one person." It was felt that created beings could not be saved by one who is himself merely a created being, and so he cannot have been just a man, but must also somehow be God as well, and hence must always have existed. And so Athanasius repudiated the view of Arius that there was a time when the Son "was not"; and the Nicene creed made him not merely God but "very God", "of one substance with the Father", thus giving us a Son who is the same age as (coeval with) his Father! Maurice Wiles shows how, over centuries, the process was repeated whereby each doctrine about the nature of Jesus raised a further question about his nature, and that, of the possible answers, only one was, on each occasion, tolerated, others being vilified. He concludes that, for the church, the overall result is "a well thought out but over-defined concept of orthodoxy", and "a penchant for mutual vilification and the multiplication of division, together with a built-in resistance to change in the face of new circumstance" (1994, p. 73).

2 The Question of Miracles and the Work of David Friedrich Strauss

1. This miracle, on which Pascal has based his defence of Jansenism, consisted in the sudden cure of his little niece (on 21st March, 1656) of an ulcerated eye

after touching a relic from the crown of thorns in the convent chapel at Port Royal des Champs, a Cistercian convent near Versailles.

2. John Wilkins (died 1672) said that miracles were limited to the days when Christianity was young and in need of supernatural testimony. Robert Boyle too thought that miracles ceased "with the foundation of Christianity". Newton wrote to Locke that "miracles of good credit continued in the Church for about two or three hundred years" (Westfall 1958, pp. 89f, 203).

3. 'The Value of Witness to the Miraculous', and his own comments on this essay in his 'Agnosticism and Christianity'; both in Huxley 1900, pp. 184–86, 329.

4. Strauss 1840, section 13. The first edition of this work, published in Tübingen in 1835–36, was reprinted in 1969 by the Wissenschaftliche Buchgesellschaft, Darmstadt. But the fourth edition of 1840 gives a fuller account of these and other matters. The numbering of the sections is not identical in these two editions. The table of contents at the beginning of the book specifies the substance of each section, and it is not necessary for me to give, additionally, page references either to the German fourth edition or to George Eliot's 1846 translation of it in three volumes. These have recently (2005) been reprinted by Continuum International.

5. The article 'Resurrection-and Ascension Narratives' in Cheyne and Black's *Encyclopaedia Biblica* notes (col. 4041) that Reimarus "enumerated ten contradictions, but in reality their number is much greater." The most striking of them are conveniently listed by Wedderburn (1999, pp. 24f) who goes on to record Strauss's conclusion that they cannot be harmonized.

6. Burger, 1970, has shown that the location of the Messiah's birth at Bethlehem was not universal in pre-Christian Jewish tradition. But it was not uncommon, and this suffices for Strauss's argument. More recently, Pomykala has shown that even Davidic descent was not expected of the Messiah until about the middle of the first century B.C., and was represented at Qumran during the Herodian period (1995, p. 270).

7. Details in VanderKam and Flint, 2002, pp. 281, 303.

8. In this chapter of some thirty pages on Strauss, Barth tells us that he was not a historian, nor a thinker; that he was in many respects a failure, that many of his opinions were the result of anger or touchiness, and that his second *Life* is a trite biography of Jesus. As for his first *Life,* it is lacking in the vision which perceives that "what truly gives human history its greatness, worth and power is the great personality of genius." At the time when he wrote it, Strauss, poor

fellow, had "not yet read any Carlyle!" (1972, p. 560). But he did at least perceive that Mozart is superior to "the dreadful Wagner", and "anyone who has understood that can be pardoned much tastelessness and much childishly critical theology" (p. 567). James Barr, who was Professor of Hebrew at Oxford, justifiably complains (1993, p. 202) of "the contemptuous ignoring of the main tradition of biblical scholarship by Barth and his followers", and finds that "New Testament scholarship made a fatal mistake when, in the aftermath of the First World War, it turned its back on the liberals and the history-of-religions school" and succumbed to the "rhetorical-theological appeal" of Barth's "dialectical theology". Cf. my discussion of Barth in my 2004 book, pp. 146f, 175–77.

3 The Virgin Birth

1. I discuss such wishful thinking on the part of C.E.B. Cranfield and others in my 1999 book, pp. 116, 273–75. David Wenham's equally wishful thinking on the subject has been effectively criticized by R. Barry Matlock, 2000, pp. 49ff.

2. Cf. Brown 1979, p.36: "In Matthew there is no hint of a *coming* to Bethlehem, for Joseph and Mary are in a house at Bethlehem where seemingly Jesus was born (2:11). The only journey that Matthew has to explain is why the family went to Nazareth when they came from Egypt instead of returning to their native Bethlehem (2:22–23)."

3. Some have tried to bring the census reported at Lk. 2:2 to within the reign of Herod by translating this verse as: "This census was earlier than the one under Quirinius", or "was before the governorship of Quirinius". Feldman has commented that these renderings necessitate an unparalleled use of the Greek word *prōtos* ('first'), and also that it does not make much sense to say that the census took place earlier than when Quirinius was governing Syria rather than stating who was governor at the time (1984, p. 712). Robin Lane Fox, who discusses the birth and infancy narratives in some detail, calls these alternative translations "attempts to evade the meaning of the third Gospel's Greek", and declares that nobody has ever entertained them for non-doctrinal reasons (1991, pp. 29f). *Prōtos* can mean 'before' if it governs a following noun or pronoun (in the genitive case): for instance Jn. 1:15, 'he was before *(prōtos)* me', i.e. 'first of me'. Luke, however, follows *prōtos* with a participle phrase grammatically quite independent of this *prōtos*.

Another way out of the problem is to take Luke as saying not that Quirinius was governor of Syria at the time, but that he was 'in charge' or 'in office' there, but not as governor, so that the reference could be to some 'office' he held in Herod's time. Brown regards this as an "unlikely hypothesis", and as "another ingenious attempt to save Lucan accuracy" (p. 395n). Also, in the updated 1993 edition of this 1979 book, he reviews recent discussion of the proposals that Quirinius was twice governor of Syria and that there were two censuses, and concludes that they are "better given up" (p. 668).

4. Attempts by Christian apologists to make Quirinius goveror of Syria in Herod's lifetime include adducing an inscription from Tivoli, which does not state any name, but records the career of "a legate" with the words: "[legatus pro praetori] divi Augusti iterum Syriam et Ph[oenicem optinuit]" . This does not mean that the unnamed man was twice legate of Syria, but that his second legateship was that of Syria (Schürer 1973, p. 258). Feldman quotes scholars who think that the man was Lucius Calpurnius Piso, who was governor of Asia and later of Syria (1984, p. 713). Syria was governed from 10/9 to 7/6 B.C. by Sentius Saturninus and from 7/6 to 4 B.C. by Quintilius Varus. This leaves no room for a governorship by Quirinius during the last years of Herod's reign, when Matthew, and most probably Luke too, require Jesus to have been born. Vogt supposes that not only the inscription from Tivoli but also "the short biographical sketch" which Tacitus gives of Quirinius suggest that he had been imperial legate in Syria in Herod's time, and "in this position had conducted a war against a tribe in the Taurus mountains" (1971, p. 5). Although no details are given of the "short biographical sketch", the reference can only be to *Annals*, iii, 48, where Quirinius is said to have subjugated the Homonadenses (Cilician brigands on the southern border of the province of Galatia). It is not said that he was legate of Syria at the time; indeed the war was presumably conducted from the north, from Galatia, not from Syria in the south; and according to Feldman (p. 712) it has been "convincingly shown" that he was governor of Galatia at that time.

5. Some have argued, for instance, that Josephus had in mind a *second* census, made only after Herod's death. That leaves us asking why he omitted such a notable event as the census in Herod's lifetime would have been. Another argument has been that the relevant census took place in two stages: the first in late B.C. will have consisted in drawing up the electoral roll by requiring all persons to register; the second followed only in A.D. 6, and consisted in the official tax assessment. These two stages, it is claimed, are distinguished by Josephus as *apographē* and *apotimēsis* (assessment), and it is only the second that he reports, whereas Luke is referring to the first. Unfortunately for this view, Josephus uses these two terms to refer to different aspects of the same situation: Quirinius, he says, came to Judea to make an *assessment* of the property of the Jews, who in consequence submitted to the *registration* of their property (*Ant.*, 18:1–4).

6. The Roman historian R. Syme, in an article of 1973, quoted by Fitzmyer, pp. 404f.

7. Some have defended the journey to Bethlehem by appealing to an Egyptian papyrus which records the edict of Vibius Maximus (A.D. 104) that those who

for any reason are away from their own *idia* should return home to enrol themselves. Someone's *idia* can mean either his private property or his 'peculiar district'. The former meaning seems required by the context here, since the census returns that have been preserved show that the owners of houses had to give their names, the names of those living with them, and the address of the house as well; and the correctness of the entries was everywhere assured by official inspection by the local authorities. Obviously, such inspection would have been difficult unless the returns were made where the property was situated. Luke does not suggest that Joseph had property in Bethlehem. On the contrary, he represents the couple as trying to put up at an inn (2:7).

8. Brown gives a very full discussion of the evidence as to which of the two women is the one who speaks the Magnificat. He is quite undogmatic on the matter, but thinks that there are better arguments for its ascription to Mary than to Elisabeth (pp. 334–36).

9. The only problem in this section of the genealogies is that, instead of Matthew's "Ram" (1:3, taken from the list in 1 Chronicles 2:9), Luke (3:33) has "Arni", and many manuscripts have, additionally, "Admin". Both are otherwise unknown. There is considerable manuscript variation in respect of both names, probably because copyists could not identify these two persons with any in the Old Testament.

10. On all this see Brown, pp. 70, 82f, and Burger, pp. 94–97.

11. For details of Rowan Williams's very qualified defence of the doctrine of the virgin birth see my 2004 book, pp. 191f.

12. Robinson is concerned to avoid two common views of Jesus—that he was God in disguise, or that he was no more than a perfect man (1973, p. 3). If he had been God in disguise, and therefore not truly human, his temptations and his suffering could only have been mere play-acting and his whole life "a charade" (1973, p. 39). If he is to appeal to mankind, he must have been himself truly a man. This means that we must not be obliged to regard him as a pre-existent being who came from heaven, nor as virgin-born on Earth. Robinson admits that Matthew states clearly enough that Joseph was not the father of Jesus, and had no intercourse with Mary until after Jesus's birth. But he holds that this does not exclude prior intercourse between Mary and some unknown male which Joseph subsequently condoned on the basis of the angel's statement to him that the foetus was "of holy ghost"—a statement which, in Robinson's view, does not exclude normal conception, but may simply affirm "the initiative of God in and through it all" (p. 46). In other words, holy spirit may have done no more than bless the intercourse of the parents, not make superfluous the role of the human father. Luke's narrative presents Robinson

with greater difficulties, and he admits that its first three chapters may represent a combination of conflicting traditions (p. 45n). He of course does not wish to offend older-type Christians by categorically denying either that the evangelists allege a virgin birth, or that this allegation may be true (p. 138). His claim is that they are not unequivocally committed to it; and this claim is, for him, of the greatest importance, since he realizes that many traditional Christian ideas (including "the mythology of the pre-existent person") have "very limited cash value in our world", and he aims to put something "in the place of this currency for those for whom it has lost its purchasing power" (p. 196).

Robinson knew that the idea of a God who exists outside his creation and has occasionally intervened in it has lost much of its former credibility; and so he argues that God is within creation, as the progressive development of "spirit". He is "to be represented no longer as a personified being over man's head, but in and by man and his responsibility. . . . God is thereby made dependent on man and man's response." God is "the power of nature and history, the Logos or principle of the evolutionary process". What happened at the Incarnation was that this 'principle' "began to be represented in a new way", in that Jesus was "a new mutation in the development of spirit" (pp. 217f). Jesus thus owed his superior nature not to any miraculous birth, but to a (Darwinian) mutation. Hence, although we may be good Darwinians, we can go on believing that Jesus was God incarnate.

13. Eric Mascall, writing as Professor of Historical Theology at London University, and describing himself as "a traditional theologian", referred (in the BBC journal *The Listener,* December 23rd, 1965) to Boslooper as a typical exponent of "the new theology" he deplored. Boslooper, he says, "holds that it is of the utmost importance that we should continue to recite the affirmation in the Creed that Jesus Christ was 'born of the Virgin Mary', but he also holds that, when we do this, we should not mean by these words that he was in fact born of the Virgin Mary but that God has acted in history and that monogamous marriage is civilization's most important social institution."

4 The Resurrection

1. P.W. Schmiedel, in Cheyne and Black 1899, cols. 4050, 4055.

2. *Ibid.,* col. 4071.

3. *The Nature of Christian Belief* (A Statement and Exposition by the House of Bishops of the General Synod of the Church of England), London: Church House, 1986, p. 21.

4. Details about Rowan Williams in my 2004 book, pp. 190–95.

5. It is Luke who turns 'the third day' into the time of the first resurrection appearances. At Lk. 24:21 two disciples are said to be in the presence of the risen Jesus on "the third day" after the crucifixion. In Paul, 'the third day' refers only to the interval between the crucifixion and the resurrection, not to the commencement of the appearances, which follow only later. Evans notes that if the Pauline passage is "read on its own and not in the light of other New Testament passages", it is possible to regard the appearances "as intended to cover a considerable period of time, perhaps even a number of years" (1970, p. 50).

6. Price (1995) argues that the whole passage (1 Cor. 15:3–11) is not a (supplemented) pre-existing creed, but a post-Pauline interpolation. Paul introduces these verses by saying that they comprise the substance of what he had preached to the Corinthians, the fundamental tenets, belief in which ensures their salvation (verses 1–2). He designates this "gospel" as what he had himself "received" and what he has in turn "handed on". Price argues that the terms 'receive' and 'hand on' are technical language for the transmitting of rabbinical tradition, and so imply that Paul had learnt his gospel from human predecessors, whereas at Gal. 1:11f the real Paul says quite emphatically that he did not "receive" his gospel from human sources at all, but from revelation. It is, however, clear that the term 'receive' can be used of what someone derives from either a supernatural or a human source. Hence Paul may in 1 Cor. 15 not be denying that his knowledge of Jesus's salvific death and of his resurrection (verses 3–4) reached him from revelation, while allowing that appearances to persons whom he knew personally (Cephas, James) came to him from human testimony. It is surely unlikely that he would claim that what he knew about the experiences of such acquaintances reached him in any other way than directly from them or by hearsay. If I read Price correctly, he holds that not only the supposed interpolator, but also Paul himself regarded Cephas as the gospel Peter and James as the blood brother of Jesus; whereas I hold that—whatever may be imputed to a latter-day interpolator—this is not true of Paul himself.

7. The burnings of the Inquisition were prompted by motives which, however deplorable, are still to us intelligible, namely desire to enforce orthodoxy or to appropriate wealth. But the systematic mythology about demons and their dealings with mankind which underlay the great witch hunt is now so alien that the torturing and burning of innumerable women seems today little better than collective insanity. In earlier centuries Catholics and Protestants alike saw the influence of demons in any beliefs but their own.

8. Wright nevertheless exaggerates when he says, on this same page (2007, p. 56), that no first-century Jew, prior to Easter, expected that one person will rise from the dead in advance of all the rest; for at Mk. 6:14–16 there is the strange tradition that, when people heard of Jesus's miraculous powers, some said he was "John the baptizer . . . raised from the dead." And when Herod (Antipas)

heard of it, he agreed, saying: "John, whom I beheaded, has been raised" (RSV and NEB).

9. David Jenkins, transcript of his 'Credo' interview broadcast on London Weekend Television on 29th April, 1984; quoted from Conor Cruise O'Brien's article in *The Observer*, 5th August, 1984.

10. It was Schopenhauer who, although himself firmly within the German metaphysical tradition, insisted: "I cannot too often repeat that all abstract ideas are to be checked in the light of experience" (Details in my 2006 article, as referenced in note 7 on p. 348 below).

Q, the Sayings Gospel

1. On the existence of Q, see Kümmel's clear account, 1975, pp. 63ff. Much more detailed but less readable is Catchpole 1993. Tuckett gives a helpful survey in Chapter 1 of his 1996 book. The case against the existence of Q is stated by Goodacre, 2001, Chapter 6.

2. For instance, the accusation that Jesus works miracles by "Beelzebub, the prince of the devils" is met by him with four responses (Q 11:17–20), followed by a saying about binding a strong man and then by the logion "he that is not with me is against me." Matthew has all these items in the same order.

3. The request for a sign appears at Mk. 8:11f and is placed by Matthew (at 16:1–4) in the Markan sequence. But the request also appears in Q 11:29, paralleled of course in Matthew (at 12:38–40).

4. Cf. J.M. Robinson 2001, pp. 27–30. Guenther's 1992 article is a lucid account of the history of the futile quest for Aramaic originals behind the New Testament writings. Reiser, 1984, finds the style and syntax of Mark characteristic of simple current everyday Greek.

5. Q 14:27 reads: "Whosoever doth not bear his own cross and come after me cannot be my disciple." Does this presuppose an image of Jesus carrying his cross, or merely indicate willingness to follow a teacher to death if necessary? Tuckett thinks that "what is probably intended is a stark and powerful metaphor to impress upon the audience the hardness of the Christian calling, the harsh life to which the Christian may be summoned" (1996, p. 321). Mack holds that the phrase 'bear his own cross' means no more than 'bear up under condemnation' (1993, p. 99).

6. The "rulers *(archontes)* of this age" are said to have crucified "the Lord of glory" because they failed to understand the hidden and secret wisdom of God

(1 Cor. 2:8). On attempts to interpret these "rulers" as meaning Caiaphas and Pilate (and thus to ascribe to Paul knowledge of the historical situation in which, according to the gospels, Jesus died), see my 2004 book, pp. 35–37. The phrase "the rulers of this age" (verses 6, 8) is not found elsewhere in Paul's letters, and the removal of the whole passage in which it is embedded (verses 6–16) "leaves a smoothly connected passage . . . dealing with Paul's initial visit to the Corinthians and emphasizing both his own 'weakness' and the 'fleshly' nature of his hearers"; whereas verses 6 to 16 constitute "an exposition of the exalted status and role of the Christian pneumatic as one who is privy to divine mysteries" (Walker 2001, p. 134). These verses certainly do stand out, as has often been noted, both in style and in content from their context, and it is hardly satisfactory to account for them, as is often done, by supposing that here Paul is suddenly adopting, 'tongue in cheek', alien formulae. Walker adds that much of both the terminology and the ideas of verses 6–16 strongly resembles 'gnostic' concepts familiar from the deutero-Pauline letters and the fourth gospel. At Jn. 12:31 and 16:11 the supreme demonic being is called "the ruler *(archōn)* of this cosmos", or (RV) "prince of this world". At Ephes. 2:2 we read of "the prince *(archōn)* of the power of the air" to whom the recipients of the letter used to be beholden; and Ephes. 6:12 declares that "our wrestling is not against flesh and blood, but against . . . the world-rulers of this darkness, against the spiritual hosts of wickedness in the heavenly places". It is, then, quite possible that verses 6 to 16 of 1 Cor. 2 were added after Paul's life so as to bring him into the fold of the 'pneumatikoi' (Walker, p. 145). Recall that our earliest manuscripts of the Paulines date from the late-second or early-third century.

7. I discuss the strange details concerning Judas in my 1986 book, pp.132–140. I would further note that, in the synoptics, after having deliberately chosen and empowered him with the others (Mk.. 3:13f), Jesus suddenly shows awareness, at the Last Supper, that Judas is going to "deliver him up" (Mk. 14:18ff and parallels in Mt. and Lk.), but makes no effort to dissuade him, and simply allows him to proceed. Nor do the eleven, who witness these words of Jesus, take any restraining action, but remain unnaturally passive in the matter. Judas remains at the meal, unmolested. Only in the fourth gospel is it said that he left the company and "went out" (13:30). In this fourth gospel Jesus expresses awareness of Judas's forthcoming behaviour at a much earlier stage (6:64–71), but nevertheless allows him to continue in his company until the final end.

Matthew and Luke complicate Mark by introducing Jesus's promise that "you my followers" (thus including Judas) will sit on thrones judging the twelve tribes of Israel (Mt. 19:28; Lk. 22:30). In Luke this promise is made even after we have been told (at 22:3) that Satan had entered into Judas. This illustrates clearly enough that independent and, to some extent, incompatible traditions are being combined. The references to Judas in the synoptic narratives of the Last Supper show likewise that they did not originally belong in that context. Mark begins with "And as they were eating, Jesus said, Truly I say to you, one of you will deliver me up" (14:18). He continues in this vein for a further three verses, after which the text repeats "And as they were eating" in order to introduce the institution of the eucharist. Nineham notes *(ad loc.* in his commentary) that, if these two sections had originally belonged together, the second of them would not have been introduced by repeating the opening words of the first, which have already made it clear that the setting is a meal. Matthew has reproduced the same incongruity: 26:21, "as they were eating" introduces the knowledge of Judas's forthcoming treachery, after which we again have "as they were eating" to introduce the institution of the sacrament.

The Judas traditions serve to show that Jesus did not die because he was outwitted, but knew in advance what would happen. But these traditions fit very poorly into the overall narrative. The Pauline phrase that Jesus was "delivered up" by God to martyrdom for our trespasses (cf. above, p. 333n2) may have given the first cue to the formation of the gospels' story that he was delivered to the Jewish authorities by a human associate. It is striking that the Greek of the gospels, unlike most English versions, does not represent Judas as 'betraying' him, but as "delivering him up", or "giving him over" to them. The verb used is, as in Paul, *paradidōmi,* not *prodidōmi;* only at Lk. 6:16 is Judas called *prodotēs,* a traitor (by the narrator, not by Jesus). Nevertheless, Judas's actions do amount to a betrayal, for—as the distinguished Catholic exegete Raymond Brown notes—he "gave Jesus over by two actions according to the Synoptics. He went before or with the arresting party to show them where and when to seize Jesus (in a remote place on the Mount of Olives late at night); and once there he identified who Jesus was, distinguishing him from others who were there (the disciples)" (1994, p. 1399). Brown finds these acceptable as historical facts, even though he notes that Mark's account (the earliest of the four) gives no indication of why Judas did what he did. Wrede likewise accepted that the authorities could not dare to arrest Jesus when he was among the people. He withdrew at night to somewhere unknown to them—perhaps to a hiding place. But Judas will have known where this was (1907, pp. 131f). Against this we may note the significance of the fact that Jesus was not there alone, but went there with his disciples (Mk. 11:11. At verse 19 some English versions have "he went out of the city", but the RSV gives the reading "they went out", and this is certainly implied by the context, for in the next verse "they" are returning to it the following morning; 14:13 implies that they are again outside it). If, then, the whole company withdrew at night, anybody could easily have tracked them, and there was no need for the services of Judas. Moreover, as Jesus was well known as a public teacher (14:49), he did not need to be identified, unless lights were needed to compensate for the darkness and the arresting party had failed to equip itself with them.

Bart Ehrman has argued that "Judas did not simply lead Jesus's enemies to him privately. He disclosed insider information that the authorities needed to arrest Jesus", namely that he had taught the twelve disciples that he "was to be the future king". His enemies needed this information "in order to have him brought up on charges before the Roman governor" (2006b, pp. 162, 168). This is a variant of Schweitzer's theory that what Judas betrayed was Jesus's secret that he was the Messiah.

William Klassen's article in a 2002 synposium on Jesus's activities gives a good overview of the continuing endless discussion of the Judas episode, and supplements his 1996 book on Judas. He urges us to "take the evidence seriously that Judas handed Jesus over and did so with Jesus's full knowledge", since he "increasingly saw himself as the suffering servant who had to lay down his life for his people." Hence "Judas acted in obedience to Christ's will" (2002, pp. 394f, 407), and must be considered a friend rather than a betrayer. But Jesus himself, although he declared Judas's deed to be necessary, also pronounced it to be culpable (Mk. 14:21)—a combination which, as we saw (above, p. 5) raises its own problems. Brown's succinct review of Klassen's 1996 book (in the *Journal of Biblical Literature,* 117 (1998), pp. 134-36) justly notes that his "passion" to make of Judas "a sympathetic figure" involves some very unconvincing exegesis, as, when Jesus calls Judas a devil (Jn. 6:70–71), this is not understood as hostility, in spite of the negative use of *diabolus* at 8:44 and 13:2.

It remains to note that the recently discovered Gospel of Judas Iscariot is a gnostic work written in the middle of the second century "by someone who did not have independent access to historical records about the events he was relating" and so "is not a book that will provide us with additional information about what really happened in Jesus' lifetime." It does, however, add yet another piece of evidence to our knowledge of how "remarkably diverse Christianity was in its early decades and centuries" (Ehrman 2006b, pp. 172, 178).

7 The Prelude to Jesus's Public Ministry

1. For Paul, mystical assimilation, achieved through baptism, makes the believer a participant in Christ's destiny, and opens eternal life to him. Wedderburn's 1987 book argues persuasively that such assimilation to the god is not documented in paganism. Yet, as Hurtado—who describes himself as "a worshipping Christian" (1999, p. 9), and is well acquainted with Wedderburn's work—shows, the influence of pagan ideas on Christian baptismal rites is not to be altogether discounted. As we saw (above, p. 9), Hurtado also notes, commenting on 1 Cor. 10 and 11, that "the cult-meal of the Christian congregation is emphatically one in which the Lord Jesus plays a role that is explicitly likened to that of the deities of the pagan cults" (p. 85).

2. Justin, *Dialogue with Trypho,* where the orthodox Jewish speaker says: "Christ, if he is come, and is anywhere, is unknown, nor does he know himself, nor can he be indued with any power until Elias shall come and anoint him and make him manifest to all men" (Chapter 8). Cf. Chapter 49: "We Jews expect Christ will be a man of men, and that Elias must anoint him when he has come."

3. 2 Samuel 24 tells that the Lord, angry with the people, ordered David to number them, then punished him for doing so by sending a plague which killed seventy thousand of them, and finally "repented him of the evil". 1 Chronicles 21 recasts this story so as to exonerate Yahweh. Here it is Satan who "moved David to number Israel". This seems to be the one instance in the Old Testament where Satan figures as a power that tempts man to sin; and he is clearly given this role because it had come to be felt unbecoming to assign it to Yahweh. Elaine Pagels's 1991 article gives an informative account of the origin and role of Satan.

4. The discourses of the fourth gospel comprise whole chapters in which Jesus expatiates on his own importance and his closeness to "the Father". To allow that they are mere "poems", compiled by the Johannine Christian community, would ruin the thesis of Ratzinger's whole book, which "sees Jesus in the light of his communion with the Father, which is the true center of his personality; without it, we cannot understand him at all, and it is from this center that he makes himself present to us still today" (p. xiv). Ratzinger begins his book by noting that Moses promised that God will "raise up . . . a prophet. . . . like unto me" (Deuteronomy 18:15). Now Moses was on particularly close terms with God, had conversed with him "as a man speaks to his friend" (pp. 1, 3f); and so the new prophet, to be like Moses, must be at least as privileged. And in fact "what was true of Moses only in fragmentary form has now been fully realized in the person of Jesus: He lives before the face of God, not just as a friend, but as a Son; he lives in the most intimate unity with the Father" (p. 6, with reference to Jn 1:8: "the only begotten Son, which is in the bosom of the Father"). One may think in this connection of the discourse in Chapter 17 of John, where Jesus reminds the Father of their primordial life together, of "the glory which I had with thee before the world was"—a passage which drew from Strauss the comment that, if it is an authentic utterance, then Jesus must have been mad (1997, p.56). This and kindred statements in John confirmed Strauss in his view that "the veritable Christ is only to be found, if at all, in the first three Gospels" (p. 57).

5. Not only the Devil, but also hell, associated with him, is "something that has either atrophied or entirely disappeared in the vocabulary and doctrinal repository of most churches" (Marty, 1985, p. 393). He adds: "To put it crudely: Hell disappeared—no one noticed", in the sense that it is "unavailable for civic discourse" ("not culturally available"), and "the public has not noticed this disappearance." But while mainstream churches now say little or nothing about hell, the more fundamentalist ones are not so reticent. Witness the report *The Nature of Hell,* issued by the Evangelical Alliance (ACUTE Publications) in 2000, which insists that hell involves "severe punishment" and holds that we are not at liberty to presume that God will condescend to "save some who have not explicitly professed faith in Jesus Christ", such as people who died never having heard of him, or those with "severe mental disabilities" (pp. 130–133). Apropos of the American scene, Kathleen Boone mentions the "proudly funda-

mentalist" tabloid *Sword of the Lord* and its "unrelenting and gruesome descriptions of hell" (1990, p. 8). All this comes from accepting the Bible as inerrant and from the conviction that, if people did not fear hell, they would have a licence to sin. For liberal Christians, however, the doctrine of eternal torment is morally intolerable and makes belief in a good God impossible.

8 Jesus as Apocalyptic Prophet

1. J.W. Colenso (1814–83), bishop of Natal, author of *The Pentateuch and the Book of Joshua Critically Examined*, 1862–79. Intelligent questioning from one of his Zulu converts had brought him to reject the historical accuracy of these six Old Testament books. In his account of the controversy that followed, Rogerson concludes that Colenso "exhausted the credibility of the older defences of orthodoxy, and showed to a younger generation of scholars facts in the Bible that orthodox schemes could no longer explain" (1984, p. 234).

2. The editors' Introduction runs to p. 54, so that the text of their English translation, pp. 56–136, is still quite short.

3. 4 Ezra 4:26. This is a late first-century Jewish work consisting of reflections prompted by the disastrous outcome of the Jewish War with Rome. Chapter 5 tells that signs of the approaching end will include a great increase in wickedness, universal panic, and confusion—the sun will shine at night and the moon by day, trees will drip blood, etc. etc. Those who survive these ills will witness the arrival of the Messiah, who will bring happiness and reign for four hundred years, but then die, and all mankind with him. After seven days of silence, God will then awaken all for the final judgment, consigning the wicked to "the furnace of hell" and the righteous to "the paradise of delight" (7:26–36). Here, then, the old idea of a national restoration under a Messianic king is combined with the more recent apocalyptic expectation of a new creation. Collins observes that "we find a similar two-stage eschatology in the roughly contemporary NT book of Revelation", where (Chapter 20) "Christ reigns on earth for a thousand years before the resurrection and a new creation" (2003, p. 82).

4. The expectation that God would soon intervene and bring an end to the evil in the world is expressed in many of the Qumran Scrolls, and is among the ideas that "seem to have profoundly shaped the world-view" of the sect there, which "considered itself to be living in the last period of history" (Garcia Martinez 2003, p. 101).

5. The fourth book of the *Sibylline Oracles,* dating in its present form from the period after the destruction of the temple in A.D. 70, concludes with a prediction of cosmic conflagration and resurrection. Collins notes that "there is evidence that an older Hellenistic oracle has been updated", although one cannot be sure

that this older oracle included these predictions (2003, p. 79). The *Testament* of *Moses* (originally from the second century B.C. and reworked in the early first century A.D.) represents Moses as transmitting secret prophecies to Joshua about "the consummation of the end of days". Israel will be exalted to the stars (10:9), so that heaven will become the dwelling place of God's people, while Earth will be converted into the place of punishment for their enemies (Nickelsburg 1981, p. 82).

6. 2 Baruch resembles 4 Ezra. Their "common eschatological presuppositions show that such ideas were widely shared in Palestinian Judaism at the end of the first century" (Collins 2003, p. 82). According to 85:10, "the youth of the world is past, the strength of the creation already exhausted, and the advent of the times is short." After times of tribulation the Messiah is revealed, but "after a time he will return in glory." This presumably corresponds to the death of the Messiah and its sequel in 4 Ezra. In *The Apocalypse* of *Abraham,* Abraham is told about a Messianic leader at the end of time. There will be some twelve periods of impiety leading up to the end.

7. On Schopenhauer, and on Schweitzer's similar view of the will, see my article 'A Critique of Schopenhauer's Metaphysic', *German Life and Letters,* 59 (2006), pp. 379–389.

8. A. Drews, *Die Christusmythe,* 1910. Jena: Diederichs. On Robertson, see *J.M. Robertson (1856–1933). Liberal, Rationalist, and Scholar,* an assessment by several hands, edited by G.A. Wells (London: Pemberton, 1987).

9. Jesus also speaks of "my kingdom" in his address to Pilate at Jn. 18:36 (three times in this single verse). But the phrase 'the kingdom of God' is "not characteristic" of this gospel (Lindars 1972, p. 150). Dunn (1985a, p. 34) contrasts it in this respect with the synoptics, noting that the word 'kingdom' is spoken by Jesus forty-seven times in Matthew, eighteen times in Mark, and ten times in Luke. In John's gospel "Jesus is *never* shown as preaching or proclaiming the kingdom" (p. 35).

10. Dunn finds the sole unifying factor to consist in "Christ", in particular in "the unity between the exalted Christ and Jesus of Nazareth" (2006, p. 218). This "unifying core" is "an abstraction" (p. 247). Once it is given concrete shape, differences appear. Dunn stresses that, by 'Jesus' in this core, he means "Jesus of Nazareth". Hence he strenuously denies the discontinuity which I have posited between the Jesus of the early epistles and the Jesus of the gospels. I have discussed his arguments in my 1999 book.

11. Allison notes in his 2003 article (p. 165) that Bultmann's 1951 *Theology* of *the New Testament* "contains a very influential portrait of Jesus as an eschato-

logical prophet"; that Joachim Jeremias's *New Testament Theology* (1971), which "summarizes his conclusions after a lifetime of study", interprets "the entire message of Jesus in terms of the expectation of a near end"; and that E.P. Sanders's *Jesus and Judaism* (1985) portrays Jesus as "an eschatological prophet who looked forward to the restoration of Israel". Allison refers also (p. 165) to the 1994 "major work" of the Catholic scholar J.P. Meier, in which, he says, "Jesus looks much more like Schweitzer's Jesus" than "a non-apocalyptic ... sage". Meier, he adds, "concludes that Jesus believed both in the presence of the kingdom and in a near end."

12. For Dunn, it suffices that Jesus, unlike the gods of the pagan mystery religions, was a historical figure, "of Nazareth"; for "by applying the same sort of (mythical) language to a *historical* individual, the New Testament writers in effect demythologize it" (1985b, p. 294. Italics original). This does not do justice to the fact that the dying and rising Christ of the earliest Christian documents is not the recently deceased preacher 'of Nazareth' at all, but a more remote figure (cf. note 10 above; also pp. 18, 216f above), although admittedly still represented in these early texts as a historical one. But quite apart from this, does resurrection language really become less mythical when applied to someone who lived more recently than Osiris or Dionysus?

13. Ben Witherington III in Shanks and Witherington 2003, p. 91. This book enthuses about the so-called 'Jesus Box'—an ossuary with the inscription 'James, son of Joseph, brother of Jesus'. In June 2003 the Department of Antiquities in Israel made it pretty clear that the inscription is later than the ossuary, the provenance of which is in any case unknown.

14. According to the article 'Second Coming of Jesus in Current Belief' in Houlden's 2005 handbook, "countless millions" believe that "the world as we know it will decline further and further into moral and spiritual chaos until the coming of Christ." The author, K.G.C. Newport, adds that "even the shallowest of trawls of the Internet" will quickly reveal that the 'rapture' is very much a "live issue to millions of people across the globe."

9 Concluding Thoughts

1. Even John Macquarrie, who insists that it would mean "the collapse of Christian faith" to abandon the ruling of the Council of Chalcedon (A.D. 451)— that "Jesus Christ is one with God the Father and yet is also one with us human beings"—nevertheless concedes that the gospel birth narratives "are manifestly legendary in character. The stories of apparitions of angels or of the star that led the wise men to Bethlehem, however much they have come to be loved in Christian tradition, have no historical value, and ... very little theological value either" (1990, p. 393; 2003, p. 142). It is significant that not one of the nine

contributors to G.J. Brooke's 2000 symposium on *The Birth of Jesus* makes any attempt to defend the gospel birth and infancy narratives as history. One of them, Arthur Peacocke, concludes that "for Jesus to be fully human he had, for both biological and theological reasons, to have a human father as well as a human mother, and the weight of the historical evidence strongly indicates that this was so" (p. 66). Another contributor, R.B. Matlock, points to the "lateness" of the two narratives, to their "divergence" from each other, and to the obvious ignorance of Paul on the matter, who wrote "perhaps before the Christmas story had come into view at all." Matlock notes that this "heightens the irony of a cultural situation where for many the last remaining personal attachment to the story of Jesus is in the annual celebration of Christmas" (pp. 54, 56).

2. I again quote Macquarrie: "The theologian or preacher has to be honest and to admit that we do not know enough about God's action or even about the mystery of our own humanity to be able to explain what happened on Easter Day." His own view is that "a continuing sense of the presence of Christ . . . had convinced the disciples that in Jesus Christ they had indeed beheld the glory of the Father" (1998, pp. 112f).

3. The social instinct is an adaptation to social conditions, and as such no more mysterious than the countless adaptations familiar from plants and animals. It was (and is) produced by the pressure of hostile forces too strong for the individual to resist, but capable of being defeated by common action. Thus territorial interests, when threatened, promote territorial cohesion, class interests and religious interests promote class- and religious cohesion. The behaviour of mammals (including man) is determined by instincts, by habit, and by rational experiment (the endeavour to adapt means to ends). To claim that all human actions are the outcome of self-interest would be to imply a prevailing rationalism that is in fact uncommon. The impulse of sympathy or attraction, which may be quite devoid of rational basis, is an important factor. In the same manner, the impulse of hatred, equally without rational basis, prompts many actions, both individual and collective. Hatred admittedly often originates from struggle between factions of interest, but it may persist even when the interests have ceased to conflict.

4. From the late eighteenth century British evangelicals campaigned against the evils of industrialization: "Dr.Barnado founded a network of children's homes. The Quaker Elizabeth Fry led in penal reform and prison visiting. Octavia Hill and George Peabody promoted improvements in working-class housing. Hannah More pioneered free schools for the poor." It was recognized that private philanthropy was insufficient, and that "the grossest abuses . . . could be prevented only by legislation." Hence "the campaign of William Wilberforce and his colleagues to ban slavery, and their promotion of factory acts" (Steve Bruce 2002, p. 96). He adds that Wilberforce's successor Anthony

Ashley (Earl of Shaftesbury from 1851), although "a puritanical narrow-minded gloomily devout Evangelical", did sterling work of this kind over many years.

5. Oliver McTernan, a Catholic priest writing from thirty years of experience in the field of conflict resolution, notes that the roots of religious intolerance and militancy "are embedded in the history and sacred texts of each of the world's faiths. Today's extremists can find in their own traditions sufficient texts and in their own religious history sufficient exemplars to justify their adoption of a world view that allows them to annihilate those who think or act differently" (2003, p. 158). The Catholic scholar Eamon Duffy is glad to note that "the age-old insistence of the Church on the obligation of Christian states to enforce and promote the Catholic religion was overturned by the Second Vatican Council's 1965 Declaration on Religious Liberty, which taught clearly and unequivocally that freedom of religious thought and practice was not a matter of pragmatic concession in an imperfect political world, but a fundamental human right." But he also observes that many Catholics have been affronted by this break with "the constant teaching of a millennium and a half of Christian civilization", and have asked: "How could 1,500 years of consistent Catholic teaching and practice on religious freedom be so radically mistaken? Was St. Augustine, was St. Thomas, were the popes who had established the Inquisition and the Index, who had promulgated Bulls permitting torture and the use of force in the service of gospel truth, were these all in error?" (2004, p. 164).

Reservations of this kind influenced—as he himself subsequently admitted—Pope Paul VI's condemnation, in his 1968 encyclical *Humanae Vitae,* of artificial methods of birth control; for although this condemnation went against the majority advice of the commission which he had himself appointed to investigate the matter, to have ruled otherwise would have been to disavow the traditional teaching of the church, which had even been expressly endorsed by his three immediate predecessors, and which condemned such practices on pain of eternal damnation (Details in Küng 1994, pp. 40ff). The ever-increasing world population—it has doubled since the end of World War II—is an obvious source of severe and disastrous conflict.

6. As a Christian priest, Young is understandably discomfited by the evidence he adduces and the conclusions he draws from it. It is not just the Bible that worries him, for "God's creation" is itself violent, full of "disease, suffering and death", mostly "inherent to the structure of the cosmos", so that God must take responsibility for it. "The animal world is intrinsically violent" and lives by predation. Young alludes here (pp. 189f) to Darwin, whose consciousness of all this alienated him from the belief that the world was created by an all powerful and all-loving God. What Young finds so disconcerting is that the Bible seems to make any such belief even more difficult. Jesus's crucifixion,

he says, "presents God as a child abuser and murderer" and raises the "agonising question": "Can anyone believe in such a God? Can a religious tradition with such a central narrative continue to be inhabited by one who has woken up to what it means in human terms?" (p. 185). To regard the scriptures as mere human misrepresentations of God is no answer, for this would make it "difficult, if not impossible", to use them as "guides to the nature of God, let alone to regard them as revelation." On the other hand, to argue that they do not in fact represent God as violent is quite unconvincing. "Even if in some texts the apparent violence of God can be argued away, the general presentation of God as violent is so ubiquitous in the Bible that it is not credible to dispense with it altogether" (pp. 187f). Yet Young cannot abandon the Christian tradition, seriously flawed though it is: that option is "not a real one for those of us who have also found grace and forgiveness and meaning within it". He wants us to "hold God to account", and not believe uncritically all that the Bible says of him, our ideas of him being "provisional and liable to revision" (pp. 192, 194). If we "exercise some form of discrimination" in approaching the texts, then we will find that, in both the Old Testament and the New Testament, there is "a genuine, if often obscured witness to a God who is non-violent and genuinely loving" (pp. 196f).

Epilogue

1. I have given a number of examples in this book of the way in which religious apologists denigrate the Enlightenment and thus continue the attitude prominent in what is known as nineteenth-century European Romanticism. Franz Grillparzer, who claimed to represent common sense viewing German intellectualism at that time from the sidelines of Austria, was very conscious of living when Enlightenment and rational thinking were derided, when Fichte, Schelling, and Hegel were being read instead of Locke and Hume, and when one metaphysical system was rapidly succeeded by another, which equally rapidly became obsolete. Although we need not endorse Schopenhauer's embittered comment that the man who can read Hegel without feeling that he is in a lunatic asylum ought to be in such an institution, we can hardly deny that much writing of that time made for lack of clarity and for pretentious statement. If the Enlightenment writers are generally more intelligible than so many of their successors, it is not because the latter are more profound but because the former try to keep in touch with the concrete. This is precisely what some religious apologists, now as then, have deplored. Thus in the final chapter of their 2008 book on Jesus's Passion and Resurrection, Marcus Borg and J.D. Crossan complain that "in the Enlightenment, Western culture began to identify truth with 'factuality'." Against this, they deliberately leave open the question of the factuality of the Easter stories, and propose that they should be read as conveying a message, as parables do. They instance the stories of the Good Samaritan and the Prodigal Son, where, as everyone agrees, the inci-

dents and personages may well be entirely fictitious. Read as parables, the Easter stories may be seen as embodying "truth claims"; first that "Jesus lives", the truth of which is "grounded in the experience" of those Christians "throughout the centuries" who "have experienced Jesus as a living reality"; and second that God has "vindicated" him and has "said 'no' to the powers that executed him". It is not explained how either claim can be anything more than wishful thinking if the stories may well not be factual. Yet Borg and Crossan cannot here dispense altogether with factuality. Parables such as the stories of the Good Samaritan and the Prodigal Son, aim merely at inculcating certain moral attitudes or certain beliefs about the nature of God, whereas the Easter stories, even in the interpretation of our two authors, claim that, as a matter of fact, God has actually acted in certain ways. Such 'facts' are not of the clear and concrete kind, and are more like those perceived in visions, to which our two authors also, in this context, appeal, saying that visions "can be disclosures of reality". Once contact with the concrete has been lost, the meaning of words becomes indeterminate. It does not follow that such words answer to no persistent plexus of notions in the mind of the user. But without the possibility of reference to the concrete, it is very difficult for anyone else to determine what that plexus is.

Concrete experience is particularly necessary as the basis of generalizations. If these are voiced before a sufficient stock of remembered experiences has been acquired, the result can be that empty verbal formulas are repeated under the impression that these are the true content of ideas. This is why 'teaching children to reason' is a questionable ideal. Apart from needing a good memory (which is hardly likely to be taught if the gift is not present), they need first to be supplied with memories of real events, processes, and physical operations and their results; and this takes time. Knowledge of how conditions and events are correlated is what constitutes science, which is not a method limited to certain restricted spheres of nature which needs to be supplemented with other methods outside those areas.

2. Papias's writings survive only as a few quotations in other authors. Apart from his statement about Mark (cf. above, p. 320), "virtually everything else he says is widely, and rightly, discounted by scholars as pious imagination rather than historical fact" (Ehrman 2006c. p. 9). In his latest book (2009), Ehrman concludes that Papias relied on what was little better than gosspip. He "passes on stories that he has heard, and attributes them to people who knew other people who said so. But when he can be checked, he appears to be wrong" (Ehrman 2009, p. 110).

3. Dunderberg controverts a number of American scholars who have recently argued that the communities behind the canonical gospel of John and the Coptic Gospel of Thomas were in conflict with each other and engaged in mutual debate which is reflected in these two gospels.

4. The scholarship of the Vatican also remains unequivocally hostile to any relaxation of traditional doctrine, as one may see from the Declaration Dominus Jesus of 2000, signed by Cardinal Joseph Ratzinger, Prefect of the Congregation for the Doctrine of the Faith (the ancient Inquisition), now Pope Benedict XVI. The English version, published by the Catholic Truth Society in 2000, states that "Holy Mother Church . . . accepts as sacred and canonical the books of the Old and New Testaments, whole and entire, with all their parts", for, "written under the inspiration of the Holy Spirit, . . . they have God as their author" (pp. 10f). Their teaching is "without error", and this applies even to passages of dubious attestation, to which Ratzinger confidently appeals—as when he twice (pp. 3, 29) quotes, as authentic words of Jesus, the statement in an appendix to Mark that "he who believes and is baptized will be saved; he who does not believe will be condemned" (Mk. 16:16). Believing involves "faith" as "a free assent to the whole truth that God has revealed". It must be distinguished from "belief", which is all that other religions can rise to. Faith involves "the full submission of intellect and will to God", whereas belief is based on human wisdom and is "still in search of the absolute truth" (pp. 9f). To regard reason as the only source of knowledge is mere "subjectivism"—by which is meant relying on one's own investigations instead of accepting what is proclaimed by the one Catholic and Apostolic Church. Other Christian communities are admittedly "true particular Churches" if they have preserved "the valid Episcopate and the genuine and integral substance of the Eucharistic mystery" (otherwise they are "not Churches in the proper sense" at all), but are nevertheless not part of the "single Church of Christ" (pp. 23f). As for other religions, they often contain "a ray of truth which enlightens all men" (pp. 4, 10), but even that ray derives ultimately from "the mystery of Christ" (p. 11). "No one . . . can enter into communion with God except through Christ, by the working of the Holy Spirit" (p. 17).

According to L. Boff, "this document provoked utter outrage both inside and outside the Roman Catholic Church" (2006, pp 9f). Nevertheless, Ratzinger insists that what the document specifies is binding on Catholics, and so "must be firmly believed"—a phrase he reiterates in italics throughout.

Bibliography

Allingham, W. 1907. *A Diary.* Edited by H. Allingham and D. Radford. London: Macmillan.

Allison, D.C. Jr. 1992. Peter and Cephas: One and the Same. *Journal of Biblical Literature,* 111, 489–495.

———. 1997. *The Jesus Tradition in Q.* Harrisburg: Trinity International.

———. 1998. *Jesus of Nazareth: Millenarian Prophet.* Minneapolis: Fortress.

———. 2003. The Eschatology of Jesus. In McGinn et al. 2003, 139–165.

———. 2005. *Resurrecting Jesus: The Earliest Christian Tradition and Its Interpreters.* New York: Clark.

Anderson, H. 1976. *The Gospel of Mark* (New Century Bible). London: Oliphants.

Andreski, S. 1972. *Social Sciences as Sorcery.* London: Deutsch.

Ashton, J. 1991. *Understanding the Fourth Gospel.* Oxford: Clarendon.

Austin, J. 1996. Review of Crossan 1991 in *Lexington Theological Quarterly,* 31, 145.

Avis, P., ed. 1993. *The Resurrection of Jesus Christ.* London: Darton, Longman, and Todd.

Badham, P. 1978. *Christian Beliefs about Life After Death.* London: SPCK.

———. 1993. The Meaning of the Resurrection of Jesus. In Avis 1993, 23–38.

Baker, T. 1975. See Morna Hooker et al. 1975, 187–197.

Bammel, E., ed. 1970. *The Trial of Jesus.* London: SCM.

———. 1984. The Revolution Theory from Reimarus to Brandon. In Bammel and Moule 1984, 11–68.

Bammel, E., and C.F.D. Moule, eds. 1984. *Jesus and the Politics of His Day.* Cambridge: Cambridge University Press.

Barnikol, E. 1998. The Non-Pauline Origin of the Parallelism of the Apostles Peter and Paul. Galatians 2:7–8. English translation of the German of 1931. *Journal* of *Higher Criticism,* 5:2, 285–300.

Barr, J. 1981. *Fundamentalism.* Second edition. London: SCM.

———. 1983. *Holy Scripture: Canon, Authority, Criticism.* Oxford: Clarendon.

———. 1993. *Biblical Faith and Natural Theology.* Oxford: Clarendon.

Barrett, C.K. 1975. *The Gospel of John and Judaism*. London: SPCK.

Barry, F.R. 1965. *Questioning Faith*. London: SCM.

Barth, K. 1956. *The Doctrine of Reconciliation*. Volume 4, Part 1 of *Church Dogmatics*, edited by G.W. Bromily and T.F. Torrance. Edinburgh: Clark.

———. 1972. *Protestant Theology in the Nineteenth Century*. English translation of the German of 1947. London: SCM.

Barton, J. 2007. *The Nature of Biblical Criticism*. Louisville: Westminster John Knox Press.

Barton, S., and G. Stanton, eds. 1994. *The Resurrection: Essays in Honour of Leslie Houlden*. London: SPCK.

Batey, R., ed. 1970. *New Testament Issues*. London: SCM.

Bauckham, R. 2001. The Future of Jesus Christ. In *The Cambridge Companion to Jesus*, edited by M. Bockmuehl. Cambridge: Cambridge University Press, 265–280.

———. 2006. *Jesus and the Eyewitnesses: The Gospels as Eyewitness Testimony*. Grand Rapids: Eerdmans.

Bauckham, R., and T. Hart. 1999. *Hope Against Hope: Christian Eschatology in Contemporary Context*. London: Darton, Longman, and Todd.

Beare, F.W. 1964. *The Earliest Records of Jesus*. Oxford: Blackwell.

———. 1970. Concerning Jesus of Nazareth. In Batey 1970, 57–70.

———. 1973. *A Commentary on the Epistle to the Philippians*. Third edition. London: Black.

———. 1981. *The Gospel According to Matthew: A Commentary*. Oxford: Blackwell.

Bernheim, P.A. 1997. *James, Brother of Jesus*. English translation from the French of 1996. London: SCM.

Bezzant, J.S. 1963. Intellectual Objections. In *Objections to Christian Belief* by several hands, with an introduction by A.R. Vidler. London: Constable, 79–111.

Blomberg, C., and D. Wenham, eds. 1986. *The Miracles of Jesus*. Volume 6 of *Gospel Perspectives*. Sheffield: JSOT.

Boff, L. 2006. *Fundamentalism, Terrorism, and the Future of Humanity*. London: SPCK.

Boone, Kathleen C. 1990. *The Bible Tells Them So: The Discourse of Protestant Fundamentalism*. London: SCM.

Borg, M. 1994. *Jesus in Contemporary Scholarship*. Valley Forge: Trinity International.

Borg, M., and J.D. Crossan. 2008. *The Last Week*. London: SPCK.

Boring, M.E. 1991. *The Continuing Voice of Jesus: Christian Prophecy and the Gospel Tradition*. Louisville: Westminster.

Boslooper, T. 1962. *The Virgin Birth*. London: SCM.

Bowden, J. 1988. *Jesus: The Unanswered Questions*. London: SCM.

Boyer, P. 2003. The Growth of Fundamentalist Apocalyptic in the United States. In McGinn et al. 2003, 516–544.

Bradshaw, P.F. 2002. *The Search for the Origins of Christian Worship.* Revised and enlarged edition, London: SPCK.
Braun, H. 1971. Vom Verstehen des Neuen Testaments. In *Gesammelte Studien zum Neuen Testament und seiner Umwelt.* Third edition. Tubingen: Mohr, 283–298.
Brooke, G.J., ed. 2000. *The Birth of Jesus: Biblical and Theological Reflections.* Edinburgh: Clark.
Brown, R.E. 1970. The Kerygma of the Gospel According to John. In Batey 1970, 210–225.
———. 1979. *The Birth of the Messiah.* Garden City: Image.
———. 1994. *The Death of the Messiah* (Anchor Bible Reference Library). Two volumes with continuous pagination. London: Chapman.
Bruce, F.F. 1952. *The Acts of the Apostles.* Second edition. London: Tyndale.
Bruce, S. 1995. *Religion in Modern Britain.* Oxford: Oxford University Press.
———. 2002. *God Is Dead: Secularization in the West.* Oxford: Blackwell.
Bryan, C. 1993. *A Preface to Mark: Notes on the Gospel in Its Literary and Cultural Settings.* New York: Oxford University Press.
Bultmann, R. 1960. *Jesus Christ and Mythology.* London: SCM.
———. 1963. *The History of the Synoptic Tradition.* Oxford: Blackwell.
———. 1968. *Theologie des Neuen Testaments.* Sixth edition. Tubingen: Mohr.
———. 1972. New Testament Mythology. In *Kerygma and Myth,* edited by H.W. Bartsch and R.H. Fuller. London: SPCK, Volume 1, 1–44.
Burger, C. 1970. *Jesus als Davidssohn.* Gottingen: Vandenhoeck and Ruprecht.
Burkitt, F.C. 1924. *Christian Beginnings.* London: University of London Press.
Byrne, P. and L. Houlden, eds. 1995. *Companion Encyclopedia of Theology.* London: Routledge.
Cadbury, H.J. 1937. *The Peril of Modernizing Jesus.* New York: Macmillan.
Caird, G.B. 1963. *Saint Luke.* London: Penguin.
———. 1980. *The Language and Imagery of the Bible.* London: Duckworth.
Campenhausen, H. von. 1964. *The Virgin Birth in the Theology of the Ancient Church.* English translation of the German of 1962. London: SCM.
Cane, A. 2005. *The Place of Judas Iscariot in Christology.* Aldershot: Ashgate.
Carnley, P. 1987. *The Structure of Resurrection Belief.* Oxford: Clarendon.
Carrier, R.C. 2005. The Spiritual Body of Christ and the Legend of the Empty Tomb. In Price et al. 2005, 105–231.
Casey, M. 1996. *Is John's Gospel True?* London: Routledge.
Catchpole, D.R. 1993. *The Quest for Q.* Edinburgh: Clark.
Chadwick, H. 1965. See Origen 1965.
———. 1966. *Early Christian Thought and the Classical Tradition.* Oxford: Clarendon.
Cheyne, T.K. and J.S. Black, eds. 1899. *Encyclopaedia Biblica.* London: Black.
Chilton, B. and C.A. Evans, eds. 1994. *Studying the Historical Jesus.* Leiden: Brill.

Collins, J.J. 1992. The Son of Man in First-Century Judaism. *New Testament Studies*, 38, 448–466.

———. 1997. *Apocalypticism in the Dead Sea Scrolls.* London: Routledge.

———. 2003. From Prophecy to Apocalypticism: The Expectation of the End. In McGinn et al. 2003, 64–88.

Cox, S. 2006. *The New Testament and Literature.* Chicago: Open Court.

Creed, J.M. 1930. *The Gospel According to St. Luke.* London: Macmillan.

Crossan, J.D. 1991. *The Historical Jesus: The Life of a Mediterranean Jewish Peasant.* Edinburgh: Clark.

Crossley, J.G. 2004. *The Date of Mark's Gospel: Insight from the Law in Earliest Christianity.* London and New York: Continuum, Clark International.

———. 2005. Against the Historical Plausibility of the Empty Tomb Story and the Bodily Resurrection of Jesus: A Response to N.T. Wright. *Journal for the Study of the Historical Jesus*, 3, 171–186.

———. 2006. *Why Christianity Happened.* Louisville: Westminster John Knox.

Davies, W.D. and D.C. Allison. 1988 and 1991. *A Critical and Exegetical Commentary on the Gospel According to St. Matthew.* Two volumes. Edinburgh: Clark.

Dempster, M.W. et al., eds. 1999. *The Globalization of Pentecostalism.* Oxford: Regnum.

Dibelius, M. 1956. *Studies in Acts.* English translation. London: SCM.

Dodd, C.H. 1932. The Framework of the Gospel Narrative. *Expository Times*, 43, 395–400.

———. 1968. *More New Testament Studies.* Manchester: Manchester University Press.

———. 1970. *The Interpretation of the Fourth Gospel.* Cambridge: Cambridge University Press.

———. 1971. *The Founder of Christianity.* London: Collins.

Doherty, E. 1999. *The Jesus Puzzle: Did Christianity Begin with a Mythical Christ?* Ottawa: Canadian Humanist Publications.

Downing, F.G. 2000. Deeper Reflections on the Cynic Jesus. In Downing's *Making Sense in (and of) the First Christian Century.* Sheffield: Sheffield Academic Press, 122–133.

Duffy, E. 2004. *Faith of Our Fathers: Reflections on Catholic Tradition.* London: Continuum.

Dunderberg, Ismo. 2006. *The Beloved Disciple in Conflict?* Oxford: Oxford University Press.

Dunn, J.D.G. 1985a. *The Evidence for Jesus.* London: SCM.

———. 1985b. Demythologizing: The Problem of Myth in the New Testament. In Marshall 1985, 285–307.

———. 1989. *Christology in the Making.* Second edition. London: SCM.

———. 2006. *Unity and Diversity in the New Testament*. Third edition. London: SCM.
Du Toit, D.S. 2001. Redefining Jesus: Current Trends in Jesus Research. In Labahn and Schmidt 2001, 82–124.
Eddy, P.R. and G.A. Boyd, 2007. *The Jesus Legend: A Case for the Historical Reliability of the Synoptic Jesus Tradition*. Grand Rapids, Michigan: Baker Academic.
Edwards, Ruth. 2003. *Discovering John*. London: SPCK.
Ehrman, B.D. 1990. Cephas and Peter. *Journal of Biblical Literature*, 109, 463–474.
———. 1993. *The Orthodox Corruption of Scripture*. New York: Oxford University Press.
———. 1999. *Jesus: Apocalyptic Prophet of the New Millennium*. Oxford: Oxford University Press.
———. 2000. *The New Testament: A Historical Introduction to the Early Christian Writings*. New York: Oxford University Press.
———. 2003. *Lost Christianities: The Battles for Scripture and the Faiths We Never Knew*. Oxford: Oxford University Press.
———. 2006a. *Whose Word Is It? The Story Behind Who Changed the New Testament and Why*. London: Continuum.
———. 2006b. *The Lost Gospel of Judas Iscariot*. Oxford: Oxford University Press.
———. 2006c. *Peter, Paul, and Mary Magdalene*. Oxford: Oxford University Press.
———. 2009. *Jesus, Interrupted: Revealing the Hidden Contradictions in the Bible (And Why We Don't Know about Them)*. New York: Harper Collins.
Ellegård, A. 1958. *Darwin and the General Reader*. Goteborg: Elanders.
———. 1993. Theologians as Historians. *Scandia*, 59, 169–204.
Elliott, J.K. 1982. *Questioning Christian Origins*. London: SCM.
———. 1993. *The Language and Style of the Gospel of Mark: An Edition of CH. Turner's 'Notes on Marcan Usage' Together With Other Comparable Studies*. Leiden: Brill.
Ellis, E.E. 1966. *The Gospel of Luke* (New Century Bible). London: Nelson.
Elwell, W.A., ed. 1996. *Evangelical Dictionary of Biblical Theology*. Carlisle: Paternoster; Grand Rapids: Baker.
Enslin, M.S. 1940. The Christian Story of the Nativity. *Journal of Biblical Literature*, 59, 317–338.
———. 1975. John and Jesus. *Zeitschrift für neutestamentliche Wissenschaft*, 66, 1–18.
Ericksen, R.P. 1985. *Theologians Under Hitler*. New Haven: Yale University Press.
Esler, P.F. 1994. *The First Christians and Their Social Worlds*. London: Routledge.
Evans, C.A. 2007. *Fabricating Jesus. How Modern Scholars Distort the Gospels*. Nottingham: Inter-Varsity Press.

Evans, C.F. 1968. *The Beginning of the Gospel.* London: SPCK.

———. 1970. *Resurrection and the New Testament.* London: SCM.

———. 1971. *Is 'Holy Scripture' Christian? And Other Questions.* London: SCM. Reissued in 1994 by Xpress Reprints.

———. 1977. *Explorations in Theology* 2. London: SCM.

———. 1990. *Saint Luke.* London: SCM and Philadelphia: Trinity International.

Feldman, L.H. 1984. *Josephus and Modern Scholarship, 1937–1980.* Berlin: De Gruyter.

Fenton, J. 2001. *More about Mark.* London: SPCK.

Fitzmyer, J.A. 1986. *The Gospel According to Luke* (Anchor Bible Series). Second edition. Garden City: Doubleday (Volume 1 is quoted unless Volume 2 is indicated).

Flynn, Tom, ed. 2008. *The New Encyclopedia of Unbelief.* Amherst: Prometheus.

France, R.T. 1986. *The Evidence for Jesus.* London: Hodder and Stoughton.

———. 2002. *The Gospel of Mark: A Commentary on the Greek Text.* Grand Rapids: Eerdmans; Carlisle: Paternoster Press.

Francis, L.J. and P. Richter. 2007. *Gone for Good? Church-Leaving and Returning in the 21st Century.* Peterborough: Epworth.

Franklin, E. 1994. *How the Critics Can Help: A Guide to the Practical Use of the Gospels.* London: Xpress reprints. Originally SCM, 1982.

Frei, H. 1985. David Friedrich Strauss. In Smart et al. 1985, 215–260.

Frend, W.H.C. 1965. *Martyrdom and Persecution in the Early Church.* Oxford: Blackwell.

Fuller, R.H. 1972. *The Formation of the Resurrection Narratives.* London: SPCK.

Funk, R. 1996. *Honest to Jesus: Jesus for a New Millennium.* New York: Macmillan.

Furlong, A. 2003. *Tried for Heresy: A 21st-Century Journey of Faith.* Winchester: O Books.

Furnish, V.P. 1968. *Theology and Ethics in Paul.* Nashville: Abingdon.

Garcia Martinez, F. See Martinez.

Gilchrist, J.M. 2007. *Jesus! What Was That? A Critical Look at the Resurrection.* Cambridge: Blue Ocean.

Glasson, T.F. 1980. *Jesus and the End of the World.* Edinburgh: St. Andrew's Press.

Goodacre, M. 2001. *The Synoptic Problem.* London: Sheffield Academic Press.

Goodspeed, E.J. 1931. *Strange New Gospels.* Chicago: University of Chicago Press.

Goulder, M.D. 2004. Did Peter Ever Go to Rome? *Scottish Journal of Theology,* 57, 377–396.

Grant, F.C. 1959. *The Gospels: Their Origin and Growth.* London: Faber and Faber. Also New York, 1957, Harper.

Grant F.C. and H.H. Rowley, eds. 1963. *Dictionary of the Bible.* Second edition. Edinburgh: Clark.
Grant, M. 1977. *Jesus.* London: Weidenfeld and Nicolson.
Graves, R. 1958. *The Greek Myths.* London: Cassell.
Guenther, H.O. 1985. *The Footprints of Jesus' Twelve in Early Christian Traditions.* New York: Lang.
———. 1992. The Sayings Gospel Q and the Quest for Aramaic Sources. In *Early Christianity, Q, and Jesus,* edited by J.S. Kloppenborg and L.E. Vaage. Atlanta: Scholars, 41–76.
Guignebert, C. 1935. *Jesus.* English translation from the French. London: Kegan Paul.
———. 1968. *The Christ.* English translation. New York: New York University Press.
Haenchen, E. 1968. *Der Weg Jesu.* Second edition. Berlin: De Gruyter.
———. 1971. *The Acts of the Apostles.* English translation of the 1965 German edition. Oxford: Blackwell.
———. 1977. *Die Apostelgeschichte.* Seventh (posthumous) edition. Göttingen: Vandenhoeck and Ruprecht.
———. 1980. *Das Johannesevangelium.* Tübingen: Mohr.
Hanson, R.P.C. 1975. The Authority of the Christian Faith. In *Theology and Change,* edited by R.H. Preston. London: SCM, 104–127.
Hanson, R.P.C. and A.T. Hanson. 1980. *Reasonable Belief.* London: Oxford University Press.
Hare, D.R.A. 1967. *The Theme of Jewish Persecution of Christians in the Gospel According to St. Matthew.* Cambridge: Cambridge University Press.
Harries, R. 1987. *Christ Is Risen.* London: Mowbray. Connecticut: Morehouse-Barlow.
Harris, H. 1973. *David Friedrich Strauss and His Theology.* Cambridge: Cambridge University Press.
Harris, M.J. 1985. *Easter in Durham.* Exeter: Paternoster.
Harvey, A.E. 1970. *The New English Bible Companion to the New Testament.* Oxford and Cambridge University Presses.
———. 1982. *Jesus and the Constraints of History.* London: Duckworth.
———. 1993. Review of Crossan 1991 in *Journal of Theological Studies,* 44, 226–28.
Hatch, E. 1895. *The Influence of Greek Ideas and Usages upon the Christian Church* (Hibbert Lectures of 1888). Fifth edition. London: Williams and Norgate.
Hennecke, E. 1973. *New Testament Apocrypha.* Volume 1, edited by W. Schneemelcher. English translation of the German of 1959. London: SCM.
———. 1965. Volume 2 of the above, edited by R.McL. Wilson. English translation of the German of 1964. London: Lutterworth.
Hick, J. 1985. *Death and Eternal Life.* London: Macmillan.
Hillerbrand, H.J. 1967. *A Fellowship of Discontent.* New York: Harper and Row.

Holloway, R. 2004. *Looking in the Distance: The Human Search for Meaning.* Edinburgh: Canongate.

Hooker, Morna D. 1981. Beyond the Things that Are Written? St.Paul's Use of Scripture. *New Testament Studies,* 27, 295–309.

———. 1983. *The Message of Mark.* London: Epworth.

Hooker, Morna D. et al., eds. 1975. *What about the New Testament?* London: SCM. Includes U. Simon, 'The Multidimensional Picture of Jesus', 116–126; M. Wiles, The Uses of 'Holy Scripture', 155–164; T. Baker, 'New Testament Scholarship and Liturgical Revision', 187–197.

Hoskyns, E. and N. Davey. 1958. *The Riddle of the New Testament.* First published in 1931. London: Faber and Faber.

Houlden, L. 1986. *Connections: The Integration of Theology and Faith.* London: SCM.

———. 1993. The Resurrection: History, Story and Belief. In Avis 1993, 50–67.

———. 2000. The Humble Role of New Testament Scholarship. In *Theological Liberalism,* edited by Jeannine Jobling and I. Markham. London: SPCK, 31–42.

———. 2002. *The Strange Story of the Gospels.* London: SPCK.

———. 2004. *Ethics and the New Testament.* London: Clark.

———. 2006. The Finger of God. *Theology,* 109 (no. 850), 273–281.

Houlden, L., ed. 2005. *Jesus: The Complete Guide.* London: Continuum.

Hurtado, L. 1999. *At the Origins of Christian Worship.* Carlisle: Paternoster.

———. 2005. *How on Earth Did Jesus Become a God?* Grand Rapids: Eerdmans.

Huxley, T.H. 1900. *Scripture and Christian Tradition.* London: Macmillan.

Jacobson, A.D. 1992. *The First Gospel: An Introduction to Q.* Sonoma: Polebridge Press.

James, W. 1902. *The Varieties of Religious Experience.* Garden City: Doubleday. No date.

Jeffery, C. and P. Dunn. No date. *Fatima: A Story of Hope.* Woking: Gresham Press.

Jenkins, D. 1967. *The Glory of Man.* London: SCM.

———. 1976. *The Contradiction of Christianity.* London: SCM.

———. 1986. Re-Searching the Question of God. In *In Search of Christianity,* edited by T. Moss. London: Firethorn, 82–95.

John, J. 2001. *The Meaning in the Miracles.* Norwich: Canterbury Press.

Johnson, L.T. 2003. *The Creed: What Christians Believe and Why It Matters.* London: Darton, Longman, and Todd.

Johnson, M.D. 1969. *The Purpose of the Biblical Genealogies.* Cambridge: Cambridge University Press.

Käsemann, E. 1964. *Essays on New Testament Themes.* London: SCM.

Keck, L.E. 2000. *Who Is Jesus?* Columbia: University of South Carolina Press.

Kee, H.C. 1977. *Community of the New Age: Studies in Mark's Gospel.* London: SCM.

———. 1983. *Miracle in the Early Christian Church.* New Haven: Yale University Press.

Kent, J. 1982. *The End of the Line? The Development of Christian Theology in the Last Two Centuries.* London: SCM.

———. 1987. *The Unacceptable Face: The Modern Church in the Eyes of the Historian.* London: SCM.

———. 1992. *William Temple.* Cambridge: Cambridge University Press.

Klassen, W. 1996. *Judas. Betrayer or Friend of Jesus?* London: SCM.

———. 2002. The Authenticity of Judas' Participation in the Arrest of Jesus. In B. Chilton and C.A. Evans, eds, *Authenticating the Activities of Jesus.* Leiden: Brill, 389–410.

Kloppenborg, Verbin, J.S. 1987. *The Formation of Q: Trajectories in Ancient Wisdom Collections.* Philadelphia: Fortress.

———. 2000. *Excavating Q.* Fortress Press edition. Edinburgh: Clark.

Koester, H. 1990. *Ancient Christian Gospels.* London: SCM. Philadelphia: Trinity International.

Kümmel, W.G. 1973. *The New Testament: The History of the Investigation of Its Problems.* English translation of the German of 1970. London: SCM.

———. 1975. *Introduction to the New Testament.* English translation of the revised seventeenth German edition. London: SCM.

Küng, H. 1976. *Christ Sein.* Zurich: Buchclub Ex Libris.

———. 1994. *Infallible?* A new expanded edition. London: SCM.

Labahn, M. and A. Schmidt, eds. 2001. *Jesus, Mark, and Q: The Teaching of Jesus and Its Earliest Records.* Sheffield: Sheffield Acadamic Press.

Lampe, G.W.H. 1966. *The Resurrection: A Dialogue Arising from Broadcasts by G.W.H. Lampe and D.M. Mackinnon,* edited by W. Purcell. London: Mowbray.

———. 1984. A.D. 70 in Christian Reflection. In Bammel and Moule 1984, 153–171.

Lane Fox, R. 1991. *The Unauthorized Version: Truth and Fiction in the Bible.* London: Viking.

Lieu, Judith et al., eds. 1992. *The Jews among Pagans and Christians in the Roman Empire.* London: Routledge.

Lieu, Judith. 1992. History and Theology in Christian Views of Judaism. In Lieu et al. 1992, 79–96.

Lightfoot, R.H. 1935. *History and Interpretation in the Gospels.* London: Hodder and Stoughton.

———. 1952. *The Gospel Message of St. Mark.* Corrected from the first edition of 1950. Oxford: Clarendon.

Lindars, B. 1961. *New Testament Apologetic.* London: SCM.

———. 1971. *Behind the Fourth Gospel.* London: SPCK.

———. 1972. *The Gospel of John* (New Century Bible). London: Oliphants.
Lindsey, H. 1974. *Satan Is Alive and Well on Planet Earth*. New York: Bantam.
Lüdemann, G. 2001. *Paulus der Gründer des Christentums*. Lüneburg: Zu Klampen.
Luz, U. 1995. *The Theology of the Gospel of Matthew*. Cambridge: Cambridge University Press.
Lyons, W.J. 2004. On the Life and Death of Joseph of Arimathea. *Journal for the Study of the Historical Jesus*, 2, 29–53.
Macchia, F.D. 1999. The Struggle for Global Witness: Shifting Paradigms in Pentecostal Theology. In Dempster et al. 1999, 8–29.
Mack, B.L. 1993. *The Lost Gospel: The Book of Q and Christian Origins*. Shaftesbury: Element.
Mackey, J.P. 1987. *Modern Theology*. Oxford: Oxford University Press.
Macquarrie, J. 1990. *Jesus Christ in Modern Thought*. London: SCM. Philadelphia: Trinity International.
———. 1998. *Christology Revisited*. London: SCM.
———. 2003. *Stubborn Theological Questions*. London: SCM.
Manson, T.W. 1956. The Life of Jesus: Some Tendencies in Present–Day Research. In *The Background of the New Testament and Its Eschatology*, edited by W.D. Davies and D. Daube (C.H. Dodd Festschrift). Cambridge: Cambridge University Press, 211–221.
Marshall, I.H., ed. 1985. *New Testament Interpretation*. Exeter: Paternoster.
Martinez, F. Garcia. 2003. Apocalypticism in the Dead Sea Scrolls. In McGinn et al. 2003, 89–111.
Marty, M.E. 1985. Hell Disappeared. No One Noticed. *Harvard Theological Review*, 78, 381–398.
Matlock, R.B. 2000. The Birth of Jesus and Why Paul Was in Favour of It. In Brooke 2000, 47–57.
McCown, C.C. 1941. Gospel Geography: Fiction, Fact, and Truth. *Journal of Biblical Literature*, 60, 1–25.
McGinn, B.J. et al., eds. 2003. *The Continuum History of Apocalypticism*. New York: Continuum.
McTernan, O. 2003. *Violence in God's Name*. London: Darton, Longman, and Todd.
Meagher, J.C. 1979. *Clumsy Construction in Mark's Gospel: A Critique of Form- and Redaktionsgeschichte* (Toronto Studies in Theology, Volume 3). New York: Mellen.
Meier, J.P. 1991. *A Marginal Jew: Rethinking the Historical Jesus*. Volume 1 (Anchor Bible Reference Library). New York: Doubleday.
———. 1999. The Present State of the 'Third Quest' for the Historical Jesus. *Biblica*, 80, 459–487.
Metzger, B. 1971. *A Textual Commentary on the Greek New Testament*. London: United Bible Societies.

———. 1987. *The Canon of the New Testament: Its Origin, Development, and Significance.* Oxford: Clarendon.
Metzger, B. and M. Coogan, eds. 1993. *The Oxford Companion to the Bible.* New York: Oxford University Press.
Miethe, T.L., ed. 1987. *Did Jesus Rise From the Dead? The Resurrection Debate Between Gary R. Habermas and Antony Flew.* San Francisco: Harper and Row.
Milgram, S. 1974. *Obedience to Authority.* London: Tavistock.
Mitton, C.L. 1975. *Jesus: The Fact Behind the Faith.* London: Mowbray (First published, Eerdmans, 1973).
Montefiore, H. 2005. *The Miracles of Jesus.* London: SPCK.
Moody Smith, D. 1984. *Johannine Christianity.* Columbia: University of South Carolina Press.
———. 1986. *John.* Second edition. Philadelphia: Fortress.
———. 1995. *The Theology of the Gospel of John.* Cambridge: Cambridge University Press.
Moorhead, J.H. 2003. Apocalypticism in Modern Protestantism, 1800 to the Present. In McGinn et al. 2003, 467–492.
Morgan, R. 1970. 'Nothing More Negative' . . . A Concluding Unscientific Postscript to Historical Research on the Trial of Jesus. In Bammel 1970, 135–146.
———. 1973. See Wrede 1897.
Moule, C.F.D., ed. 1965a. *Miracles. Cambridge Studies in their Philosophy and History.* London: Mowbray.
Moule, C.F.D. 1965b. *The Gospel According to Mark.* Cambridge: Cambridge University Press.
Nickelsburg, G.W.E. 1981. *Jewish Literature between the Bible and the Mishnah.* London: SCM.
Niederwimmer, K. 1967. Johannes Markus und die Frage nach dem Verfasser des zweiten Evangeliums. *Zeitscbritt für neutestamentliche Wissenschaft*, 58, 172–188.
Nineham, D.E. 1963. *The Gospel of Mark.* London: Penguin.
———. 1976. *The Use and Abuse of the Bible.* London: Macmillan.
———. 1977. *Explorations in Theology* 1. London: SCM. Includes: 'The Order of Events in Mark's Gospel' (7–23); 'Eyewitness Testimony and the Gospel Tradition' (24–60); 'Schweitzer Revisited' (112–133).
———. 2000. Foreword to J. Bowden's edition of Schweitzer's *The Quest* (see Schweitzer, 2000), ix–xxx.
Nongbri, B. 2005. The Use and Abuse of P^{52}. *Harvard Theological Review*, 98, 23–48.
North, G. 1990. *The Hoax of Higher Criticism.* Tyler: Dominion.
O'Collins, G. 2003. *Easter Faith.* London: Darton, Longman, and Todd.
O'Neill, J.C. 1991. *The Bible's Authority: A Portrait Gallery of Thinkers from Lessing to Bultmann.* Edinburgh: Clark.

Origen. 1965. *Contra Celsum*. Translated with an introduction and notes by H. Chadwick. Cambridge: Cambridge University Press.

Overbeck, F. 1974. *Über die Christlichkeit unserer heutigen Theologie*. Darmstadt: Wissenschaftliche Buchgesellschaft. Reprint of the second edition of 1903.

Pagels, Elaine. 1991. The Social History of Satan. *Harvard Theological Review*, 84, 105–128.

———. 2003. *Beyond Belief: The Secret Gospel of Thomas*. London: Macmillan; New York: Random House.

Pannenberg, W. 1972. *The Apostles' Creed in the Light of Today's Questions*. English translation of the German of 1972. London: SCM.

———. 1987. Response to the Debate. In Miethe 1987, 125–135.

Parrinder, G. 1992. *Son of Joseph: The Parentage of Jesus*. Edinburgh: Clark.

Peacocke, A. 2000. DNA of our DNA. In Brooke 2000, 59–67.

Perkins, Pheme. 1994. The Resurrection of Jesus of Nazareth. In Chilton and Evans 1994, 423–42.

———. 2000. *Peter: Apostle for the Whole Church*. Edinburgh: Clark.

Perrin, N. 1970. *What Is Redaction Criticism?* London: SPCK.

Polkinghorne, J. 1992. *The Way the World Is*. London: Triangle, SPCK.

———. 2002. Eschatological Credibility: Emergent and Teleological Processes. In T. Peters et al., eds. *Resurrection: Theological and Scientific Assessments*. Grand Rapids, 43–55.

Pomykala, K.E. 1995. *The Davidic Dynasty Tradition in Early Judaism*. Atlanta: Scholars Press.

Price, R.M. 1995. Apocryphal Apparitions: 1 Corinthians 15:3–11 as a Post-Pauline Interpolation. *Journal of Higher Criticism*, 2:2, 69–99. Reprinted in Price et al. 2005, 69–104.

Price, R.M., et al., eds. 2005. *The Empty Tomb: Jesus Beyond the Grave*. Amherst: Prometheus.

Prickett, S. 1995. The Bible as Holy Book. In Byrne and Houlden 1995, 142–159.

Räisänen, H. 1987. *Paul and the Law*. Second, revised edition. Tübingen: Mohr.

———. 1990. *The 'Messianic Secret' in Mark's Gospel*. Edinburgh: Clark.

———. 1995. The New Testament in Theology. In Byrne and Houlden 1995, 122–141.

———. 2000. *Beyond New Testament Theology*. Second edition, London: SCM.

Ratzinger, J. 2007. *Jesus of Nazareth*. English translation of the German. London: Bloomsbury.

Reimarus, H.S. 1970. *The Goal of Jesus and His Disciples*. Introduction and English translation by G.W. Buchanan. Leiden: Brill.

Reiser, M. 1984. *Syntax und Stil des Markusevangeliums*. Tübingen: Mohr.

———. 2001. Eschatology in the Proclamation of Jesus. In Labahn and Schmidt 2001, 216–238.

Richardson, P. and J.C. Hurd, eds. 1984. *From Jesus to Paul*. Studies in Honour of F.W. Beare. Waterloo, Ontario: W. Laurier University Press.

Robertson, J.M. 1910. *Christianity and Mythology*. Second edition. London: Watts.

———. 1916. *The Historical Jesus: A Survey of Positions*. London: Watts.

———. 1924. *Ernest Renan*. London: Watts.

———. 1925. *Gibbon*. London: Watts.

Robinson, James M., et al., eds. 2001. *The Sayings Gospel Q in Greek and English*. Leuven: Peeters. The Introduction (11–72) and the English translation are by Robinson.

Robinson, John A.T. 1963. *Honest to God*. London: SCM.

———. 1973. *The Human Face of God*. London: SCM.

———. 1976. *Redating the New Testament*. London: SCM.

Rogerson, J. 1984. *Old Testament Criticism in the Nineteenth Century. England and Germany*. London: SPCK.

Russell, D.S. 1971. *The Method and Message of Jewish Apocalyptic*. London: SCM.

Sanders, E.P. and M. Davies. 1989. *Studying the Synoptic Gospels*. London: SCM; Philadelphia: Trinity International.

Sanders, E.P. 1985. *Jesus and Judaism*. London: SCM.

———. 1993a. *The Historical Figure of Jesus*. London: Lane.

———. 1993b. The Life of Jesus. In *Christianity and Rabbinic Judaism,* edited by H. Shanks. London: SPCK; Washington DC: Biblical Archaeological Society, 41–83.

Sandmel, S. 1965. *We Jews and Jesus*. London: Gollancz.

———. 1970. Prolegomena to a Commentary on Mark. In Batey 1970, 45–56.

Schmidt, K.L. 1919. *Der Rahmen der Geschichte Jesu*. Berlin. Photographic reprint 1964. Darmstadt: Wissenschaftliche Buchgesellschaft. There is no English translation, but brief quotations are given in English in Kümmel 1973.

———. 1923. Die Stellung der Evangelien in der allgemeinen Literaturgeschichte. In *Eucharisterion*. Festschrift for H. Gunkel, edited by H. Schmidt, Volume 2. Göttingen: Vandenhoeck and Ruprecht, 70–90.

Schmithals, W. 1971. *The Office of Apostle in the Early Church*. English translation. London: SPCK.

Schneemelcher, W. 1965. Apostle and Apostolic. In Hennecke 1965, 25–31.

Schramm, T. 1971. *Der Markus-Stoff bei Lukas*. Cambridge: Cambridge University Press.

Schürer, E. 1973. *The History of the Jewish People in the Age of Jesus Christ*. New English version revised and edited by G. Vermes and F. Millar. Volume 1. Edinburgh: Clark.

Schweitzer, A. 1913. *Geschichte der Leben-Jesu Forschung*. Tübingen: Mohr.

———. 1954. *The Quest of the Historical Jesus* (English translation of *Von Reimarus zu Wrede,* 1906). Third English edition. London: Black.

———. 1968. *The Kingdom of God and Primitive Christianity.* London: Black.

———. 2000. *The Quest of the Historical Jesus.* First complete English edition. Edited by J. Bowden. London: SCM.

Schweizer, E. 1971. *The Good News According to Mark.* English translation, London: SPCK.

Scobie, C.H.H. 1964. *John the Baptist.* London: SCM.

Shanks, H. and B. Witherington III. 2003. *The Brother of Jesus.* London: Continuum.

Shaw, G. 1983. *The Cost of Authority: Manipulation and Freedom in the New Testament.* London: SCM.

Sim, D. 1996. *Apocalyptic Eschatology in the Gospel of Matthew.* Cambridge: Cambridge University Press.

———. 1998. *The Gospel of Matthew and Christian Judaism.* Edinburgh: Clark.

Smart, N., et al., eds. 1985. *Nineteenth Century Religious Thought in the West.* Volume 1. Cambridge: Cambridge University Press.

Stanton, G.N. 1992. *A Gospel for a New People: Studies in Matthew.* Edinburgh: Clark.

———. 2002. *The Gospels and Jesus.* Second edition. Oxford: Oxford University Press.

———. 2004. *Jesus and Gospel.* Cambridge: Cambridge University Press.

Steele, D.R. 2008. *Atheism Explained: From Folly to Philosophy.* Chicago: Open Court.

Stewart, R.B., ed. 2006. *The Resurrection of Jesus: John Dominic Crossan and N.T. Wright in Dialogue.* London: SPCK.

Storr, V.F. 1913. *The Development of English Theology in the Nineteenth Century, 1800–1860.* London: Longmans, Green.

Strauss, D.F. 1840. *Das Leben Jesu kritisch bearbeitet.* Fourth edition, two volumes. Tübingen: Osiander.

———. 1846. *The Life of Jesus Critically Examined.* English translation of the above by George Eliot. Three volumes. London: Chapman. Reprinted 2005 by Continuum.

———. 1861. *Hermann Samuel Reimarus und seine Schutzschrift für die vernünftigen Verehrer Gottes.* In *Gesammelte Schriften*, edited by E. Zeller in twelve volumes. 1876–78 (Bonn: Emil Strauss). Volume 5, 1877, 229–409.

———. 1879. *A New Life of Jesus.* English translation of the German of 1864. Second edition in two volumes. London: Williams and Norgate.

———. 1997. *The Old Faith and the New.* Reprint of the English translation of 1873 of the German of 1872. With an introduction and notes by G.A. Wells. Two volumes bound as one. Amherst: Prometheus.

Strecker, G. 1960. William Wrede. Zur hundertsten Wiederkehr seines Geburtstages. *Zeitschrift für Theologie und Kirche,* 57, 66–91.

Sweet, J. 1979. *Revelation.* London: SCM.

Sykes, N. 1963. The Religion of Protestants. In *The Cambridge History of the Bible.* Volume 3. *The West from the Reformation to the Present Day,* edited by S.L. Greenslade. Cambridge: Cambridge University Press, 175–198.

Sykes, S. 1997. *The Story of Atonement.* London: Darton, Longman, and Todd.

Talbert, C.H. 1997. *Reading Acts.* New York: Crossroad.

Taylor, A.J.P. 1970. *English History, 1914–1945.* Harmondsworth: Penguin.

Taylor, Joan E. 1997. *John the Baptist within Second Temple Judaism.* London: SPCK.

Taylor, V. 1920. *The Historical Evidence for the Virgin Birth.* Oxford: Clarendon.

———. 1966. *The Gospel According to St. Mark.* Second edition. London: Macmillan.

Telford, W.R., ed. 1995. *The Interpretation of Mark.* Second edition. Edinburgh: Clark.

Telford, W.R. 1999. *The Theology of the Gospel of Mark.* Cambridge: Cambridge University Press.

Theissen, G. and A. Merz. 1998. *The Historical Jesus: A Comprehensive Guide.* English translation of the German of 1996. London: SCM.

Tillich, P. 1968. *Systematic Theology.* Volume 1. Welwyn: Nisbet.

Toit, D.S. du. See Du Toit.

Toynbee, A.J. 1939. *A Study of History.* Volume 6. London: Oxford University Press.

Tuckett, C.M., ed. 1983. *The Messianic Secret.* London: SPCK; Philadelphia: Fortress.

Tuckett, C.M. 1996. *Q and the History of Early Christianity.* Edinburgh: Clark; Peabody: Hendrickson.

———. 2001. *Christology and the New Testament.* Edinburgh: EdinburghUniversity Press.

Twelftree, G.H. 2003. The Miracles of Jesus: Marginal or Mainstream? *Journal for the Study of the Historical Jesus,* 1, 104–124.

Tyrell, G.N.M. 1953. *Apparitions.* Revised edition. London: Duckworth.

Valantasis, R. 2005. *The New Q.* New York: Clark.

VanderKam, J.C. 1994. *The Dead Sea Scrolls Today.* London: SPCK.

VanderKam, J.C. and P. Flint. 2002. *The Meaning of the Dead Sea Scrolls: Their Significance for Understanding the Bible, Judaism, Jesus and Christianity.* New York: Harper Collins.

Van Voorst, R. 2005. Nonexistence Hypothesis. In Houlden 2005, 639–41.

Vermes, G. 2008. *The Resurrection.* London: Penguin.

Vielhauer, P. 1965. Gottesreich und Menschensohn in der Verkündigung Jesu. In *Aufsätze zum Neuen Testament.* Munich: Kaiser, 55–91.

Vogt, J. 1971. Augustus and Tiberius. In *Jesus in His Time,* edited by H.J. Schultz. English translation. London: SPCK, 1–9.

Walker, W.O. Jr. 2001. *Interpolations in the Pauline Letters.* London: Sheffield Academic Press.

Ward, K. 1992. *Is Christianity a Historical Religion?* London: Dr.Williams's Trust
Weatherly, J.A. 1994. *Responsibility for the Death of Jesus in Luke-Acts.* Sheffield: Sheffield Academic Press.
Weaver, W.P. 1999. *The Historical Jesus in the Twentieth Century, 1900–1950.* Harrisburg: Trinity International.
Webb, R.L. 1994. John the Baptist and his Relationship to Jesus. In Chilton and Evans 1994, 179–229.
Wedderburn, A.J.M. 1987. *Baptism and Resurrection.* Tübingen: Mohr.
———. 1999. *Beyond Resurrection.* London: SCM.
Weiss, J. 1971. *Jesus' Proclamation of the Kingdom of God.* Translated, edited and with an Introduction by R.H. Hiers and D.L. Holland. London: SCM.
Wells, G.A. 1982. Reissued in 1988. *The Historical Evidence for Jesus.* Buffalo: Prometheus.
———. 1986. *Did Jesus Exist?* London: Pemberton.
———. 1989. *Who Was Jesus?* La Salle: Open Court.
———. 1996. *The Jesus Legend.* Chicago: Open Court.
———. 1999. *The Jesus Myth.* Chicago: Open Court.
———. 2004. *Can We Trust the New Testament?* Chicago: Open Court.
Wenham, D. 1991. *Redating Matthew, Mark, and Luke.* London: Hodder and Stoughton.
———. 1995. *Paul: Follower of Jesus or Founder of Christianity?* Grand Rapids: Eerdmans.
Werner, M. 1957. *The Formation of Christian Dogma.* London: Black. An abbreviated translation of *Die Entstehung des Christlichen Dogmas. 1941.* Bern and Leipzig: Paul Haupt.
Westfall, R.S. 1958. *Science and Religion in Seventeenth-Century England.* New Haven: Yale University Press.
Whealey, Alice. 2003. *Josephus on Jesus: The Testimonium Flavianum Controversy from Late Antiquity to Modern Times.* New York: Peter Lang.
Wiles, M. 1967. *The Making of Christian Doctrine.* Cambridge: Cambridge University Press.
———. 1974. *The Remaking of Christian Doctrine.* London: SCM.
———. 1994. *A Shared Search: Doing Theology in Conversation with One's Friends.* London: SCM.
Wilkinson, A. 1986. *Dissent or Conform? War, Peace, and the English Churches 1900–1945.* London: SCM.
Williams, R. 2007. *Tokens of Trust: An Introduction to Christian Belief.* Norwich: Canterbury Press.
Wilson, S.G. 1973. *The Gentiles and the Gentile Mission in Luke-Acts.* Cambridge: Cambridge University Press.
———. 1984. From Jesus to Paul: The Contours of a Debate. In Richardson and Hurd 1984, 1–21.

———. 1995. *Related Strangers: Jews and Christians, 70–170* C.E. Minneapolis: Fortress.
Wink, W. 1968. *John the Baptist in the Gospel Tradition*. Cambridge: Cambridge University Press.
Witherington, B., III. 1992. *Jesus, Paul and the End of the World*. Exeter: Paternoster.
Witt, R.E. 1971. *Isis in the Graeco-Roman World*. London: Thames and Hudson.
Wrede, W. 1897. *Über Aufgabe and Methode der sogenannten Theologie*. Göttingen: Vandenhoeck and Ruprecht. English translation 'The Task and Methods of New Testament Theology', in *The Nature of New Testament Theology: The Contribution of William Wrede and Adolf Schlatter*, translated and edited by R. Morgan, 1973. London: SCM, 68–116.
———. 1901. *Das Messiasgeheimnis in den Evangelien*. Göttingen: Vandenhoeck and Ruprecht.
———. 1903. *Charakter und Tendenz des Johannesevangeliums*. Tübingen: Mohr.
———. 1907. *Vorträge und Studien*. Tübingen: Mohr.
———. 1971. *The Messianic Secret*. English translation of Wrede 1901. Cambridge: Clarke.
Wright, N.T. 1992a. *The New Testament and the People of God*. London: SPCK.
———. 1992b. *Who Was Jesus?* London: SPCK.
———. 1996. *Jesus and the Victory of God*. London: SPCK.
———. 2003. *The Resurrection of the Son of God*. London: SPCK.
———. 2007. *Surprised by Hope*. London: SPCK.
Yarbro-Collins, Adela. 1992. *The Beginning of the Gospel*. Minneapolis: Fortress.
Young, J. 2007. *The Violence of God and the War on Terror*. London: Darton, Longman, and Todd.
Zahrnt, H. 1963. *The Historical Jesus*. English translation. London: Collins.
Ziesler, J.A. 1979. Luke and the Pharisees. *New Testament Studies,* 25, 146–57.
Zwiep, A. W. 1997. *The Ascension of the Messiah in Lukan Christology*. Leiden: Brill.

Index of New Testament References

Matthew

1 : 3	339n9	
6	99	
17	102	
18	105	
20	92	
21	13, 223	
22–23	94	
2 : 1	84	
2–3	36, 49, 81, 84	
5–6	96	
8–11	85	
11	337n2	
13–15	97	
16	81, 90	
17–18	97	
21–23	83, 97	
3 : 2	230f, 249	
3	222	
6–7	223, 225	
10–12	224f	
15–17	226f	
4 : 1–4	236	
5–7	238	
8–11	239	
17	231, 249	
24	7	
5 : 1	123	
1–16	35	
3	40	
13–14, 22	35	
17–19	36, 250	
22	35	
32	32	
38–42	35	
39	4	
43	225	
43–48	35f	
44	50, 52	
6 : 2, 5	4	
9ff	232	
25ff	4	
7 : 1–5, 13–14	35	
7–11	4	
15	303	
28–29	30, 36	
29	34	
8 : 1–2	197	
20	279	
28	321	
9 : 26	192	
10 : 2–4	147	
7–8	250, 258, 266	
9–11	267	

373

13	269	24	199
14–15	151	27–28	35f, 254
15–16	294		
17–22	268	17 : 1	123
18, 21–22,		12	262
26	268f	13	224
23	266ff	23	183
24–42, 39	268f	24–27	323
33	54		
34–35	285	18 : 1–4, 21–22	35
37	260, 285	15–17	34
		21	35, 323
11 : 2–6	231		
3	226	19 : 19	36, 225
9–10	222, 291	28	148, 259, 280
12	231, 262		
12–13	231	21 : 16	33
14	224, 271	31	261, 294
21–24	298		
29	4	22 : 1–14	33
		39–40	36, 52
12 : 1–8	32, 52		
24–28	261, 263, 281,	23 : 2–3	52, 225
	294	6, 34	34
30	31	15	225
40	159	16, 28	52
42	4		
		24 : 23–26	222
13 : 13–15	187	27	278
40–43	36, 279	29	255
52	34	29–34	3, 266
54–56	81	30ff	254
		34	35, 255, 283
14 : 1–2	81	36ff	35
28–31	323	37–39, 44	278
33	181	43	8
		48	34
15 : 6–9	52		
		25 : 14ff	230
16 : 1–4	342n3	31–32	260, 280
6	52	41, 46	260
12	52, 182f		
16–18	34, 138, 181	26 : 21	344
17–19	323	28	223, 333n1

36	322	2	188
56	125	5–7	223
		6	322
27 : 25	35, 54	7	194
37	49	10	198
45ff	162	13	200
46	242	17, 23	197f
51–53	121, 133, 162	23–28	32, 197
57	155	24	199
62	202	27–28	201
62–66	120		
		3 : 6	202
28 : 1	120	7–12	200
3, 7, 15	121f	11–12	191
9	127, 136	13–14	343n7
10	144	15	235
14–15	121	16–19	147
16	136, 145	21	82
16–20	122, 132	23	188
17ff	129	27	281
19–20	250, 280	31	82

Mark

		4 : 10	147, 189
		11	30, 189
		11–13	180f, 186
1 : 1–4	221ff	14	30
4	333n1	14–20	181
6	223, 230	15	188
7–8	224	17	30
9	226	33–34	181, 188f
10	106, 233	36	189
10–11	227, 250	41	181, 189
12–13	234, 238		
15	230, 249, 258, 289, 298	5 : 1–2	321
		1–20	60
16–20	148	7, 17	191
21–22	30	19–20	192
24	235	43	191
25	191		
27	30, 36, 191	6 : 3	143
39	30, 200	4	82
40, 45	196	7	43, 235
		7–11	148, 194, 268
2 : 1ff	191	12–13	148, 181

14–16	341n8	19	36
30	181, 267	23–24	40
32–44	58	25	153
35–37, 52	181	29–30	30, 285
43	182	31	281
		32–34	161, 183f
7 : 1–23	32	35–45	184
3–4, 7	24f	45	41, 259, 333n1
14	188	47	192
17	197		
18–19	181, 189	11 : 1–16	147
24–25	193		
24–30	25, 197	12 : 1–12	26
27	295	12	187, 194
31	25	13	202
		13–17	196
8 : 1	196	25	259
4	65, 181	26–27	169
8	182	33	50
11–12	61, 342n3	37	188
14–21	181f		
29	183, 189	13 : 2	26
30	186	3	335n7
31	161, 184, 279	6–27	26
32	183	9–13	27, 268
34	230	10	26, 284
35	30, 260	14	27f, 38
38	261, 278	24–25	259
		24–27, 30	278
9 : 1	283, 289, 293	30–37	26
2–7	185		
5	119	14 : 12–17	147
9	186, 190	13	344
9–13	230	18ff	343n7
11, 13	224	21	5
31	161, 183	24	223, 333n1
31–35	147	25	281
36–50	199	28	115, 324
38	335n7	32, 34	322f
38–41	31	35–36	5
43, 48	260	50	125, 184
		61	193
10 : 1	188	62	192, 283, 289
1–12	32	66–72	320

15 : 34	40, 242, 323	16	12, 224
39–40	323	17	225
43	154	21–22	227f
47	323	23ff	99
		33	339n9
16 : 3	155		
7–8	115f, 118, 142, 162, 320	4 : 1–4	236
		5–8	239
11–13	184	9–12	238
		15	230

Luke

		5 : 1–11	130
		3–9	323
1 : 1–2	36	12	197
5	87, 90, 99		
13, 20, 24	91	6 : 14–16	47
24–25	87	20	40
27, 31, 35	91f	22	212
32	103	24–25	40, 281
32–35	92	27	50
36–37	91		
39–40	87	7 : 16–17	70
39–45	93	18–19	231
41, 44	82	19	82
42–43	87	22	209
46–55	92	26–27	222, 291
56	87, 93	34–35	211f
57–80	93		
67–79	92	8 : 2–3	117, 321
		9–12	187f
2 : 1	86f		
1–2	38	9 : 18–23	321
2	88, 337n3	23	230
3–5	89	27	283
7	339	45	183
11	90	57–60	214
22–23, 39–40	90	58	212, 279
41–51	107		
48–50	92	10 : 9, 11	230, 258
		12	294
3 : 3	12	13–15	215, 298
4, 6	222f	18	281
7, 9	225	21–22	215f
10–14	230		

11 : 1	232	
9–13	214	
17–20	342n2	
20	237, 281	
29	342n3	
49	213	
12 : 1	183	
8–9	212	
9	54	
22–31	214	
40	212, 278	
51–53	285	
13 : 31	53	
14 : 11	281	
16–24	33	
26	4, 214, 260, 285	
27	342n5	
16 : 16	231	
23–24	260	
24–25	40	
17 : 21	262f, 281	
24–27, 30	278	
18 : 31–34	184	
19 : 11	230, 283	
41–44	39	
21 : 20–21	39	
24	38	
32	230, 283	
34–36	279	
22 : 3	218	
19–20	41, 333n1	
24–27	333n1	
28, 30	148	
69	283	

23 : 27–31, 48	39	
34, 46	40	
43	136	
50–51	151	
24 : 1–10	122	
6–7	116, 321	
9	118	
11–32	118	
16	119	
20–21	184	
21	250, 341n5	
22–24	122	
24	125	
25–27	159, 193	
30	132	
31–32	119f	
34	142	
36–43	120, 129	
39	125	
44–45	185, 193	
47	118	
49	114, 116	
51	114	

John

1 : 1–18	324	
8	219	
13	80, 109	
14	44	
19–23	229	
29	46, 48	
29–34	228	
30	48	
31	229	
35–40	325	
36, 45	80	
41	44	
42	139	
2 : 11	46, 186	

3 : 3, 5	275	42	80, 100
14–16	47		
16–17	5	8 : 12	44f
18	151	17	51
22–24	229	20	48
28	229, 232	32	45
30	229	44	50
31–36	47	58	45
36	151		
		9 : 1, 5	44
4 : 1	229	22	42, 49
9	44		
22, 24	51	10 : 8	4
23	274	18	48, 277
29	48	20	46
		27, 28	275
5 : 1	50	30	250
5	44	34	51
10	49		
23–24	44f, 275	11 : 23–26	275
25	274	39	44
28–29	275	42	48
46	51	57	42
6 : 6	48	12 : 23	48
21, 26	44	31	242, 295
29	44, 46	32–33	47
31–38	44	42	42
39–40	275		
40	44	13 : 1	46, 51
41	50	18, 27	218
44	45, 275	23	130
47–50	44	30	343n7
51–52	50	34–35	50
51–59, 54	275		
64	48	14 : 1	46
64–71	343n7	6	45
65	45	16–18	276
67–70	43	24	44
		26	276
7 : 2	50	30	242
5	80		
30, 44	48	15 : 1	46
39	276	26	276

16 : 2	42	8	280
11	46, 49, 242, 295	9, 26	145
		13	147
12–13	276	15	132
33	46	16	12
		18–20	121
17 : 1	46		
3	47, 275	2 : 1–4	116
5–6	45f, 229, 277	14ff	153
9	45	22	11
20–21	50	23	5
		27–28	73
18 : 6	48	32	185
20, 32	46f	36	185, 276
36	348n9	38	122
36–37	48	41	116, 153
19 : 11	48	3 : 13–14	12
14, 31	46		
26–27	130	4 : 4	116, 153
		27	12
20 : 1–11	126f		
12	116	5 : 34, 39	53
15	127	37	88
17, 18	127, 144		
19, 26	119	6 : 14	12
19–23	128		
22	276	8 : 1	145
24	43	16	122
26	136		
27	127	9 : 3ff	135
29–31	128f, 160, 166	26, 31	145
21 : 7	130	10 : 38	11f
14	129	40–41	114, 125, 135
20–23	131, 324		
24	44, 130f	11 : 19	145, 188
25	131		
		12 : 2	146
Acts			
		13 : 25	12
1 : 1–3	114f, 234	33	227
6–7	283	34	252

16 : 4	146	

19 : 1–7	219
4	12, 226
11–12	37
23 : 6, 9	53
26 : 23	162

Romans

1 : 3–4	79, 100, 329
4	13, 185, 233
16	138
3 : 25	5, 210
4 : 24–25	210, 333n2
5 : 6–9	7
6 : 3–4	135
8 : 9	137
32	5
9 : 6ff	51
18	190
10 : 9	143
11 : 7, 23	190
13 : 11–12	282
15 : 3–4	71
19, 24, 28	284
16 : 25–26	71

1 Corinthians

1 : 11–13	143
20	295
20–25	138
22–23	61
23	7, 333n2
24	211
2 : 2	7
6, 8	295
13	8
16	47
3 : 18–19	295
6 : 11	122
7 : 10	7
29–31	282
40	8
8 : 6	328
9 : 1	133
5	143
14	30
10 : 11	282
21	9
11 : 23–26	9
12 : 7–10	137, 334n6
14 : 6	47, 137
13–14	334n6
18	334n6
24ff	137
28–31, 37	8
15 : 1–2	134
3–5	134, 146, 214

3–8	133f
3–11	341n6
6	149f
12	153
17	133
20	136, 146, 162, 167
43, 50	135

2 Corinthians

4 : 4	295
5 : 1–10	135
8 : 18	143
11 : 14	295
12 : 1–4	151
9	8

Galatians

1 : 4	5
6–9	139
8–9	50
11–12	9, 341n6
17–18	148, 160
18	142
19	143
2 : 6–9	138, 140
9	139ff, 144
11–14	31, 140ff
4 : 4	79, 217, 329
22–29	79

Ephesians

2 : 2	295
3 : 5	8
6 : 12	295

Philippians

2 : 6–11	46, 136, 185
7	7
9–10	13
3 : 5	52
21	135

Colossians

1 : 15–20	10f, 328
19–20	5
2 : 2–3	180, 211, 328
12	135
14–15	144
18	151
20	144

1 Thessalonians

4 : 15–17	281f, 300
5 : 2–3	282

1 Timothy

6 : 10	314
13	11

Titus

2 : 13	128

Hebrews

1 : 2–3	328
5	227
8–9	128
2 : 18	242
4 : 15	242
9 : 26	217
10 : 37	287

James

1 : 6	151
5 : 8	282

1 Peter

1 : 20	217
4 : 7	282

2 Peter

1 : 16–18	11
3 : 3	284
7–12	297
8–10	254

1 John

2 : 18	282
5 : 7–8	128

Jude

14	246

Revelation

2 : 2	133
6 : 12–17	259
13 : 15	29
14 : 20	293
16 : 3	316
15	8
22 : 9, 16, 20	8

General Index

Abomination of Desolation, 26, 28f, 38
Abraham, apocalypse of, 259
Acts of the Apostles: adoptionism of, 185, 276; author, 37; on the enrollment, 88; gentile mission in, 250; on Jesus's ministry and passion, 11f; on Jesus's parousia, 274; on Jesus's resurrection appearances, 114f; on the Jews, 53; miracles in, 37; on Paul, 38; on Pharisees, 53; speeches in, 74, 153; on the Twelve, 146; 'we' passages in, 38
Ahaz, 94f
Alexander the Great and his empire, 246
Allingham, W., 77
Allison, D.C., Jr., 11, 134, 140f, 153, 167f, 243, 250, 259, 273, 280f, 284, 291
Andersen, Hans, 150
Anderson, H., 24f
Andreski, S., 21, 163
Antioch, the quarrel at, 140f
Antiochus IV (Epiphanes), 18, 26, 28, 65
Antipas, tetrarch of Galilee, 83, 89, 220
antisemitism: in Christianity, 54; in the New Testament?, 50ff
apocalypse, meaning of, 246
Apocalypse of Weeks, 246, 297
Apocalyptic, Jewish, 121, 152, 163, 245ff
Apocrypha of New Testament, 43, 149
Apollonius of Tyana, 2
apostles: authority of: 43, 63; meaning of the term, 133

Apostolic Fathers, 61, 148
Aquinas, St. Thomas, 54, 108
Aramaic originals, none of New Testament, 208
Archelaus, enthnarch of Judea, 83, 87, 89, 97
archontes, 295, 341, 342n6
Arius, 355n8
Arnobius, 16
Articles of religion, Anglican, 125
asceticism, Christian, 257
Ashton, J., 127, 129
Assyria, 94, 96f, 221, 246
Athanasius, St., 335n8
Atonement, Christian doctrine of, 4f, 41, 48, 316
Augustine of Hippo, St., 54
Augustus Caesar, 86f
Austin, J., 305
authentic life, 74, 287
authority, submission to, 309f
Avis, P., 62

Babylson, Jews' exile in, 65, 69, 100ff, 221, 297
Badham, P., 113, 117, 126
Bain, A., 273
Baker, T., 307
Balaam, 67, 84
Bammel, E., 254
baptism, efficacy of, 135, 219, 225, 249
baptismal formula of early church, 122, 250

Barnabas, epistle of, 12, 148
Barnikol, E., 138f
Barr, J., 110, 249, 300
Barrett, C.K., 275
Barry, F.R., 5
Barth, Karl, 78, 113, 170f
Barton, J., 307
Barton, S., 172f
Baruch, apocalypse of 259
Bauckham, R., 292, 319ff, 326, 330
Baur, F.C., 75f, 256
Beare, F.W., 23, 33f, 52, 84f, 95ff, 120f, 146, 155, 212, 221, 283
beliefs, practical and other, 310
beloved disciple, 118, 126f, 130f, 325, 331
Benedictus in Luke, 92f
Bernheim, P.A., 146
Bethlehem, 68, 80ff
Bezae, Codex, 53
Bezzant, J.S., 304
bias and reasoning, 21
Blomberg, C., 61
Boone, Kathleen, 309
Borg, M., 175f, 305
Boring, M.E., 7, 143
Boslooper, T., 105, 110f, 340n13
Bowden, J., 2, 98f, 265, 271, 304f
Boyd, G.A., 19, 326
Boyer, P., 39, 300
Boyle, N., 313f
Bradshaw, P.F., 106
Braun, H., 75
Brooke, G.J., 209
Brown, D., 107
Brown, Raymond E., 54, 80ff, 122, 128, 232
Bruce, F.F., 37
Bruce, S., 176
Brunvand, J.H., 204
Bryan, C., 204
Buchanan, G.W., 248ff
Bultmann, R., 15, 74, 146f, 159, 175, 258, 275, 287f, 297f, 327
Burger, C., 96, 102
Burkitt, F.C., 304
Butler, S. 149
Byrskog, S., 319f, 330

Cadbury, H.J., 233, 331
Caird, G.B., 242f, 294f
Caligula, 31
Campenhausen, H. von, 81, 91, 99f
Cana, wedding feast at, 46
Cane, A., 5
Carlyle, T., 77
Carnley, P., 135, 172, 174
Carrier, R.C., 135
Casey, M., 54
Catchpole, D.R., 342n1
catchword connections, 199
census decreed by Augustus, 38, 86ff
Cephas, not the gospel Peter, 138ff
Chadwick, H., 277
Cheyne, T.K., 108, 151
Christ: Jesus recognized as, 183, 185; meaning of the term, 210
Christianity: cult origin of, 9, 196; whether dependent on historical events, 265, 272, 305; factions in early, 31; intolerance of early, 28; Jewish origin of, 51, 54; pagan influence on, 9; survival of, 75, 171, 176, 306
Christmas: carol services at, 111, 308; date of, 106
Christology, traditional problems of, 4
Chrysostom, St. John, 28, 54
Church in the New Testament, 34
Clement of Alexandria, 28, 277
Clement of Rome, 27f, 61
Colenso, J.W., 77, 248
Collins, J.J., 246, 280, 297
Corinth, the church at, 152f
Cox, Stephen, 305
Cranfield, C.E.B., 337n1
Creed, J.M., 92f
creeds, Christian, 256
Crossan, J.D., 156, 177, 290f, 305, 327
Crossley, J.G., 31f, 132f, 171
crucifixion, pre-Christian, 18
Cynic philosophers, 214f, 286
cynicism not entailed by atheism, 312, 314

Daniel, book of, 26f, 29, 65, 252, 280, 300

Darwin, Charles, 66, 76f, 176
David, King, and Jesus, 36, 68, 73, 84, 92, 96, 103, 329
Davies, Margaret, 210f
Davies, W.D., 268f
Da Vinci Code, 107
dead, raising the, 153
Dead Sea Scrolls, 9, 18, 259
death, life after, 137, 168ff, 248, 306
Decapolis, 25
deism, 247f, 264
demons: defeat of, 46, 60, 235; their recognition of Jesus, 191. *See also* exorcism
demythologizing, 293, 297
Deuteronomy, book of, 154, 213, 237ff, 303
Devil: defeat of, 48f, 235; power of, 240. *See also* demons, Satan
dialectical theology, 337
diaspora of Jews outside Palestine, 24
Dibelius, M., 132
disciples: and apostles, 133, 253; multiple roles of in gospels, 189f
docetism, 217
Dodd, C.H., 58, 123f, 131, 200, 241, 261, 275, 288f
Doherty, Earl, 328
Domitian, 27
doublethink, 74f
doublets in gospels, 65f
doubt, sinfulness of, 151
Downing, F.G., 286
Drews, A., 272
Duffy, E., 351n5
Dunderburg, I., 45, 331
Dunn, J.D.G., 171, 270, 277, 297, 300, 348n10
Du Toit, D.S., 304

Eddy, P.R., 19, 326ff
editing, a theological euphemism, 82, 116
Edwards, Ruth, 128
Ehrman, Bart D., 6, 16f, 23ff, 40, 54, 140ff, 152, 158, 228, 278, 281, 284f, 291

Einhard, 59f
Einstein, Albert, 293
Elijah, 70, 72, 223f, 262
Eliot George, 63, 78
Elisha, 70, 72
Ellegård, A., 67, 217
Elliott, J.K., 93, 114, 134, 137f, 227, 232, 321
Ellis, E.E., 334n1
Elwell, W.A., 110, 254
Emmaus, appearance of risen Jesus at, 118f, 132, 159
emotion: and belief, 107, 167, 175f, 305; contagious, 8, 287; easier to convey than ideas, 311; and flimsy ideas, 164f, 175; and liturgy, 111, 308; role in behaviour, 164, 305, 311
Enlightenment, supposed prejudices of the, 62, 163f, 167, 292, 307, 313f, 325ff
Enoch, book of, 211, 213, 246, 259, 280
Enslin, M.S., 105, 233f
epistles: early ones specified, 7, 10; differences between earlier and later, 11
Ericksen, R.P., 305
eschatology: inaugurated, 281; 261
Esler, P.F., 334n6
Eucharist, 9, 132, 275
Eusebius of Caesarea, 27, 330
evangelism, unreceptiveness to, 45, 213
Evans, C.F., 41, 63, 87, 116, 123, 134, 147, 155, 157f, 235, 299
existentialism, 74, 287
exorcism in the New Testament, 41, 59f, 261
eyewitness claims anent the New Testament, 20, 24, 33, 36f, 65, 269f, 305, 319ff, 330
Ezra, apocalypse of, 259

Fadus, 37
faith: characteristics of, 315; independent of historical evidence, 113, 128, 257, 272, 305
Fall, man's, 73, 289
Fatima, alleged miracles at, 150
Feldman, L.H., 337n3, 338n4

Fenton, J., 289
first fruits of resurrection, 136, 167
Fitzmyer, J.A., 37f, 87ff, 229f, 237, 243
Flynn, T., 328
footwashing, 46
form criticism, 201
France, R.T., 23f, 162, 334n5
Francis, L.J., 307
Franklin, E., 109, 111, 303
fraud not to be imputed to evangelists, 68, 124f
Frei, H., 63, 177, 278
Frend, W.H.C., 27f
Fuller, R.H., 114, 117, 123, 148, 152
fundamentalism, 1, 20, 39, 309
Funk, R., 288
Furlong, A., 274
Furnish, V.P., 143

Gabriel, archangel, 64, 87, 91
Galilee and Jesus, 7, 14f, 210, 216
Gamaliel I, 37
Genesis, book of, 276
gentile mission in New Testament, 122, 132, 139, 141, 250
Gerasene, demoniac of, 60, 191f
Gethsemane, Jesus at, 5, 7, 115, 130f, 322f
Gibbon, E., 128, 304
Gilchrist, J.M., 125
glossolalia (speaking with tongues), 18, 137, 334n6
Gnosticism, 43, 45, 217
Goeze, J.M., 247
Goodacre, M., 207
Goppelt, L., 11
Gore, C., 109
gospel, meaning of the term, 30, 249
gospels, canonical : anonymous, 23, 65; literary relations among, 24, 42, 75, 79, 179, 207, 266, 330; use of Old Testament in, 3, 68ff, 98. *See also* doublets
Goulder, M.D., 172, 207, 334n3
Grant, F.C., 71
Grant, M., 71
Graves, R., 241

Guenther, H.O., 146, 342n4
Guignebert, C., 13, 136, 148, 151, 156, 161, 308

Habakkuk, 69
Habermas, Gary R., 177
Haenchen, E., 27ff, 43, 55, 61f, 73f, 120f, 126f, 132, 141, 177, 233, 237, 252, 325
Halley's comet, 85
hallucinations, 119f, 128, 150
handwashing, 24
Hanson, A.T., 286
Hanson, R.P.C., 63, 286
Hare, D.R.A., 35
Harries, R., 119
Harris, H., 64ff, 256
Harris, M., 174
Hart, T., 292
Harvey, A.E., 7, 70, 113, 291
Hatch, E., 172
hatred: endorsed in New Testament, 3, 50, 260, 285; and religious belief, 54, 315
Hebrews, gospel of, 145, 149, 291
Hegel, G.W.F., 74
Heidegger, M., 287
Helena, mother of Constantine, 160
Hell, 35f, 260, 346n5. *See also* salvation
Hennecke, E., 105, 145
Hercules, 64, 111
Herod the Great, 38, 81f, 97
Herodians, 42, 53, 182, 202
Hick, J., 152, 334n7
Hillerbrand, J.H., 77
history and science, 165f
Hitler, Adolf, 164, 170, 300, 313
Holloway, R., 98
Holy Spirit. *See* spirit
Homer, 208, 329
Homonadenses, 338n4
Hooker, Morna, 98, 233, 242f
Hosea, 36, 97
Hoskyns, E., 71, 289
Houlden, L., 2, 4, 8, 26, 30f, 34, 40, 50, 68, 151f, 229, 304
Hume, David, 164, 325f

Hurtado, L., 9, 19f, 219, 328, 345n1
Huxley, T.H., 59f, 150, 311
hypocrites, 34, 226

Ignatius of Antioch, 11, 61, 80, 217f
illusory ideals, 314
Immaculate Conception, doctrine of, 107f
Immanuel, prophecy in Isaiah, 94f
immortality. *See* death, life after
Incarnation, doctrine of, 172, 339n12
independence versus conformity. *See* authority
interpolations: in Josephus, 17, 220; in New Testament, 140, 341. *See also* manuscript evidence
Irenaeus, St., 23, 139
Isaiah, 69f, 94, 221. *See also* servant of Yahweh
Isis, 151
Islam, 161, 190, 316

Jacobson, A.D., 216
Jairus, daughter of, 44, 130f, 180, 191
James, apostle, son of Zebedee, 129f, 146
James of Jerusalem, 143ff
James, W., 314f
James, epistle of, 281
Jechoniah, 101ff
Jeffery, C., 150
Jenkins, D., 174
Jeremiah, 97
Jeremias, J., 349
Jerusalem, destruction of, 6, 26, 33, 38f
Jesus: arrest, 48; ascension, 114f, 127, 135f; authority, 30, 34; baptism, 226ff; betrayal, 9, 333n2, no biography possible, 64, 77, 202f; birth, 2, 68, 79ff; brethren, 80ff, 143; burial, 70, 134f; chronology of ministry, 196ff; and creation, 10f, 79, 106, 328; crucifixion, without historical setting in earliest documents, 7, 10, 82; death as ransom, 41, 333n1; 'delivered up', 9; ethical teaching, harsh, 214, 260, 289; ethical teaching, imperfect, 3f, 265f; as exorcist: *see* exorcism; and family values, 256, 284f; historicity, why unquestioned in antiquity, 15f; historicity, dispensable?, 78, 265; and the law: *see* Jewish law; as magician, 16, 20, 237; miracles, 2, 59ff, 182, 208f; name, 13; parables, not in earliest documents, 7; parables, not in fourth gospel, 41; parables, meant as unintelligible, 186f; parables, settings of, 202; pre-existence of, 10f, 45f, 48, 211, 228f, 277; as proclaimer and as what is proclaimed, 30; prophecies concerning, 69, 71, 94ff, 119; prophecies by, 3, 183f, 324; psychology of, whether ascertainable, 64, 269; resurrected body, 120, 125f, 159f, 169; second coming, 14, 26, 34, 263, 282, 286; as son of David: *see* David; as son of God, 185, 192, 227f, 233, 250; as Son of man, 26, 259, 279; transfiguration, 11, 70, 119, 130f, 185; words from the cross, 40f. *See also* Christ, Christology, Emmaus, Galilee, Gethsemane, Lord's Prayer, Moses, Nazareth, Sabbath
Jewish law, 14, 24, 31f, 36, 141
Jewish war with Rome, 6, 145
Joel, 224
John, apostle, son of Zebedee, 43
John the Baptist, 12, 41, 47f, 80, 82, 209ff, 219ff, 249, 282, 291
John, gospel of: appended chapter, 44, 129ff; author, 43f, 129, 131, 319; Christology, 4, 45, 80, 106, 166, 228, 242, 275ff; date, 42, 49; discourses in, 20, 41f, 46f, 242, 276; eschatology, 3, 41, 274ff; and the Jews, 42, 49f, 54; miracles in, 41, 44, 59; relation to other gospels: *see* gospels; and the synagogue, 42; and the Twelve, 43; unhistorical, 48f, 129, 201
John, J., 72f
Johnson, L.T., 165
Johnson, M.D., 103
Jonah, 159
Joseph of Arimathea, 70, 153ff

Joseph, husband of Jesus's mother, 79f, 84, 87, 97
Josephus, Flavius, 17f, 37, 39, 83, 88f, 220, 298
Joshua, 13
Judas of Galilee, 37f, 88
Judas Iscariot, 5, 121, 145f, 218, 330, 343n7
Jude, epistle of, 50
Judgment. *See* Last Judgment
Justin Martyr, St., 81, 232f, 251, 277

Käsemann, E., 201
Keck, L.E., 15, 100, 290
Kee, H., 60, 98
Kent, J., 58, 165, 172, 274, 289, 308, 315
kerygma, meaning of the term, 287
Kingdom of God: imminence of, 259, 266ff, 282; meaning of, 30, 258, 260, 262ff; whether present, 261ff
Klassen, W., 345
Klein, G., 146
Kloppenborg Verbin, John S., 208, 215, 235f
knowledge, varieties of, 163ff
Koester, H., 45, 218
Kümmel, W.G., 25
Küng, Hans, 108, 132, 291f, 318

Lampe, G.W.H., 39, 117, 120f
Lane Fox, R., 337n3
Last Judgment, 26, 280
Last Supper, 41, 223, 281, 333n1
law. *See* Jewish law
Lazarus, brother of Mary and Martha, 43f, 275
Lazarus and Dives, 40
leaders, trust in, 309
Lecky, W.E.H., 314
Lessing, G.E., 68, 77, 247
Lewis, C.S., 255
Lieu, Judith, 51
life-of-Jesus research, development of, 258
Lightfoot, R.H., 194, 200

Lindars, B., 43, 47, 71, 128, 144, 275
Lindsey, Hal, 1
literary criticism, make-believe in, 72, 176, 205
Locke, John, 164
Loisy, A., 153, 155f, 274
Longley, C., 125, 318
Lord's prayer, 232
love: and knowledge, 163f, 167; of neighbour, 36, 50, 52, 225
Lüdemann, G., 304
Luke, gospel of: adaptation of Mk., 38f, 115ff, 230, 283, 321; adoptionism in, 228; appearances of risen Jesus in, 118ff; date, 38f; eschatology, 230; and Jerusalem, 39, 116; on Pharisees, 53; sources (*see also* Q), 37; sympathy with the deprived, 40
Luther, Martin, 54
Luz, U., 35, 268
Lyons, W.J., 155f

Macaulay, T., 314
Maccabees: books of, 28f; martyrs, 137, 248
Macchia, F.D., 308
Mack, Burton L., 214, 342n5
Mackey, J.P., 111
Macquarrie, J., 137, 163f, 288, 349n1, 350n2
magi. *See* Matthew
Magnificat, 93
Malachi, 93
Manson, T.W., 194, 271
manuscript evidence of New Testament, 42, 131f, 140
Marcion, 139
Mariolatry, 93, 107
Mark, gospel of: appendix to, 116; and community tradition, 24, 200; date, 26, 28f, 284; doublets in, 65f; gentile orientation, 24; geographical errors, 25; on the Jews, 51; literary character, 203, 205; miracles in, 58f, 61f, 320; oldest extant gospel, 24; and persecution of Christians, 28f; and Peter, 28, 200, 320f, 323; and Q, 209

Martinez, F., Garcia, 347n4
Marty, M.E., 346nf4
martyrs, Christian, 161f
Mary, mother of Jesus, 79f, 87ff, 143, 150
Mary Magdalene, 116f, 126f
Mascall, E., 340n13
Matlock, R.B., 350
Matthew, gospel of: adaptation of Mk., 31, 121f, 268, 322; appearance of risen Jesus in, 122f; Christian community of, 35; date, 33f, 121, 267f; discourses in, 123; and 1 Enoch, 280; on guard at Jesus's tomb, 120f; on hell, 35f; Jewish orientation, 36, 75; on the law, 36; magi in, 46, 83ff; on scribes and Pharisees, 34, 51f, 225f; and social cohesion, 35
McCown, C.C., 25
McTernan, O., 351n5
Meagher, J.C., 187, 189, 191, 205
Meier, J.P., 17, 42, 349
Melito, 27
Messiah, ideas of, 68f, 77, 95, 254
Messianic secret. *See* secrecy motif
metaphysics as basis for religion, 272
Metzger, B., 39, 53, 84, 107, 211
Micah, 96
Middle East, present situation in, 249
Miethe, T.L., 37
Milgram, S., 310
miracles: in antiquity, 2, 58; attempts to explain away biblical, 58f, 64f; belief in, 57, 66f, 173f, 254; of Jesus. *See* Jesus
Mitton, C.L., 25
monotheism, 128
Mons, battle of, 150
Montefiore, H., 62
Montgomery, J.W., 330
Moody Smith, D., 43, 49, 51
Moorhead, J.H., 301
morals: and instincts, 312, 350n3; and religion, 312
Morgan, R., 71, 173
Moses and Jesus, 70, 72, 83f, 169, 346n4
Moses, Testament of, 259

Moule, C.F.D., 173, 182
mountains and revelation, 77, 123
mystery religions, 219f, 298
myth in the New Testament, 72, 255, 303
mythological process, 110, 125

Nathaniel, 43, 129f
Nazareth and Jesus, 36, 80ff
neighbour. *See* love
Nero, 27
Newman, J.H., 63
Newport, K.G.C., 349n14
Nicodemus, 43, 275
Niederwimmer, K., 25
Nietzsche, Friedrich, 76
Nineham, D.E., 24f, 28, 65, 69, 154, 194, 196, 202f, 234, 257f, 269f, 282f, 306, 324
Nongbri, B., 42
Non-recognition, motif of, 119, 127, 160
North, G., 1

O'Collins, G., 122f, 132, 156
Old Testament, use of in New Testament, 3, 68ff, 94ff, 252
O'Neill, J., 138, 257
Origen, 28, 39, 277
Osiris, 161, 329
ostracism of unbelievers, 75f
Overbeck, F., 256ff

Pagels, Elaine, 45, 308, 315
Pannenberg, W., 79, 124
Papias, 42, 320, 330
paraclete, 276
parousia. *See* Jesus, second coming
Parrinder, G., 79f, 84
Pascal, Blaise, 335n1
Passover, Jesus's death at, 46, 154
pastoral epistles, 11
Paul, the apostle: author of earliest extant Christian documents, 6; on baptism, 135; Christology, 7, 133, 281; on crucifixion of Jesus, 7, 144;

on divorce, 7; and Jerusalem, 6, 145, 160; on Jesus's birth, 79; on the Jewish law, 14; and miracles, 61; mission to gentiles, 284; and Pharisees, 52; on prophets in the church: *see* prophets; silence concerning most of Jesus's life, 7, 16; and the Twelve, 145ff; and Wisdom literature, 15, 211; on wives, 282
Paul VI, Pope, 351n5
Paulus, H.E.G., 64f
Peacocke, A., 350
Pentateuch, 77, 233f
Pentecost, 116, 128
Pentecostalism, 276, 308, 334n7
pericope, meaning of the term, 196
Perkins, Pheme, 173, 320
Perrin, N., 29
persecution: of Christians, 26ff, 145, 268; by Christians, 54, 303, 341n7
Peter, the apostle: denial of Jesus, 131, 320; and the empty tomb, 118, 126f; martyred?, 131; mentioned by Paul?, 138ff; and the resurrection appearances, 142; speeches in Acts, 73; and the transfiguration, 185. *See also* Mark
Peter, epistles of, 10, 254, 284, 297
Peter, gospel of, 151, 291
Pharisees: importance of, 42; Jesus's abuse of, 52; Jesus's relations with, 25, 32, 61, 182, 202, 261. *See also* Matthew
Philip, disciple, 43, 48, 80
Philo, 105, 217
Pilate, Pontius: not mentioned in early epistles, 7, 10; not mentioned in Q, 3
Pius IX, Pope, 108
Platonism, 273, 328
Pliny the younger, 17, 27
Plutarch, 105, 161
poetry and religion, 304
Polkinghorne, J., 168ff
Polycarp, St., 61
Pomykala, K.E., 336n6
Popper, Karl R., 157
population, limitation of, 318
predestination, 45, 187, 190

Price, Robert M., 149, 331, 341n6
Prickett, S., 304
prophets, early Christian, 8, 137
Proverbs, book of, 211
Psalms, use of in New Testament, 73

Q (document drawn on by Luke and Matthew): as hypothetical source, 2, 15, 207ff; alleged compositional history of, 214ff, 235f, 286; message of, 3, 216; on temptation of Jesus, 235f
Quartodecimans, 63
Quirinius, 38, 88
Qumran, 69, 71, 96, 208f, 222

rabbis, their methods of arguing, 235, 241
Rachel, 97
Räisänen, H., 25, 30, 136, 179ff, 237f, 264, 304
Ramsay, W., 38
'rapture' of believers, 300
Ratzinger, J., 42, 242
Reformation, 62
Reimarus, H.S., 68, 77, 122, 158, 247ff, 258
reinterpretation: importance of in religious history, 36; of old doctrines as symbols, 58, 72, 75f, 109, 172, 264, 289, 292, 304; as ongoing process, 1, 36, 294
Reiser, M., 298, 342n4
Renan, J.E., 76f
resurrection. *See* death, life after
riches and salvation, 40, 260, 281
Richter, P., 307
Ricoeur, P., 304
Ritschl, A., 264
Robertson, John M., 58, 77, 240f, 272, 303, 315
Robinson, James M., 148, 208ff, 268f
Robinson, John A.T., 4, 74, 109, 267, 289, 339n12
Rogerson, J., 347n1
Russell, D.S., 297

Sabbath and Jesus, 32, 52
Sadducees, 42, 169, 225
salvation, to whom vouchsafed, 40, 223
Samaritan, parable of the good, 196
Sanday, W., 194, 200
Sanders, E.P., 180, 201ff, 261f, 279, 286, 349
Sandmel, S., 52, 142
Satan: meaning of the word, 234; persistence of belief in, 242f
Schmidt, A., 209
Schmidt, K.L., 2, 195ff, 270
Schmiedel, P.W., 113, 124f, 138, 151, 159
Schmithals, W., 146
Schneemelcher, W., 146
Schopenhauer, A., 272, 342n10
Schramm, T., 237
Schürer, E., 86ff, 220, 222
Schweitzer, Albert, 2, 4, 49, 78, 179, 195, 247, 249, 252, 255, 258, 264ff, 278, 295f, 298, 303
Schweitzer, E., 142
science and religion, 165, 303
Scobie, C.H.H., 232
scribes, Christian and Jewish, 34
scriptures, meaning of term in New Testament, 134
secrecy motif in the gospels, 46, 185ff, 224, 251
Septuagint, 25, 33, 94f, 100f, 187, 235
Sermon on the Mount, 30, 35, 46
servant of Yahweh, 4f, 155, 269
Shaw, G., 137, 303
Sibylline oracle, 259
silence of an author, when significant, 14
Sim, D., 34f
Simon, U., 177
sins, power to forgive, 129, 132, 223
Sitz im Leben, 201
social cohesion, 35, 313
social instincts, 312
Solomon, book of Wisdom of, 137, 211, 213
Son of God, 250
Son of man, 3, 26, 212f, 252, 279
soul, the, 153, 168

Sower, parable of the, 29f
spirit: imparting of, 276; and prophecy: see prophets, early Christian; witness of, 8, 137
Stalinism, 315
Stanton, G.N., 14f, 52, 173, 328
Steele, David Ramsay, 316
Stewart, R.B., 177
Storr, V.F., 63
Strauss, David Friedrich, 1f, 63–78, 100, 108, 171, 176f, 179, 240, 248, 251, 254ff, 303, 246n4
Strecker, G., 179
summaries, in gospels, 199f
Sunday, 160f
Sweet, J., 29
Sykes, N., 62
Sykes, S., 5
symbols, religious ideas as. See reinterpretation
Syme, R., 338n6

Tacitus, 17, 73, 86f, 265, 320, 338n4
Talbert, C.H., 38
targums, 96, 187
Taylor, A.J.P., 150
Taylor, Joan E., 42, 210, 219ff, 231f
Taylor, V., 109, 147
Telford, W.R., 24, 26, 51, 284
Tell, Wilhelm, 109f, 115
Temple, W., 58, 165, 172, 274, 307f
temple of Jerusalem: cleansing of, 7; destruction of, 6, 26; veil of, 162
Tertullian, 139
Text of New Testament, attestation and variants, 62, 228
Theissen, G., 298
theology, not to be constrained by creeds, 194, 256f, 263, 307
Theudas, 37
Thomas, apostle, 43, 125, 128, 130, 166
Thomas, Coptic gospel of, 3, 33, 152, 211, 214, 284f
Tiberius, 17
Tillich, Paul, 305
Toynbee, A., 241
tradition and doctrine, 63

Trajan, 27
Trevor-Roper, H., 59
Trinity, doctrine of, 50, 128, 250
Trypho, 251
Tübingen school, 256, 258
Tuckett, C.M., 10f, 194, 210ff, 225, 231
Turner, C.H., 321ff
Twelftree, G.H., 61
Twelve, the, 43, 145ff, 162
twelve tribes, Jewish, 148, 280
Tyrrell, G.N.M., 149

unbelief, punishable, 150f

vague affirmations, 172, 174ff, 272
Valantasis, R., 216
Valentinus, 43
VanderKam, J.C., 9
Van Voorst, R., 14f, 17, 21
Vatican Council II, 54f, 351n5
Vermes, G., 171
Vielhauer, P., 146f
Vincent, St., 63
violence and human nature, 316

Walker, W.O., 140, 341
Watson, F., 173
Ward, K., 286
Weatherly, J.A., 53
Weaver, W.P., 59, 110
Webb, R.L., 12
Wedderburn, A.J.M., 135, 299, 345n1
Weiss, J., 256ff
Wellhausen, J., 146

Wenham, D., 11, 325, 337n1
Werner, M., 49, 163
Westcott, B.F., 200
Westfall, R.S., 336n2
Whealey, Alice, 17
wilderness, theological significance of, 222
Wiles, Maurice, 107, 120, 173, 177, 335n8
Wilkinson, A., 170
will, doctrines of, 272f
Williams, R., 18f, 106, 130, 174
Wilson, E.O., 317f
Wilson, S.G., 16, 53, 230
Wink, W., 229
Wisdom literature, Jewish, 15, 137, 211, 329
witchcraft, 150
Withrington, B., III, 293, 299
Witt, R.E., 151
Wittgenstein, L., 157, 164
women, testimony of, 118, 138, 159
words and ideas, 175f
Wrede, William, 2, 30, 48, 179ff, 209, 262ff, 272, 282f, 303
Wright, N.T., 2, 62, 157ff, 195, 295ff, 306, 326f

Yarbro-Collins, Adela, 5
Young, J., 315f

Zahrnt, H., 78
Ziesler, J.A., 53
Zoroastrianism, 235
Zwiep, A.W., 135f